FIFTY YEARS AGO TODAY:
The Sixties Then and Now

Michael Eric Stein

Streetlight Books

New York

FIFTY YEARS AGO TODAY: THE SIXTIES THEN AND NOW.
Copyright © 2017 by Michael Eric Stein. All rights reserved. Printed in the United States of America. No part of this book may be used or reproduced in any manner whatsoever without written permission except in the case of brief quotations embodied in critical articles or reviews.

For further information on Michael Eric Stein, please contact
E-mail: mericstein@streetlightbooks.com
www.streetlightbooks.com

Book Design by Kurt E Griffith,
Fantastic Realities Studio
www.fantastic-realities.com
Cover Concept by Michael Eric Stein
Earthrise images courtesy of NASA/JPL

Back Cover Photo Credits
Power to the People: Irvin Trigueros. Student Protest Crowd in Sacramento, CA., March 2014, via *Nation of Change*.
Give Peace a Chance: Evan MacPhail, Peace Protest, Oct. 27, 2007.
Black Lives Matter: Fibonacci Blue, Black Lives Matter Protest, Minneapolis, Minnesota, November 15, 2015. Creative Commons Attribution License.
No Justice, No Peace: Ron Anthony Bautista, Eric Garner Protest in New York, 2014.

ISBN-13: 978-0692859728 (Streetlight Books)
ISBN-10: 0692859721

Published in 2017 by Streetlight Books
Printed by CreateSpace, An Amazon.com Company
Available on Amazon, CreateSpace e-store, and other retail outlets.

Also by Michael Eric Stein

Continuous Trauma, a novel

All Good Things,
the stage musical story of the Remains

Cats' Eyes, a novel

Author Michael Eric Stein has been a novelist, playwright, screenwriter, television writer (*Miami Vice*, the CBS television movie *Higher Ground*), and a journalist writing on film, rock, jazz, and Hawaiian music and culture for *Films In Review*, the *Los Angeles Times*, and *Maui No Ka Oi Magazine*. He is a graduate of Yale University and the New York University Graduate School of Film and Television, and currently lives in New York City.

4 | **FIFTY YEARS AGO TODAY**

"Songs to aging children come..."
— **Joni Mitchell**

Dedicated to the young.

FIFTY YEARS AGO TODAY

"In a dark time, the eye begins to see."

— **Theodore Roethke**

8 | FIFTY YEARS AGO TODAY

Table of Contents

Preface and Acknowledgments	13
Introduction: We Wanted the World	21
The Music	37
Why the Music Isn't Over	39
Sweet and Dirty Water	43
Dylan, Cash, and the New Nashville Skyline	48
When Britain Rocked the Waves	53
Farewell Starman	59
Farewell Starship, and Hail *Blackstar*	63
Love and Mercy and California Nightmares	69
Music Hyphenation and the Changing of the Bards	74
Get Off Our Great Lawn	83
On Hearing Jimi Hendrix in a Cologne Commercial	88
The Velvet Motherland and the City of Dreams	92
It Was Fifty Years Ago Today	108
The Media	123
The Ultimate '60s Filmmaker	125
Bonnie and Clyde: From Theme to Meme	133
Lawrence of Arabia to W of Iraq	138
Gumping on the '60s	146
War is Hell Yeah	150
Tomorrowland: Beauty and the BS	154
Our Fair Lady	159
Selma and the '60s.	163
Selma and the Dramatization of History	166
The '60s and the Films of 2014	171
Loved It Madly, But Not the History	175

The N-Word and Other Shocks to The System	180
Marshall McLuhan: Medium of the Media	192

The Issues — 199

JFK: 1963, 1991, and the Twenty-First Century	201
Ferguson Won, Occupy Nothing	214
The New York PBA: Bringing Back the Ghetto	218
99 *Homes* and America Ain't One	223
Black Mass for Citizens	228
Fury Road Lingo and American Ecospeak	233
Punch the Hippie, Kill the Planet	240
Helluva Good Country Once	248
Peace Then	254
Hiroshima	263
Sticking to Our Guns	265
Generation Gapped	274
When Students Struck and Won	283
When Teachers Struck and Won—and Lost	298
Tom Hayden and American Freedom	304

The Counterculture: Back-And-Forward — 311

Bad Xanadus	313
Moon Age Daydreams and TV Reality	318
The Left Is Senator Goldwater Now	326
Woodstock and All After	344

Postscript — 369

Notes — 371

References/For Further Reading — 389

12 | FIFTY YEARS AGO TODAY

Preface and Acknowledgments

ifty Years Ago Today came about as a result of my blog, "Sixties Sense," an ongoing attempt to link the music, the movies, the ideas, and the issues of the '60s to the present day, using aspects of the cultural and historical richness of that decade to help understand the present. I was advised (with a touch of bemusement) that if I were really going to try to turn those blogs into a collection of essays, I would have to "drill deeper." Sixteen additional essays and many revisions later, I know the truth of that. The blogs radiated into related contexts, immediately suggesting additional essays, while blogs that seemed a good idea at the time turned out to be no more than that.

My interest in the decade stemmed first of all from the writing of my novel _Cats' Eyes_, set in the New York of the '60s, but also from my own experiences during the period itself.

The first few years of the decade were the last time I had a complete family; by the time I was thirteen my mother had died of a long, slow case of cancer. Faced with that strangely and sadly broken home life, I found my refuge in '60s New York. It wasn't totally without risk in a crime-ridden era, but I could run a lot faster then, both away from muggers and toward antiwar and civil rights activities and rock concerts.

My first anti–Vietnam war demonstration was at age thirteen, largely to be with the cool older kids, but by the time I was fourteen, thanks in part to encounters with the American Friends Service Committee and other antiwar groups, I was the anti-war-of-choice person I am today; pacifism in all but self-defense was from then on my main personal and political principle, and I would participate in many antiwar demonstrations and activities in New York and Washington DC. At one point during those years I rode my bicycle into the midst of the 1967 Be-In in Central Park; what I saw in Sheep's Meadow persuaded me to walk the bike and to gape in amazement for the rest of the day, and I would never stop enjoying the most creative and playful and loving aspects of that counterculture.

As for the music, my initial exposure to it was an extremely hip fellow summer camper who played us the Doors, the Butterfield Blues Band's *East-West*, Country Joe and the Fish, and *Freak Out* by the Mothers of Invention on the small (but stereophonic) record player in the Camp Winaco Rec Hall. All of it from record companies we'd never heard of (Elektra and Verve), which made it all the more fascinating. My first live show was the Blues Project, Wilson Pickett, and The Who and Cream's first American appearance at the Murray the K "Fifth Dimension" show at the RKO 58th Street. When the Who smashed their instruments I rushed the stage and never looked back. I would see Cream again (incredibly improved) at Hunter College, the Chambers Brothers at my high school, and soon after would become a weekly concertgoer at the Fillmore East. And I would be at Woodstock two of the three days and nights. All this before my seventeenth birthday.

It's not an exaggeration to say that for hundreds of thousands of young people The Music and the culture engendered by it was everything in the '60s. Not just the titans—the Beatles, Byrds, Stones, Dylan, Hendrix, Pink Floyd—but lesser bands (if you can call them lesser) from Quicksilver Messenger Service to Canned Heat, and even garage bands of the day, the one-hit wonders whose appearances on the hoary '60s music TV shows *Shindig* or *Hullabaloo* are a staple of YouTube.

With the music all we need to do is look back in pleasure and be grateful that such great popular art also had an influence on cultural history for decades (in short, it's the most upbeat part of the book). The efforts to link '60s music—including jazz, funk, soul, salsa, and even late classical compositions—to the present day need not be too strenuous. It's a given.

But beyond that there's the profound question of what does an era whose thinking was so dedicated to elaborating left-wing ideas of resistance to authority, the military-industrial complex, and capitalism have to teach the America of Donald Trump and the "free market"? How can the '60s visions of love and justice impact our far more cynical and irrational period? The fact is that in realms from resistance to wars of choice to the rise of a new civil rights movement, from the impact of new media to the disaffection of youth, the '60s and the early 21st century echo each other in ways that are almost uncanny.

Anyone who can answer "yes" to the old saying "Vass u dere, Cholly?" can confirm this. In a fly-on-the-wall, good-hearted high school way, I participated in Urban League "Give A Damn" ghetto (then) cleanups, which might have been a minor volunteer effort, but it made me aware for the rest of my life of the plight of people of color a few subway stops from where I lived, and just how intractable entrenched poverty, in its very geography of pain and anger, can be. I also worked as a volunteer for liberal-moderate-Republican (yes, it did exist once) Mayor John Lindsay, and learned that, whatever his mayoral shortcomings were, when he effectively kept urban peace in 1968 when every other city was rioting, it was something to be proud of; over the years I would learn that those efforts kept my city on the road to being the most open, tolerant, and multicultural American city for the rest of my life. Remembering the efforts of Mayor Lindsay and his aides, I can help but contrast them and their results to those of white (but sometimes black) mayors' and governors' policies toward de facto segregated and poverty-stricken cities like Baltimore and Ferguson.

Still I realize that when it comes to writing about the issues of the period, it's here where, given I'm mainly a writer on cultural issues with experience in film and television, I'm on my newest ground. So this is one reason why, in this book, these issues are often perceived through music and media, both from the '60s and the present day, especially since relatively recent movies and television shows have often revisited the period, and in movies like *Selma* and cable television films like *All The Way*, many of the historical issues. Finally, for anyone who doubts media's power over recent history I have three words: President Donald Trump.

And now the caveats. You won't find any essays in this book on gay rights and feminism, not just because they were only starting in the '60s (Stonewall and the first major new feminist demonstrations around 1969) but because, given my sex and sexual orientation, I have no experience to even begin to tell that story. I'm also no guide to the great African American literature and political thinking of the period, except to say if you haven't read writers like James Baldwin or the letters of Martin Luther King, Jr., do so as quickly as you can. As for Latino issues, no two-cents-or-less for similar reasons—but remembering the heroic struggles of Cesar Chavez and the United Farm Workers in the '60s, and the inhumanity they dealt with every day, I urge you to read literature and the latest political thinking relating to issues and threats facing them and their descendants.

And as you probably can tell if you've read this far, no one reading on should expect a smartly detached sangfroid about the era. I was fortunate enough, due to being a New Yorker and a budding writer with adventurous curiosity, to be able to be 'almost almost famous' during that time, Kid Zelig. The '60s formed my sensibilities forever, and even though I was quite young, I've never since felt more connected to the wider world. In part that was because my years of drug 'experimentation' (why do they call it that when if it totally succeeds you nonetheless keep wanting more proof?) had not yet begun. So I was alert during the '60s, in fact probably as alert as I'd ever be again. If you want ironical detachment about the era, this is not the book.

Given how the era did so much for me, my first debt of thanks is to Louise Tanner, the mother of my oldest friend in the world, who became my unofficial godmother in life once my own mother, her dear friend, had passed away. One aspect of this book of essays that gives me pleasure is that Ms. Tanner, an excellent and noted writer of her day, published a nonfiction book, *All The Things We Were*, that looked back on the decades of her life from the 1920s on and included a very sympathetic afterword on the then unfolding '60s (in fact, as a birthday present to her son, she took me and him to one of the original performances of *Hair* at New York's Cheetah discotheque). So I feel as if I'm continuing a fine extended family tradition.

It's also thanks to her that my dad ultimately did not veto my going to Woodstock. And I owe him a debt of thanks for, among many other things during that difficult period in our lives, telling me "I would have hated myself had I kept you from going to that." My dad was a post-FDR moderate "Rockefeller Republican" and no fan of the era's left-wing activity or most of the music (except for the Beatles, and later Steely Dan because, in his words, "they swing"). Yet he was also a piano prodigy whose parents had not allowed him to play pop or jazz, and the way I bonded with the old man was always through music (and his wise realization I needed somewhere else to be, that I needed, in the right way, to "go play in traffic.")

While I'm solely responsible for the writing, research, copy editing, and publication of *Fifty Years Ago Today*, I'd like to thank again Kurt Griffith for his excellent work on the cover, interior design, and website. As I mentioned in my '60s novel *Cats' Eyes*, I'm lovingly indebted to all my friends and family of the period, and owe thanks to everyone I personally interviewed for and acknowledged in that novel, and whose generously offered information I drew on once again for this book.

Finally I would like to extend a special thanks to what once was an American institution, *Life* Magazine. In an eccentric but eerily prescient move, I saved as much as I could (in excerpted form) of my old *Life* Magazine issues, which my mother had previously saved for me. As a writer and researcher decades later, I found there was nothing like going back to original materials, whether on microfilm or crumbling in the palms of my hands, to reawaken my consciousness of the period and to truly get a feel for the pulse of history beneath it. Those who want to put everything in digital form on Google and other (for now) free services and dispose of other archives should bear than in mind.

In the case of *Life*, what was startling was not just how good the photographs were: the best of the period, from the first corps of heroic black-and-white photographers to the countless nature photographers whose works are full-color treasures and the visual sagas of courageous war photographers like Larry Burrows. It's the writing that's really remarkable after all these years. If in the once mighty Henry Luce media empire *Time* was meant to be the boardroom-and-smoke-filled-room voice of the Establishment, *Life* had a broader mandate to reflect the full spectrum of American events in words and pictures, from nature to the first computers, from fads to consuming passions, from the lighthearted to the tragic.

Life thus became a full-on transmitter of the counterculture, devoting major coverage in 1969 not just to the moon landing but to Woodstock (an entire special issue) and the Vietnam Moratorium—and the magazine had a stance, depending on who was invited to write the article (which once became, in the famous 1968 "New Rock" issue, Frank Zappa) from moderate to pretty far left. From the perspective of our utterly antagonistic politics, it's remarkable to go back to what was very much a middle-of-the-road publication of the period and see how passionately, conscientiously, even lyrically its writers attempted to understand the new music and media and political upheaval of the time. Meanwhile other writers, combining with photographers outdoing themselves in series like "The Wonders of Life on Earth," gave us all a vision of the natural world that made everyone who immersed themselves in them environmentalists forever.

And in the spirit of those journalists and photographers, who never meant for their work to be definitive, the last word, or the paramount image, I hope that this book will not serve as a conclusive summary for anyone interested in studying the era and its relation to present-day America. It's meant to be a thought-provoker, a straw that stirs the drink, and those who want richer, deeper, and more scholarly insights into the period are directed to the "References and Further Reading" pages, which mention, just as examples, Marshall McLuhan's *Understanding Media*; Greil Marcus's *The Old Weird America*, a close and beautiful study of the work of Dylan and The Band; and Taylor Branch's *Parting of the Waters*, at nine-hundred-pages-plus only the first part of a magnificent Herculanean trilogy on the civil rights era that one could spend years studying.

Clearly the era still has much to teach us. We have never been in such dire need of its lessons.

20 | FIFTY YEARS AGO TODAY

INTRODUCTION

*"The old get old
And the young get stronger
May take a week
And it may take longer
They got the guns
But we got the numbers
Gonna win, yeah
We're takin' over
Come on! . . ."*

— Five to One, **The Doors**

*"Come mothers and fathers
Throughout the land
And don't criticize
What you can't understand
Your sons and your daughters
Are beyond your command
Your old road is
Rapidly agin'
Please get out of the new one
If you can't lend your hand
For the times they are a-changin'. . ."*

— **Bob Dylan**

22 | FIFTY YEARS AGO TODAY

We Wanted the World

Once upon a time, in an America far far away, a generation was told it was wonderful and that all its problems could be solved at their parents' knees or in the halls of government and science.

Television showed harmony nested in cozy suburban dens. Science (as showcased in *Life* Magazine, especially in the International Geophysical Year) seemed to have answers for everything, and outer space was the backdrop for a triumphal march to the moon. Jet travel would open up the world for us. The Kennedys' Camelot was in command. Prosperity saturated a wonderful New York World's Fair—as in literally full of wonders to a child's eyes. In fact the top comedy album we all listened to and laughed to was called *Wonderfulness*, a celebration of the joys of our baby boomer childhood by a comedian who was not only at the top of his game but was, as a TV star on *I Spy*, an emblem of successful "Negro integration."

And if our parents were agitated a little bit at something called the Cuban missile crisis; if we did shelter drills in the halls of our public schools in case the Bomb dropped, while wondering if, given images of the Bomb we'd seen, that would really help; if the Negro housekeeper dropped hints she came from another, more disturbing home environment; well, that missile crisis ended with a sigh of relief all around, and there was civil rights and James Meredith and Martin Luther King and that comedian, Bill Cosby. All would be well.

Maybe there were hints in every family of certain shadows if you looked hard enough. A war veteran at the card table whose odd behavior you were gently alerted to. Your parents' worries about what your dad called "The John Birch Society." A feeling of anger and pain in the folk music played at summer camp campfires. There was prosperity and the World's Fair in the early '60s, but it was laced with all sorts of "Age of Anxiety" aspects from just a few years before.

Then the anxiety and anger and grief exploded.

We were let out early from school to learn Camelot had been shot dead. There was the beautiful woman who'd showed us the White House with blood on her beautiful coat. We watched the assassination aftermath and funeral for four days—nothing else on television, no dens, no *Great Adventure* or *Bonanza* or *My Three Sons* or *Leave It To Beaver*, although those three days were not without a moment of what we would later call reality television. The assassin of the president was led out of the police station by Texas lawmen in white hats to face swift and sure American justice—until he too was murdered right before our eyes. One moment an image at a slight low angle to show the march of correction in all its power, then the blur of an unwanted extra and the crack of a gunshot and the villain of the hour's face contorting in anguish as he went down. Then that frame of the TV screen disintegrating to the stunned roars of the lawmen. The image of postwar peace and prosperity cracking up.

Much later, despite the hit we'd seen on television that implied (we all knew from the movies) some sort of mob justice, we were assured by a Commission true justice had been on the verge of completion and Lee Harvey Oswald was the lone assassin. But we weren't told that in the den, nor in the school, nor in the halls of science—and even the governor of Texas, who had been in the car with the president when he was slain, and had been shot himself, left us in our beloved *Life* Magazine with questions, not reassurances.

Soon after, the president's successor led the passage of a civil rights bill which we thought would solve the problems and quell the anger of that other race of people across town. It didn't. Science began warning of the threat of air pollution (and there were even some glimmers of worries about pollution and the climate) but we trusted science and the government would take care of that. They didn't. And when America's attempts to keep order in the world resulted in a war that we learned was ill-advised, immoral, and illegally undeclared, but we might be drafted to fight in it anyway, an Age of Rebellion began.

We had been told we were wonderful, on commercials, in those happy suburban family television shows, at the New York World's Fair. We were the inheritors of the World War II-winning, automobile-building, United Nations-hosting Americans, and the world was waiting for us. There was just one catch: it was the world our parents wanted us to have.

But in that world the war in Vietnam was a stalemate and a slaughter, where young American men were expected and compelled to put their bodies on the line. The outrages of lynchings and beatings directed against the civil rights movement in the South fought for TV time with those happy fictional suburbs. And then, on the same variety shows that had showcased Frank Sinatra and the Rat Pack and ring-a-ding-ding pass-the-highballs-and-the-stewardess came the Beatles, Stones, Airplane, Doors, sex for everybody, and intoxicants which were very different.

So in the same way our parents wanted the world they had won, we wanted another kind of world. A world in opposition to one we were supposed to be grateful to have. And when did we want it?

> *I hear a very gentle sound*
> *With your ear down to the ground*
> *We want the world and we want it...*
> *We want the world and we want it...*
> *Now*
> *Now?*
> *NOWWWWWWWWWWWWWW!*[1]

What do you expect from kids whose problems were solved in half-hour increments on television, who were promised the world, and now were being stunned into renewed awareness of that by the howl of Jim Morrison?

And we thought we could have that world, at least vicariously, through The Music.

"Pop is funny. It's a tease," Bruce Springsteen would later say, "It's an important one, but it's a tease, and therein resides its beauty and its joke."[2] But first came the beauty. The boys of the "British invasion," led by The Beatles, were, depending on your sex (or sexual orientation, though we didn't say that then), undoubtedly beautiful, excitingly sexy, or at least enjoyably goofy.

And when it came to The Beatles, the music was undeniably beautiful, by any formal or informal criteria you can name. Aided by the "fifth Beatle," producer and arranger George Martin, the orchestrations of the songs became more and more complex and ravishing. As for the compositions, it's hard to listen to songs like "If I Fell" or "In My Life," the interplay of harmonies and lyrics, and not think you're listening to the most perfect songs in the world.

But the Beatles proved to be far more than ultimate teen sensations and musical prodigies; they would share their private, privileged, first-off-the-block experiences of what would become the new mass Eastern-world-influenced, "free-love"-influenced, and marijuana-and-

LSD-influenced culture of the '60s and lead us personally to those new ways of seeing, hearing, and thinking. Their most beautiful and humane and yet also surprisingly complex expression of all that, *Sgt. Pepper's Lonely Hearts Club Band*, managed, in its fourfold brilliance, to both record, symbolize, satirize, and catalyze that transformation, and accelerated the changes by making them both pop and popular. Gentleman Paul, George the Seeker, and good old Scoutmaster Ringo wanted us to love it and make peace with it, and so make love and peace. But there was also in Rebel John's day in the life the awareness it might all happen way too hard and fast. I'd love to turn you on. Bring on the acid orchestra shrieking.

Many of the record albums of the '60s teased us into seeing, hearing, learning different truths, and thinking we could build that new world from them alone. The Stones and Cream brought our African American r & b back to us in newly crafted forms, followed by Jefferson Airplane and the San Francisco sound with its psychedelic and political anthems, and that would help stimulate a political revolution long before Senator Bernie Sanders used that phrase. 1967 through 1969 was a transformative moment and movement, a phase of doubt and liberation where Americans genuinely tried, in the words of Czechoslovakian dissenter and later president Václav Havel, to "live in truth"; some, like Havel, even got prison sentences for their struggles. It was a time long sought for and intensely fought for, transpiring in a fever dream. Morrison roared it. He and many others tried to live it.

You'll forgive the rhapsodic prose but it's truly appropriate for that period, especially as experienced by an adolescent. It really felt sometimes like creation, destruction, and improvisation in between streaming together in a time when America learned to see with the eyes of its artists, marginal people, native Americans, and rebels. Perceptions widening and colliding, sometimes engendering true peace and love, sometimes fostering madness, with countless discoveries both inside and outside of books and music. Compassion and synthesis tried to soften the process, but like tye-dye and light show ectoplasmic shapes and colors ingesting each other in a swirl of energy, all these perceptions and revelations bled into each other, sometimes badly, sometimes beautifully.

Adjustment to different colored faces, different foods, different art (and body paint), different pleasures, above all different music, people of different backgrounds learning (even if mocking) each others' experiences, it was a United Nations of America—and all about the value of diversity as it was comprehended then, and not simply because of the need to get beyond racism and sexism and xenophobia. It was the old Hawaiian saying "Knowledge does not come from one *halau* (school)." It's one reason one of the primary metaphors of the '60s was that of the tapestry: disparate fabrics and lives woven together in unprecedented integration, racial and otherwise, with London, New York, San Francisco, and Los Angeles the host Anglo-American cities of the splendid time guaranteed for all.

And part of the tapestry was on the other side: not only did we still, no matter how we felt about "Amerika," love that moon shot technology— we wanted to take it. Or as Paul Kantner would put it in his post-Jefferson Airplane *Blows Against The Empire*. "Hijack the starship … And our babes'll wander naked through the cities of the universe."[3] Hardly a realistic or drug-free view. But ominous pleasures in the Doors, aching for love and liberation in the music of the Airplane and the Dead—it was all different faces of a quest for ecstasy and new frontiers, psychological and technological, in what was perhaps the most mass-utopian phase of American history. And, although many were, you didn't have to be on marijuana or LSD to feel caught up in that.

Yes, we wanted the world now/then, and music and mass movements and popular philosophies and visions promised to give it to us. But right from the beginning, putting it in perspective, was a world-weary voice of remarkable knowledge and power. Even in his early twenties, Bob Dylan was the proverbial adult in the room: tough, relentlessly skeptical, owning up to consequences. That he could also be happily leading us in a chant of "everybody must get stoned" ("Rainy Day Women") or become downright exultant ("Chimes of Freedom") didn't mean he couldn't then chill us with the anger and despair of "Masters of War" or the ruefulness of "Blowin' In The Wind."

Our future Nobel Prize-winner was, as Elia Kazan said of that other great Midwestern popular artist-hero, Marlon Brando, a great channeler of human experience—as well as the songs of Hank Williams and Woody Guthrie combined with the poetry of Arthur Rimbaud and Allen Ginsberg. And as a result of all those influences he was more allusive and circumspect about the changes of the '60s.

Darkness at the break of noon
Shadows even the silver spoon
The handmade blade, the child's balloon

> *Eclipses both the sun and moon*
> *To understand you know too soon*
> *There is no sense in trying*
>
> *Pointed threats, they bluff with scorn*
> *Suicide remarks are torn*
> *From the fool's gold mouthpiece the hollow horn*
> *Plays wasted words, proves to warn*
> *That he not busy being born is busy dying.*[4]

Here, in one of his signature works, a proto-rap talking blues explosion of surreal poetry, was the balance to the wild desire and rage incarnated in Morrison's full-throated and almost infancy-seeking lyric scream: the constant forward motion with awareness of the choice and risk involved. *It's Alright Ma, I'm Only Bleedin.'*

There was in Dylan, however much he joined in the fun, an astringency to chase all that excess: the putdown, the put-on, the sadness of an old man's blues even in his twenties, the corrective sensibility that nonetheless found poetic escape and reverie in the love songs, some of the best ever. He was the first to organize the inchoate anger in the very best "protest" songs. He could puncture pretension, even about his own exalted status, as well as anyone.

And his career, its provocations, the literacy of his songs, was a reminder of the reason the passion of art (fired up by The Music) and protest (fired up by the Draft and the Bomb) and sexual liberation (fired up by The Pill) could spring forth in the '60s: there was a *balance* in the form of a divided but still basically tolerant, literate, and well-educated middle-class America. Ideals honed and nationally unified by resistance to fascism and in support of the United Nations, an excellent and financially accessible university system, a generalized approach of comity and team spirit, all allowed a disruptive but still mostly within-the-bounds appeal to be made for tremendous change. *Dionysus in '69* (an appropriate name for a theatrical piece about primal drives and liberation and excess) was balanced by *Apollo in '69* (an appropriate name for the brilliant science of the space program that would get us to the moon). Even and especially at Woodstock, what made the temporary city based on free love, free drugs, and free music work was ... good behavior. Yes, for all the furor of the "generation gap" of the time, Woodstock was a testimony to American parenting.

That balance also existed within the great rebellion, where it took the form of logical and rigorous knowledge and planning behind the protest and nonviolent resistance movements, as surely as knowledge of folk music and literature informed Dylan's songs: from the southern African American civil disobedience led by Martin Luther King (influenced by Mahatma Gandhi and Reinhold Niebuhr); to student strikes and building seizures led by the Students for a Democratic Society and Tom Hayden; to community organizing and the organizing of a massive national protest, the Vietnam Moratorium, according to principles derived from everyone from Thomas Paine to Saul Alinsky. And it was rooted in middle-class values and lawmaking and education. Bourgeois (as in "boozh-wa") might have become a putdown in the '60s, but it was the bulwark of all the values that allowed the era to flourish, along with a government that essentially supported institutions like city and state universities and labor unions.

And when so-called "rugged individualists" (often from states that have benefited from government largesse since the Homestead Act and railroad land grants) or law-and-order advocates (who saw nothing wrong in drafting young men to fight an unconstitutional war) or misguided labor unions (pitted against the college kids who might have supported them or might have even been their kids) or the police fought the political expressions of the changes of the '60s in the courts and streets, only smartly wielded legal defense could protect them. That was another achievement of the '60s: lawyers like Martin Garbus, William Kunstler, and Gerald Lefcourt, continuing the tradition of left-wing lawyers like David Scribner. They defended creative dissent as voiced and fought and enacted in media and religious circles by Lenny Bruce, Dr. Benjamin Spock (yes, a real Doctor Spock), William Sloane Coffin (the "bus-riding chaplain" of Yale), Fathers Philip and Daniel Berrigan, and the Chicago Seven.

The events that challenged America in the '60s happened at a speed that might seem fast even to America today, and that blizzard of changes happened to an America that was still—even after the Great Depression, World War II, and the atomic bomb—used to a much more tranquil pace of life. That drive for as fast a transformation as possible led to fanaticism and politically to extremism and equally extreme backlash, It's a line that, as Jim Crow found after one too many lynchings, and the Black Panthers found after one too many displays of guns, and as America found in Vietnam, could way too easily be crossed.

The exhortation to surrender your old self, especially in the quest to want and then possess a world, and with drugs and beautiful bodies to urge it along, is powerful. But, as the Dylan song suggests, in his ever dry and prematurely timeworn voice, what are the costs if you do? And what happens to the people who can't lose themselves, or who do a lousy job of it? Especially since there are no guarantees even for the people who can?

So the transforming moment and movement never completed itself, at least not in America. It achieved liftoff, orbited the planet, but landed hard and badly. The kind of fully achieved transformation that might have built a more just and free and economically inclusive and thriving society, that could've sustained middle-class comfort and scope of action—well, seen any presidential inaugurations lately?

Its promise was blocked by everything from white backlash to black activist overreach, from extremist acts of terror to an out-of-control FBI (and yes, we are talking about the '60s here), from drug trips that some never came down from to back-to-nature movements that became permanent withdrawals from society, from wasteful government antipoverty programs to not enough help where it was needed, from too militant schooling to destructive teacher union strikes.

Only in music could the great synthesists like Dylan, the Beatles, the Stones, Miles Davis, and Frank Zappa survive and build a legacy. For all the attempts to combine music and politics—John Sinclair of the MC5 declaring a rock band should be a revolutionary unit, the Airplane's songs about revolution—it never happened. For in the non-music-and-art-world, only strict discipline, high moral stature and intelligence, and heroic courage could have imposed a fruitful program on the wild onrush of events, and the three main figures who could've done that were assassinated. Instead we got Richard Nixon, a figure with that level of sagacity, perhaps, but obviously not the answer we were seeking.

So the '60s leaves us, fifty years on, with a triumphant cultural legacy, but, in the world beyond culture, with warnings and lessons about mistakes we definitely need to avoid. If this book's Music section contains most of the joy and hope, The Media and The Issues sections, which in many ways comment on each other, are more problematic, more troubling. The Issues section in particular reflects all the '60s turmoil, all the "who's side are you on?" pressures that were reflected in the lines in Buffalo Springfield's "For What It Worth" about young

INTRODUCTION | 31

people speaking their minds and paranoia striking deep and all sorts of battle lines drawn.⁵ And back then without social media you proclaimed that on your shirt or jacket, wearing buttons, from candidate buttons to antiwar buttons to buttons with slogans like the African American Urban League's "Give A Damn" to "Question Authority"; polarization then was literally more out front. Now that we're in another "whose side are you on?" era, the "Issues" section comments on what the '60s tell us about not just resistance and trying to change the system, but (surprisingly) thinking past conflict to mediation and solutions.

Still, when it comes to issues, and the temptation to fall into ideology, this, then and now, is where the beautiful tease falls short. This was where—as Springsteen's line surely evokes the era's great fantasy villain—the Joker was and still is laughing. And what perhaps amuses the Joker the most is how we're in danger of repeating the four main mistakes of the '60s, especially since we've already repeated the first two.

The first mistake would be ignoring the lessons of Vietnam and the Middle East simultaneously. In a ghastly irony that approached classic tragedy, the soldier who remembered well the lessons of Vietnam, Colin Powell, and who, as a result, had led our troops to a well-defined and well-ended victory in the first Gulf War—this soldier was persuaded (perhaps because he was a soldier) to forget those lessons, that need for a clear mission and exit strategy, public support, and a case of self-defense—and so would lend his credibility as Secretary of State in the United Nations to a second Iraq war that heeded none of those criteria and gave us thousands of dead and wounded troops, a decimated Iraq, and a quagmire in the desert with no end in sight. For, unlike the Viet Cong, our enemy from Iraq II would become a worldwide terrorist organization with a capacity for endless destruction.

The second mistake we've made goes back to the split in the '60s between the workers and unions and the New Left and their supporting intelligentsia, which has now become a split between the working/middle classes and their unions (what's left of them), and left-wing intellectual and political class and media mavens (what's left or will be left of them).

In the '60s, many unions hated the New Left and embraced Nixonian law and order, which eventually engendered Reaganomic conservatism—which led to the near-destruction of those unions. Meanwhile the New Left turned its back on the unions, if somewhat understandably after one too many beatings by construction "hardhats," which eventually contributed to the New Left's isolation and defeat. The fruit of this fifty years later is the election of President Donald Trump mostly by working and former middle-class groups who feel disempowered and forgotten by the intellectual and political Left—a man whose career was built on grinding down his working and middle-class vendors and construction firms or not paying them through bankruptcy and whose catchphrase became "You're fired!" Meanwhile students align themselves with potentially absolutist and alienating identity-politics-related campaigns.

After the '60s, the result of such a split, rather than collaboration between the intellectuals and working/middle classes, was that we did not get, as in France, Germany, and most of the then "developed" world, the goods and the protections of modern middle-class life, such as universal health care and a decent income safety net. Especially under a Trump administration, we now have a system of ideas and values and a government where almost any American not super-rich can at any time stand on the edge of an economic abyss.

Our police and criminal justice and for-profit-prison systems are now forgetting another great lesson of the '60s: that if you ghettoize people of color and treat them as an underclass there will be awful consequences. This time, since everyone has more destructive weapons (don't discount the ability of an underclass pushed to the wall to access those arms, not to mention cyberhacking), if '60s-era rioting and national disorder ensues, the losses may be unprecedentedly severe, especially since many of the old "ghettoes" are now fully diverse. The second Jim Crow of police abuses and mass incarceration will in all probability result in what the abuses of the '60s caused: disturbances approaching civil insurrection.

The fourth mistake is potentially the worst of all: the terrible denial of the environmental issues we once faced willingly and collectively after the publication of Rachel Carson's *Silent Spring* in 1962 and the first Earth Day at the end of the decade, in responses such as the Clean Water and Air acts during the Nixon administration, measures to stop acid rain in the Bush 1 administration, and collective efforts to restore the ozone layer. Now that a truly enormous economic conversion needs to be made to avoid climate cancer, land and ocean destruction, and atmosphericide, our government has been captured by powerful interests who could have enough of a cushion of profits to sustain them while they diversified their energy profile, but will now in all probability continue to block all political attempts to create such policies. The current American equating of fighting for the environment with "tree huggers" and hatred for regular American jobs is helping to drive the world to epochal disaster. A look back at the '60s can provide insights, even if neither so-called liberals or conservatives may one hundred percent approve of what they find.

Such a look back can also avoid a final mistake: succumbing to the negative consequences of our modern media. As the great '60s thinker Marshall McLuhan pointed out, our very use of the media influences history in the way it influences our perceptions, our attitudes, and the way we communicate and behave. McLuhan became our guide to how our own modes of communication and entertainment, particularly in the mass media, can rewire us in a neverending feedback loop, and warned us of its consequences. These need to be heeded now more than ever as we transform our very ways of absorbing information and thinking and seeing in a way even McLuhan, although he came close, never quite imagined. Our responses to new media are now conditioning our response to the most fundamental historical choices; just think of President Donald Trump's devastatingly effective use of Twitter, or the weird persuasiveness of false news on Facebook. So considerations of media and history are inseparable, then and now.

The '60s clarify the stark choices of the early 21st century more than any other era.

But there was inspiration there too, and not just from the music. Thomas Jefferson said in matters of style be flexible, in matters of principle be absolute; the trick is knowing which is which. The '60s had a ton of style, as the great TV show *Mad Men* displayed. But they also laid down enduring principles, even if they modulate according to circumstances. I might have understood why it wasn't a war of choice to kick Saddam Hussein out of Kuwait, and certainly why Osama Bin Laden had to be disposed of, but I will always be as antiwar as I was in the '60s. I may feel the Black Lives Matter movement, born of Ferguson, occasionally makes tactical mistakes, but I will always be for them and against Jim Crow no matter what party or region he's from, or what prison or corrupt court or police department he hides behind.

Above all, as many of us learned from hitchhiking and camping and meeting "back to nature hippies" or just educating ourselves in the ecological texts of the era, I will always be an unswerving environmentalist and conservationist—and if the '60s achieved nothing else, the beginning of the modern ecological movement marks them as the first decade of the glimmer of a hope of humanity's survival.

Let's look back with pride, if with a little skepticism, perceiving the present day through the lens of the '60s and the '60s in terms of the present day—and with an attempt at the honesty of the era, free of "parsing" of "nuances" and cynical '80's-style "irony" (surrender) and media "process" discussions. Most of these essays don't confine themselves only to the '60s. To revel in nostalgia, however pleasant it is to look back, is to do no more than feed on the glow of one's aging memory neurons in trying to recapture, as Max Bialystock said in Mel Brooks's *The Producers*, one last thrill on the way to the cemetery.

Still ... how to remember best those values? How to recognize and see through the reduction of '60s culture into commercial cues (Hendrix songs selling cologne), advertising signifiers for feeling sexy and rebellious (Bonnie and Clyde as mere images of badassness), and "slacktivist" world-saving with little or no effort (Global Citizen)? How to instead take the real thing into the future? Now that that American future is governed by President Donald Trump and his cabinet, such '60s values may be a vital bulwark against the kind of division and repression even the '60s generation has never experienced. To put it bluntly the Left, especially the old '60s baby boomer Left, lost big time—and for a long time, especially in dog, cat, or remaining baby boomer years. But the section "The Counterculture: Back and Forward" aims at ideas, consolation, and hope for the days and nights ahead.

To find the contemporary relevance, value, and lessons of history is the task of every aging generation. We can and must pass them on. In the case of the '60s, it's to remember all those attempts at liberation, both successfully achieved and still aspirational, remember all the fun (as the end of the Directors' Cut of *Woodstock* memorializes after its roster of dead musicians, "R.I.P. it up. Tear it up. Have a Ball.") but also remember the consequences and to fight to preserve the best of those values.

Above all, to just *remember*, especially to help a new generation that definitely needs more extracurricular non-politically-correct-censored historical awareness. The tone should be one of a celebration and an elegy. The American '60s were, in many ways, a classic tragic character, great and noble and brought down by the very flaws inherent in that greatness. The furious impatience. The heaven-storming hubris. The race to want and transform and rise up and take the world that all too often, especially on the most powerful drugs, became trips to nowhere and the ultimate coming down.

But during those years a lot of people were busy being born.

36 | FIFTY YEARS AGO TODAY

THE MUSIC

"That's what rock 'n' roll is, a promise, an oath."

— Bruce Springsteen

Why the Music Isn't Over

What is it about the staying power of '60 music that transcends boomer nostalgia?

> "*Let's all get up a dance to a song
> That was a hit before your mother was born.*"[1]
> – **Lennon-McCartney**

One of the hottest tickets on StubHub in 2015 was for the Grateful Dead 50th anniversary reunion in Chicago in July. Such a fan response was a remarkable testament to what the Dead, their music, the feelings behind it, and the music of the 1960s mean in American cultural history and in the rock pantheon of music fans everywhere.

I got a sense of this when I saw the production of *Hair* a few years back in New York. As a teenager, I'd gotten to see one of the original performances of *Hair* at the Cheetah discotheque. The Broadway revival was faithful to the set of the old show, to the renditions of all the tunes, even to the "Flower Power" and other counterculture leaflets handed out to the theatergoers, which completely took me back to the period. But the audience didn't. I was surrounded by kids and young adults in their twenties and thirties. They were wearing '60s-era fashions and completely getting into this almost fifty-year-old show.

All too many of my generational comrades believe that after classic rock of the '60s and the early '70s, rock turned to crap. A short of list of examples of why that's not the case could include Elvis Costello, The Pretenders, The Police, The Clash, Peter Gabriel, U2, Pearl Jam, Radiohead, TV on the Radio, and St. Vincent.

But there's no question that '60s music has a hold on the public and a staying power that's truly extraordinary, and which suggests that after the last baby boomer shuffles off to the eternal Buffalo, it will still be a touchstone in American lives. And the reasons have as much to do with the music's matrix of time and circumstance as the music itself.

The music of the '60s came out a crucible of constant live performing, a hard-ass work ethic behind the hedonism, that forged enduring bonds between the performers and their audience. The Beatles in Hamburg; the Stones' constant gigging around England and braving of a nightmare gig on American television's *Hollywood Palace* (which nonetheless helped break them out in America); the folk-rockers and Bob Dylan's campaign of concerts at Greenwich Village clubs and folk clubs throughout the country; and the fact that bands like the Yardbirds and the Doors would even play local high schools en route to big city performances, all cemented the early fan bases that propelled them to stardom. Even as they got more popular, groups like Jefferson Airplane and the Dead did so many free and low-priced concerts, many in venues where they were allowed to play spontaneously for hours, that you really got to love the bands and feel like you knew them. By the time of Woodstock, a solidarity had been created that would last decades, and that adults would inevitably want to pass on to their kids.

The musical potpourri '60s rockers could draw on in creating their sound was incredibly rich, not just historically but in terms of the confluence of music(s) occurring at the time: jazz, Latin, Broadway, pop, rock, folk, and soul were all having fertile periods, and even composers like Igor Stravinsky and Aaron Copland were still at work. And it was all available on mass-produced LP records and radio for the first time. The Beatles not only listened to, played, and transformed music from Buddy Holly and Chuck Berry but also the "Great American Songbook"; there on the old *Ed Sullivan Show* videos is Paul charming every skeptical adult in America with his version of "'Til There Was You" from Broadway's *The Music Man*. And of course he learned and copped from it—just listen to "And I Love Her."

The Rolling Stones aimed straight at American r & b and performed and copped from every source of blues and "race music" they could lay their hands on. Talk about, to quote Dylan's later album title, love and theft: Chuck Berry, old Chess Records, Bo Diddley—it was all fair game for the Stones as they basically repurposed America's roots music and brought it back to "US."

So did Eric Clapton with the blues, Bob Dylan with folk and many other strands of music, and Simon and Garfunkel not just with folk and early guitar rock like the Everly Brothers but folk music's awareness of styles like calypso music, which translated to an openness to international sounds that would go into Paul Simon's greatest solo achievements, *Graceland* and *The Rhythm of the Saints*.

This was the era of the first rapid access to world music and performers. When an Indian master of the sitar, Ravi Shankar, was able to come to America in what was the first age of jet travel and play major concert halls, and when his records could then be mass-produced and sold first to connoisseurs and then the public, rock music was transformed. George Harrison learned the sitar and brought it to the Beatles' music; its modalities then became a part of "raga-rock," named after the musical pieces played on the sitar, a heady strand of playing that runs through the work of bands like The Byrds and The Doors. This kind of serious and seriously fast transmission of foreign music throughout an entire music scene was up to this point unprecedented.

Along with increased ability to provide the music came a whole new level of absorbing it made possible by enhanced leisure time and music education in high schools and colleges. As was mentioned in the *New York Times* obituary of John Renbourn,[2] one of the founders of the folk-rock-jazz '60s group The Pentangle, from the very beginning he had been a scholar of medieval and Renaissance music, with a respect for and access to middle-class music education that's increasingly difficult to come by today.

And '60s rockers were able to freely experiment with what they knew and combine it with other sounds. The relative newness of studio technology, and greater time and space both physically and fiscally, allowed what Jerry Garcia once called the greatest gift to the Dead in the recording studio: freedom to fail. And the business consented to it. Frank Zappa once stated that a music executive had told him he didn't know what the hell Zappa was doing, but the kids seemed to like it, so go ahead.

And so they learned. Rock was studio-produced music in a way that hadn't been seen before, taking advantage of then new electronic technologies like overdubbing and sixteen-track music soundboards (not to mention all the new tricks that could be done with wa-wa pedals and feedback). The new music absorbed and recreated and altered the sounds of all the other music before it with an adventurousness that still sounds fresh today.

And the most media-connected generation up to that point could listen to just about any and all previous music on vinyl LPs and radio and recognize, enjoy, and make new hit song incarnations out of it. A Hammond organ could not only sound like Jimmy Smith or Booker T, but Johann Sebastian Bach, and it did on Procol Harum's chart-topping "A Whiter Shade of Pale." The Who created a rock opera, *Tommy*, while Sly and The Family Stone took soul music, itself an amalgam of gospel and r and b, and added rock to create an irresistible sound. Frank Zappa and his Mothers of Invention cooked up in the studio a mix of rock and jazz that pioneered jazz fusion with Stravinsky and Edgar Varese thrown in for good measure. Santana brought the Afro-Cuban influence ... it was all a smorgasbord of sounds, which to contemporary ears can tie '60s music to any number of other musical traditions, in the same way rap and hip hop's sampling links to pop music of the '60s through the '90s.

And no compendium of the virtues of '60s music would be complete without the p-words: Passion. Politics. Protest. Love songs for young adults that brought the adult part in, of which Dylan, the Beatles, and John Phillips of the Mamas and Papas were the masters. Fury at the Vietnam War and the civil rights struggle can constantly be heard in the songs of the era, which, to use one of the code words of the '60s, are still relevant: "Fortunate Son" by Creedence Clearwater Revival speaks to the military of today as powerfully as "What's Going On?" by Marvin Gaye can speak to black kids in Detroit or Ferguson.

Finally, the songs just plain hold up. From the Beatles' beauty to the Stones' sinew to Dylan's poetry to the Doors' ingenious use of the blues, the songwriting just doesn't get old. Their music will indeed be one of our only friends until the end.

But here's what's good about knowledge of why '60s music is so powerful and enduring: it can be a guide for success for new bands. The recipe goes something like this: constant live performing; unselfishly forming a nucleus of a "scene" with other bands (look at that Williamsburg rock explosion of the 2000s); insisting on freedom to experiment and grow; getting as deep a music education as one can, even if it's less formal songwriting or instrument classes and workshops—such as are offered in New York by local songwriters and bandleaders—or just endlessly listening to stuff on the Web; and drawing on real passion and a connection to what's happening in one's community, one's city, one's nation.

And for those who remember the '60s, those are certainly also reasons to (inclusively) defend the music of their youth. Not just "your mother should know."

Sweet and Dirty Water
An Idiosyncratic Genealogy of '60s Music

2015 seems to be the year to remember the Grateful Dead, signified by the video from Playing for Change in which musicians around the world joyously perform the Dead tune "Ripple." That signifies an enormous achievement: A band that had started out fifty years ago playing free-form variations on rock 'n' roll and jug band music, and then brought in elements of acidhead anarchy, studio experimentation, and the blues, evolved over the decades into perhaps the all-American band of all time. And true to the title of that song, their music became a river into which flowed folk, bluegrass, acid rock, country music, bass player Phil Lesh's classical training, even elements of jazz improvisation.

It seemed to me (also thinking of the title of that song) that the Dead's music has always aimed for that kind of flow. The plashing of a mountain stream, the evanescence of sunlight on the waves, divergent strands of peaceful and beautifully adorned melodic phrases in constant motion and harmony. A musical goal that could be summed up in the phrase "sweet water."

There was an actual band named Sweetwater, a group that was a warmup act at the Fillmore East and that played at Woodstock. That reflected a kind of pastoral ideal that much of the music of the time aimed for: harmony with nature and natural resources and an older, purer and closer-to-the-earth American tradition. The Grateful Dead's music exuded that kind of feeling, and found its east coast equivalent in the songs of The Band, harder rocking and tighter, but still harkening back to that connection to the land and to earlier kinds of music, from gentle folk lays to square dances to marching bands in songs like "Whispering Pines," "Rag Mama Rag," and "The Night They Drove Old Dixie Down." Still tighter, simpler, but rural- and country-oriented in all their work was Creedence Clearwater Revival.

And David Crosby (who plays on the "Ripple" video) exemplified what might be called the more sophisticated Laurel Canyon brand of that kind of "sweet water" folk-leaning pastoralism, from his work in The Byrds, who initiated country rock with *Sweetheart of the Rodeo*, to his songs with Crosby, Stills, Nash, and Young ("Guinevere"). The Mamas and the Papas (with exceptions for John Phillips' most bittersweet romantic ballads), Joni Mitchell in her early albums, Gram Parsons and the Flying Burrito Brothers—all were a part of that tradition.

But along with the sweet water flowed the dirty water—exemplified by the tune "Dirty Water," a '60s singles hit by The Standells with a great slap-happy backbeat that I've always enjoyed except when it signals that the Red Sox have beaten the Yankees. It was part of an urban rock tradition that accepts the grit and shadows of a life far removed from pastoral pleasures, that revels in it, that finds in its energy and pulse and intellectual and political undercurrents a source of wit, protest, passion, all filtered through many different types of musical influences.

The tune "Dirty Water" is basically a 12-bar blues, and rhythm and blues, along with the edginess absorbed from songs by Bob Dylan and social protest folk-rock singers, were the essential elements of '60s urban rock. For the Brits of Liverpool and London, American r & b and early rock 'n' roll was their folk music. That "hard stuff" was the legacy reinvented by the Beatles, the Stones, the Kinks, Cream, and The Who; major American bands didn't rock that hard in the same way during this period, except for Sly and the Family Stone and Santana, whose grooves came from whole other sources, and "America's lost band," the proto-garage-rock band The Remains.

In the States, the Paul Butterfield Blues Band and their offshoot the Electric Flag broke out blues-rock, along with, on the West Coast, Janis Joplin and Big Brother and the Holding Company. Another great blues-rock band, although they artfully disguised the form in so many ways that they're not known for it ("Love Me Two Times," "Riders of the Storm"), was Los Angeles's The Doors.

Talk about the ultimate "dirty water" band. L.A. music before The Doors had been primarily influenced by the cheerful and instantly hummable tunes of the Beach Boys, and the more melancholy and sophisticated but still healing impulses Brian Wilson brought to *Pet Sounds*.

That was not what Jim Morrison and The Doors were about. In a remarkable article from *Life* Magazine, "Wicked Go The Doors," Fred Powledge described going with his daughter to a Doors concert, becoming fascinated by their sensuality, genuine poetry, challenge to the audience, and "social comment," and then sharing his daughter's outrage when Morrison got arrested for taunting the police.[1]

The music of the '60s, as everyone knows, was heavily influenced by marijuana and LSD "acid trip" experiences. If the more "sweet water" groups saw bad acid trips as occasional nightmares in a dreamscape, roadblocks on a fantastic journey toward visions and harmony with the universe, the Doors' songs seemed to see them as opportunity: while you're there, have a look around. Jim Morrison's lyrics seemed inspired by the kind of drug experiences that fueled Rimbaudesque poets looking into the abyss. Even the Doors' rare happier visions, like "The Crystal Ship" with "a thousand girls, a thousand thrills"[2] had that shadow of pain, a more louche kind of hedonism, a darker edge. Even a hit teen romancer like "Hello I Love You" had that tinge of depravity.

The Doors' "weird scenes inside the gold mine" were filled with a primal dread and sexuality, their long album-ending oratorios were full of sociopolitical and even ecological protest, and their musical walk or lope or swing was definitely on the wild side. Much of the mystery and feeling of alienation in their music came from its exotic (at the time) influences beyond the blues, like Baroque harpsichord music, Brecht-Weill songs, and above all a raga feel, borrowed from the Indian classical sitar music played by Ravi Shankar.

That Indian-Near Eastern musical influence was also powerfully felt in The Doors' East Coast musical cousins The Velvet Underground in songs like "Venus In Furs," along with a heavy blues backbeat in "I'm Waiting For The Man" and "White Heat/White Light." Both bands had elements of confrontational theater in their stage acts, especially Morrison in his furious rock shaman mode, and both bands weren't afraid of offending anybody, from the hippies who found the Velvets too downbeat and scaggy to (in the case of The Doors) the master of '60s Sunday night television, Ed Sullivan.

But the greatest and most conscious offenders and exponents of "dirty water" music, so outrageous that there was no chance of them landing conventional radio or tv airplay, were Frank Zappa and the Mothers of Invention. Zappa's fertile musical genius combined elements of rock, L.A. greaser music, comic opera, Igor Stravinsky, sonic experiments, any mouth noise he found disgusting and funny, and compositions and improvisations that would help engender fusion jazz-rock and even yield a conservatory-based body of work.

There was no classifying him, but there was plenty of resistance to him, which he actively courted. He went on the attack against Top 40 radio, religion, and conventional sexual morality to the point that in his oratorio "Brown Shoes Don't Make It" on *Absolutely Free* he characterized a "City hall mind" politician as a pederast (shocking back then). His shows were, for those of us who saw them, a blend of great music, scathing black humor, and sociopolitical views that grew more and more articulate until he wound up testifying before Congress against censorious labeling of rock records (with Twisted Sister's Dee Snider and yes, John Denver at his side).

And while he was not one for conventional political protest, his angry mid-'60s song about the Watts riots, "Trouble Comin' Every Day,"[3] was one of the best of the genre, with brilliant ricochets of lyrics that condemned not just racism but the general stupidity that allowed the riots to happen ("... the color of your skin just don't appeal to him no matter if it's black or white because he's out for blood tonight."). His attacks on con-artists and the gullibility that fostered their creeds were aimed at the counterculture as well; *We're Only In It For The Money* is the all-time anti-hippie record, and its title and outrageous *Sgt. Pepper* parody cover is a deliberate putdown of "flower power" and "beautiful" pastoral musical ethereality. As a final grace note to his musical legacy—given he valued humor above almost anything else—the record he did with his daughter Moon in the '80s, "Valley Girl," became his one huge hit, mocking as it did a particular mode of girlspeak, and that girlspeak is now the default mode of talking for young women throughout New York City. (Hope you're having a good laugh over that one somewhere, Frank.)

So you can almost look at American '60s rock as pastoral sweet water from The Grateful Dead, the later Byrds records, CSNY and the Band versus the urban dirty water of the blues-rock bands, the Doors, the Velvets, and Frank Zappa. Of course, that would be overly simplistic, especially since the greatest acts found ways to fuse both strands in their work.

John Sebastian of the Lovin' Spoonful wrote one of the all-time kickass urban anthems, "Summer In The City" (it may not seem to rock hard now, but it sure did then), but primarily the band played "good time music" based on jauntier strains of folk that they distilled into irresistible Top Ten singles. Simon and Garfunkel were known for their beautiful vocal and guitar harmonies, with an English madrigal pastorality, but sharp New York wit, age of anxiety angst, and social protest were a part of Paul Simon's writing from "Sounds of Silence" to "Mrs. Robinson" and beyond. And of course Bob Dylan wrote music and lyrics based on everything from romantic folk songs to blues to early rock and roll to poetry and Shakespeare.

Two bands of the '60s blended the pastoral and urban strands so well that the first band led the American pack in terms of '60s hits and is very fondly remembered, while the second band is one of rock's immortals. San Francisco-based Jefferson Airplane were thoroughly imbued with the pastoral, summer-of-love, acid-rock influences of the Bay Area. But thanks to Marty Balin's Broadway background and Grace Slick's east coast education, there was plenty of New York/Brill Building smarts and urban influence in the band's sound; you can hear it in Slick and Balin's soaring and soulful harmonies, or a truly arresting experiment like "Rejoyce," Slick's musical setting of the Molly Bloom soliloquy. Like the most urban bands, they dipped heavily into raga-rock grooves, which lead guitarist Jorma Kaukonen, rhythm guitarist Paul Kantner, and bassist Jack Casady played with a jazz-level adventurousness complemented by Spencer Dryden's drumming.

Fronted by the beauteous and daring Ms. Slick, they became the most popular and commercial of the '60s bands, while putting out albums like "After Bathing at Baxter's" (aka "Ignition") which are still stunning in their combination of songwriting chops, acid-rock interplay, and a moving evocation of the spirit of the times.

But none of the above, as Bill Graham, impresario of the Fillmores East and West, once stated, nobody could touch Jimi Hendrix. Hendrix began by playing the chitlin' circuit behind everyone from the Isley Brothers to Little Richard, absorbing every kind of American blues and r & b. When he moved to England and formed the Jimi Hendrix Experience (Noel Redding on bass, Mitch Mitchell on drums), he took in whole other ways of writing and playing songs, famously learning the lead tune from *Sgt. Pepper's* right after the album was released. His music was primarily urban, fusing blues, r & b, raga-rock, psychedelia, and Beatles-level studio experiments, but songs like "Little Wing" and "Angel" show he could play in a yearning, folk-influenced vein as well. In Hendrix and his incredible guitar, all the voices of the '60s met, and his *Cry of Love* album led the way for much of '70s funk and carried hints of his own kind of jazz as well.

We might have had a whole other genealogy of sweet and dirty water music had Jimi Hendrix lived past his twenty-eighth birthday.

Dylan, Cash, and the New Nashville Skyline

Remembering a truly remarkable musical exhibit at the CMA Museum and Hall of Fame.

Not to criticize my beloved Jefferson Airplane/Jefferson Starship or San Francisco, but despite the song "We Built This City on Rock and Roll," contemporary San Francisco owes more to silicon than vinyl. There's only one city that's been built on music, that's been called Music City for centuries, and that's still more than earning the name today.

Nashville has not only kept its identity as the home of classic country music, gospel—its first international touring group was the Fisk Jubilee Singers, who moved Queen Victoria to dub Nashville "a musical city"—bluegrass, and the Grand Ole Opry. It's also home to the most powerful songwriting community in the country, grounded in the legacy of everyone from Hank Williams to Kris Kristofferson to Zac Brown. And as an exhibit at the Country Music Association Museum and Hall of Fame, "Dylan, Cash and the Nashville Cats," shows in detail, Nashville owes much of its resurgence to a series of fortuitous musical conjunctions that began in the mid-to-late 1960s.

You might not expect to see an exhibit headlining Bob Dylan at the CMA Hall of Fame, which has been dubbed "The Smithsonian of Country Music," and was formed in part to help stem a rock 'n' roll tide that once threatened to relegate country music to archival backwaters. Now that country music is glitzily prosperous, and the CMA has a giant building with continuous hallways of exhibits and educational centers (one from Taylor Swift)—not to mention an annual CMA festival that attracts 80,000 people a day—you might expect them to stress their own heritage. Country music's history after all includes the King of rock 'n' roll, Elvis Presley, and his solid gold Cadillac on display right there in the Hall, and features plenty of musicians whose beliefs are, to say the least, to the right of the rock world.

But here's the first surprising fact you learn at the CMA Hall of Fame: country music has always been more inclusive than you'd suspect. It's a real people's tradition, with the occasional prejudices but all the universal sorrow, anger, and joy that suggests. In fact,

Gene Autry, the '50s singing cowboy who began his career in the '30s, compared himself to President Franklin D. Roosevelt in his caring for the common man. For those who think country music has always been right wing, here are some of Autry's words: "While my solutions were a little less complex than FDR ... I played a kind of New Deal cowboy who never hesitated to tackle many of the same problems."[1]

The CMA Hall's screen stanchions featuring video and audio performances, its displays of artifacts (everywhere in Nashville is a kind of living country music archaeology, with costumes of famous stars, letters, musical instruments)—and, in glass walls beyond the nearest exhibits, its still more and still bigger artifacts—all track a richly multivariate vision of country music heritage: fiddle-oriented Appalachian music met jazz to create western swing; Memphis Beale street r & b met hillbilly music to create the rockabilly of Presley; "race music" and Scotch-Irish music happily miscegenated where the actual races were forbidden such things. Visitors to the Hall should steep themselves in that history before entering the Dylan and Cash exhibit to appreciate how the stage was set for the next and maybe most important step in modern Nashville's evolution.

"Dylan, Cash, and the Nashville Cats" is as thorough and entertaining a study of a music scene as you're likely to see, with all the usual artifacts on display—guitars, sheet music, period photographs, and videos—but also a series of listening booths, where one can wander in and hear tracks from both the Nashville musicians themselves and the famous artists that they played behind. The walls and ceilings are adorned with paintings and posters from Jon Langford, founding member of the Mekons, which have the punky edge you'd expect from an artist from that era, but also a density of colorful detail and a roughewn quality to the portraits that recall the passions, commitment, and restless seeking of that earlier time.

It was a time when Dylan had stopped doing what he called "finger-pointing songs" and had become a rock musician, alienating his original fan base even as he achieved stardom. Now he was once again uneasy and needing a new musical direction. He wrote a series of letters to Johnny Cash, whom he revered ("Johnny was and is the north star,"[2] he would later say) stressing he was from Hibbling, Minnesota, and that he loved to sing Hank Williams's "I'm So Lonesome I Could Cry." He wanted to come down to Nashville and record cuts of his new album *Blonde on Blonde* with the Nashville session musicians, made famous by the Lovin' Spoonful's mid-'60s hit "Nashville Cats."

As Dylan and Cash became friends and Dylan shifted away from more left wing music, Cash was able to defend him and introduce him to the more conservative Nashville community. When Cash began his variety show from the Ryman Auditorium in the 1970s and wanted to introduce the new singer-songwriters to his huge country audience, Dylan was one of his first guests, followed by stars like Neil Young and Joni Mitchell. And as Dylan changed the culture of Nashville, he was changed by it. On "One Too Many Mornings" and other songs like "Lay Lady Lay" from his album *Nashville Skyline*, Dylan changed the timbre of his voice, and, in a move that was shocking to many back then, even cut his hair. Meanwhile he encouraged the tightly rehearsed Nashville musicians to improvise more with him and Al Kooper and Robbie Robertson, his standbys, and they learned from Dylan and grew to admire him.

Johnny Cash would go on to break down all sorts of musical divisions in his career. His bravery and musical smarts played a big part in creating the new country music and merging the cultures of Nashville and rock. Of course it wasn't all smooth sailing. Kooper, then Dylan's organist, recalled when he was walking down a Nashville street and got catcalled and chased by thugs for his long hair and psychedelic garb until other musicians showed up and helped protect him. But in the long run musicianship overcame the divisions of the '60s because everyone wanted to play with the laid-back, professional, virtuosic "Nashville Cats."

The Nashville musicians Dylan brought into his *Blonde on Blonde* sessions—Charlie McCoy, Kenny Buttrey, Wayne Moss—soon found plenty of work. San Francisco's youth-oriented stars, like the band Moby Grape, made the trip down there. Gordon Lightfoot came from Canada, and Dylan liked his music so much he called him an influence on his album *John Wesley Harding* (my choice for Dylan's greatest Nashville-oriented work), which in turn made a Dylan-lover of Jimi Hendrix, who recorded two of that album's songs.

Then came Simon and Garfunkel ("The Boxer"), Fred Neil, Ian and Sylvia, Neil Young (*Harvest*), and The Byrds (*Sweetheart of the Rodeo*). As Fred Carter Jr. said "They came in, we recorded 'em, they got hits and then they left. For twenty years we turned 'em out like water."[3] There's a bit of anger there at the lack of credit and money (welcome to Hollywood, Fred) but also pride in how the Nashville Cats became such an integral part of America's musical DNA.

Their influence continued into the '70s. Linda Ronstadt, Leonard Cohen, and George Harrison in his solo period went to Nashville to play with the "Nashville Music Machine." Cohen called the atmosphere "free from judgments, free from criticism" while Steve Miller said in awe "they learned a song in seven minutes."[4] Country rock and a renaissance of acoustic singing/songwriting came out of that music scene, along with of course a whole new wave of powerful and profitable country music, from Kris Kristofferson to Garth Brooks and beyond.

The pride and warmth from that period, that memory of a playful, ingenious, creative musical communion, glows from the exhibit and creates an ambience that leads visitors to congregate and hang out. By the walk-in open-sided listening kiosks people of all generations sometimes sit on the ground chatting as they listen to the music or remember events of forty-five years ago; the exhibit has an informal, relaxed feeling unlike any museum exhibit I've gone to since, well, maybe the '60s.

In 2015, the Nashville skyline that Dylan showed on the back of his album of the same name is now completely transformed. Nashville has emerged from the disaster of the 2010 flood stronger than ever. And it has weathered all the cross-cultural collisions that were part of the great Robert Altman movie *Nashville* to become the ever-diversifying and more sophisticated city of the television show *Nashville*. Since 1925, the Grand Ole Opry has been and still is the magnet that draws the classic country musicians, from Hank and Waylon to Faith and Carrie. And there's no question that Nashville's resurgence owes a lot to classic country's bounceback—you can feel that at an Opry show with new act Canaan Jones, some international bluegrass, and enduring country stars Larry Gatlin and Reba McIntyre playing to a packed house.

Still it's hard to imagine the Nashville of today without going back to the events of that literal harmonic convergence of Dylan, Cash, and the Nashville Cats over forty-five years ago. The new Ryman Auditorium, which has hosted so many rock and especially '60s-era superstars (Jeff Beck having been the latest as of this writing). The world-famous Bluebird Cafe, with its emphasis on the kind of commercial yet unplugged and personally performed songwriting that first emerged in the '60s and '70s (not to mention that its performing songwriters, like Gordon Kennedy, have written huge hits for stars like Eric Clapton).

The fabulously successful annual CMA Hall of Fame Music Festival, which would not be as successful if only the Opry's audience showed up. Studios like Blackbird, headed by Martina McBride's husband John, with absolutely state-of-the-art facilities that have attracted not just country stars, but rockers, rappers, and Aretha Franklin. A booming city with a workforce 65% of whom are musicians.

The modern Nashville is built on all kinds of music. And Bob Dylan, Johnny Cash, and the Nashville Cats of the '60s are its architects.

When Britain Rocked the Waves

After the British blues-rock band Ten Years After were catapulted to success by their appearance in the film *Woodstock*, which immortalized Alvin Lee's solo guitar work on the jam number "Goin' Home," the band made many tours of the United States and discovered a puzzling gap in fans' awareness of their music.

"The strange thing was we had gone to what I considered to be the home of the blues, but they'd never heard of most of them, and I couldn't believe it—'Big Bill who?' [as in Big Bill Broonzy]" Mr. Lee recalled in a 2003 interview with *Classic Rock* magazine. "We were recycling American music and they were calling it the English sound."[1]

Mr. Lee wasn't the first to have his music so misnamed. All the British bands who'd come before him, and who'd developed their styles from American early rock 'n' roll and r & b, were in part the beneficiaries of American fans' ignorance of their own r & b and rock 'n' roll songs, which in some cases were no more than a few years old. The "British invasion" of the mid-'60s was rooted in Americans having forgotten or neglected their own music, leaving their ground to be occupied by a frenemy. The redcoats came but in this case they brought us freedom: a return to awareness of the roots of our music and musical liberation.

To see how this happened—beyond the fact that the British bands, led by The Beatles, had a foreign and irresistibly appealing charm, and rode a wave of fondness for Britain going back to World War II and beyond—it's important to remember just how sanitized and "whitened" American music had become in the early to mid-'60s. America had pioneered the mix of rockabilly and r & b "race music" that in the '50s, spearheaded by the phenomenal Elvis Presley, became early rock 'n' roll. But by the onset of the '60s, America was already trying to escape from it, especially after trailblazing piano rock 'n' roller Jerry Lee Lewis faced a wave of moral condemnation over his "child bride" and numerous politicians inveighed against "the devil's" (i.e., black) music. Chuck Berry and a host of African American acts were being marginalized, ripped off, tamed, cleaned up, and anaesthetized by "Brylcreem brigade" acts like Fabian, Bobbys Rydell-Vee-Vinton, and Pat Boone. Elvis Presley was past his early rock 'n' roll prime and churning out some of his more forgettable music in his mostly forgettable series of films.

And so American young people, seeking a more authentic music to address their growing concerns, were not about to turn to this new homogenized clean-clear-through version of rock 'n' roll, which was not that much different than the studio confections of Patti Page or Dean Martin in his ring-a-ding-ding mode. They chose folk music, which was free of control by the record companies, playable on guitar and banjo and other non-orchestral instruments, and had simple and powerful chords and melodies that either had weighty lyrics of their own or that could be adapted to satirical or angry comments on the news of the day. Even Bobby Darin and Dion, "Brylcreemers" and members of the early '60s teen idol wave, were quietly undertaking a study of the folk scene that would lead Darin to record Tim Hardin's "If I Were A Carpenter" and Dion to have a surprise '60s hit with his gentle elegy to America's slain leaders "Abraham, Martin and John." Years later the Beach Boys' career as top-20 hitmakers would gain another dimension with the folk- and-Beatles influenced *Pet Sounds*.

There was a clear strain of African American influence in folk music, especially songs by artists like Leadbelly, but overall the folk phenomenon was young white people discovering a music embedded in British, Scotch-Irish, and European traditions that they could play and sing and build on wholeheartedly and unaffectedly. There was of course a strong and similar folk revival in Britain too, especially among female singers like Marianne Faithful. But British lads looked for inspiration in very different sources, in a way that seems all the more mysterious when looked at from a fifty-years-on perspective.

Listen to something as raw and craggy as Robert Johnson's backwoods holler on the original "Crossroads," perhaps his most well-known song, and however hard the guitar hand thumps, you can't help but be amazed at how young Brits like John Mayall and Eric Clapton figured out how to adapt this sort of music to propulsive rock rhythms and flying jazz-length solos. Delta blues, especially Robert Johnson's, existed in a totally different geographic, sonic, affective space than postwar British cities; to tap into the greatness of a Robert Johnson or Howling Wolf was to reach out not only to a different era but a different world. It wasn't like Scotch-Irish-descended folkies warming up to Scotch-Irish folk lays; it was white urban Brits adopting the music of black ex-slaves. The tension and beauty of Johnson's music is in the empty space of implied beats and fragmentary, allusive picking and chords; for Cream to have added a driving rock beat and fulsome improvisation to a song like "Crossroads" seems an almost impossible feat of musical alchemy.

But of course Clapton, Bruce, and Baker had plenty of help in learning the electric blues techniques of Muddy Waters and Buddy Guy, not to mention the up-and-coming fully "integrated" Butterfield Blues Band. They could hear how, in the words of Chuck Berry, there was a "backbeat you can use it,"[2] and like the Beatles and Stones before them, they had not chosen to forget Elvis, or Chess Records, or Little Richard-Jerry Lee Lewis-Chuck Berry, or their own chugging skiffle music. And the fact that many blues forms had a kind of swing built into them naturally suggested extended solo techniques, always anchored to those rock-ribbed chords and harmonies.

Still, it took dedication and passion and plenty of (to be non-British) chutzpah, in part explainable by the way that young and hip British music lovers brought the same passion to collecting blues as folk was collected stateside, in part because their gritty postwar upbringing more instinctively connected them to this hard-lived music.

There were plenty of British bands who "invaded" America with pop and folk and British music-hall influenced tunes, some real beauties and charmers, like Billy J. Kramer's "Little Children," Herman's Hermits "Mrs. Brown You've Got a Lovely Daughter," Freddie and the Dreamer's "I'm Telling You Now," and the New Vaudeville Band's "Winchester Cathedral." If you're below a certain age and drawing a blank on these, you're forgiven. What you're not going to draw a blank on is the r & b-influenced music: The Beatles singing Chuck Berry's "Roll Over Beethoven," which led directly to their "A Hard Day's Night." Or The Kinks' initial burst onto the scene; though leader Ray Davies would later rollickingly fold in Brit music hall traditions into some of their biggest hits, their first chart-toppers turned the basic r & b "Louie, Louie" beat in two different hard-rocking directions for "You Really Got Me" and "All Day and All of the Night." And the Zombies mixed jazz and folk with tougher rock beats for "Tell Her No" and "She's Not There."

Above all there were The Rolling Stones and The Who. The Stones' dedication to bringing American blues and r & b into their music was an absolute landmark of the music of the era and paved the way for the Yardbirds, Eric Clapton and Cream, Led Zeppelin, and all blues rock and heavy metal to follow. The first Jagger-Richards song, "The Last Time," took its refrain from an African American spiritual. Their reworking of delta blues and Chess Chicago blues tunes led the pack. But oddly, after their megahit "Satisfaction" and great *Out of Our Heads* album, they sometimes seemed in the '60s a prematurely spent force. They were bogged down in personal problems and (especially in the case of the doomed Jones) drug issues, and they appeared to be camp-following the Beatles, especially with their "flower power" albums; of course they were actually engaged in a creative rivalry with them, pushing folk-influenced pop songwriting more in their own musical directions. Anything Jagger saw as seductive he would try, and he quickly saw the possibilities of the troubadour mode; the Stones had a few very successful madrigalesque folky compositions, from "Ruby Tuesday" to "Sitting On A Fence." But the late '60s were an uneven ride for them, culminating in the much-maligned, drowning in musical excess, but adventurous and quite beautiful *Their Satanic Majesties Request.*

Starting in 1969 they would leave their medieval modes, pipes of Joujouka, and impressionistic jams behind. With *Beggars' Banquet* and *Let It Bleed* they recovered their own voice and embarked on a triumphant tour, although marred at its climax by the Altamont concert with its miserable conditions and Hell's Angels homicide. But with *Banquet* came the fusion of great songwriting that tapped into music of people of various colors, the hard rock riffs, and lyrical baditude that would rule the '70s and incorporate black music into their own urban sound; you don't come up with a masterpiece like *Exile on Main Street* through mimicry.

A (rock) generation later, The Who similarly went back to hard-rocking basics, like their cover of "Summertime Blues," but with Carnaby flash, Mod and Day-Glo colors, some of the Beatles symphonic musical palette, and folk's beauty to fight the British postwar greyness. Their "aggressive r & b" was overlaid with everything composer and musical polymath Pete Townsend heard, from the chords of lyrical ballads, to music of a classical bent carried by John Alec Entwhistle's French horn, to parodies of other kinds of music and vaudeville music (as in "A Quick One While He's Away," Townsend's Brit kitchen sink mashup of *The Odyssey*), to long-held-chorded refrains and anthems made possible by Keith Moon's sustained blasts of drumming. He and the band would pour it all into the full-blown "rock opera" score of *Tommy* and the song cycle of *Quadrophenia*.

And no survey of British rock is complete without the magnificent '60s outliers the Moody Blues, King Crimson, and above all Pink Floyd, who quickly skipped from tuneful rock to exploring the long lines and darkly wide-open spaces of a more psychedelic and symphonic mode and, through everything from lineup changes to venturesome leaps into worldbeat rhythms to incorporating Brian Eno's ambient music, kept going into the '80s and '90s and beyond. But the root was always a heavy rock beat.

Meanwhile American music of the '60s never was quite that hard-rocking. It turned toward cheerfully swinging jug band-based music (the Lovin' Spoonful and the early Grateful Dead), heavily folk-influenced psychedelia and acid and raga rock (Jefferson Airplane), and a more archival closer-to-the-bone kind of blues (Canned Heat, Janis Joplin, Johnny Winter). Not that the last three, especially Janis with Big Brother and The Holding Company, couldn't rock hard, and Creedence Clearwater Revival would soon bring back their own kind of mix of rockabilly and blues to the palette of American music. America's sheer cornucopia of regional musics complicated the mix: Creedence dipped into a New Orleans sound, Big Brother included in its repertoire a great version of Gershwin's "Summertime," and Santana and Sly and the Family Stone came from totally different influences altogether.

With the punk music of the late '70s American rock would come roaring back. But before then perhaps our only rockers in the Brit sense would be the Stooges; the MC5; the Doors and The Velvet Underground in their harder-edged moments; American proto-punk one-hit wonders like the Music Machine, Count Five, and the Castaways in top 20 radio; and the pioneers of what would be called garage rock, "America's great lost band" The Remains.

But to prove that any distinction or generalization like this asks to be challenged—in the most outrageously brilliant form of reverse musical alchemy, Britain birthed one of the greatest and hardest-rocking of all rock bands when the sort of American player they copped from came to Britain and copped from them. It wasn't until Jimi Hendrix came to London and absorbed British pop and psychedelia and, specifically, *Sgt. Pepper's* (along with a solid bassist, a great drummer, and the support of Paul McCartney) that the Jimi Hendrix Experience was born. Coming back to America, his act was revealingly dubbed by *Life* Magazine "musical miscegenation," a term that referred to racial intermarriage, only recently legal in the United States. In Hendrix was the best possible fusion of the British return to rock and America's reclamation of it, mixed with all the musical experimentation that had gone on on both sides of the pond, to produce Hendrix' roaring and soaring sound.

Still, taking early rock and roll and r & b into hard rock, in the '60s and beyond, would be led by the Brits and the Irish. They were the rock purists and leaders, as they would be in their seminal punk bands (the Ramones notwithstanding), as they would carry on with Bowie and The Clash and U2 (Bruce Springsteen, who started out with jazz-rock, notwithstanding). The British Invasion, as it turned out, was more like a homecoming.

Farewell Starman

"Just remember, duckies, everybody gets got."[1] – **David Bowie**

David Bowie was only barely a '60s rock figure, releasing his breakout hit "Space Oddity" in November of 1969. But he first came to the public's notice years earlier on a charming self-promoting British television clip as the leader of a club refusing to cut their hair, where he was introduced as David Jones. Thanks to another lesser icon of '60s rock, he later chose his magnificent name change.

You'll be reading (or have already read) plenty about his biography, his many guises (Ziggy, The Thin White Duke), and his musical legacy, so here's some memories around the edges.

One time back in the '70s I was watching television when I saw something that I thought was a stunt someone was playing with what was then called trick photography. It was David Bowie singing Christmas carols with Bing Crosby. It was a strange encounter both on screen and off, but Crosby had nothing but good things to say about Bowie, and Bowie was happy to try to move his career a little closer to mass popularity, and besides, as he said, his mother really liked Bing.

This was decades before the pairing of any two performers like, for example, Lady Gaga and Tony Bennett. It wasn't going to the extreme, as he often would do in his later career; it was daring (and caring) because it was the opposite.

Bowie's wildness and experimentalism was always balanced by his humanity and that empathy for issues close to the earth that, in his various personas (as in his great sci-fi film), he pretended to have fallen to. It's what gives his early song "Life On Mars" it's poignancy; like the great Beatles song "A Day In The Life" it's about the pain and fears of ordinary existence, balanced by some aspiration or wish toward transcendence ("Is there life on Mars?").[2] That kind of warmth is what gives the song "Starman" its joyousness: it's sung from the point of view of a wishful child.

Bowie was very much a figure of the '70s and decades beyond in the artifice and distancing that went into the creation of and immersion into personas like Ziggy Stardust. Within those personas, though, he wrote and sang with a very transparently accessible passion. It helped that no one with perhaps the exception of Keith Richards was better at rock hook riffs (think of "Rebel Rebel" or "Suffragette City" or "Heroes"). But there on the Ziggy album, in the midst of a very strange death-haunted sci-fi fantasy myth Bowie concocted, are songs that speak to self-affirmation ("Hang On To Yourself"), love of music ("Ziggy Stardust"), courage in the face of marginalization and death (the "you're not alone" refrain from "Rock and Roll Suicide"), perseverance ("It Ain't Easy"), and trying to make the most of out whatever you've got left ("Five Years").

This is not to take the wonderful strangeness and artistic invention out of his work and reduce it to moralizing. This is the man who after all brought theater and film and fashion to rock, and created and mimicked truly alien figures onstage and in film, most notably in *The Man Who Fell To Earth,* maybe his finest acting performance, which was shrugged off by smartass critics as Bowie playing himself. When it came to self-stylization and consciously artificial dramatization, the whole Brechtian bag of tricks, there was no one like him in music then or even now. Albums like *Aladdin Sane* or *The Man Who Sold The World* are irreducibly fascinating and theatrical and strange.

But even here, because Bowie was so thoroughly a narrative poet behind all his shape-shifting, is at least one theme; when the man who sold the world tells you he never lost control, it's a hollow boast. Aladdin Sane is after all ... well, you can hear the play on words.

When you replace the ecosphere we all share with an egosphere, however high you rise, you're headed for a fall. In "Ashes and Ashes," going back to his old hit "Space Oddity," Bowie sings "We know Major Tom's a junkie/Strung out in heaven's high, hitting an all time low."[3]

And yet, this is after all the Major Tom who, presumably, walked out into the ether, at least in his mind, once in orbit. Major Tom's message in "Ashes to Ashes" is "I'm happy, hope you're happy too/I've loved, all I've needed: love." His mock-'funeral' in the video is decidedly on the glam side. Bowie, poised between the attempts at drug-enhanced transcendence of the '60s and the dark coke-and-heroin decline of the '70s, saw it both ways. In *The Man Who Sold The World,* one of his darkest albums, there's nonetheless an exhilaration to "All the Madmen," where he sings "'Cause I'd rather stay here/With all the madmen/Then perish with the sad men roaming free."[4]

Moments of exploration and improvisation and art—these are ways to escape deadening boredom and conformity. If you can be a sane Aladdin, you can control what the genie's throwing at you and rise above the rest. Encouraging thoughts to anyone who would follow in Bowie's direction—and they were legion, most of the major New York and London rock figures of the 1970s and 1980s, from Lou Reed in the new identity Bowie (as producer) helped him craft in the appropriately named album *Transformer*, to Madonna in her videos and beyond.

And yet again ... "Ashes to Ashes" ends with the chorus, "My mama said, to get things done/You better not mess with Major Tom." And in the intro to his song "Modern Love," there it is again: "I know when to go out. I know when to stay in. To get things done."[5] So sing with Bing. Adapt to MTV, brilliantly, in the *Let's Dance* album. Write a song with the modest but truly inspiring line "We can be heroes/Just for one day..."[6] and sing it with heartbreaking conviction in a concert celebrating the fall of the Berlin Wall, and truly earn the tribute paid by the leadership of Germany with the statement that David Bowie helped lead the imprisoned half of that country to freedom.

In his great 2013 return-to-form album, *The Next Day*, the human and humane Bowie roars off the tracks, aware of and fighting his mortality in the title song, pledging his loyalty to what Springsteen called the "tease" of pop in "The Stars (Are Out Tonight)," lamenting his lost Berlin past in "Where Are We Now?", showing cold fury at mass individual and state killing in "Valentine's Day" and "Heat," and ending with a rousingly cheerful and hopeful and now very haunting vision of going to another country in "I'll Take You There" ("What will I become in the USA?/Hold my hand and I'll take you there"[7]). This is the Bowie much of whose music was rooted in "soul" in every sense of the word.

So remember him for whatever songs or images you most remember, for like all the best single artists of the '60s and the '70s— Bob Dylan, Hendrix, Zappa, Springsteen, Joni Mitchell—he contained multitudes. He was all about art, including his very fine collection, but he was also about doing his bit for grittier causes, like his last charity gigs. And he once said his favorite leisure time activity was spotting new bands, so whatever else was going on with him, he was always all about the music and about helping lead others to musical appreciation or success.

For me the song that best illustrates how David Bowie was, along with being a man and artist of his times, a rocker who recalled the '60s at its best, is a song on not one of his earlier albums but *The Next Day*. It's a song that in one refrain combines outrage at war, desire for an altered state of madness and inspiration, and great compassion. The song is "I'd Rather Be High."

> *I'd rather be high.*
> *I'd rather be flying.*
> *I'd rather be dead, or out of my head*
> *Than training these guns on these men in the sand*
> *I'd rather be high…*[8]

The man who fell to earth is now as high as it gets.

Farewell Starship, and Hail *Blackstar*

Ashes to ashes in triumph.

It was a very sad coincidence—losing "Starman" David Bowie and then, barely two weeks later, one of the pilots of Jefferson Airplane and Jefferson Starship, Paul Kantner. But at least, in the wake of these deaths, comes what may very well be Bowie's masterpiece.

Jefferson Airplane was a group that founding rock impresario Bill Graham called one of the original San Francisco bands of the 1960s (the others being the Grateful Dead, the Charlatans, Quicksilver Messenger Service, and Big Brother and the Holding Company featuring Janis Joplin). We all have music groups we fall in love with and mine was the Airplane; I saw them at least twelve times that I can recall.

The dazzling Grace Slick (and whipsmart and funny and a brilliant songwriter—listen to "Rejoyce") certainly got to my teenage hormones, but it was the music as well. The Airplane's songs had the pristine folk chords and harmonies and ringing guitars that bands like the Byrds had already primed me to love, but then came that dizzy dance, that angular, agile, exotic … as the band named it, taking off and flying. Jack Casady's propulsive bass lines that sounded like jazz in an afterburner, one of the influences on the filigreed but hard and heavy bass of Jaco Pastorius and all the rapid-fire electric bass playing afterwards. Jorma Kaukonen's lead guitar, weaving through the basic folk chords in Kantner's "DCBA 25," more haunting and seductive than anything I'd ever heard—and then cutting loose faster and harder and more unpredictably on other tunes than anything else on record at the time. Spencer Dryden's jazzy drumming drove the music along, and anchoring it all was Paul Kantner's rhythm guitar. It was rock steady, as the *New York Times* obit credited Kantner with, but also filled with the kind of delicate and adventurous picking that Kantner, a devotee of the Weavers, might have picked up learning from the banjo book by Pete Seeger.

Kantner also wrote many of the harmony structures of the Airplane's songs. It was in the vocals that the band really shone. Grace Slick and Marty Balin leaned into the mike and seemed to try to top each other with soaring held notes, while Paul, holding down stage right, sang with a solid mellow baritone that grounded them. Those vocals and anthemic lyrics (many provided by Kantner) made them the group that could evangelicize for the beliefs of and desires of the era, above all for finding "Somebody To Love." That song from the album *Surrealistic Pillow* became the signature tune of the band: a song built like the hit it would become, with a simple verse and chorus structure, Grace's vocals knifing through the airwaves (I still remember the DJ, Dandy Dan Daniels of WMCA in New York, exclaiming "Listen to the pipes on that chick!"), until it surprisingly ended with (on a Top 40 radio song, no less) a beautiful instrumental break with Jorma in full acid-guitar mode.

The Airplane were gutsy, beautiful (the most romantic—not to mention romantically involved—band), and very commercial. With Kantner's reassuring college-boy handsomeness, Marty Balin's *Hair*-style-Broadway soulfulness, and Grace Slick's flat-out gorgeousness, they were the band most likely to attract the "Mad Men" '60s. They did a Levi's commercial on the radio, and there's satire but also affection for Madison Avenue in songs like "Plastic Fantastic Lover." They were never about to resist pop success's temptations. But as a result they were an effective bridge between two cultures: for all their ability to hang out with the suits, you can't listen to *After Bathing At Baxter's* or *Crown Of Creation* and not know that they embodied the look, the sound, and the politics of the counterculture with absolute conviction: whether it was acid trips, multiple sexual relationships, or the total political transformation of the country. The band combined a heady collision of different music traditions—blues, jazz, acid rock—and the charm and literacy to be the most attractive spokespeople for their generation of fans. Grace Slick in a white dress at Woodstock singing "Volunteers" seemed to embody the beauty of the era to (never) come.

And as Jorma Kaukonen said of Kantner, "Paul was the catalyst that brought the whole thing together. He had the transcendental vision, and he hung onto it like a bulldog. The band would not have been what it was without him."[1]

After the breakup of the Airplane, Kantner cofounded, with Balin and Slick, the far more commercially successful incarnation Jefferson Starship. The name was derived from Kantner's science-fiction vision of the possibility of one day hijacking an advanced starship for enlightened and ecstatic voyaging through the universe. Utopian to say the least, but that yearning engendered a beautiful transitional album, *Blows Against the Empire*, with Kantner joined by Slick, now his partner, and featuring contributions from Jerry Garcia and David Crosby. It would prove the foundation for "Miracles" to come and all the successive Starships' later hits. So with the passing of Paul Kantner, we memorialize and celebrate the passing of his two bands as well.

Kantner told the website Wales Online in 2009 that "the rock bands of the '60s supplanted the football and military heroes, and just as all those heroes had fallen when put to the test, rock musicians proved they had no more of an answer to saving the world than anybody else."[2]

He was too hard on himself, so let's give him the credit he and the Airplane deserve. What the American rock troubadours of the '60s supplanted with their musical and intellectual awareness, led by Bob Dylan and Simon and Garfunkel and the Airplane, were not football stars and generals but '50s novelists and beatnik poets. Those men and women ultimately realized they couldn't save the world either. Nobel Prize-winner John Steinbeck once famously complained that you couldn't get socioeconomic change in America because the poor viewed themselves as "temporarily embarrassed millionaires."[3] Perhaps one problem with achieving the kind of change that the rock stars of the '60s wanted is that so many Americans now view themselves as temporarily embarrassed rock stars (or, given their violence fixation, temporarily retired action heroes).

So maybe the best a great rock musician/performer can do is change people's perceptions and attitudes toward the life around them. And those still in the game and trying to chart new frontiers can take comfort from the last act of David Bowie, his posthumous album *Blackstar*.

Not that *Blackstar* is about any kind of social or political change. Bowie had put out those views before, throughout his body of work, from "Changes" to, especially, *The Next Day*. The theme of *Blackstar* is life's passing, created by a man who knew he was directly experiencing it.

In that sense it's unprecedented. The only work of popular art that comes to mind when thinking about it is the film *Boyhood*, which showed the passage of time through its having been filmed in brief intervals over twelve years, so that the characters and settings actually aged onscreen. That film was an extraordinary blend of filmmaking concentration, grace, and courage. Bowie's album, with equal grace and courage, and almost unbelievable energy and stamina (he was in the final stages of liver cancer when he did it), incarnates time's end, the thousand-yard stare. This isn't Jacques Brel singing "My Death" (a song once covered by Bowie) or Dylan singing that "it's not dark yet, but it's getting there."⁴ This is testimony from fully in the dark, done not through any extraordinary act of technique (though great craftsmanship), but simply by having the boldness and endurance to do it.

Bowie's suppleness with hook riffs lends itself well to the composition of the eerily and beautifully flowing "Blackstar" suite. The music begins with a near-Eastern motif boosted with great jazz-over-march-time drumming and stuttering sax, which will later resolve to a steady jazz-rock march at the song's conclusion. In the middle portion the music ceases to be ominous and starts to soar with hymnal organ chords and a more soulful beat, as Bowie and the chorus ultimately proclaim "I'm a blackstar,"⁵ deathbound but creatively shining at the same time. It's a theme that even the album cover's graphic design echoes: with its black reflective letters etched on a black background, it's a void until the light catches it right.

The video adds an underlying story to the phases of the song, which seems to tell a version of the Crucifixion story—only when the three crucified figures are shown, the central one is not a nobly suffering Jesus, but a grotesque mocking figure swathed in rags, less an image of resurrection than the ragged end we all will come to. For in this video there is no resurrection, though there is a kind of transubstantiation through art and memory, almost like Shakespeare's "sea-change" in Ariel's song in *The Tempest* ("Those are the pearls that were his eyes."). A beautiful woman in a lunar setting finds an astronaut with a '70s "smiley face" pin (Major Tom?) lying dead beneath a black star. As a bandaged-and-button-eyed ravaged-looking Bowie sings, the woman brings the astronaut's skull to a ritual space in a medieval desert city. Spasmodically dancing male acolytes, but also women dancing in a circle, will celebrate the relic, which will ultimately be revealed to be a bejeweled object of art.

When the dance dissolves with rising organ music, an aging and clearly very ill Bowie, with his eyes unbound, holds the "Blackstar" book as an offering to the sky. He sings prayerfully until he briefly assumes the identity of what seems to be a preacher offering some kind of salvation, at which point he camps it up as only he can. The music alternates between a hymn and a vamp, gently mocking the preacher, but then the true focuses of the video become the now no-longer-jittery but strong rhythm of the "I'm a blackstar" chant, and images of the dying (once again bandaged) Bowie, the women, even the crucified figures reacting to the music—and Bowie's eyes, the eyes of the girl, the eyes that in the video's world are the center of life, all offering their own black stars to the heavens.

The bandaged button-eyed Bowie returns in the video of "Lazarus," singing to a bass heavy rock dirge accompanied by a mournful sax and wails and shots of feedbacked guitar. Here something briefly frees him from the eyeless death state (and literally from a cupboard), so he can do a spasmodic dance and take stabs (as in stabbing motions), at writing, envisaging his own death. He rises up from a bed at one point, having, in a great lyric, "dropped my cellphone down below." The state he evokes is a blend of agony and excitement, awful restriction yet feelings of liberation ("This way or no way/Someday I'll be free/Just like that bluebird/Ain't that just like me.").[6]

Other songs seem to recall the struggles of life as a kind of infernal, if thrillingly lustful machine. It's a theme begun in "Lazarus"'s line "But I used up all my money/I was looking for your ass." "'Tis A Pity She Was A Whore," describes a sexual encounter turned to violence. The mysterious "Sue" seems to be a hard-rocking time-telescoped track of a relationship ending in the death of a lover (or simply love) and perhaps disappointment, perhaps rage at one's own conduct, perhaps just "mindless faith in hopeless deeds."[7] In the rock march of "Girl Loves Me," the carnival drunkenness and sexual ferocity of youth is depicted in Nadsat, the language of the young juiced-up ultraviolent "droogs" in *A Clockwork Orange* (and is it any surprise Bowie's love for Kubrick continued after *Space Odyssey*?).

The song ends with two beautiful heartbreakers. "Dollar Days" begins with Bowie's actual labored breath and the crinkling of dollar bills, and the dry details of a last act that one hopes wasn't exactly true for him (as in "Cash girls suffer me"). But then, with the lilting soul of the *Young Americans* album and a gorgeous sax solo, Bowie sings a haunted farewell to love and continuing work, the bruised and painful goodbye of someone with more disguises to create, climaxing with "I'm trying to/I'm dying to,"[8] two thoughts that, accompanied by a guitar riff that recalls the "... wonderful" last chorus of *Ziggy Stardust*, stand together and apart. Bowie, who had long experimented with cut-up and spliced-together language, uses the couplet's play on words (and the lyric "the bitter nerve ends never end") to suggest both resistance to death and inevitable surrender. In the album's final song, "I Can't Give Everything Away," the chorus similarly "cuts up" into "I can't give everything," the plaintive cry of an artist who (apparently) was still very much attached to life and working on one more album to "give" his fans, and "away," a word which echoes off into the distance that Bowie knows is taking him.⁹ The music ends in an exuberant freeform guitar solo, but then a classic 'dying fall' and one last pealing organ note fading into the distance.

David Bowie was one of the greatest true artists of rock. And it's fitting that, given his canvas was his identity, he leaves us with a self-portrait, fearfully revealing, generous, and indelible.

Love and Mercy and California Nightmares

Brian Wilson's hard-earned smile

There was a lot of mythology around the Beach Boys right from the start, and not just in their portrayal as a happy family versus boys actually growing up in the shadow of an abusive father. As a California friend who knew them in the early days pointed out to me, they were thought of as "hodaddys"—guys hanging around surfers for the scene—who knew about cars, not the beach; the Bondo Boys would've been a more accurate name for them. Among many other aspects of the Beach Boys' story that *Love and Mercy*,[1] the Brian Wilson biopic directed by Bill Pohlad, gets right is the dichotomy between their lives and their image. Wilson, at one point insisting to cousin and band member Mike Love that they have to grow creatively and not go back to their old stuff, screams "We're not even surfers!"

And while that manufactured image had its authentic side in the brothers' happiness over their music, success, and California lifestyle, underneath it was the specter of Brian Wilson's fusion of genius and illness. The movie captures that right in the beginning by presenting early images of the Beach Boys frolicking and playing their hits and being a family in a halcyon home movie format—but just before that bouncing a barrage of voices through the multitrack speakers, suggesting both a typical '60s album's use of "trippy" vocalizations but also the voices inside Wilson's head that would undo his sanity.

Love and Mercy thus starts out ominous and ambivalent, and then develops that ambivalence through the early years' portion of the film. The Beach Boys were at the outset a hitmaking machine drilled by a father who sometimes smacked them into their paces, elevated by songwriting and parts-arranging by Brian that were initially, as Mike Love says, "clever." Of course all the mid-'60s groups then were tight musically and in performance, but given the brutal sternness of their dad, the Beach Boys hit their surfer themes and onstage marks as if their lives depended on it.

No wonder Brian Wilson embraced the liberation he found in The Beatles' *Rubber Soul;* Paul Dano, playing the younger Brian, in a great moment exclaims that it's like a new kind of modern folk songs album, but absolutely solid, not a moment wasted. You can see the light going on in his eyes. At the same time his vocal parts writing, composing, and arranging went from clever to inspired, the inspirations being the harmonies of the Four Freshmen and Phil Spector's "wall of sound" production.

But when the film crosscuts to Brian Wilson decades later, you can see the light and inspiration have gone out. John Cusack, who seems to be channeling Peter Sellers's performance in *Being There*, renders the older Brian as the helpless puppet of psychiatrist Eugene Landy, played by Paul Giamatti as a monster of manipulation and exploitation of Brian's wealth and stature.

In cross-cutting throughout the film these two phases of Brian Wilson's life and getting at how these two types of person could coexist in one lifetime, *Love and Mercy* is refreshingly nondogmatic about the two major conflicts Wilson endured: the one between his dawning art and the blend of sun, fun, and romance that the Beach Boys wanted to embody and their fans wanted to see and hear; and the way that Wilson's art and the increasing solo responsibility he took on fed his schizoaffective disorder, so that the dream of greater music that rose above the popular connection was the seed of the madness and nightmare to come.

In exploring those conflicts, the movie seems of two minds about the classic album *Pet Sounds*—as, frankly, I've always been. On the one hand, it's a wonder of gorgeous songwriting and harmony and totally adventurous use of the studio; in one sequence, Wilson places bobby pins on piano strings and plucks them while someone's holding down the keys to the piano to create a sound never heard before. His brilliance and sheer playfulness in the studio, presented in a semidocumentary fashion, is great and instructive fun to watch. Meanwhile, the movie takes time to (literally) introduce The Wrecking Crew, the fabled studio musicians who backed the Beach Boys and so many other groups, the West Coast equals of the Nashville Cats. *Love and Mercy* beautifully and democratically shows just what went into creating *Pet Sounds*.

But for a classic album, I always found *Pet Sounds* slowed and weighed down by sentimentality and childishness (that annoying clippity-clop rhythm from cheesy Westerns), and you can hardly say that it doesn't have a wasted moment. It also doesn't have the canniness, humor, discipline, and sophistication of the Beatles records it was influenced by and that it later influenced. Paul McCartney loves the album and says it was a huge influence on *Sgt. Pepper's*, but so also was John Lennon.

The weakness of Wilson's method is summed up in his defense of keeping collaged candid vocals from the studio on the tracks, a common '60s hip record album technique. Was it flip and cheerful, or a scattershot and sloppy impression of the insane pace and confusion of events of the time? Was it making fun of acid trips or reflecting them? Did Wilson know the difference?

And cousin Mike Love, who should probably be called "Tough" Love for the role he plays in the movie, has a point when he declares that *Pet Sounds* needs a hit. Love's insistence that the sun and fun part of their music was genuine, beloved, and necessary is even underscored by Wilson's behavior when he's not trumpeting his musical goals: he has beach sand under his piano in his home, and he's never happier than when he's in the pool with his brothers. Wilson ultimately answered Love by knocking off a beautiful version of "Sloop John B," and that, plus a goofy Monkees-like video, kept the Beach Boys in the charts even as *Pet Sounds* became a critical darling but commercial flop.

The fault lines that *Pet Sounds* created would persist, as the film foreshadows by cutting back to the adult Brian Wilson and suggesting the long-lasting damage to come. As Wilson takes on more and more auteurist responsibility, only uses the group for their voices, and grows increasingly solitary, he becomes more and more vulnerable. And Paul Dano plays him as an achingly sensitive blank slate on which any impression, whether artistically nurturing or outright cruel, would leave far too lasting a mark. You cringe when you hear he took LSD, and know it will spin him out of control.

The song "Good Vibrations" is a great release in the movie because it's the last time Wilson's brilliance and the discipline and team spirit necessary for the band converge, producing their biggest-selling hit. Then he goes off into the (at that point) failed solitary creation *Smile*, which destroys him so that he can't even rouse himself from his near-catatonia to see the first true smile of his baby daughter. And since the movie has captured so well the confidence of a master musician with *Pet Sounds*, the most painful moment of *Love and Mercy* is simply a pan down a row of tapes that mark the multiple versions of songs on *Smile* that Brian records as he becomes lost even in his studio home.

His unlikely salvation begins years later when he meets car saleswoman Melinda Ledbetter. Well, not that unlikely—who wouldn't reach out for love when it's offered by a sweet, kind Elizabeth Banks, an incarnation of blonde beauty in 2015, and very much the ideal of the Beach Boys' "California Girls" song. But the casting does seem to deliberately recall that song, and suggest that the most genuine impulses of Brian Wilson's music—the happiness, the fact that he called his planned masterwork *Smile* "a teenage symphony to God,"[2] the embrace of life and love that went into his hits—will ultimately free him as much as this lovely woman.

And what she tries to free him from is one of the darkest aspects of the '60s. Many writers, most famously Joan Didion in her collection of essays *The White Album* (named after the Beatles' pre-breakup 1969 double record), have said that in California the '60s died with the Manson murders. But a contributing cause of death had to be the narcissism, the navel-gazing, the cultivated vulnerability and passivity in the rush of consciousness-expanding (and drug-taking)—all of which would ultimately attract cultist predators.

The problem with personal liberation movements is that they can all too easily shade into self-indulgence on the one hand and terror at being too free on the other. At that point the frightened freedom-seekers turn to the sort of people they feel can stabilize them or keep them safely freewheeling—hustlers, quacks, and dictatorial substitute fathers like Eugene Landy—and that became one of the many factors that ultimately undercut the promise of the '60s.

The movie ends with the beginning of Wilson's renewal, summed up as his reaching out to Melinda when she frees him from Landy. "Wouldn't It Be Nice?" plays as he finally claims his love, and captions at the end summarize the passage to Wilson's ultimate triumph, the live performance of *Smile*, shown briefly along with Wilson's encore playing of the song "Love and Mercy." That's the way a lot of biopics end now, and it's a bit of a weak tea choice. On the other hand, a 2.5 hour Brian Wilson biopic would have definitely been too much of a good thing.

There is at least one documentary that shows how Wilson ultimately reconquered the studio and his own terrors—not to mention a stroke—to finally produce *Smile*, and it should be seen as a complement to *Love and Mercy*. For ultimately the liberation of Brian Wilson is not just personal, but personal and musical. It's sufficient that *Love and Mercy* shows he did it, and that Wilson's life suggests, as Neil Young has sung, that "this old guitar's not mine to keep,"[3] but while you have it, it's not about the musician, it's about the music, whether your music is music, painting, novels, medicine, politics, or whatever you do to keep body, soul, and, if you have one, family together.

Love and Mercy, an excellent film overall, gets across that there were ways in the fullness of time to get past the '60s California nightmare and to reconcile '60s musical genius with being a trouper for your fans and with basic human connections. When Wilson performed the finished *Smile* at Carnegie Hall, according to a friend of mine who saw it, there wasn't a dry eye in the house during the standing o.

There are genuine '60s happy endings.

Music Hyphenation and the Changing of the Bards
The recombinant DNA of '60s music

The first music hyphen brand I ever heard of, and perhaps the most successful of them all, was "folk-rock."

To set the scene: in the early '60s America's major hotbed of cultural and intellectual ferment was New York's Greenwich Village. It was the main node of a network hooked up to San Francisco, Los Angeles, London, Paris, Taos, and wherever intellectuals, mystics, musicians, and poets gathered. It was where Timothy Leary looked for support for his unauthorized psychedelic experiments, where experimental filmmakers and playwrights had their turfs, where Warhol's Factory met the Kennedys' Camelot. You know—the high-rent area now boasting plenty of NYU real estate.

Its symbols were the young (largely) men who called themselves "Beats," after an attitude of weariness with postwar America and in imitation of black jazz lingo; they soon became known as "beatniks," a comic corruption from the Soviet satellite Sputnik. Some were merely scavengers nibbling at crumbs of experience everywhere from jazz to 42nd Street's Hubie's Freak Show, very much absorbing local paranoia, and wearing the beards and berets of French intellectuals and bebop musicians and the dark garb of hipsters of all times and places. They were objects of curiosity, satire, and occasional ridicule; my playgroup members would lean out our carry-all bus and if we happened to see one shout "Beatnik!" the same way kids shout "cows!" during a drive in the country.

But the best of these Villagers and beatniks also produced landmark abstract art, film, comedy, theater, and poetry, some of which, like the work of Ginsberg and Ferlinghetti, would enter the American literary canon. They were also embracing a trend going back to the Depression, but slowly coming back out of the shadow of McCarthyism, of communal singing of American folk ballads and politically angry songs from the likes of Leadbelly and Pete Seeger and The Weavers.

In acoustic music hangouts like the Gaslight and Café Wha, musicians seeking an authentic tradition in which to play old songs and write their own songs of protest or spiritual uplift or romantic love began

Music Hyphenation and the Changing of the Bards | 75

to rediscover folk music and hold "hootenannies," folk singing jams. Songs from English madrigals to Negro spirituals were triumphantly reinterpreted in the music of performers like Peter, Paul, and Mary, and Joan Baez.

High culture and urban music often is built from town or improvised street music, from Bach and Brahms composing gigues and rhapsodies based on peasant dances, to Irving Berlin making show tunes out of ragtime. In the folk movement, there was a lot of plugging into what Greil Marcus would later call "the old weird America," as a generation of mostly all-American college kids started singing in the voices of backwoodsmen and sailors and lovelorn swains, which was fine with the conservative establishment until they picked up on Woody Guthrie, who'd played a guitar emblazoned with "This Machine Kills Fascists." At that point the folk singers must have driven the establishment crazy, looking so clean-cut and collegiate and putting out such left-wing music, to the point where kids would sing along in summer camp, led by folkie-wannabe counselors, to "If I Had A Hammer," "This Land Is Your Land," and "Puff the Magic Dragon," preparing, without knowing it, for membership in a civil rights-antiwar-army, not to mention their later drug of choice.

Original songwriting was a particularly fertile extension of the scene, borrowing as it did from not just folk revivalism but currents of anger and satire in the Village's theatrical productions and comedy stages. The current-events-based humor of Mort Sahl, whose main props were a sweater and a newspaper; the "sick-nick" and often profane attack comedy of Lenny Bruce; the incisive if at the time tamped-down anger of African American comedians like Dick Gregory; the brilliant "egghead" improvisations of Nichols and May; all found an echo in the satirical lyrics of Tom Paxton (whose "Daily News," for example, poked fun of the right-wing New York tabloid of its day) and the fury of folk singer Phil Ochs.

Oh here's to the land they tore out the heart of,
Mississippi find yourself another country to be part of. [1]

Ochs saw topical songs as a pertinent and militant editorial mode, and he and Tom Paxton and Pete Seeger sang about issues like "automation"; escalation of the Vietnam war and the stupid arrogance of the President; white supremacy organizations; and unions not sufficiently supporting civil rights (Ochs's prescient "Links On The Chain"). It was neighborhood journalism in song, with the international community of intellectuals, artists, and musicians then living there casting their attention on the wider "neighborhood" of American and world issues in general.

As the folk scene began to attract a media spotlight, some older folkies called the younger ones opportunists, which hurt, since peer approval was the main measure of success at the Gaslight, Folk City, Lion's Head, and Mill's Tavern. But while everyone knew after a certain point that there were talent agents and variety television scouts hanging around, there was a real solidarity and a feeling of being in a movement linked by common beliefs and (largely liberal and humanitarian) political goals. Folk also celebrated the natural, the pure, the rejection of artifice and superficiality so on display in the TV variety shows of the period.

The folk movement became a folk craze that swept through colleges and then mainstream American music. In part that was because, unlike the subtle and sophisticated harmonies of the best American standards, folk songs were built out of chords that most musicians could quickly learn to play on piano, guitar, or (for the more nimble-fingered) banjo. In part that was because the music, while including its share of fierce-looking solidly built men like Theodore Bikel and Burl Ives, increasingly was fronted by young photo- and telegenic faces. Joan Baez was no dummy about the seductive effect she was having on the men in the audience with her white-dress-clad beauty, waif gypsy eyes, and "I Never Will Marry" sort of songs. Judy "Blue Eyes" Collins and Joni Mitchell weren't ignorant of that either, and Mary Travers was so heartbreakingly dazzling that one record producer famously dubbed Peter, Paul and Mary "two rabbis and a hooker." Meanwhile, among what we'd now call folk acts "of color," Harry Belafonte was swooningly handsome to all races, colors, and creeds, while Odetta was charismatically powerful. And John Denver was the face any mother could love of The Mitchell (originally Chad Mitchell) Trio.

In short, the folk scene soon gained enough "wattage" to have its stars on the Ed Sullivan Show and all over the radio. But it was soon to be upset by a different kind of wattage coming from one of their own who'd come up in another kind of people's music altogether.

Bob Dylan has often stated, as some rediscovered not exactly stellar efforts of his reveal, that his first influence was rock 'n' roll. But rock 'n' roll had gone flat in the early '60s, as the ornery Chuck Berry, the morally condemned Jerry Lee Lewis, the gone-Hollywood Elvis Presley, and the way too early taken from us Buddy Holly and Ritchie Valens gave way to "teen idols" like Frankie Avalon and Fabian.

Dylan found new inspiration in folk music and the ballads of Woody Guthrie, not to mention a whole new persona; he was one of the great sponges, absorbing everything he heard and putting it right back out there, especially the songs and the attitude of Guthrie. Wearing and playing his harmonica, he also harkened back to rural black blues troubadours. But for all his seemingly artless but very self-aware stage presence, he had real folk credentials, playing down south for civil rights, most memorably in the documentary *Don't Look Back*. After Joan Baez helped jumpstart his career, his songs became the folk movement's anthems, his 1963 appearance at Newport Folk Festival catalyzing an onstage singing of "We Shall Overcome" by him, Baez, Peter, Paul and Mary, and other acts, all linking hands. That became the peak moment of the folk movement, the point at which it went out from the Gaslight and Café Wha to the world.

But Dylan had never forgotten rock and roll; he has mentioned, and one can clearly hear, that the basic musical structure of "Like A Rolling Stone" is shaped by Ritchie Valens's "La Bamba." His Guthriesque persona was the act of assumed identity of a boy from a Jewish home in Hibbling, Minnesota, not insincere at all, just mutable; Dylan was always "processing." Moving toward more and more original songwriting he filtered folk storytelling, truth-telling, and protest into increasingly poetic symbolism, and he had his detractors, but above all he had Baez as partner and ally, the strong young woman literally hoisting him up in a famous photo.

Dylan's surrealist, post-Bomb way of lyric writing, by the time of *Bringing It All Back Home* and *Highway 61 Revisited*, got to a level that, as he stated with an interview with the late Ed Bradley on *60 Minutes*, he would never equal again. Dylan merged classic songwriting chops with his own experiments in letting writing simply flow into dreamlike images and plays on words; at a time when even someone as cerebral as Mike Nichols was an improv artist and had as his motto "revere the unconscious," Dylan experimented with "automatic writing" in a long poem called "Tarantula" and that method spilled over into his songs. He also saw where blues, Hank Williams, Arthur Rimbaud's surrealism, and beatnik poetry converged: honesty, a feeling of being alone in the universe, images of loneliness and passion and the need to, if not take action, at least own up. As he shrewdly articulated in a *Life* Magazine interview, people his age and younger had a fear of lies and "things that are kept back. Kids have a feeling like me, but they ain't hearin' it no place."[2]

And he built up that kind of lyric writing as much through his knowledge of rock as folk. Rock was good at allusiveness, thanks to years of using slang and other censorship-evading lingo to disguise sex acts in the lyrics. Poetic ambiguity and compression wasn't that big a next step (as pointed out by Frank Zappa in *Life* Magazine's "New Rock" 1968 issue). Dylan added to that the ecumenicism of being open to many worlds and discarded and suppressed histories. And though he would be too sarcastic in those days to see his music as a way to foster hope, compassion, synthesis, and unity, you can hear all that in his protest songs ("Pawn in Their Game," "Masters of War"), love songs ("Visions of Johanna"), and in his blazing live "Chimes of Freedom" performance at Newport. Dylan would ultimately combine in his words and music so many influences from Shakespeare to the blues that he would earn the Nobel Prize in literature for his songs.

But back in the mid-'60s, in service to the music rather than the lyrics, he would take his first huge step toward musical synthesis. He would throw away all the musical 'political capital' and goodwill his folk writing and performing had earned by plugging into electric guitars, amps, and speakers. And it wasn't just electrification of folk songs, it was full-on fusing them with rock 'n' roll, even including old r & b classics in the repertoire.

His fellow folk musicians felt he'd led them to the mountaintop only to throw them off a cliff, and justifiably recognized a threat to their careers. And folk fans hated it. One cried "Judas!" in a memorable live performance. "I don't believe you! You're a liar!" Dylan shouted back, attacking the folk fans' lack of the kind of conviction he brought to his music as much as defending himself. Then he cried "play it fucking loud!" and he and the band—as in members of The Band—launched into "Like A Rolling Stone," and folk-rock began.[3]

The greatest of all synthesists would prompt an injection of startling literacy into all acoustic and electric songs thereafter and stimulate all the amazing combinations and recombinations of music that rock would incorporate into its repertoire. The fusion of folk and r & b-based rock and roll, the two greatest American people's musics other than jazz, spawned all sorts of electric bands: the Lovin' Spoonful, with John Sebastian hunched over an electrified autoharp, the band doing what they called "folky but pick-y" banjo and jug band music-influenced tunes and topping the charts. The Mamas and Papas doing the same with plaintive, fully orchestrated love songs. The Byrds above all—formed by Jim McGuinn, who had worked with the Chad Mitchell Trio and Judy Collins; Gene Clark out of the New Christy Minstrels; and solo act David Crosby—copped to what Dylan was doing by literally copping him. They played arrangements of his songs and Pete Seeger's "Turn, Turn, Turn" with bell-like twanging guitars, a less edgy and more mellifluous arrangement, choral harmonies, and a Beach Boys-like backbeat, and brought Dylan fully into the mainstream right before Dylan would crack that mass audience himself with a 45rpm single version (the longest single done as of that time) of "Like A Rolling Stone."

The Byrds would go on to fuse the influence of John Coltrane's solos on "India" and Indian music's ragas into the classic song "Eight Miles High," McGuinn stating he was trying to expand the group's instrumentation with "jet age" energy. Soon would come more jazz-influenced music (the band Blood, Sweat, and Tears), classical-music-influenced songs ("A Whiter Shade of Pale"), even a rock bolero ("White Rabbit"), with blues and country rock yet to come.

A band I loved, and perhaps the band that most wildly combined, combusted, and reinvented sounds and—in their legendary conflict-ridden way—personnel was The Yardbirds. Eric Clapton, Jeff Beck, and Jimmy Page passed through this mini-maelstrom of blues, hard-rocking dystopic marches ("Shapes of Things"), minor key Beatlesque songs ("For Your Love"), Near Eastern bongo-laden pop ("Heart Full of Soul"), raga/gypsy rave-ups ("Over Under Sideways Down"), and general druggy, cranky, entertaining experimentalism that made for a bunch of brilliant singles hits but was so out of control that it seems tragically fitting that lead singer Keith Relf electrocuted himself onstage.

And it would all climax with the Jimi Hendrix Experience, the ultimate synthesis of not just many kinds of music but the biraciality of rock. Still that was only the beginning of rock's explosion of agglomeration and eclecticism made possible by the players' musical literacy and all the then-new studio techniques like multi-track recording. As Frank Zappa dryly put it, "the audience is being exposed to an assortment of advanced musical and electronic techniques that five years ago might have sent them screaming into the streets." Zappa called it audience education.[4]

And so it would seem that, with the audience reeducated to the new palette of electric music, folk-rock would simply shade into rock. But the folk part of folk rock had one more triumphant peak left to it, in a songwriter in many ways, if not as flamboyant as Dylan, lyrically as smart and sensitive and with a deeper breadth of musical knowledge and influences. He had also had, with his partner, a far better early rock 'n' roll experience than Dylan, when in high school, calling themselves Tom and Jerry after the cartoon, they'd had a minor hit with "Hey Schoolgirl." Their main influences were the acoustic rockabilly Everly Brothers, but their own beautiful guitar picking and harmonies fit seamlessly into the New York folk scene. And for their new name, which could've easily fit into either the intimate two-first-name bracket of folk acts (Ian and Sylvia) or the semi-Biblical pattern of Peter, Paul and Mary had they simply called themselves Simon and Arthur, they committed an edgy and arresting act of showbiz rebellion by putting an outright Jewish name up front as Simon and Garfunkel.

The rest is of course a history that is sometimes forgotten—as in Simon and Garfunkel, not the Stones or Dylan, were the act that challenged the Top 20 primacy of The Beatles. And while they would have their tunes which would both swing and rock, they would never be considered rockers, at least not until Simon dipped into Latin music for songs like "Me and Julio Down By The Schoolyard." Simon's writing, ranging through influences from Bach melodies to pop standards (*Still Crazy After All These Years*, an album evoking the best of New York in the '70s) would always be anchored in folk music. Whether in the lushly beautiful troubadorial "For Emily" or the gospel of "Bridge Over Troubled Water" or the groundbreaking and exquisitely crafted worldbeat music albums out of South Africa in *Graceland* and Brazil in *The Rhythm of the Saints*, he would carry on the old folk scene's guitar styles and warm embrace of international influences.

And as the successful early rocker who upheld the acoustic folk standard versus the dilettante early rocker who overturned it, he and Dylan would be frenemies for many years until finally playing together on a tour in 1999. In "Roll on John" Dylan's tribute to Lennon on his recent *Tempest* album, Dylan also honors Simon and Garfunkel in quoting "Slow down, you move too fast" from "The 59th Street Bridge Song." The twain of folk and rock once again and forever meet.[5]

So what does all this have to do with the present day? What the music of the '60s tells us is never underestimate the power of musicians to ride that hyphen, to recombine and synthesize different music into new forms. The basis now may be not as congenial to baby boomer sensibilities, deriving intensely from rap and hip-hop and the beats of electronica, but my aging ears were first educated to what one might call new hyphenates and syntheses by the band I absolutely loved in the '90s, Radiohead. Their *OK Computer* was truly the *Sgt. Pepper* of its day, with its unparalleled studio techniques, its weaving in and out of an allusive central topic and character, this time the mordant perceptions of an "uptight" subterranean "paranoid android" figure instead of a playfully soaring-over-it all marching band. The compositions were lushly arranged but still rocked hard. And unlike the Beatles, who never broke much new ground after 1967, Radiohead (especially Johnny Greenwood) and Thom Yorke in his individual and Atoms for Peace work have experimented more and more with unusual song structures that blend what seem to be their old influences—John Lennon, U2, prog and art rock—with new modes of electronica and most recently string orchestra voicings in songs like "Burn The Witch" off the album *A Moon-Shaped Pool.*

Meanwhile hip-hop and rap, which started, like rock, by fusing street-level musical expression with electronic technology, have become increasingly sophisticated to the point where the pulses of the rhythm itself have become mini-musical compositions, the "beats" of producers and artists like Timbaland and D'Angelo. And as they've dethroned rock as the main popular music, nonetheless somewhere along the way came an explosion of new rock from Brooklyn where you could hear in, for example, the fast-tumbling lyrics and funky drive of TV on the Radio's "Dancing Choose" from *Dear Science,* the infusion of rap into rock. The music of St. Vincent often has an electronica dance beat and a kind of chanting quality melded into the lyrics, in the same way the torrents of rap from Kendrick Lamar quick-change to the rhythms of electronica, funk, and even jazz.

There are whole new syntheses and hyphenations and hybridizations going on, made possible, in the same way classic rock was, by whole new recording techniques, and instead of merely ragas coming from India and Latin music from south of the border, international sounds flowing in from every corner of the world. Its bardic leading figures may not have the foundational musical and literary knowledge of a Bob Dylan or Paul Simon, but then again they don't have a music education-record company infrastructure to help them grow that body of work.

What they they have is the benefit of another kind of musical learning that they make use of as best they can: that cross-breeding of influences mixing and interpellating spontaneously from all sorts of sources, to which the term "rhizomatic" has lately been applied. It's horizontal rather than vertical growth, bricolage rather than "roots to the fruits" construction, not the way trees grow but the way mushrooms and lichens flourish as they interlace and overspread and conquer the forest. And the music that influences them and to which they contribute streams 24/7 to devices they can carry wherever they go. How else does an orthodox Jew like Matisyahu become a rapper? How else does MIA become an international star? How else does Beyonce move from basic soul and funk diva status to becoming the kind of musician who can mix various adventurous compositions and sound designs (and also throw in a country rock tune) in her mini-film "Lemonade"? We've had bards in this era like Chuck D, Ice Cube, Beyonce, K'Naan, St. Vincent, Eminem, and Kendrick Lamar who may never have the body of work of '60s, '70s, or '80s artists—that depends on, among other things, survival of peacetime in western civilization.

But rappers have poured out enough words already so that, for devotees, there are websites devoted to "decoding" all their lyrics. We've had, among other international and cross-generational collaborations, Robert Plant and Bono working with the "Festival in the Desert" musicians of Mali; those musicians have now been driven underground or into exile by ISIS-allied fanatics, but at least the performances and the traditions live on.

As we learned in the '60s, he great thing about The Music and its endless hyphenations—other than, as Bob Marley sang, "when it hits you feel no pain"[6]—is that even when it looks back, it goes forward.

Get Off Our Great Lawn

Global Citizen urges inactive action with an unfree free concert.

In New York City, a great tradition of free and charity outdoor concerts dating back at least to the 1960s, along with its most celebrated free concert venue, the Great Lawn in Central Park, is being annually taken over by the star-studded festivals of a smiling horde of "Global Citizens."

The festivals are dedicated to the goal of ending "extreme poverty." So it would seem that the enterprise is a worthwhile one, or at the very least merits the Seinfeld Defense: *not that there's anything wrong with that*. But considering what free concerts have always meant (like, for example, you can just show up because it's free) and what the goals are of a concert for a worthy cause (like raising money for a specific purpose), the verdict is not so simple. For Global Citizen, co-founded by CEO Hugh Evans and Ryan Gall, promotes concerts that are earned but with no guaranteed admission, and its campaigns are based on the belief that the message, the social platform, can be not just the medium but the whole effort.

I participated in Global Citizen its first year to try to get into its first New York free concert. As a website cryptically named "I Love Free Concerts" said about "The largest free music festival (and our favorite),"[3] in order to obtain tickets you had to "earn them by completing actions on the Global Citizen Festival website. These actions are fun, educational, and easy." I did it by writing a couple of letters, and then was able to put my "points earned" into the concert lottery draw for a spot at the Great Lawn free concert.

That's right, it's a "free concert" for which you pay with advocacy for Global Citizen, and afterwards, to paraphrase an NYC expression, you got nuthin'.

So again, per Jerry logic, is there anything wrong with something that devoted to a worthy cause, even if you don't win the draw?

For one thing, how every MSNBC commentator and Global Citizen celebrity guest says if you perform actions you will get into the concert, which is not true; Global Citizen's most recent instructions explain "Users win tickets to the festival through taking action to end extreme poverty. You can choose from a range of actions that earn you points. Once you earn 25 points from festival actions, you can enter the *draw* for festival tickets."

But also how about the loss of a whole set of values behind free concerts, especially in New York and Central Park? For me they began with nights in the '60s and '70s spent enjoying an aspect of New York civic pride: sitting with my family listening to the Philharmonic Orchestra on the Great Lawn. Jefferson Airplane gave a particularly memorable free concert in the '60s at the Central Park bandshell. And through subsequent decades, Sheep Meadow and The Great Lawn in Central Park played host to free concerts by, among others, Barbara Streisand, James Taylor, Paul Simon, and the Dave Matthews Band.

Free concerts by great bands, or even less-known local bands, always had a glow to them beyond their 'free-ness.' In the '60s and '70s, they helped many top bands cement their fan allegiances and also aided communities such as Haight-Ashbury in San Francisco and New York's East Village, if only by boosting morale; the late '60s and '70s were hard times for New York and for the country. It's corny, I know, but "free concerts" were almost '60s shorthand for good times-good people-let the sunshine in. They also enhanced the counterculture community's solidarity and well-being—at Woodstock, impresarios willing to take a big economic haircut turned what could've been a disaster if they'd tried to collect tickets into a miracle of cooperation when they didn't and declared the event, as shown in the movie *Woodstock*, "a free concert from now on."[1]

A close cousin to such free concerts were the charity events of the '70s through the '90s where you'd buy a ticket—maybe even a steeply priced one—but you'd know you were getting to see an extraordinary show and you'd know exactly to what good cause the money was going. George Harrison's Concert for Bangladesh. Farm Aid. At both free and charity concerts you often felt so motivated that you'd contribute even more money or volunteer efforts.

And when Bob Geldof built a giant US-UK concert in 1985, Live Aid, around the specific cause of alleviating hunger in the Horn of Africa, he announced how many millions were raised at the show and stressed the direction the money would take. Famine in that region has proved an endless problem, but Geldof came back twenty years later with an even more massive seven-continent effort, Live 8 2005, including a great little band from Antarctica performing amid penguins. How well did the concerts do? Live Aid had presented a heartbreaking photo of a dying little girl swarmed with flies; at the Live 8 show she bounded onto the stage, a vibrantly beautiful young woman. There wasn't a dry eye on the planet.

But now at Global Citizen, both a free (sort of) and charity (sort of) concert, designed for television and about as real and spontaneous as "red carpet" (they literally use that phrase) interviews, and Ariana Grande happening to show up to sing with Chris Martin, the point is not to get together and cheerfully create a communal event, or pool your ticket money with the likeminded and unite for a righteous cause. The whole free-and-charity-concert brand, so to speak, has been degraded to a meme whose content is publicity and low-effort conscience-salving on behalf of an organization with maximal possible connection to celebrity and minimal possible connection to the audience.

Now you "earn" points for the "free concert ticket in New York" (as in lottery ticket) by anonymously and at a cyber-distance "taking an Action Journey" (as in a series of tweets and letters and phone calls) for a potpourri of "goals" which often amount to, Ponzi-scheme style, getting other action-takers on the network. If free concerts on the Great Lawn in New York are associated with any "action" now, it might be action against the English language.

And if Global Citizen's rhetoric prompts any queasy memories, it's of '70s cults like Werner Erhard's EST ("Interested is interesting"), as do the endless shots of happy crowds. On one of the website videos, even the extreme-poverty-stricken are smiling. Then there are the testimonies of how Global Citizen changed action-takers' lives: whatever you did before, it's all better post-Global Citizen. The interviews with "action-takers" and the MSNBC chat breaks were reminiscent of telethons if, for example, the pledge moments in the old Jerry Lewis telethons had been all about Jerry Lewis.

And those telethons raised real money, whereas, as ceo Evans said before the 2016 concert, it's one thing to do specific projects in specific countries (digging wells, as he put it) but raising the hundreds of billions required to end "extreme poverty" by 2030 requires "calling on" global leaders in politics and finance. That may be true, but it's also true that while it may be on everyone's bucket lists to see the end of extreme poverty through massive contributions by global leaders, in poverty and drought-ravaged villages, it's more about an actual bucket of clean water from a new little well.

Again, okay, Global Citizen is a world-famous well-intentioned social platform for tweets and letters and pledges by Rihanna to help girls' education and phone messages to Congress and *not that there's anything* ... One can hope that, in economist Jeffrey Sachs's words supporting Global Citizen, "people get to the Park because they're engaged ... building a community ... the idea is when you get to that concert you've done something ... it brings Global Citizens together to say we can get things done ... "[2] Unity of purpose to create change is a worthy goal. Still at best Global Citizen is what Chris Evans, MSNBC pundit, paradoxically (and quite accurately) characterized it as during Global Citizen 2016: a program of "concrete asks."

And this gets into just how well intentioned Global Citizen is. What does New York get by letting Global Citizen take over one of the only huge Central Park concert occasions it can afford each year? What cause do concertgoers ultimately most benefit by spraying Global Citizen-related messages on social media? Could it be ... Global Citizen?

How much of any money raised is specifically directed to action-oriented efforts rather than, say, "focus" on sanitation and gender equality? "Commitments" are made: for example in 2015 Norway's Prime Minister Erna Solberg committed to double her country's contribution to the Global Partnership for Education, and increase sanitation funding by at least 6 million USD, and European Commission Vice President Frans Timmermans pledged to increase support for the refugee crisis by 500 million euros.

But what's the follow-up? It's great to see Beyonce and Pearl Jam and Kendrick Lamar put on terrific shows, and hear from Bono, the Gateses, and Malala Yousafsai, who will probably go anywhere to urge mass support for a philanthropic program as long as they get to mention their own much more substantive efforts.

But I defy anyone to find one substantive "action" or even plan in this 2015 paragraph from the Global Citizen website. "2015 is the year for the movement to end poverty. This September at the UN General Assembly in New York, world leaders from 193 countries will announce new GLOBAL GOALS designed to fight inequality, protect our planet, and end extreme poverty by 2030. The festival is a critical lever for achieving policy and financial commitments that will shape the success of the Global Goals over the next fifteen years."

Finally, not even the most generous application of the Seinfeld Defense can justify World Bank President Jim Yong Kim's presence at the concert. He announced that the World Bank would lead in efforts to lift twenty million people out of poverty next year, but that leaves out many millions more the World Bank's austerity programs have put into poverty and misery. The lineup of hipsterish-looking corporate honchos also appearing to show their kinder, gentler selves at the 2015 concert was also non-Seinfeldable. Cheers to the New York crowd for their lusty boos.

Ultimately we have no idea what the results of Global Citizen's concerts will be, other than leaving the followers feeling good about themselves—though probably not as good as how Global Citizen's founders feel about themselves.

If I may quote to Global Citizen a figure from wish-fulfillment scenarios who really "takes action": Make my day. Get off our Lawn.

On Hearing Jimi Hendrix in a Cologne Commercial

When '60s music spirit is for sale the music itself suffers.

The images, bathed in several shades of blue (the product is Bleu de Chanel) show a hunk actor dressed in the height of fashion filming a love scene. He flees the movie set pursued by a crowd of paparazzi and desperate fans; one woman even flings herself on his car. Driving away at top speed, he's haunted by the image not of the icily beautiful actress he did a love scene with, but the woman he really loves—who looks pretty much like the icily beautiful actress, but let that pass. In a mysterious corridor, he pursues her, his dream, so that, away from all the paparazzi and insane fans, he can be who he really is.

The music behind this commercial: "All Along The Watchtower," written by Bob Dylan, performed by Jimi Hendrix.

Hearing classics from great musicians of the '60s behind commercials is nothing new. Nike used John Lennon and The Beatles' 1968 "Revolution"; the result was a great lack of acclaim, even fury, and the three surviving Beatles sued to stop its use in the television commercial in 1987, although it kept playing until 1988. The Rolling Stones "I'm Free" has been deployed in a credit card commercial—anyone who's ever been in debt knows how free that makes you feel—and the Who's "I'm Free" was trotted out in a cable company commercial to celebrate the freedom of choice given you by your friendly cable provider.

But to understand why this commercial is particularly annoying, it helps to first check it out in its entirety (on YouTube it's actually called The Film).[1] Its accompanying ad copy (originally combined with it on the website) talked about how, for a man who wants to be truly out of the ordinary, this is the fragrance that expresses liberation, determination, and desire.

Okay, typical ad language. But then you can play the video "The Interview,"[2] and hear the French actor/star, Gaspard Ulliel, discoursing on the art and the meaning of the commercial.

First of all, anyone who finds a certain kind of French intellectualism in itself funny is urged to go straight to this video, where Ulliel compares the commercial's drive for "extreme liberty" to Chanel herself (wait, wasn't she drawn to fascism?) and goes on about the realm of abstraction and fantasy in the second half of the commercial. It makes you think maybe the commercial should've been called "*un film*" and ended with "*fin*." Trust me, you'll have a laugh, even though, if you know anything about Jimi Hendrix and the song itself, you might want to take a *Wayne's World*-size hurl into the nearest toilet afterwards.

If you had to sum up the '60s in one musician, Hendrix is whom you'd pick. He incarnated in his own career almost all the strands of music that went into '60s rock. When he broke through, he also broke the pop color barrier decades before Michael Jackson: a black musician fronting white guys in a rock band was up to then unheard of. Along with figures like Mick Jagger and Jim Morrison (on a good night) he was one of the greatest live performers of that period (I saw Hendrix on a night he wasn't at his best, and still have never forgotten it). He achieved a whole new level of musicianship on the guitar, in both rock and blues, and technically, with his unprecedented fingering and chording and his use of every resource available on the electric guitar at the time, he blazed a trail for all other guitarists to follow; as shown by guitarists like Vernon Reid, formerly of Living Colour, "Hendrix" has become a whole mode of guitar-playing.

But it was in his personal style that Hendrix also incarnated the best of the era. Down-home earthiness; he came out of awful poverty. Live-and-let-live acceptance of all kinds of people. A stoned-out but also artistic detachment, wildly costumed flamboyance, omnipresent sexuality, daffy humor, peacefulness mixed with gentle defiance (from his "If 6 Was 9": "They're hoping soon my kind will drop and die/ But I'm gonna wave my freak flag high...")[3] and total commitment to his music—he had it all. In his performance of "The Star Spangled Banner" at Woodstock, he fused a genuine love for America and even honoring of military service (he'd done some) with a generation's horror at the "rockets' red glare" raging over Vietnam and made an entirely original and explosive tone poem out of the song using only the strings and feedback of his guitar.

Hendrix's cover of "All Along The Watchtower" came from Bob Dylan's album *John Wesley Harding*, the first major album by Dylan after he had nearly died in a motorcycle accident. The album, with its pared-down acoustic instrumentation and sparse aphoristic lyrics, remains for many the most spiritual and existentially haunted of all of Dylan's albums. It's filled with biblical references in songs like "The

Ballad of Frankie Lee and Judas Priest," and the valley of the shadow of death makes its presence felt, especially in "All Along The Watchtower":

> *There must be some kind of way out of here*
> *Said the joker to the thief*
> *There's too much confusion*
> *I can't get no relief.*[4]

That's the stanza that plays over the images in the Bleu de Chanel commercial of Gaspard the stud fleeing his greatest existential threat: greedy photographers and turned-on super-fans. To paraphrase a lyric from Dylan's "Watchtower," talk about businessmen drinking his wine—and French businessmen at that.

Everyone wants the allure of the '60s. As Thom Yorke sang (half sarcastically, half ardently) in "Anyone Can Play Guitar" on Radiohead's *Pablo Honey*, "I wanna be Jim Morrison."[5] Yorke and Radiohead honored in their own way the underground spirit of the Doors music and achieved that kind of charisma and power and then some. But the advertising and business world wants the glamour of that authenticity, that rebellion, that nonconformity, that knowledge of the dark side, that integrity, without wanting any of those values themselves to rear their ugly heads. Chanel knows how to use ominous hard-driving music that's also a cultural touchstone to make men feel that they gotta somehow have the essence of that in their cologne.

It's a kind of anti-education. Every time songs are plundered that way, they lose their original meaning, especially for people who never heard or saw the original in the first place. They become memes incorporated into the matrix of commercial business as usual, tamed sometimes beyond recognition, even completely inverted and sent into Bizarro world ("I'm Free" with credit cards). There's an old story about how a song celebrating the legendary radio dj Wolfman Jack, "Clap For The Wolfman," was ruined the night another dj cracked a joke on the air about "penicillin for the Wolfman." Or imagine the song "Have Yourself A Merry Little Christmas" as background for one of those "just the right amount of wrong" Vegas commercials. Pairing Hendrix and "Watchtower" with fifty shades of bleu is that kind of bastardization.

And finally, just how does the essence of what men want in their Chanel cologne— determination, desire, independence, supermodels— just how does what is being sold in that commercial compare to what is being conveyed in the song? Dylan's *John Wesley Harding* joined Doors albums in the pantheon of music that troops in Vietnam loved to play. Its frequent theme, especially in "Watchtower," of trying to grasp what life really means while facing death truly spoke to men for whom that was part of the job description:

There are many here among us who feel that life is but a joke
But you and I, we've been through that, and this is not our fate
So let us not talk falsely now, the hour is getting late.

The song, like its previous verse had stated, gives no relief from that theme right to the end:

All along the watchtower, princes kept the view
While all the women came and went, barefoot servants, too.
Outside in the distance a wildcat did growl
Two riders were approaching, the wind began to howl.[6]

In Hendrix's cover of the song, though, what gives a kind of relief—and maybe this is why Dylan loved it—is the guitar orchestration. The sheer minor key thrill of it captures the implicit defiance of a song that faces such a dark theme so squarely. The layering of the shimmer of the acoustic strum and flight of the electric guitars is gorgeous, and in the break there are three kinds of guitar solos, one a kind of swooping evocation of vertigo (the high view of the watchtower, the storm), one a wa-wa line like a wild cat growling, and finally an almost gleeful funky solo that soars briefly above the darkness. The song and Hendrix's cover of it suggest Albert Camus' thought that, however absurd and meaningless mortal life may be, especially in a time of plague or war (which Camus knew personally), it's up to us to fill it with our own efforts and visions and live a life of dignity and unity with the rest of humankind.

Now go buy some cologne.

The Velvet Motherland and the City of Dreams
A European Son Essay in Four-Part Harmony

The Prague Spring

When I was fourteen years old, as one of the "senior" campers at Camp Winaco in West Baldwin, Maine, I was fortunate enough to go on a trip to Expo 67 in Montreal. That's when I fell in love with Czechoslovakia.

We know it now as the Czech Republic and Slovakia, but back then it was one nation, and one of a kind, as Expo 67 proved. The Czech pavilion, as all the magazine and newspaper coverage pointed out, was one of the highlights of this greatest of world's fairs I ever saw (with apologies to my beloved New York 1964 World's Fair—let's just say the technology had moved ahead).

First came a Hall of Centuries, with gold and silver objects from the Great Moravian Empire of the eight century, and manuscripts from the Middle Ages and the Renaissance, and a Hall of Tradition, a room of craft displays, jewelry, lace, ceramics, and Bohemian glass. Then came the Trebechovice Bethleham, an incredible wooden Nativity scene with two thousand figures, three hundred of them animated, carved over forty years, and portraying glimpses of everyday life in the 19th century down to the tiniest detail.

But that was only the warmup act for this traveling roadshow, which climaxed with examples of then new film technology that, except in one case, haven't been equaled (or at least duplicated) even today. Polyvision was a room of films projected on spinning hoops and other moving surfaces; it was impossible to know where to look first. One then wandered into the hypnotic Diapolyecran, an interpretation of Creation on a wall 32 feet wide by 20 feet high. A mosaic of over one hundred two-foot-square cubes, each fitted with two slide projectors, glided back and forth, constantly changing images in a way that created interlocking and vanishing and reemerging pictures that washed over the wall in waves: volcanoes to greenery, amoebae to insects to animals, all the way to modern man. I can still remember the hushed clicking that predicted each new image.

Then came (and the line was too long to even get in) Kino Automat, an early experiment in combined theater and film and interactivity, where the audience got to vote on the various turns and ending of the plot of a movie. As a cooldown from all these eye-popping attractions, the pavilion had four restaurants, a fashion show, and an outdoor area of playful statues.

There were other impressive pavilions, like the US one, surprisingly gentle in spirit (rock guitars rather than guided missiles) and contained in a mighty geodesic dome by Buckminster Fuller. There were certainly other dazzling experiments in film: Kaleidoscope, with its mirrored all-encompassing screens, and Labyrinthe from the National Film Board of Canada, a film experience synchronizing a multistory vertical screen 38' by 20' high with another equally giant screen on the floor.[1] But here was a small country from behind what we were always told was a cultural dark age zone, beneath the shadow of the Iron Curtain, beating all the rest with native wit and imagination. I figured, in words later to be made a song title by David Byrne, this must be the place.

1968's Prague Spring, as showcased in *Life* Magazine, did not disappoint me: beautiful bare-midriffed and miniskirted girls (really? there?) and brave longhaired youth challenging the Soviet-era apparatchiks, while looking hip as can be by Hradcany Castle and on the Charles Bridge. Eastern European youths congregated in Prague and wrote in collective notebooks about their feelings upon the death of "Red Fascism," while at a confrontation of two Politburos at Cierna that summer, Alexander Dubček charted a course to a benign middle way: "revisionist" freer socialism and *"stikhiinost,"* or spontaneity not controlled by any political vanguard. And it all seemed to make so much sense, this "socialism with a human face." Of course Leonid Brezhnev, premier of the Soviet Union (the former empire controlled by Russia) was going there to shake hands with Dubček and make peace with what was going on. What could be better for them than such humanization? The Soviet world was prepared to enter the modern one.

Well, no. That was just the con before the storm. Perhaps, while entranced by the Prague spring and Dubček, I should have remembered the other son of Prague who'd recently entered my imagination: Franz Kafka. The driving force of his masterworks *The Trial* and *The Castle* is the man who thinks he can talk to the right person, who thinks he has a case. The most effectively oppressive system is the one that makes the people think they have a chance to defend and protect themselves just before the iron grip descends. And, as Kafka's dreamlike stories suggested, within the human mind itself lay the seeds of that self-deception, that rejection and yet secret embrace of total control.

We'd soon see the heartbreaking news headlines, especially on the cover of *Life*: "The Death of the Bright Young Freedom."[2] On August 30, 1968 came the Soviet Union's crushing invasion (so frighteningly depicted in Phil Kaufman's film of Milan Kundera's *The Unbearable Lightness of Being*). The Prague Spring was gradually replaced by a harsh clampdown that included the immediate jamming of radios and later rounding up of reformers.

1968 was a terrible year for democracy and civil disobedience by young people. In France, a huge popular resistance movement started by students and joined by millions of Renault workers and other labor unions prompted a harsh pushback by the DeGaulle regime and was ultimately defeated by a referendum. In Mexico City, ten days before the summer Olympics, hundreds of students were killed by the military and police in the Plaza de las Tres Culturas in what became known as the Tlatelolco massacre, named after the section of the city where this worst suppression of Mexican political opposition took place. And here in America, at the Chicago Democratic convention that rammed Senator Hubert Humphrey down the electorate's throat, the police smashed into waves of demonstrators in a "police riot" later condemned by the whole nation, a major factor in the election of Richard Nixon as President. One of the protesters caught by the TV cameras held a sign that said "Welcome To Prague."

But while the anti-Vietnam war dream gradually surrendered to Nixon's machinations—slowly pulling our troops out while continuing the war and bombing Cambodia, a strategy whose end result, after more needless sacrifice of troops, was North Vietnamese victory and the Khmer Rouge—the long-term dream of democracy never died in Prague. For twenty-two years, despite imprisonments of leading dissidents, stripping intellectuals of all their rights, and ironclad surveillance to the limits possible at the time, a resistance flickered in the darkness that would ultimately triumph over its own traitors, even the Soviet Union itself. And it was sustained in part by American rock music influences one would never suspect. To see what those influences were and how they worked, let's briefly go back to how I learned about Franz Kafka.

The Unexpected Soundtrack of Resisting

In 1968, one of my favorite bands was The Mothers of Invention led by Frank Zappa, and that year saw the release of perhaps his most satirically pointed album, *We're Only In It for the Money*. From the album's cover, an astonishingly detailed nasty parody of *Sgt. Pepper's*, to songs like "Who Needs The Peace Corps?" "Concentration Moon," "Flower Punk," and the strangely beautiful "The Idiot Bastard Son," this was Zappa's most direct broadside against American stupidity, repression, consumerism, and conformism of every stripe, whether beauty products or his favorite target, Top 40 radio; whether dressed up in flower-power hippie garb, all-American bow ties, or police uniforms.

The album ended, very oddly, with one of Zappa's compositional and studio experiments, an experimental piece named "The Chrome-Plated Megaphone of Destiny." Zappa first urged listeners to read the Kafka short story "In The Penal Colony," about a Commandant of the Penal Colony guiding an Explorer through the intricacies of a giant machine that, over six hours, tortures inmates by carving the names of their crimes on their backs, but also, according to the Commandant, instils mystical visions of justice and correction. Zappa's accompanying liner notes made reference to "Camp Reagan" (Reagan was then the right-wing governor of California) and a "recreational device" that might do the same thing as part of a "Final Solution to the Nonconformist Problem."

The music itself was an intriguing mix of Cecil Taylor-ish percussive piano, early industrial noise-rock summoning the image of that infernal machine (a lot of clanging and banging), and roving guitar lines that proved early on that Zappa would be one of the most fiendishly brilliant utilizers of time signatures in any field of music. But did it track the story? Well ... transmuting Kafka's deep, surrealistic unease and horror at the excesses of the human psyche into a sonic portrayal of cartoonish legal persecution, Kafka's poetry aligned with Zappa's commentary ... not one of his more successful musical experiments.

Still, it got me into Kafka. And after reading Kafka's stories I fell in love even more with Prague—and thus was both bitterly disappointed, but maybe less surprised at the next sad dictatorial turn in Prague's history.

What was surprising—and what I didn't learn until decades later—was that in the same way Frank Zappa had found some sort of intellectual and maybe even spiritual sustenance in Kafka, the homeland of Kafka, in the midst of a Kafkaesque phase of its history, turned to Frank Zappa. Why? The protest that was part of Zappa's musical universe was not of the strictly American '60s left-wing counterculture kind. For example, in *We're Only In It For The Money* Zappa railed against hippies, who raised Zappa's ire in part because he believed they were well-off phonies creating their own conformity and adopting a quasi-religious creed ("I will love everybody. I will love the cops as they kick the shit out of me on the street.") But Zappa had limitless compassion for "creeps," genuinely nonconforming oddballs at the extreme end of the unacceptability spectrum. For them and their friends he had the utmost compassion:

> *Mama, mama*
> *Your child was killed in the park today*
> *Shot by the cops as she quietly lay*
> *By the side of the creeps she knew*
> *They killed her too.* [3]

Zappa may have inveighed against psychedelic hippie bullshit but he never stopped caring about personal and cultural outcasts. How to resolve the contradiction, how to be nonconformist but not an official hippie pseudo-rebel? Wit, detachment, righteous anger, and braininess. Or as Zappa once put it "You can't be busted for awareness. Maintain your aristocratic coolness."[4]

And so Zappa, who had in his adolescence appeared on the *Steve Allen Show* as a "wiggy" but clean-cut teen genius making music out of a bicycle and playing cards, who had been raised fairly conventionally by, in his words, "pretty religious" parents, became the covered with facial hair, dirty-mouthed, angry totem of the phrase he coined for the Mothers of Invention's first album, *Freak Out* (though in a totally workaholic drug-and-drink-abstaining way). He was in many ways the Lenny Bruce attack comic of rock, sometimes insulting his audiences ("If your children knew how lame you were, they'd murder you in your sleep"), sometimes just laying on them a nightmare vision of establishment whitebread America. His protest was simultaneously his own Apollonian form of beautifully intricate music—like the xylophone, celeste, and harpsichord passages on the album *Uncle Meat*—combined with a Dionysian immersion in fantasies of dirty sex (especially in his one movie, *200 Motels*), furious (but usually funny) rants, and disgusting mouth and bowel noises.

And nowhere was his self-chosen independent outsideness, his anger at a system of thought control rather than particular targets, his vitriolic attacks on censored media, his love of Kafka and his seeing Kafkaesque repressiveness everywhere, and his outrageousness more appreciated than in the underground music circles of oppressed Czechoslovakia. Their main underground band was Plastic People of the Universe, formed by Milan Hlavsa and Ivan Jirous, who named themselves after Zappa's song "Plastic People" ("You're Plastic People/ Oh baby now you're such a drag"), a song that targeted mass-culture-influenced conformity and craven acceptance of American norms, violence, and oppression ("Take a day/And look around/Watch the Nazis/Run your town." and later "I know that love/Can never be/A product of/Plasticity.").

Zappa's lyrics thus became an inspiration to the Plastic People and other bands. Zappa's music, on the other hand, while loved and appreciated, was not what underground bands needed. On an album like *Absolutely Free*, the music's design could become insanely complex. A piece like "Brown Shoes Don't Make It" was literally an oratorio of interlocking musical parts and recording effects: a politician father, singing his dream of incest with his sixteen-year-old daughter in a lyric set against an Alban Berg-like string quartet background, suddenly then starts singing, to cheesy barbershop quartet music in four-part harmony, that he wants to "smother that daughter in chocolate syrup."[5] Another part of the album features a jam between a guitar and soprano sax in part based on a motif from Stravinsky.

While admiring Zappa and absorbing his lyrics and his gut-level indignation, Czech musicians needed a more accessible model than this phenomenal musical genius whose bands would always be, however hard they rocked, highly rehearsed studio bands often conducted onstage by Zappa himself. Zappa's influence on underground Czech bands' philosophy was thus supplemented by an influence on their sound and attitude that came from another '60s band—a band with a highly experimental but much simpler sound; a band that also had its problems connecting with "flower power" and psychedelia; a band that ironically competed with Zappa for the American fringe audience on the same record level, Verve; a New York vanguard band that would ultimately provide the name for Czechoslovakia's Velvet Revolution.

The Velvet Underground were, like Zappa, self-chosen denizens of the darkness. Their leader Lou Reed was a Long Island kid who'd cut his teeth in the music business trying to write and even perform commercial tunes. But in college he'd discovered the poetry of Delmore Schwartz and in New York found he could write in that vein about the world of New York's East Village back when it was truly a low-rent and occasionally scary haven for artists, proud sexual "deviants," and left-wing politics. In what Ice Cube would later term journalism from his neighborhood, Reed wrote songs about the immigrants, artists, and renegades all around him; about Andy Warhol's pansexual clan and heroin addiction and the freaks that haunted Reed's streets and his dreams. The sound he and violinist John Cale fashioned was part blues, part raga, part basic four-four rock, and always urban, minimal, and raw (or eerily poignant, as in "Pale Blue Eyes") in a way that could never fit into the lush and sweet and largely bucolic paeans to peace and love that the record companies preferred in the late '60s. Were it not for Andy Warhol's fervent support (they basically became his house band) they would've had trouble even getting gigs.

Like Dylan, Lou Reed was in part cultivating an image, wearing a sneer and singing in a deadpan drawl, but his songs are full of troubling emotions, especially those in perhaps his greatest song on the Velvets' first landmark album, "Heroin." In the voice of a hopeless addict, he wishes he'd been born a thousand years ago sailing on a ship away from the evil of New York even as he simultaneously succumbs to and embraces yet another fix. Reed's minimalizing voice is balanced by the maximal metaphors, as the music accelerates in a two-chord stringendo and John Cale supplies the screeching viola of the smack flow.

The band's classic first album was recorded in eight hours live in the Scepter studio at a point when the place was literally falling apart. Despite the recording schedule there was time for musical tinkering and experimentation, including dowtuning the guitar to the viola to get the eerie drone effect in "Venus in Furs." The Velvets recorded excursions into hard-rock blues and early noise rock experimentation to create a sound with an edge and a fascination unlike any other, and when Nico, she of the Teutonic icy blonde glamor and ennui-laden voice, joined them, the outre-ness couldn't be more extreme.

This kind of complete marginality was embraced by Czech bands. Lou Reed felt that anyone should be able to play his songs, and so they were fairly easy to cop and to learn from. The balance of nihilism and orneriness in the music that somehow also shimmered with the downbeat allure of tunes like "All Tomorrows Parties" spoke to people with a vibrant cultural tradition forced to lead drably controlled lives. There was despair in a song like "Heroin" ("Thank God that I'm good as dead/Thank you God that I'm not aware/Thank God that I just don't care.") but also an openness to new experience ("And I guess, but I just don't know") and, in a song like "Venus in Furs," a reawakening of passion no matter how painful ("Different colors made of tears").[6]

But perhaps the Czechs really absorbed the Velvets because, like any great artist, Lou Reed had absorbed the world around him: in the '60s New York had its similarities to Prague, with the East Village playing host to marginal writers and outsiders and real "European Son"s (as in one of their songs) going back to World War II refugee days—with all the bitterness and melancholy that entailed. That angst and menace was there in the Velvets' music in the flight both mental and physical (as in "Run, Run, Run"), in the paranoia (as in "Sunday Morning"), in the hard-edged beat of the junkie tune "I'm Waiting For The Man" (back when "Lexington 1-2-5" was not a gentrified Harlem), and the noise-rock explosions venting the cognitive dissonance of the city's promise and crime in "Sister Ray."

Zappa and the Velvets didn't have too many touchpoints (except perhaps for those noise-rock jams), but the Czechs adopted them both and Reed and Zappa were among the first foreign notables invited to the new Prague by Václav Havel in the '90s. But the process by which Havel, one of Prague's major dissident writers, became Czechoslovakia's president and was able to welcome the two alt-rockers of their day as visiting dignitaries was as hard and long as it was improbable.

For among the many ways the Czech authorities ensnared and entrapped their people for over two decades was driving a wedge between the artists and the political dissenters. As a performance artist from Prague would later tell me, the authorities went after the writers circulating their unauthorized underground manuscripts and usually left the visual and musical artists alone. Musicians, painters, performance artists, and sculptors signed papers pledging loyalty, learned how your art might transgress in ways that would piss Gustáv Husák and his apparatchiks off, and stayed out of prison. Only if you incorporated into your lyrics, for example, messages that sounded too challenging would you incur their wrath.

And taking on the aggressive hard edge of the Velvets and the provocative attitude of the Mothers and Zappa, the Plastic People of the Universe were uncompromising in doing just that. Their underground world and style was an attack on official culture of communist Czechoslovakia. Yet even when the authorities came down on them, in their pride they never quite made common cause with the political dissenters, claiming theirs was a different kind of rebellion.

The story of how these strands of rebellion, the political and the musical, broke apart but ultimately found common ground and combined to help deliver the Czech people is fiendishly complex, and would seem to resist any distillation into powerful drama that would explore those contradictions and their triumphant resolution. Fortunately we have Tom Stoppard. In his late, great, and extraordinarily entertaining play *Rock 'n' Roll*, he made vivid art out of the careening but stubborn progress to Czechoslovakia's intellectual and spiritual survival, and just how important the music of the '60s was to that renaissance.

The Pipes of Pan in Eastern Europe

Stoppard himself was a bit of a rockstar in the mid-'60s, when he captivated the theater world with his first play, *Rosencrantz and Guildenstern Are Dead*. The play, which inverts Hamlet by looking at it comically from the point-of-view of the play's most inconsequential characters, had a kind of mod-London irreverence mixed with playful and relentlessly brilliant Oxford don-nish idea-and-wordplay. It has plenty of delightful moments that suggest British humor of the time like *Beyond The Fringe* and the sketches of Peter Cook and Dudley Moore.

Yet it also entered that bleak Samuel Beckett *Godot* territory in a way that was very Czech and Kafkaesque in spirit. Stoppard was, in his words, originally "a little Czech schoolboy"—his parents fled Czechoslovakia when he was young. Rosencrantz and Guildenstern, like permanent cosmic expats and maybe Stoppard himself, can't remember home. They have no desires and feel part of a mechanism of a play beyond their control, desperately seeking meaning for their plight, sometimes from a group of Players, but not getting logic, or art, only come-ons. Half-hoping the mechanism of the play will assign direction to their destinies, but fearing (rightly) the consequences, they quibble and theorize; meanwhile every act and scene blackout, insofar as it gives them any direction at all, brings them closer to their almost tossed-off deaths. Amusing us all the way, Tomas of Czechoslovakia conjures up a Kafkaesque vision of men at the mercy of infernally incomprehensible changes.

Stoppard's plays have ever since mixed comedy and tragedy, have often had surrealistic passages, and have always shared George Bernard Shaw's incorporation of "social utility" and fulsome rhetorical and even teaching impulses. His characters constantly voice their visions and ideas, sometimes with the most passionate seriousness, often with a generous dose of wit or even near-slapstick bumptiousness; Monty Python's Anne Elk and her theories could easily have stepped out of one of his plays. And one of Stoppard's great themes, coming directly from his background, is the noble nineteenth-century vision of building a new society out of class consciousness, economic theory, and revolution that plummeted toward disastrous communist twentieth-century reality—the great theme of his trilogy *The Coast of Utopia*.

Rock 'n' Roll, as befits its subject, is playful, passionate, and deadly serious in equal measure. The play begins with an almost hallucinatory scene of a piper playing a love song to a beautiful sixteen-year-old flower child, Esme. He may be an incarnation of the god Pan, or just maybe Syd Barrett, the original leader of Pink Floyd. In one scene Stoppard captures all the promise and halcyon delights of the '60s and in subsequent scenes incarnates everyone's love of the Music back then. But Esme's foreign student boyfriend and Stoppard's lead character Jan has something else on his mind; despite the apparent crushing of the Prague Spring, he thinks there's hope for socialism yet if people of goodwill band together to save it and (and this was the play's starting point for Stoppard) unlike Stoppard he decides to go back to his homeland.

It's a high-minded and fateful decision and a bad one, as Jan becomes part of the repressive downward spiral of his nation, internalizing many of the self-deceiving strategies through which Czechs, especially intellectuals, somehow hoped the repression would lift. In one scene Jan refuses to sign a petition for prisoners imprisoned by Husák's "government of normalization." Jan tells himself it's narcissistic and won't help the prisoners. The scene is based on an actual exchange between Milan Kundera, the nation's main writer, and Václav Havel, its main playwright and dissenting prisoner; Kundera had declared the new politics had retreated, but not disintegrated, in the same way Jan insists the Prague Spring was not defeated by the Russian invasion. Jan always seeks the middle ground: decency, not heroism. For Jan, such heroism is not honest work and doesn't accomplish anything. Still, unlike the Bohemian underground of the time, who put down the official opposition of banned writers and intellectuals, Jan, as a dissenter, doesn't type other dissenters as a bunch of losers.

But he's also a journalist who compromises with the authorities, at one point simply to get his rock records back. Jan and his friend Ferdinand are fanboys constantly discussing '60s music. There's as much discussion about and allegiance pledged to groups like the Velvets, the Fugs, Pink Floyd, and above all the Stones as in any American setting, for to the Czechs of the time, those bands were truly important. But for Jan the fact that the Plastic People, named after Zappa, played "Venus in Furs" by the Velvet Underground publicly is evidence that the Czech puppet leader "Husák'll keep the hardliners on the B side." And so he won't sign any petitions, even though the Plastic People have just lost their professional license to play in public (the equivalent of the New York '60s cabaret card but worse) because of their extreme nature.

Of course he'll be proved wrong. The concept that the push for Havel, dissent, and reform was opposed to the push for free music in Prague was a false dichotomy. (Havel himself perceived that clearly; he saw in the Plastic People a "disturbing magic," a kind of "inner warning ... metaphysical sorrow and longing for salvation." He felt that "truth was on their side."[7]). In so far as *Rock 'n' Roll* tackles politics, it's to break down that wall between nonpolitical music (or even political like the Mothers, if slathered in offensive comedy) and political resistance. Jan, a classic liberal in a Communist Iron Curtain setting, refuses to sign a loyalty pledge, and is "purged" to kitchen work, no longer allowed to teach. Though he refused to sign the petition to release dissidents, he later circulates one against a mass arrest of the Plastic People and their fans in 1974, and in 1976, after attending another mass arrest concert, his records are smashed, and he serves time in prison.

Rock 'n' Roll is a complex play where ideas constantly play against each other and explode and pinwheel like some kind of mental psychedelic light show. But always Stoppard connects on an emotional level, especially in the story of the intellectual but also deeply personal conflict back in England between Max, an old British Communist teacher who's kept his diehard integrity and strategies for defending his old creed, and Eleanor, his wife who teaches Sapphic poetry and believes above all in earthly passion and beauty and love despite the fact her own body is falling apart grotesquely from cancer.

This truly generous-hearted and sophisticated play has compassion for Max as he defends the Czech occupation. A "decent fit" between "theory and practice" is what Max seeks, just like Tom Hayden and SDS did with the New Left (it's hard to believe now, but trying to resolve paradoxes in Marxist Communist theory was a major preoccupation of activists in the '60s). Max, the recalcitrant Communist, can't win the argument but is touching in his faith, and Stoppard honors his commitment while unsparingly revealing the cruel contradictions he can't overcome.

Inspired, as Stoppard says in his introduction to the play, by Václav Havel and his essays "Dear Dr. Husák" and "The Power of the Powerless," Stoppard uses the history to put Jan and Max into corners where resistance to delusion and dogma is the only option, whether one accepts it or not. In the play's darkest phase in the '80s, Esme's beautiful memory of Syd Barrett as the Piper is now an old nut case on a bike, Jan despairs of Gorbachev's perestroika, Havel is in despair with the Czech people, the Plastic People have been brutally punished and finally driven apart, and, for Max, Communism has died with Margaret Thatcher. The characters admit major and minor betrayals of each other in the name of or in opposition to Communism.

But these passages build up to the play's high note; if musicians wanted to compromise, the music didn't, even when, like Barrett, musicians went mad. The music was an emotional and mental space for finding the passion that was Eleanor's life and, in the words of Havel, for "living in truth."[8] The play ends with an explosion of light and sound as Jan, after decades, reunites with Esme and they go to a newly freed Prague to see the Rolling Stones play Strahov, where the Communists had once had big shows. That moment of onstage spectacle is counterpointed with a quieter moment in a Cambridge garden where a student recites a poem from the classics that intones, in a passage from Plutarch, "Great Pan is dead"—but not when the Rolling Stones hit the stage.

Václav Havel, when he was a prisoner, had said the petition Kundera had criticized gave them satisfaction; renewed their solidarity and ability to survive their sentences; showed civic backbone; and also publicized the practice of long prison terms, which then got to the press, which then exerted successful pressure on the authorities. And so Havel would also fight to get support for the Plastic People, seeing them not as drug addicts or layabouts but independent thinkers, and would help to get three of them released from prison. He would in his own efforts unify artistic and political resistance and ultimately, when he became president of the new Czechoslovakia after the Velvet Revolution, celebrate its success by inviting Zappa and Lou Reed to join the festivities. Meanwhile a member of the Plastic People would later form the band Pulnoc and play in America, another fusion of political and artistic liberation.

And Havel would become the humane and successful example of a philosophy, as stated by Stoppard, that sought to "return life to its human scale and language to its human meaning; to recognize that socialism and capitalism in its selfish forms are different routes to global totalitarianism.... The equivalence of theory and practice is nowhere harder to achieve than in 'living in truth' in a society which lies to itself. In the Czechoslovakia of 1968 to 1990 a rock 'n' roll band came as close as anyone."[9]

4. This Must Be The Place

As part of the macro-consummation of Eastern Europe's dreams of liberty under the great writer/leader Václav Havel and the immortally great statesman Mikhail Gorbachev in 1990, a micro-consummation occurred: I finally got to visit Prague.

It was an extension of a research trip I made to Berlin in the course of writing a screenplay. Pretending to be a journalist, and hiring an interpreter when necessary, I interviewed cops, Auschwitz survivors, and ordinary Berliners.

Berlin alternately fascinated, delighted, and spooked me. I stood on the Berlin Wall, which I'd always thought would be around long after I was dead. I saw the East Germans voting, in pencil on long sheets of medieval-looking paper, for the first time in forty years, absolutely inspiring. I then saw the (at that time) still smoke-blackened Reichstag, walked past buildings in Prinzlauerberg riddled with bullet holes, and visited the East German museum with its truly awful Holocaust room, and was reminded of just how much darkness had been passed through to get to that vote. But in a Berlin club I saw a shaven-headed young woman dancing with broken chains around her feet. I saw the first exhibit by a West German artist, Rainer Fetting, in one of East Germany's magnificent museums. All of which was extraordinary, not to mention the fact that, being of German-Austrian descent on one side of my family, and having grown up in the Yorkville "Germantown/Berlin Bar" neighborhood in Manhattan, my Berlin trip felt, despite my Holocaust-related research, almost like a homecoming.

But it was in visiting Prague that I felt sheer exhilaration and an affinity of spirit. The beautiful medievality of the city, its narrow near-deserted lamplit streets at night. Seeing Kafka's grave, and knowing that in this country an artist whose most famous work tells the fable of a man transformed into an insect was one of the culture's greatest heroes. Walking the Charles Bridge with a cup of grog in hand and watching the swans on the Vlatva River, while noticing signs that translated as "Václav to the Castle" (a slogan of Havel's election campaign, referring to the Hradčany Castle complex), and then seeing that Castle, and later being transfixed by the beauty of St. Nicholas Church and the Old Town Square. There it was: the same glow-in-the-dark brilliance—no wonder this was the city of the original Black Light theater—the same preservation of wit and art and basic human values under the heel of oppression that I'd seen at Expo 67. Above all, there was Prague's Jewish Museum, perhaps the greatest in the world, for Hitler had planned, after he'd killed the last European Jew, to build a Museum of the Dead Race in Prague, and the Czechs had turned his hoard of relics into a testament to Jewish survival, resilience, and achievement. But just outside was a cemetery so filled with Jewish dead that the gravestones were tilted on top of each other, a reminder of the depth and also the price of that European experience.

For me the soul connection was only in part about Judaism (the museum was there by historical accident) but more about the cherishing and cultivation of that museum and Kafka and art and beauty, curating it somehow against the nightmare of not just the Holocaust but so much subsequent adverse history.

Could the trip get any better? In a bar sipping some Slivovicz, a plum brandy strong enough to be one way the Czechs survived Communism, I got some anti-American shade from someone at the bar, gave him some shade back, and heard applause and noticed the presence of movie lights.

I had become a part of a documentary on the man next to me, a

Czechoslovakian performance-artist. We were soon in conversation, and I asked him if the Czechs were at the time feeling nervous or good. He answered that they were feeling nervous because they were feeling good.

We became fast friends for eight hours. He took me to a theater where Václav Havel's plays had been performed; I didn't understand a word of the production but didn't care. He and two beautiful actresses then toured me around Prague one more time. I certainly wanted to stay longer, but my ticket was booked. I'd finally embraced Prague, Prague had embraced me back—it was time, in a very good frame of mind, to go home.

I know that, even if I get to Prague again, the Prague I saw, just tremulously opening to freedom, but still with only (superb) beer and (mediocre) beef on most restaurant menus, is gone, having been replaced by the "Amsterdam of Eastern Europe." But its lessons remain with me, above all the power and value of '60s music, or indeed any music, in providing energy for intellectual and political changes, and making you at last, if nervously, feel good. As Ziggy Marley sang, "when the lights gone out, and the food run out, all you have is just the music."[10] It sounds sappy until you think of Prague from 1968 to 1990, or *Hair* being performed during the siege of Sarajevo.

New York likes to think of Paris as its sister city; I'd vote for Prague as another sibling. And how are those related cities and countries faring? France's system is now being severely tested by homegrown Islamic terrorism, but in the wake of that temporarily suppressed revolution of 1968, socialist administrations sprang up under Francois Mitterand and his successors, and France emerged with a government still highly protective of workers and middle-class rights and lifestyles, including health care. Czechoslovakia went through its share of troubles, and indeed had to split apart, but the Czech Republic is now a stable and prosperous democratic society.

It's America that's experimenting with Orwellian and Kafkaesque perversion of the language of institutions that can lead to breakdown and violence. It's America that is turning toward slicing and dicing of the federal government, mass incarceration of people of color, impoverishment of the middle class to feed the interests and coffers of one tenth of one percent of its population, the crushing of future generations under enormous educational debts, and the embrace of "law and order," bigotry, anti-media sentiments, and potential legal and quasi-legal repression.

In one of my photo albums of my trip to Berlin and Prague is a picture of me standing on top of the Berlin Wall, while below people chip at the Wall to get their bits of Soviet empire history and Red Army caps are sold as souvenirs. It all seems immortal until it's Disneyland. As Radiohead, once sang, "We are standing on the edge."[11]

What can we learn from the Prague Spring and *Rock 'n' Roll*? Jan finally achieves this wisdom. "How did the propaganda paper and the capitalist press arrive at the same relation to the truth? Because all systems are blood brothers. Changing one system for another is not what the Velvet Revolution was for. We have to begin again with the ordinary meaning of words."[12] And as Havel stated in his "The Politics of Hope," this must be in service to a constant application of that virtue, which is an "orientation of the heart" and "an ability to work for something because it is good, not just because it stands a chance to succeed."[13]

The Czechs outlasted opression with spiritual sustenance from their greatest dissenters, quietly sustained resistance, and a hefty dose of '60s rock. We could do worse than look to *Rock 'n' Roll* and the history of Prague since 1968—musical, cultural, and political—to find ways to help get us through what may be coming.

It Was Fifty Years Ago Today

On June 2, 1967, time pretty much stopped in New York City. My friend and I, as I recall, heard one of the songs on someone else's portable radio, learned what brand new album it was from, and immediately ceased our handball game to go up to his apartment to listen on his dad's KLH stereo system.

The power of that day in pop music was a confluence of many factors: the still massive popularity of the great group who'd become men of mystery no longer performing; the strangeness of the music and its orchestration and the fascinating possibility that it all might be linked to marijuana and LSD; the fact that so-called "underground" FM radio stations had emerged that were not hamstrung by the Top 40 format, so they could play the whole album cut by cut over and over until much of the city was entranced.

Sgt. Pepper's Lonely Hearts Club Band sounded like novelty music, other kinds of music we'd heard, and nothing we'd ever heard before, even if it did sound like The Beatles. Believe the fifty-year-old hype: this was *the* album of the '60s. Not because it matched the verbal brilliance and richness of Dylan's *Highway 61 Revisited* or *Bringing It All Back Home*, or the storytelling and song-by-song power and gemstone brilliance of the Who's *Tommy*, or the blazing musicianship of Hendrix's *Electric Ladyland*. But in its luxuriantly arranged, meticulously crafted, mischievous, sometimes lilting, sometimes frightening, beautifully designed and orchestrated tracks it opened up a whole new way of listening to pop music and even of seeing the world. *Sgt. Pepper's* was a meeting of the playful Beatles universe with the spirit of the *The Twilight Zone*; in its songs and stories and music extraordinary things happened to ordinary people, and we were all invited to sing along.

But this album didn't just pull in an established audience; it created a new one. It was the Woodstock of vinyl, consolidating the counterculture in music fandom before the massive rock festival revealed it to be a living breathing body in the millions. It popularized for all time the concept album (even if, technically, the Sgt. Pepper's motif was more a frame than a concept); Frank Sinatra had had thematically organized collections (*September of My Years*), but this sort of imaginative structure, emanating right through to the Edwardian costumes of the band and famous-and-infamous-of-the-century cover tableau, was a new approach that made possible the appreciation of each song as the vital part of a whole.

****

Of course by then the Beatles had been surprising everyone for years. For awhile it was simply by not vanishing, not becoming, as George Harrison one day admitted, a temporary craze that would soon be over, after which he was planning on opening a business.

The Beatles were a process of discovery. They lifted the mass audience created on television by the Kennedy funeral from grief to happiness. When they came to our shores on that Pan Am plane, they prompted so much female teenybopper screaming that they at first exasperated young males, but then proved so fresh, buoyant, and funny, with the specificity of (as they at one point made themselves) cartoon characters, you couldn't help but be hooked. And the Beatles rode their unprecedented wave through sheer talent, hard-won skill, musical awareness, and a great sense of humor to a whole new mass market level. Their process of artistic evolution, reflected in their songs and album covers, was fascinating and a little bewildering. After all, previous groups had come and gone so fast they simply didn't change.

At first, they were there just to have fun for us, just like the Rat Pack for our parents, but less ritzy and sleazy. And they were a perfect and perfectly congenial mesh of different personalities, even John with his hard-edged willingness to give offense (to this day Paul and Ringo have an ineffable gaffe-free mastery of their personas). We loved the fun and games at first, and the way that in their movies they lampooned everything from their pop fame to their private world of ultimate 'bachelor pads.'

But then the fact that the songwriting chops of the band—influenced by everyone in early rock from Chuck Berry to (above all) Buddy Holly—were ridiculous, and the fact that the songs got more and more beautiful (*If I Fell* is just about a perfect piece of music), slowly came through. I remember I became aware of the surprising new depths of the Beatles with "Help"—not the movie, which was silly fun but actually a step down from *A Hard Day's Night*—but the song. Not just its quick-changing hooks and interplay of guitar, drums, and harmonies, but one line: "But now these days are gone I'm not so self-assured."[1] Not only did it precisely reflect my adolescent sensibility, it was so ... literate. "Self-assured." Wow.

And as gifted students and mimics as they were performers they were hoovering up all the sounds they could, trying to extend their shelf-life beyond that of the usual "teen idols" of the time. So gradually they also absorbed the seriousness of the folk movement, the mysticism of Indian music, the adult passion of standards, and made them their own.

****

The Beatles' long march to *Sgt. Pepper's*, all the experimentation and songcraft, is most on display on the English *Rubber Soul* and *Revolver*; those albums had many more songs than the American versions—although the American market caught up with those tunes with the release of *The Beatles: Yesterday and Today*, which included four singles, most prominently "Yesterday," not on the American albums. It's on those two releases we first became aware of George's beautifully etched guitar leads in any number of styles, Paul's lissome bass parts and excursions into neoclassical chamber music, Ringo's coloristic use of the drums and high hat, and, most remarkably, John's adapting of hard rock and folk rhythms to a whole cornucopia of influences that made the Beatles the most ecumenical synthesizers in rock.

They also started to become subversive. The very title of the album *Rubber Soul* (not a great pun, but informative) suggests their resistance to the pushmi-pullyu pressures of their fame: not only were their musical ambitions and thoughts undermined by all the hooplah, but, as their music became more sophisticated, the by now old-hat screams made it impossible for them to play live with the equipment of the time and hear their own harmonies. And the album cover's distorted pictures of the Beatles' faces against a hazy green forest setting suggested another kind of stretching altogether.

Their way out of biggest-boy-band-ever-world (besides that forest haze) was folk rock. Listen to the strumming of the guitars and the yearning harmonies on a good Peter, Paul and Mary tune and then listen to the combination of skiffle and folk strum on "I've Just Seen A Face" or "I'm Looking Through You," or the folk feeling in the harmonies and bridge of "Nowhere Man." The other kind of "folk" they were listening to (as in borrowed music from another tradition) was French pop as performed by artists like Charles Aznavour and

Serge Gainsborough. John channeled that influence and a Harrison sitar motif into the madrigalesque but world-weary "Norwegian Wood," which seems to be a long sigh about a romantic and sexual misfire, and the languorous "Girl," complete with dramatic puffs on some kind of cigarette—not to mention the beautiful mix of folk and a touch of bossa nova in "In My Life," which would become the secular wedding song of a generation.

Meanwhile Paul broke into out-and-out pop with the similarly French-accented "Michelle," the other side of the plaintive chamber music seriousness of his hit "Yesterday." And Ringo, the happy medium of the band, put his warm signature on the rockabilly "What Goes On." The variety of it—there were also plenty of pop rock tunes—the depth, the fact that the US market bought into it without singles being released, led many listeners to react to it as a new kind of record, above all Brian Wilson of the Beach Boys, who saw it as an artistic challenge for his own songwriting.

With *Revolver* (another not so great pun, but informative—as in this spinning disc is a bit dangerous) the Beatles began to exemplify the old Tolstoy quote about all happy families being alike, but unhappy families being unhappy in different ways. They hadn't looked very happy on the cover of *Rubber Soul*, and on this album cover, they were chilled out Aubrey Beardslian sketches from whose heads spouted all sorts of manufactured images of themselves, perhaps a comment on how all the hype was threatening their very identities; by now they'd stopped performing and were recording, as one colleague said, as a very intense hobby. It was, of course, a very high-class problem of discontent, but it could be felt in their work. And while the collaboration, overseen literally and musically by "fifth Beatle" producer-arranger George Martin, never stopped, you started to really hear whose songs were whose, although it almost didn't matter when the songs were this good.

Harrison's driving blues-rock song "Taxman" with its furious raga rock lead, and his sitar-driven "Love You Too" made his musical direction clear. Paul came up with perhaps his neoclassical masterpiece, the string orchestra working-class vignette of "all the lonely people" in "Eleanor Rigby," with a compassion for the lonely and the loveless and the lost that would always be in his music. And in the same way Brian Wilson had reacted to *Rubber Soul*, Paul was responding to Wilson and the Beach Boys' landmark album *Pet Sounds*. He has written about how he took in how non-obvious bass lines could sprout melodies, and how he learned more about going from the "intro" to the "verse"; the influence is clearest in Paul's "Here, There, and Everywhere," with its prelude, its soft deliberate phrasing, its elegant harmonic structure and bridge (reminiscent of Beach Boys songs like "In My Room" and "God Only Knows"), and backing harmonies.[2]

But it's John who truly soars on this collection. In the same way his later experiments in poetry, not to mention his lyrics on his most surreal songs, would collage all sorts of wordplay together, he had an amazing ability to stitch together different kinds of music. When you hear John's songs you also hear all the others; he really does seem to be the leader and orchestrator, bringing out George's most adventurous use of the guitar, Ringo's most nimble drumming, Paul's most eloquent bass lines, and George Martin's most powerful string arrangements.

With "I'm Only Sleeping" he was back to his *chanson* mode but with a rocking bluesy shuffle and George's first backwards guitar. "Dr. Robert" is one long blues-rocking sneer at a pep-pill-dispensing fraud with a parodic churchly organ break in the middle. In "She Said She Said," Lennon plugs into George's raga vibe for a lyrical yet spooky song about when love becomes frightening drug-free consciousness expansion, jumpstarting and shifting between three-quarter and four-four time in a musical bipolarity that had even Leonard Bernstein amazed, with a melody like a cry in the dark to a woman that's "making me feel like I've never been born." And "Tomorrow Never Knows" ended the album with a flat-out acid-trip raga chant that's still a hair-raising one of a kind; the camp counselor with whom I first listened to the album on a tiny record player just shrugged his shoulders. "Or play the game existence to the end/Of the beginning..."[3] This was whole new territory.

Still *Revolver* was so sonically and musically, however brilliantly, all over the place, one could wonder how they would ever pull it together again. The Beatles had been in a bubble so long that they seemed to be broadcasting they didn't need their fans anymore, and they maybe they were also tired of each other and ready to pack it in. But fortunately that was not the way world music history was going to happen.

****

Paul has asserted that he "sort of directed *Pepper*, and my influence was basically the *Pet Sounds* album."[4] Maybe so; the album certainly bears the stamp of McCartney's (and Wilson's) whimsy and gentility.

Still it's the songs where John takes the lead that provide much of the yearning, the power, and the weight. The collaboration still had one golden period to go. And one of the ways Lennon and McCartney pulled that off, other than their assiduous joint collaboration with George Martin, was to sublimate the Beatles' discordant personalities into a fantasy entity. An act on top of an act.

It was a kind of continuation of the joking around they did on the hit "Yellow Submarine." That was more than a goofy novelty song crank-out. The Beatles, especially John, loved the fractured humor, non sequiturs, and scrambled soundtracks of the Spike Milligan/Peter Sellers BBC radio *Goon Show*; that kind of daffy lingo was part of the Beatles' whole repartee with the press. They also enjoyed any and all jokes about puffed-up British officialdom. The proof that this idea of a silly submarine commander truly worked on their imaginations and brought out the best of their humor is that it would ultimately generate a successful animated movie, *Yellow Submarine*, which I adored as a kid and which would do a lot to improve the art of film animation.

In that same spirit they came up with the concept of an imaginary silly Brit military band performing in Edwardian costumes for an imaginary audience, shown on the cover as a stylized gathering of the great and near greats of the twentieth century, including four very recognizable young mop tops. *Sgt. Pepper's*, with a very light touch, thus honored the power of but bid a colorful farewell to the Beatles franchise in a way that definitely seemed to cheer the Beatles up; whereas they looked haunted on *Rubber Soul*, and were sharing a private joke on the back of *Revolver* in a way that shut the audience out, on the inner foldout for *Sgt. Pepper's* (the first album with a gatefold sleeve), and in their Sgt. Pepper costumes, they happily face front, and on the back cover Paul's turning his back is clearly a jocular touch, even if many crazies of the era interpreted that as a clue that he was in fact dead.

Through fantasy they could once again face outward to reality. And perhaps it was an alchemical accident, but kicking the album off with such a total flight into the imagination seemed to engender an album all about imagination. The saving grace of imaginative perception. The sad consequences of when it's missing or never there.

The production, especially compared to their first album, *Please Please Me*, done in ten hours, was astonishing. Seven hundred hours in the studio creating a sonic universe where just about every sound was distorted, compressed, or equalized (vocals echoing through the revolving speaker of a Leslie organ, microphones stuck down in the bells of the horns). Snippets of musical tape stuck together in all sorts of ways like the "cut-outs" in a William Burroughs novel; as producer and arranger George Martin said, "The Beatles certainly had an eternal curiosity for doing something different."[5] The album would end with a 15 kilocycle tone at John's request "to annoy your dog" and spliced together nonsense Beatle chatter for a bit of infinite sound in the concentric run-out groove (preserved of course on CD).

An article by *Life* Magazine, titled (sorry) "The New Far-Out Beatles," caught the excitement in the lead-up to the album's release by listing the range of sounds the Beatles were exploring—from woodwinds and French horns to harmoniums, harpsichords, mellotrons, sitar, tambourine, wound-up piano, and table harp. George was quoted as saying "The future stretches out beyond our imagination. There is musical infinity as well."[6]

There's a feeling right from the start of music coming from a distant and mysterious stylized neverland: the murmur of an audience, violins tuning up (not that the first song would include them), then suddenly a heavy bluesy rock march leading to a bridge of a fanfare of Handelian horns, a vaudevillian turn in the music before going back to the blues-rock again. It cued us for a genre-crossing, era-blending, musical-alternative-universe album. And the Beatles were aware of what a new tack they were taking, which they they let us know right in the first verse, but with such a gentle touch it's almost unnoticeable:

> *It was twenty years ago today.*
> *Sergeant Pepper taught the band to play.*
> *They've been going in and out of style.*
> *But they're guaranteed to raise a smile.*
> *So may I introduce to you.*
> *The band you've known for all these years.*[7]

"Twenty years ago," the immediate postwar period when the Beatles were growing up. The "out of style ... raise a smile," couplet, gently mocking the burden of all performers: the vagaries of fame, but despite it all, the need to always aim to please. And then "So may I introduce to you/The band you've known for all these years." It's a line continuing the music hall schtick, but almost like a Zen koan: if they're so well known why do they need an introduction? Because they've completely changed. "Sergeant Pepper," whatever kind of muse he is (and he's nonsense but with a haunting resonance) has made the Beatles lonely again, walled off in their kingdom, but within those walls they've recreated themselves and their music.

Still as the music hall shout-and-bounce of the first track announces, it's all for the fun of the Fab Four who had limitless (for that time) fiscal and musical resources in the studio. Given that, it's amazing how non-grandiose most of the album will be. But some seriousness does come in when the rocking theme song and fanfare come to an end with the intro of Ringo as Billy Shears.

On come the old Beatlemania screams (the hair, the girls), but then as Ringo starts "With A Little Help From My Friends," the other dimension of the album opens up: feelings of alienation, rejection, desperation, and need for comfort. "What would you do if I sang you a tune/Would you stand up and walk out on me?" Joe Cocker knew what he was doing when he turned this tune, sung by Ringo in his usual hail-fellow-well-met style, into an agonized confessional soul gospel number. A good key to when *Sgt. Pepper's* downshifts into this deeper level is when a song becomes a call and response, perhaps suggesting the kind of internal questioning so many people were going through at the time (Other Beatles: "What do you see when you turn out the light?" Ringo: "I can't tell you but I know it's mine."). It's all done in good fun in jaunty nursery rhyme couplets and with the common sense refrain "I get by with a little help from my friends." The Beatles slip in the poetry so lightly that you don't even stop and think about it until you're ready to. They don't tell you but you know it's there, and when you turn out the light it's there for you.

Then comes John's "Lucy in the Sky with Diamonds." His feathery high voice on the verses to reverbed harpsichord and an Indian drone struck me as some of the most beautiful music I'd ever heard—followed in the chorus with a yearning version of the classic Lennon rock-march. It's all about inspiration, about pushing into a whole other way of seeing the world … through LSD? Lennon claimed it was actually inspired by a drawing by his little son, and in the animation of *Yellow Submarine* "Lucy" is depicted as a cloudlike crayon drawing. This begs the question: why didn't he call it "Nancy in the Sky with Diamonds?" But in the end, it really doesn't matter: the point is the triggering of imagination and opening up of perceptions that any inspiration can create.

Then four songs into the album, from a group that had previously, to paraphrase a later McCartney lyric, filled the world with "silly love songs," comes the first of only two true love songs on the entire album. Clearly the Beatles were on a whole other track; the successor album, "Magical Mystery Tour," would have only one song where the word "love" was even highlighted, and that in the universal sense of "All You Need Is Love."

And "Getting Better" is a love song with a sting in its tale, mainly about not love but getting over anger. There, in the middle of a "cute Beatle" Paul song nonetheless, to a menacing Indian drone, are lyrics in which the singer admits to physically abusing his "woman" but trying to change. Even in the upbeat chorus of "It's getting better all the time" is John's call-and-response counterpoint "It can't get no worse." Paul's great sliding bass propels it, George's drones and dissonant guitar plucking disturb it, and John can always be counted on for a splash of cold water on McCartney's warmth. The ultimate effect: a song about loving transformation to be sure, but with a darkly ambiguous shell over the sweet center, and so always intriguing to hear.

The next song, "Fixing A Hole," escapes beautifully into pure melodic McCartney with lyrical accompaniment by George's guitar, but again, not about the pleasures of romantic dreaming but simply ... dreaming. It swings along to a jazzy harpsichord (honestly), velvety drums from Ringo, and John lays out, biding his time ...

He returns as the chilly call-and-response counterpoint of the selfish parents in "She's Leaving Home," a song very much in Paul's "Eleanor Rigby" mode but suppler and more touching, a simple vignette of a girl running away that rang bitterly true in many homes of the generation-gapped '60s. John voicing the parents' bewildered complaints and shocked new awareness while Paul simply sings the facts of her leaving and the parents' heartbreak ... the two lines resolve in shared acceptance of the hard fact of her departure at the end.

Then John takes center stage in "Being For the Benefit of Mr. Kite," a song whose flat-out trippiness, enhanced by spliced-up backwards-forwards-sideways music tapes ricocheting across the speakers, has never been equaled. Inspired by an old circus poster, its calliope-on-acid breaks were an emblem of the time as much as any music. But it wasn't just inspired by LSD, but by the glee and artistic hilarity of an actual circus poster. The Beatles, George Martin, and engineer Geoff Emerick here treat us to an incredibly layered production that's an equivalent of abstract "all-over" painting, vaudeville music and entertainment meets William Burroughs "cut-ups" meets Stockhausen. "A splendid time is guaranteed for all" from many directions.

After that George's obligatory sitar song "Within You, Without You" seems a little too doctrinaire a recital of his new creed, although certainly beautiful and fitting the theme of a new way of seeing and knowing. The bored laughter of hipsters at the end, probably approved by George, might just be an admission that he was on a lonely path, as would be (recorded during the *Sgt. Pepper* sessions) his complaint of how his own "Northern Songs" music and music company were slighted in Lennon-McCartney-world, in "It's Only a Northern Song."

It's back to Paul and a music hall beat with clarinet serenades in "When I'm 64," which still fits that theme of new perceptions in not being a standard love song and in its imagining old age with a definite edge ("Yours sincerely, wasting away"). "Lovely Rita" is the album's other actual love song, a working-class story of a bloke trying to romance a meter maid, very light stuff about the usual courtship frustrations ("Took her home, I nearly made it/Sitting on the sofa with a sister or two"), with one of Paul's characteristic cheery music hall piano breaks—until either because it's all in the bloke's fantasizing head ("Give us a wink and make me think of you"), or more likely because she agreed to "take some tea" with him, it soars off into the echoing heavy-breathing stratosphere—and, whether thanks to the weed or the bloke's imagination, better results. But then with the blatting of horns comes John Lennon's bleakly comic ode to the morning 9-to-5 rush hour, "Good Morning," a psychedelic workup of the common drags of existence (and in the '60s, the office 9-to-5 was how almost everyone worked). It's punctuated by a quickening of the horn lines suggesting the flirtations of the workday, the flashes of the imagination that are the only solace in an existence so mechanical that even the dog, the cat, and the canary on the soundtrack get vacuumed up in it.

And as the Sgt. Pepper's band, in the album's hardest rocking number, seems to shoot off into aural orbit, the last track is left to something much deeper: "A Day In The Life," Lennon's modern-world-wasteland masterpiece, to be later accompanied, in a continuation of the *Sgt. Pepper's* recording sessions, by his mind-opening masterpiece, "Strawberry Fields Forever," and his third more extravagant and surrealistic freak-out masterpiece "I Am The Walrus."

It was an encore/coda that stunned listeners back then and has lost none of its impact: a beautifully scored ballad sung with John's unique sarcastic melancholy, like a bird chirping in a Francis Bacon nightscape, about the bleakness and ennui of modern life which then, with the line "I'd love to turn you on," brought in a crescendoing multitracked orchestra sound like nothing we'd ever heard before, but that always suggested to me a combination of orgasm and acid and air raid sirens—wonder, pleasure, and terror all at once. It abruptly cuts to a shuffling sequence of nine-to-five boredom, sung by Paul, the top end of his voice clipped by engineer Geoffrey Emerick in the studio to make it sound even flatter and sleepier—but then the singer suddenly goes into a dream, and the music launches into swirling and echoing orchestral chords yearning for transcendence. That alteration of ennui and promises of liberation gives a snappier beat to the return of the bleak ballad, and sets up a verse with a *Goon Show* black comic silliness ("Four thousand holes in Blackburn, Lancashire ... They had to count them all/Now they know how many holes it takes to fill the Albert Hall"), before one last orchestral scream and a crashing piano chord dying by slow degrees into silence.

What's it all about? No '60s truths in particular—and all of it. The song and the album resist any answers or interpretation except ... we're breaking the rules here, not with visions, but vision-ness. One's own dreams, the right mood on a happy day, all can be important and life-renovating (one has to remember how dominated the '50s and '60s were by nine-to-five work regimens and general conformity to appreciate this). We're becoming your eyes and ears in a new way—the sonic variety of the album, compared to the monotonous groove settings of so much modern pop, still reminds us of this—and we invite you to join us.

Which ultimately is the import (not message) of this album and why it's perhaps the greatest album of the period. The Beatles were not ahead of the curve on musical, political, or romantic truths. They were usually not originators, but appropriators and synthesizers. They were, like Shiek Auda in *Lawrence of Arabia*, always out to steal something honorable, and thanks to great musicianship and lyrics and the invaluable help of George Martin, they almost always got their loot.

But in *Sgt. Pepper* they became original in presenting not any specific truths but the frame of mind of the era in a new kind of musical environment, and by that and their lyrics they brought a worldwide audience to this new perception. Trips both narcotic and imaginary, flights of fear and fancy, imagining old age, learning how fragile familial bonds can be and how depressingly modern life and its conformity can turn out, but also being delighted by Lucy in the sky, seeing life flows on within you and without you, or whatever you alone see when you turn out the light.

****

Sgt. Pepper's musical cornucopia would spill over into *Magical Mystery Tour*, even if attached to a very lame movie, and four other albums laden with classics, especially from George Harrison—"Here Comes The Sun," "Something"—who on his musical and spiritual path would arrive at the greatest of all Beatle solo musical efforts, *All Things Must Pass*, and the greatest of all Beatle public musical efforts, the first great rock fundraising show, the Concert for Bangladesh. So much for "Only A Northern Song."

But the signature Beatle album of that post-*Sgt. Pepper* period would be the double album simply called the White Album. It would be a Christmas bon-bon wrapped inside photos tricked out with blue tint and high contrast, a pop and mod museum, Ringo dancing with Liz Taylor, charming grandees in their charming chateaus all too much-ly heading for "Good Night." The *White Album* featured brilliant production work, hurdy-gurdy-man goofiness from Ringo, calypso-accented cheeriness from Paul, and some gorgeous acoustic guitar songs ("Julia," "Blackbird"), but also a kind of sickly-sweet excess culminating in nine minutes of aimless experimentation and the startling capture of insanity in Paul's (yes Paul's) "Helter-Skelter," which Charlie Manson would make his private theme song. The album would dissolve in a heavenly haze that would amount to the decade's biggest musical boner-killer, and forever give the phrase "White Album" the connotation of discontent, discord, and paranoia, especially as used by Joan Didion as the title of her book and disturbing essay about the end of the counterculture.

Meanwhile the Rolling Stones, who had followed the Beatles down the path of peace and love and disorienting musical environments in their underestimated but nonetheless second-on-the-bill *Their Satanic Majesties Request*, broke out *Beggars Banquet* with songs like "Sympathy for the Devil" and "Street Fighting Man." In their albums of the '70s and '80s they triumphantly returned to their own batch of genres—honky tonk, country, African rhythms, African American soul rock gospel, and the blues—with Jagger preening and dancing in front of Bill Wyman's loping bass and any number of great lead guitarists and Charlie Watts' high-hat hiss and thump, while Keith Richards took his place as the riffmeister of them all. It would be rock's second wind, joyous and heartfelt and badass, and it was clear who would now be "the greatest rock-and-roll band in the world" even before the Beatles' breakup in 1971.

In their solo careers the Beatles would be haunted by trials and tragedies: George and Ringo would struggle with substance abuse, Paul would suffer the awful early death of his beloved wife Linda Eastman, and above all John Lennon would be assassinated just when he seemed to be at his happiest. Still there would be many great musical enjoyments and moments from them all.

But there would always be something very special about *Sgt. Pepper's*. As the various events and sexual and political undercurrents and mind-altering substances of the '60s were engendering things in heaven and earth previously undreamed of, we all thought it was passing strange—and four princes told us as strangers to give it welcome.

FIFTY YEARS AGO TODAY

THE MEDIA

"It's misleading to suppose there's any basic difference between education and entertainment. This distinction merely relieves people of the responsibility of looking into the matter."

– Marshall McLuhan

FIFTY YEARS AGO TODAY – THE MEDIA

The Ultimate '60s Filmmaker

"*The awful daring of a moment's surrender
Which an age of prudence can never retract
By this and this only have we existed...*"
"The Waste Land," **T.S. Eliot**

"*It's a friendly call. Of course it's a friendly call. Listen, if it wasn't a friendly call, you probably wouldn't've got it.*" President Muffley on the Hot Line to the Soviet premier, **Dr. Strangelove**

If you've ever enjoyed shouting out your version of Jack Nicholson's version of "Heeere's Johnny!," if limitlessly foulmouthed drill sergeants crack you up, if you can tell the theme of *Also Sprach Zarathustra* from the first note (even if you don't know its name), if you've ever used words like "strangelove" or "horrorshow," and if you've ever described a night out to your buddies as "an eyes wide shut party," then you've fallen under the influence of one of the greatest of all filmmakers, Stanley Kubrick.

And if you're old enough to remember Kubrick's heyday in the '60s, then you also remember how his films mirrored and helped define the era: its desires, its worst fears, and its hopes and dreams.

Kubrick's first '60s movie was *Spartacus* (right in 1960), although because that movie was controlled by its star, Kirk Douglas, and initially had a different director, Anthony Mann, Kubrick never considered it one of 'his.' But as a hired gun Kubrick orchestrated a film that broke from the saccharine religiosity of most Hollywood epics, took the genre into angry and tragic territory, and unforgettably depicted the terror of the ancient Roman army's phalanxes and the wiliness and viciousness of Roman politics. That Kubrick nerviness combined with Douglas's charisma and the writing of Dalton Trumbo, the leftist writer Douglas courageously hired to break the Hollywood blacklist, made for the best Hollywood epic until *Lawrence Of Arabia*.

With *Lolita* (1962) and its cheeky, scabrous reflection of the coming sexual revolution, Kubrick was back in his own territory. Vladimir Nabokov adapted the screenplay from his novel, but the movie shows the Kubrick touch in the comedy of a man caught in the maze of his own illicit desires. The movie was softened by the censorship of the times, but its fascination came not from explicit sex but the way in which James Mason's superficially civilized Humbert Humbert ensnares his adored way-too-young "nymphet" Lolita, only to have Lolita escape and trap him in a nastier snare with the help of Peter Sellers's far more depraved Clare Quilty. The film invited its audience to a decade-long party while warning them about monsters of the id beneath.

Kubrick would flourish during the '60s in part due to the greatly increased education and literacy of movie audiences. As part of its consequent adventurousness, that audience welcomed the topical "sick" humor and satire of Lenny Bruce, Mort Sahl, and *Mad* Magazine, one of the cultural touchstones of the time. Kubrick embraced that sensibility with his *Dr. Strangelove*, a comedy about America unintentionally attacking Russia with nuclear weapons, which was a sensation when it opened in 1964, and was dubbed a *Mad* Magazine view of nuclear Armageddon.

MAD also stood for Mutually Assured Destruction, the '60s Pentagon's absurd but accurate concept that the nuclear-armed United States and Soviet Union would never go into battle because they would be too successful—as in destroying each other and the entire planet. *Strangelove* was full of that kind of absurdity: perfectly symmetrical sets as the background of lunatic actions, and verbal absurd-isms like "Gentlemen, you can't fight in here, this is the war room." Peter Sellers plays three roles: the President, the eponymous weapons scientist Dr. Strangelove, and Lionel Mandrake, an archetypal Kubrick protagonist: a smart, sane, but comically faltering British military man caught in a maze of codes and regulations that protect the madness as he tries to stop the nuclear attack machine. It's no surprise how *Dr. Strangelove* ends—what seems surprising in retrospect is how much '60s audiences could enjoy it, acknowledging as it did their own dread (very much back in contemporary news) about nuclear doomsday.

Dr. Strangelove worked so well because of a great script whose main writer was Terry Southern, and because, whether in a satirical or realistic realm, Stanley Kubrick was one of the toughest and best of all directors of war films—in part because an underlying theme of all his movies was the savagery inextricably linked to human intelligence, language, law, history, and art. As if to demonstrate the truth of the old saying that the world is a comedy to those who think and a tragedy to those who feel, his films always approached that truth comically, albeit with the darkness of the term "black comedy" and with two enormous exceptions: the scalding and heartbreaking conclusions of *Spartacus* and Kubrick's early antiwar World War I film *Paths of Glory*, both of which starred Kirk Douglas and bore his influence.

Strangelove originally had the subtitle *How I Learned To Stop Worrying and Love The Bomb*, which necessitated the movie's title being done in a kind of skinny childish scrawl. How does one love doomsday? In the most positive sense, through comedy, through simply laughing at its absurdities. But in a nastier way, as the name Dr. *Strangelove* immediately suggests, through being a heartless technocratic expert who can savor the possibilities for managerial control in a post-nuclear-attack world, especially, as expressed by Dr. Strangelove himself in the end, proposing the arrangement of a mating program with tremendously enhanced sexual possibilities for elite survivors. And one can "love" the Bomb because of humanity's lust for war and destruction, immortally captured in the image of the Texas bomber captain Major Kong's gleefully riding a nuclear warhead like a rodeo horse down to the moment of impact.

Dr. Strangelove broke box office records, though called in various reviews "snide," "defeatist," "destructive of morale," and of course "anti-American." Kubrick replied: "Why should the bomb be approached with reverence? Reverence is a paralyzing state of mind. For me the comic sense is the most eminently human reaction to the mysteries and paradoxes of life. I don't see why an artist has to do any more than produce an artistic experience that reflects his thinking."[1] It's a statement that revealed Kubrick was not long for Hollywood, and indeed he would soon move to a chateau near London, never to return to the States (because of his dim and almost phobic view of air traffic control, literally never). But he still established a productive relationship with Warner Brothers, since at the time no one quarreled with a hit.

And that helped him secure the budget for the most ambitious film of its time. For all the lusts and fears of the era, there was also great hope embodied in humankind's leap into space, and Kubrick captured that in 1968 in his most beloved film, *2001*. A supreme film technician, Kubrick took full advantage of '60s innovations in filmic special effects—the 1964–1965 World's Fair and Montreal Expo 67 exhibits reveled in "trick photography" and multiscreen experiments—and innovated with special effects supervisor Douglas Trumbull many of his own cinematic illusions to create a giant-screen sci-fi epic with the immersive spectacle of a World's Fair ride movie, whose story was nothing less than a journey from the beginnings of human intelligence to infinite space. When it opened it seemed a disaster, panned by critics, satirized by *Mad* Magazine as "201 Minutes of Space Idiocy." But in part due to a clever ad line, "The ultimate trip," a catchphrase that both described its staggering visuals and referenced the LSD drug trips that every hip young baby boomer was aware of, the film broke through to younger audiences and became another classic.

The story by Kubrick and Arthur Clarke had its own man-machine battle between an astronaut and the spaceship's supercomputer "HAL," who decides, with true Kubrickian absurdity, that man's greatest mission is too important to be left to humans. But the fruit of the astronaut's victory over the machine is a final meeting with the black monolith that periodically beckons human intelligence to its next step, and a transfiguration that suggests the supposedly cynical Kubrick wanted to convey an almost spiritual belief in the perfectibility of the human mind.

In his next science fiction film Kubrick's muse grew darker. A *Clockwork Orange*, premiering in 1972 but developed from Anthony Burgess's novel in the late '60s, tells the story of Alex, played by Malcolm McDowell, a vicious young criminal made "good" by behavioral conditioning, but also turned into a powerless victim for a hypocritical and brutal society. The film pits the visual splendor of Alex's hyper-mod "ultraviolent" world and his witty "Nadsat" lingo against a satirically envisaged corrupt (and very dingy) regime to propose that the human passion for art and freedom of choice comes at the price of the urge to violence, but still is preferable to total repression. For when this thug is imprisoned, submitted to the mechanistic and cruel "Ludovico treatment," and released into society, once he's conditioned into some sort of humility and compassion society viciously avenges itself on him, and his only way out is back in: to have the conditioning smashed out of him by a near-suicide and to thus be restored to his old gleefully anarchic and destructive, but exuberant and resilient self.

When I was young I responded not only to that liberating (if chilling) thought but the excitement of an American film dramatizing so effectively such a sophisticated philosophical point; it was like hearing Dylan's "Like A Rolling Stone" on Top 20 AM radio. Over forty years later I still find the *Clockwork Orange* view of humankind's 'juiciness' as tied to potential violence but far more threatened by the machine within and without a bracing paradox and a timely warning.

In his three subsequent films Kubrick stuck with variations of that dark vision of civilized (or semi-civilized) characters fighting to escape the black hole of innate regimentation and violence. The exquisitely photographed *Barry Lyndon* (1975), with its tale of a passionate but low-class rake achieving wealth and status only to be destroyed by the aristocrats of his elegantly murderous society, remains a great Kubrick movie that it seems only photographers and hardcore Kubrick fans can love. But the horror masterpiece *The Shining* (1980) and the Vietnam War saga *Full Metal Jacket* (1987) became classic hits, perhaps in part because they're reminiscent of Kubrick's great '60s films. *The Shining* is almost the shadow of *2001* in its sense of space, pace, eerie music, and its story of a hapless writer and his family sucked into the Overlook Hotel's nightmare ghost world, which seems the opposite of *2001*'s monolith, devolving the writer into a homicidal maniac. And *Full Metal Jacket* recalls *Strangelove*'s black antiwar humor, as a marine recruit whose wit earns him the name Joker in the end can't beat but only join what the Vietnam War machine does to his platoon.

That kind of worldview earned Kubrick what Michael Herr, in his terrific articles about Kubrick following the director's death, lambasted as "strangely disrespectful" obituaries.[2] The putdowns emphasized myopic criticism of, above all, his 'coldness' as a filmmaker, which showed that the critics never were was as smart about Kubrick as the moviegoing public, who responded with fascination and laughter to the authentic harshness of Kubrick's universe and the sense that there could be a bit of hope in it after all.

Just about every Kubrick film presents its protagonist with some kind of ensnarement, a trap or a maze he has to battle his way out of. It was what gave his films such mystery and suspense. Sometimes that was literal, as in the topiary maze at the climax of *The Shining*, sometimes internal, as in *Lolita*, often an antihuman and mechanical system, as in the nuclear war procedures of *Strangelove*, the robotic protocol of interacting with HAL in *2001*, the conditioning of *A Clockwork Orange*, and the rules of the duel in *Barry Lyndon*. Savagery lay behind those labyrinthine rules, as in the elaborately strict military training of *Full Metal Jacket* that's supposed to produce disciplined warriors but instead breeds sexually maladjusted monsters.

In the great dystopic political/sc-fi trilogy of the '60s the snares and mazes are technological, and so these films still have much to say to us about how the institutions and the very language we inhabit, motivated in many cases by an ungovernable aggression, can affect our ability to create supposedly benign tech systems. All the ways which we construct to avert accidental nuclear war, the supercomputers we create to guide (potentially) a super-spaceship (or an actual super-surveillance system), the behavioral conditioning processes we might yet create to tranquilize the populace, can be infected by this innate greed and fury. And self-satisfied slavery to those systems (as in loving the Bomb) is always a bad deal, a point Marshall McLuhan would make in his '60s tome *Understanding Media* regarding people's "narcissistic" servitude to then new technology.

So where's the hope? Even Kubrick once ruefully kidded about the lack of a "rooting interest" in his films. It's certainly true that *Paths of Glory*'s Colonel Dax, defending in a military kangaroo court three soldiers falsely accused of cowardice; Peter Sellers' Lionel Mandrake in *Dr. Strangelove* trying singlehandedly to break through all the military systems gone awry; and *Full Metal Jacket*'s resourceful Joker trying to retain his humanity all get defeated by the war machine. But audiences accepted the hardbitten honesty in those films. They got that a willingness to be honest with yourself about what's really happening (as opposed to succumbing to delusions or belief systems), and an ability to learn from the folly and cruelty and from one's suffering and at least fight the machine is almost always present in Kubrick's films and their protagonists, no matter how deep the pessimism.

But here was the other affirmative theme: Kubrick's films suggest how technology run amok can be tamed by what ethicist Shannon Vallor, in other contexts, has termed "technomoral virtue."[3] *AI (Artificial Intelligence)* a film Kubrick never made, but which was made by Steven Spielberg from one of his scripts, showed how Kubrick was always questioning the nature of human intelligence, in the same way that's now being carried on by the fascinating Kubrick/*Blade Runner*-descended television series *Westworld*, which also has a central metaphor of a maze. How do you solve one of the biggest mazes of all: the difference between a machine intelligence and a truly human one?

The "technomoral virtue" and a path toward solving this problem may in part stem from what another great director of the '60s, Mike Nichols, called the need to "revere the unconscious" (from which his great improv work with Elaine May sprung). For Nichols that resulted in a highly detailed but flexible mode of direction in a slew of great plays and movies, though no philosophy per se. But in Kubrick's work it amounted to a way of behaving when confronted with a high tech war machine, a malign supercomputer, the Ludovico treatment, a hive of evil spirits, or brutal military training that leads to a death trap beneath a sniper—namely a marshaling of the unconscious resources of what he called "the comic sense": leaps of awareness, bravery, and improvisation.

It's in the way Kirk Dullea's astronaut improvises a daring way around HAL's turning the entire ship against him and throwing him out into space in *2001*. HAL the supercomputer would not, like Strangelove's nuclear war machine, run destructively amok: the astronaut's smarts and courage would make sure that if it didn't serve humanity it would (in an eerily poignant sequence) meet its own insanity and destruction. And later that same use of and reverence for the unconscious would impel the astronaut to commit his ship to entering the world of the monolith and the next step of human evolution—an act of improvisational abandonment, trusting a very deep instinct to turn over the controls to something unknown and greater.

This from the director considered one of the great control freaks of the cinema—but the fact is, as Malcolm McDowell has spoken about, that despite his meticulous control on his sets, Kubrick left room to improvise; seeing that *Clockwork Orange*'s rape scene was merely ugly and prosaic as written, he gave McDowell free rein to try something different, asking him if he could perhaps dance,[4] and the result was the "Singing in the Rain" number that not only, as it turned out, solved a bunch of script problems, but made for the most memorably horrific sequence in the film.

For the man for whom symmetry and rules were an overwhelming visual and thematic motif,[5] the hope lay in those moments when men or women confronted the ghosts in the machines with courage, action, radical intelligence, or simply honesty, when a daring humanity-centered choice was made and perverse mechanical logic was broken. Critics seemed to miss this, and so never even grasped Kubrick's return to a fully optimistic view in his imperfect, but still haunting *Eyes Wide Shut* (1999), a movie where the lusts and jealousies of *Lolita* are resolved in familial reconciliation.

That last film is a puzzle to Kubrick's devotees; given the time of Kubrick's death, it might very well have been finished by others. But the body of the film is pure Kubrick: when Tom Cruise strays from his scornful wife Nicole Kidman, who deliberately inflames his jealousy about another man, he is caught up in the maze of a sexual fever dream often shading into nightmare—threats on the streets of a slightly off-kilter, studio-created New York; a just-miss sexual tryst with a girl later revealed to be dying of AIDS; insane encounters when he tries to purchase a mask for a private orgy that turns out to be potentially lethal. At the end of the night, a cynical and sinister colleague of his, while playing a solitary game of pool (so to speak, playing with himself) supplies Cruise with a realistic logical explanation for the bizarre events to help him cover up and repress what happened and return to normalcy. But when he returns, tries to lie to his wife about his wanderings, and sees the mask he left on his pillow, an incarnation of his night's fugitive desires, he breaks down and tells the truth, thus accepting his desire and its dream logic as just that, not as a somehow rational (but probably, per his lying colleague, deceitful) sequence of events.

In that maze-breaking moment when he breaks down into his humanity, he awakens and returns to his wife, and when he asks her what they should do about where their relationship is at that point, she replies that they should immediately do the most unconscious and direct thing possible, in the last word ever spoken in a Kubrick film: "Fuck."

Not a bad way for the '60s finest filmmaker to leave us.

Bonnie and Clyde
From Theme to Meme

In 1967, movie audiences first saw the trailer for *Bonnie and Clyde*, which juxtaposed the stars' names in psychedelic fonts and colors against scenes from bloody Depression-era gun battles. The slogan was "They're young, they're in love—they kill people."[1]

The collision in styles and tones so totally flummoxed audiences and critics that at first the movie was a flop. It was only after younger moviegoers discovered it—thanks to a second wave of critics that hailed the film or even recanted their original attacks—that *Bonnie and Clyde* became a hit and then a classic of the era.

Fifty years ago the movie was an experiment in telling a dark and gory crime spree tale with an injection of youthful exhilaration and even comedy, with some borrowing from the romanticism and jump-cut kineticism of French New Wave films like Jean-Luc Godard's *Breathless*. And what gave that strange brew its popularity was both the times in which it was set and in which it appeared.

From the title photos clicking on of scenes from the Great Depression, *Bonnie and Clyde* was anchored in the sociopolitical reality of the 1930s, when farmers and banks foreclosing on them were at war, and the young guns robbing banks could see themselves as fighters for the people. Right away, then, the movie reflected the rebellious values of the 1960s, the feeling young people had that the police and the government—particularly the military draft—were out to get them, and that the only way to strike back or at least escape was to be, metaphysically and sometimes literally (to Canada), on the run.

The film also spoke to young people's sense of disconnectedness and frustration, the feeling that even in pursuing the normal blessings of life—falling in love, getting married and having a child if they wanted to—they were stalked by dangers from the threat of nuclear war to the war in Vietnam. Bonnie and Clyde were among the first antiheroes of '60s films, rebelling and challenging society, socially conscious (in their way), rejecting conventional morals in ways both dubious and energizing, and thus speaking to a new rebellious generation.

And it helped that *Bonnie and Clyde*, written by Robert Benton and David Newman (with Robert Towne as "consultant") and directed by Arthur Penn, was a great movie, blending red-hot performances, lightning pace, powerful themes, a jolting rhythm of bank-robbing ecstasy and wounded agony in the getaways, and the excitement of what are still some of the most brilliantly edited gun battles on film.

It also had, along with inevitable Hollywood romantic allure, real honesty. Bonnie and Clyde play out the audience's fantasies of young love and power but pay dearly for it; the film careens from spree to desperation as every Barrow gang casualty receives its full weight of horror and pain. The gang attracts primitive media coverage, which they enjoy, but which makes their attempts at refuge useless. And while the violence mounts, it's poignantly believable that the couple clings to middle-class dreams and familial longings (in the same way an earlier lawbreaking couple on the run did in Nicholas Ray's 1948 *They Live By Night*[2]): Clyde wants a house, Bonnie wants to see her mother. But in a weirdly elegiac soft-focus sequence at Bonnie's mother's house, in hazy dreamlike colors, Bonnie's mother throws her out, knowing if she stays at such a predictable hideout she'll be shot dead.

We never lose all sympathy for them; to substitute a gun for sexuality and normal pursuit of status and growth is clearly wrong, but it's also clear from the outset that hard times inflict lousy choices that leave them with no future and, once they start to kill, no way out. And that final exit is bloody—Bonnie and Clyde's end was the most horrific explosion of gunfire and gore yet seen in movies, and it left audiences all over the country stunned. It also sealed young moviegoers' identification with them as victims, however deluded, of a violent, heavily armed, brutally oppressive America. *Bonnie and Clyde* caught that feeling of playful rebellion (not to mention a sexual revolution) tempered with an awareness that in a violent Puritanical society the punishment may not just fit but horribly exceed the crime.

The movie was so influential that it was followed by three other movies with similar themes developed in the '60s that premiered on or around 1971. In *Thieves Like Us* directed by Robert Altman[3] (and based on the same Edward Anderson novel as *They Live By Night*), the young protagonist is a good-hearted but aimless drifter tagging along with a small-time gang, and the woman who falls in love with him has a dead-end life at a truck stop. Their love affair and courtship is winningly sweet, but unlike in *Bonnie And Clyde*, there's no romance to the crime spree that frames it—just grim robbery, flight, and violence. Altman's camera reduces the couple to figures in a pastoral but bleak landscape, and their dawning life together is soon wiped out, a victim of the cycle of poverty and crime the Great Depression breeds in this most ominous, mournful, and sociopolitically damning of the post-*Bonnie And Clyde* melodramas.

Badlands, Terrence Malick's stunning debut film,[4] takes as its basis the Starkweather killing spree of the '50s, and becomes a chilly if compassionate portrait of a young couple not just on the run from the law but civilization, seeking in every way—Kit's murders, Holly's romance novel narration, and a Huck Finn-like immersion in nature—to break loose to some frontier idyll, but dooming themselves the more they break from the social order. The roots of the Bonnie and Clyde story—the rebellion against poverty and ignorant and cruel authority, the fame Kitt wins on his killing spree—are still there. But in *Badlands* purely violent rebellion is a perversion of the American frontier impulse that might fuel a brief romantic hegira and satisfying revenge, but can't possibly help the couple escape and "ring that bell." Except for a few moments of glimmering love and illumination, the couple-on-the-run story is framed by beauty but never touched by it, for gunplay and killing can never be any kind of liberation.

Leave it to Steven Spielberg, in his debut theatrical film *The Sugarland Express*, to make the most sympathetic and even hopeful film in the post-*Bonnie And Clyde* trilogy.[5] *Sugarland*'s couple on the run is trying to reclaim the mother's birth child, who has been successfully adopted by a wealthy couple; it's a nonviolent but senseless quest that ends in senseless tragedy, despite the efforts of a humane police captain to avoid the inevitable. Spielberg brings his unique vision to the chase as it becomes a giant machine, symbolized by an ever-lengthening line of pursuing cop cars, that corners the brave if deluded young couple into their fate. And yet the film's emphasis on simple human decency and the fact that, as a note at the end of the film tells us, the mother did ultimately get back her child, offered some hope for the members of the audience engaged in their own children's crusades, whether against the draft or in defense of alternate lifestyles, in the '60s and early '70s.

Subsequent decades saw many variations of the Bonnie and Clyde theme, viewed through increasingly cynical perspectives—by the time of *True Romance* and *Natural Born Killers*, both written by Quentin Tarantino, the fusion of rebellion, sexual glee, and murder was being played for black comedy and nasty media satire, and all you could say about the new Bonnie and Clydes were that at least they weren't as malignant as their enemies. The tragic and social protest elements had been leached out of the story.

How does a plot lose so much of what made it work and still fill a movie? To some extent it had become a meme, defined by Richard Dawkins and others as an informational element of a culture passed from one individual to another by nongenetic means. Film genres do indeed mutate and evolve, but they usually hold fast to certain rules. In westerns, the gunfighter who wanted to lay down his guns for good but has to pick them up one more time to defend a family/friend/woman ... you know it every time you see it, from *Shane* to *Unforgiven*.

The Bonnie and Clyde meme, perhaps because its perfect audience is every new generation of young moviegoers in search of both rebellion and novelty, has been through a radical (d)evolution. In at least one spectacular example it's been stripped of every last shred of its original meaning; all that remains of the story is the zap of pursuit and gunplay mixed with sex boiled down to a visual and thematic accompaniment to the world's biggest pop show.

"Beyonce And Jay Z On The Run,"[6] broadcast on HBO, begins with a brief parody of images from *Breathless*, *Pulp Fiction*, and of course *Bonnie and Clyde*. "This is a stick-up" becomes a refrain of a Near Eastern hip-hop number. Beyonce and Jay Z are a gangster (gangsta) couple on the run in the video backdrops for concert numbers that occasionally take over the show. Images from Depression-era couple-on-the-run films are reduced to bare visual icons—the highway lines going by, the shot-out mailboxes, a fetishization of piles of money—all poured on in a sensual assault pile-driving behind the songs whose ultimate theme is "Die In Love and Live Forever."

The couple-on-the-run saga here is the internal warfare and battle with the media that has characterized Beyonce and Jay Z's sometimes troubled marriage, and the last explosion of gunfire that kills the gangsta video couple is an emblem of the real one triumphing over that manufactured image. Unlike B & C, Bee and Z beat back the emotional and media assaults and their own demons to proclaim their renewed love before 75,000 fans in Paris.

It's just part of the show, and Beyonce's singing and performances are good enough to defuse any criticism about what is after all merely the backdrop of the concert. But given how modern concerts pretty much seek to annihilate the differences between the live performer(s) and the lighting, sonic, and video machine behind them, it's not a trivial addition to the concert, nor is the concert's modification of the content.

And there's something depressing, even unnerving, about how a theme that was once so rich in elements of love and rebellion and social protest, and which reflected such a strong point of view about American life, can be rock-videoized and reduced, for current audiences, to nothing but its romantic wish-fulfillment aspect and symbolic images. It becomes a glitzy meme whose only content is good looks, money, young love, and baditude, suspending the audience in a universe where all that matters is the realm of almost limitless wealth and glamour and how the divine couple "on the run" blows away the media snipers in their kingdom. It sends the audience home worshiping in a trance of celebrity adoration, not mulling over serious matters in shocked silence.

Lawrence Of Arabia to W of Iraq

Fifty-four years ago an almost-four-hour, mostly British film about serious historical and geopolitical issues, with scarcely a woman in the whole cast, beat out a film adaptation of a beloved American classic, *To Kill A Mockingbird*, for Best Picture of the Year. 1962 was indeed a different time.

Lawrence of Arabia[1] was both a huge critical and popular success in part because in those years the Mideast and the Arabian Peninsula were still glamourous and exotic to Americans. Dubai was still a fishing village. Bedouin caravans still crisscrossed the Arab peninsula. And Arab destiny and potential unity was very much on people's minds during the 1960s, for the Mideast was every bit as much a trouble spot as it is now. Gamal Abdel Nasser, the British-educated President of Egypt, had forged a United Arab Republic out of Egypt and Syria, was enlisting the support of America's global enemy, the Soviet Union, and, seeking a greater destiny and an empire, had blocked the Suez Canal. When Israel, Britain and France invaded in response, he managed to fend them off and, even though the Canal was opened again, humiliate Britain. His hand strengthened, he would, in 1966, launch his armies against Israel. The resulting Six-Day War would be a shattering defeat for Egypt, Syria, and Jordan (I still remember the button circulated at my school: "See The Pyramids. See Israel") that would give Israel the West Bank, the Sinai (until Israel withdrew many years later), and the Golan Heights, shaping the Middle East to the present day.

So *Lawrence of Arabia* was a film whose time had definitely come, and, in part due to its greatness, and in part due to world events since the '60s, it's timeliness has never ended; it's proven to have legs sturdier than one of its camels. *Lawrence of Arabia* is almost universally acknowledged to be the peak of Hollywood's wide-screen epic genre, regularly revived in special presentations (it even works on an iPad for millennials who love the film, as I learned looking over my much younger seatmate's shoulder on a recent flight, although that's hardly the best way to see it).

And it still speaks volumes to us, particularly when one considers the second Iraq war and its aftermath. As *Lawrence of Arabia* tells us, T.E. Lawrence sought greatness in the deserts of the Mideast because, in his words, it was clean. One hundred years later, George W. Bush and his war council sought greatness there because it was oily. T.E Lawrence was a courageous officer, a polymath, and a genius. George W. Bush ... wasn't. But the results were so similarly disastrous for each that one has to wonder: it's unfortunate the same people who prepared a CD for President Bush on Katrina so he could figure out what was happening there didn't recommend *Lawrence of Arabia* to Bush before his Administration decided to invade Iraq. Not that it would've mattered; *alea iacta est* (the dice were cast) as a somewhat better commander-in-chief than Bush once said. But we could all say at least we tried.

***

The film begins with a death sequence as mysterious and, in a different way, spooky as that which begins *Citizen Kane*. In the bright sun, viewed from a steep overhead angle on the wide screen, which is otherwise dominated by the stone squares of a plaza, a man gets ready to ride a motorcycle while triumphant martial music plays, a peculiar contrast. When we next see him, riding along a road marked as dangerous, he's wearing goggles so we can't quite see who he is. He's a total mystery (and bear in mind this movie introduced Peter O'Toole, who would not immediately have been recognizable as the star of the picture). He goes faster and faster, clearly enjoying it, until he finally swerves and crashes, his goggles flying onto a bare branch.

In one of the film's many deliberately jolting cuts, we go to St. Paul's Cathedral, where a funeral service has just taken place for what turns out to be the legendary T.E. Lawrence. The film moves into a narrative framework that truly suggests *Citizen Kane* on a camel, although in this case we won't be seeing different narrators introduce different portions of the film. More subtly, we'll see at the funeral a reporter interviewing the film's later implied narrators in the same sequence they'll appear in in the film, as they answer his questions about who Lawrence was as briefly, politely, and enigmatically (in one case, with unintentional irony) as possible before the fourth narrator takes us flashbacking into the film itself. Like *Kane*, this will be a look back at a man trying to decipher the mystery of his character. And in the same way the dying word "Rosebud" was the symbol that triggers Kane's mystery, the motorcycle and the gradual explanation of what it symbolizes for Lawrence will figure into the mystery of Lawrence's character. With one big difference (no spoiler alert here needed); it won't attempt to wrap it up in a psychological bow like *Kane* did, but will just focus more precisely on Lawrence's contradictions.

I've always felt that *Lawrence of Arabia* is not as great a film as *Citizen Kane* was, but a better movie. Most people would vehemently disagree with that, as I will probably find out. True, you don't have the crackling juicy dialogue of Frank Mankiewicz. Instead you have the clipped, economical, occasionally sententious but always illuminating script of Robert Bolt and Michael Wilson. You don't have *Kane*'s expressionistic filmic innovations that were so startling in their day and still pop off the screen. You just have director Sir David Lean's extraordinary use of immense filmic space, shot so wonderfully by cinematographer Freddie Francis, as a character in the drama itself, as dramatic as John Ford's use of Monument Valley in his westerns, so beautiful and powerful that it influenced the eye of Steven Spielberg, especially in its contrasts of sweeping landscapes and close-in utter chaos. And *Lawrence of Arabia* is a multifaceted look not just at a man but a vital region of the world.

The intelligence of this film is reflected in the casting: a bevy of hoarily famous British and French actors play the wily colonial manipulators, while newcomer Omar Sharif and classic film wild man Anthony Quinn play his Arab friends (and unlike Ridley Scott's unwillingness to cast an Egyptian in his *Exodus* film, Lean took a chance on a then unknown Egyptian, Sharif, in a key role). These all seem obvious casting choices until one considers that the most famous of the British actors, Alec Guinness, plays the Arab King Faisal, appropriately a leader caught between a British education and his Arab nationality in the same way Lawrence is caught between his self-chosen Arab identity and British roots. Faisal also has a destiny he dreams about: he "longs for the vanished gardens of Cordoba" (not exactly the sort of mindset with which to welcome Anglo-Saxons as liberators, and worth remembering when we call Saudi Arabia our ally). But he will later resign himself to the "caution and mistrust"—what he calls the "vices of old men"—of the postwar peace that gives the Arab lands to the British and the French and puts him in power to effect a transition.

That's hardly what Lawrence has in mind. The soaring orchestral theme that just about every baby-boomer moviegoer could probably hum if asked expresses Lawrence's yearning for grandeur. Composer Alex North also put on the score some typical Hollywood epic motifs: triumphant British marches and Near Eastern exotica bellydance music. But it's significant that, in the overture and intermission music, those respectively pompous and cheesy themes are counterpointed against the grandeur motif until they literally bury it, suggestive of how the purity of Lawrence's mission will be polluted by the British and French military's designs and racist concepts of the Arabs' worth. Lean insisted these orchestral interludes be kept in the restoration, suggesting they echoed important thematic and plot points in the movie.

Initially Lawrence is a nuisance to his superiors. He's sent to help the Arabs because the Home Office feels "the Bedouin are a sideshow of a sideshow," and in part to get rid of him. But the magnificent cut from Lawrence blowing out a match to a massive desert sunrise shows what Lawrence thinks of his mission and sweeps the audience into the thrill of his ambition. From the beginning of his hegira he tries to adapt to the Bedouin. But then Sherif Ali (Omar Sharif), introduced riding across the desert in a long-lensed endless shot until he seems like destiny hovering before Lawrence (a great moment in world cinema), kills Lawrence's guide for drinking from his well. Peter O'Toole, his soon to be world-famous eyes flashing, tells Ali the Arabs will be a little people so long as they fight tribe against tribe, a "silly people, greedy, barbarous and cruel." This is a man who's come to learn from and dictate to the Arabs at the same time, the first of many dangerous (and familiar-sounding) contradictions.

When abandoned with only his compass as a guide he rejects Ali's help and makes it to Faisal's camp alone, where he initially wins the Arabs over by reciting some of the Koran. He'll assure them British and Arab interests are the same ("possibly," replies Faisal). Faisal's realpolitik balances Lawrence's "desert-loving English" idealism in almost every dialogue exchange; the writing nimbly turns just about every romantic claim of Lawrence's on its head.

Still most of the first half of the film shows Lawrence's triumph (warning: as of now this article tracks the plot). The meditating in the desert on how to defeat the Turks occupying Arabia (while watched by two boys who'll become his loyal servants, and pay for it dearly). His subsequent plan to take the Turkish town of Aqaba and its seaward-facing guns from the land. His horrific ride through the Nefut, where he not only recruits Shiek Auda's (Anthony Quinn) Howitat tribe, but goes back to rescue a man from the "sun's anvil," declaring about what appeared to be the man's certain fate, "nothing is written." He wins the Arabs' loyalty for this feat, above all that of Ali, who's virtually falling in love with him—the "love that dare not speak its name" in those days—and who gives him the name El Lawrence. But a later incident and the film's brutally precise dialog will throw that romantic claim that "nothing is written" back in Lawrence's face.

Lawrence wins Auda and his men over by goading Auda to be truly great and not be a mercenary for the Turks, and also promises him gold in Aqaba (as opposed to, say, the Bush administration firing an entire army and losing the money to the most corrupt officers and Al Qaeda in Iraq anyway). Dressed in Arab whites, Lawrence will, after a terrible sacrifice, lead the army into Aqaba. As he rides his camel by the sea, Sherif Ali throws him a victor's garland, but we already see signs of Lawrence's breakdown, symptoms that will only become worse after he loses one of his boy servants to a sandstorm while riding across the Sinai to Cairo to inform the British that the Bedouin have taken Aqaba.

And then, after this devastating loss to desert quicksand of one of the people he truly cared for, when he first arrives in Cairo, an officer heads toward him on a steep escarpment perched across a waterway, seemingly impossibly distant. He yells "Who are you?" in a way that recalls when Lawrence, riding alone in the desert, yelled at the bare mountains the refrain "I'm the man who broke the bank at Monte Carlo!" just to hear the echo of his own voice. The officer's cry though is not an echo of Lawrence's ego and dreams: it's the beginning of the summons of Lawrence's previous life and duties, and the beginning of the confusion that will plague him for the rest of the film. And the bearer of this confusion rides on a motorcycle.

Once Lawrence arrives, the trackless wastes of the desert become the rigidly enclosed courtyards and squares of British Cairo which, the way Lean and Francis photograph them, seem as menacing in their way as the desert sands. Clearly as the second half of the movie begins Lawrence is half-insane and very much a loose cannon. He proclaims "Arabia is for the Arabs" but doesn't want to stay and fight for that because he's learned he has a sadistic streak and enjoys killing. But General Allenby and his cohorts aren't about to let their useful *rara avis* fly away. Allenby won't let him go but lies that Lawrence can tell the Arabs that Britain "has no ambitions in Arabia." They walk the squares in the courtyard, similar to the squares in the opening of the film, and Lawrence is swarmed by admiring British officers in a demonstration that clearly frightens him.

And so he goes back to bring democracy—oops, independence—to the Arabs. Of course he's now in service to a lie, and Allenby even pities him, saying he will "ride the whirlwind." His plan of sabotaging Turkish railways is both a patriotic contribution to the war effort and an invitation to his Arab troops to outright brigandage. The storming of a train is a masterly cinematic sequence in which the sweeping curves of sand dunes shape a magnificent charge which then, amid the crazily distorted angles of railway cars smashed by dynamite, becomes robbery and massacre. As Donald Rumsfeld said about the looting of Iraq, it's the "stuff happens" of wartime and freedom. And, as with Rumsfeld and the Bush administration, in accepting the "stuff happens" in battle, Lawrence begins to lose his war.

For even as an American reporter, one of the implied narrators (played by Arthur Kennedy) is glorifying his myth and assisting his rise to fame, Lawrence is descending into megalomania, believing he can give the Arabs freedom all by himself. Meanwhile his troops are simply taking what they want and disappearing into the desert. Trying to spur his troops on by some kind of daring action in a Turkish city, he instead allows himself to be taken prisoner by a homosexual Turkish general and opens himself up to the kind of sadomasochistic experience he's clearly been seeking for a long time. The torture and his ambiguous reaction to it seems to chasten him and teach him he's "like any man."

But what does that phrase mean to a man whose own nature, provoked by the geopolitics of the region, has split in two? Told of the Sykes-Picot treaty that will divide Arabia between the British and French, and reminded that, if the generals told lies to the Arabs, he told "half lies," (division on division) his half-Arab glory-seeking self reemerges. He believes he can defeat the treaty and give the Arabs Damascus personally, and he beats Allenby there. But in the course of his last campaign Lawrence surrounds himself with a mercenary army of killers who, out of sheer greed, will never question him (the "private contractors" of his war), and, in a ghastly sequence, commit a massacre of Turkish troops. Sherif Ali, in an example of the film's dialog reflecting Lawrence's contradictions, throws Lawrence's "greedy, barbarous, and cruel" characterization of Arabs back at him. The journalist lionizing him now tells him (in an example of dialog reversing upon itself) "You rotten, bloody man. Let me take your rotten, bloody picture for the rotten, bloody newspapers."

Once the Arabs seize Damascus they break down into their tribal warfare, can't agree how to run the city, horribly neglect Turkish prisoners, and then melt into the desert. Without once referring to *taqiyya*, the doctrine of deceit against the infidel allowed under Islam, the movie shows how one is always at the risk of being betrayed in wartime alliances in the Mideast if one is not a Muslim, or at least not able to command enduring loyalty. Lawrence, his last campaign an atrocity, a failure, and a sham, is promoted to colonel simply so he can have a private suite on a ship back to Britain. The only praise he gets that merits his former achievements is from Faisal, who will build on the freeing of Arabia from the Turks to slowly shape modern Saudi Arabia (and accept colonialism in the bargain). But as Faisal tells him "What I owe you is beyond valuation" Lawrence is already a disappearing shadow.

Soon he's on the road away from Damascus, where he glimpses a symbol that mirrors his fatally divided nature, combining British imperialism and potential foolish daredevilry, surrender to the rush of events and an illusion of mastery—an officer on a motorcycle.

***

Lawrence's story is a great tragedy played on a worldwide canvas, and it seems reductive to mine it for lessons regarding the ludicrous blunder that was the Second Iraq War. But all such actions have at their roots the Promethean quest, often explored in great art, of a man or a group of men trying to reshape destiny and remake what's far greater (or worse) than them, whether it's Moby Dick, L.A.'s Chinatown, or the culture and geopolitics of the Mideast and the regimented architecture of the British home offices in Cairo. Lawrence knew how to adapt to the desert by sheer force of will, but could not impose that will on the reality of either world he dealt with.

As George Bernard Shaw might have put it, *Lawrence of Arabia* thus has extraordinary "social utility," a criterion for judging great art Shaw threw in the face of every art-for-art's-sake dogmatist of his day, and still very relevant for ours. So while being fascinated and moved by the artistic experience, we can appreciate, for example, its lessons regarding what Lawrence genuinely achieved; Lawrence, as his *Seven Pillars of Wisdom* showed, made a very deep study of the region, and that led to his initial successes. President Bush and his cohorts did not. Lawrence at one point understood the lay of the land enough to buy off an army rather than fire them all as the Bush administration initially did (ultimately Lawrence's strategy was done in the "surge" later in the Second Iraq War to some relative success).

Much more importantly, Lawrence's ultimate tragic fate points out the hubris and folly of Anglo-Saxons trying to unify a collection of peoples who, for all sorts of religious and geographic regions, refuse to unify. "Being an Arab will be thornier than you suppose," says Sheik Auda Abu Tayi, and he knows far more about it than Lawrence. *Lawrence of Arabia* reveals in its screenplay, its cinematography, and its direction, that one can't completely remake oneself or a country, but those influences are instead always shaping us for better or worse, and refusing to understand that leads to disaster.

The movie's very title suggests a noble quest dissolving into incongruity and then British vs. Arab impossibility. So what ultimately does that last ride on a motorcycle, the "Rosebud" of "citizen Lawrence," represent? The British empire of his birth and official status destroying him? The nearest thing he can ride to a charging camel, with which he can recapture the excitement and the speed of his Arabian conquests? Perhaps more like the confusion between the two and the desire, which even he knows is crazy, to have all of it. Perhaps it was a suicide, and if so a suicide by soldier on both ends of the rifle, with his British goggles flung onto the bare branches he so often saw in the desert.

No, the sands of Arabia and the Mideast are not conducive to conquerors, whether they be Egyptian or European, geniuses like T.E. Lawrence, or, in the words of Michael Moore, merely "stupid white men." I would urge those that have inherited the whirlwind and the White House to screen Sir David Lean, Robert Bolt, and Michael Wilson's magnificently written and poetically directed film, at least to give themselves and the country a chance to not meet the fate foretold in Rudyard Kipling's epic and romantic poem, *The Naulakha*. Kipling's words, though dealing with Asia and not the Arabian peninsula, and though using colonialist racist terms, ring as true today as they did in Kipling's time. I would pick them for W, Cheney, and Rumsfeld's memorials.

> Now it is not good for the Christian's health to hustle the Aryan brown,
> For the Christian riles, and the Aryan smiles and he weareth the Christian down;
> And the end of the fight is a tombstone white with the name of the late deceased,
> And the epitaph drear: "A Fool lies here who tried to hustle the East."

Gumping on the '60s

Now that *Forrest Gump*[1] has been re-released on IMAX, it's time to remember what's really good about the film: the opening windblown feather sequence that blends theme, image, and special effects; the great performance by Tom Hanks, and even better one by Gary Sinise; and the witty insertion of Hanks as Gump into live action footage from the '60s that was the state of the art in special effects back in the '90s.

Okay, credit for the good stuff over. The rest of *Gump* is a lowbrow, clumsy, nasty attack on the very generation and values that baby boom audiences of the time somehow convinced themselves the movie was honoring.

Leaving aside the original author Winston Groom's right-wing biases and crudely macho vision of his character (his original Forrest was a sexual superman, an astronaut journeying into space with a female astronaut and an ape, and a stuntman with a naked Raquel Welch), the movie made from his book, while softening some of that, never escapes a reactionary vision of America in the '60s.

In fact, Forrest is very reminiscent of a comic strip character of the period, Lil' Abner, created by Al Capp. Lil' Abner was a southern simpleton who reflected Capp's conservative cantankerousness about all the changes of the time, but the comic strip was an often satirical cartoon never meant to be taken too seriously. Capp was smart enough not to fall for his own joke; in fact, until he descended into destructive bitterness many years later, Capp's talk show appearances—featuring his honest, cranky disagreements with all things '60s—were an enjoyable commentary on the period, in the same way it was always good to see William F. Buckley, no matter how much you disagreed with him, because of his eloquence, sophistication, and genuine integrity.

Forrest Gump though is meant to be taken very seriously as a blend of Lil' Abner and Jesus Christ. His blunderings into history are funny—until his basement-i.q. sayings are expressed as gospel truths. This sort of sanctimonious view that a mentally "slow" person has the genuine unvarnished folk wisdom has not exactly aged well. And the way it equates good-old-boy USA common sense with—well, being retarded—was this movie really embraced by middle America?

Yes it was, probably for one main reason: Forrest's 'simple folk' wisdom is used in the movie as a blunt instrument to attack everything related to the left-wing ferment of the '60s. At an anti-Vietnam war demonstration, whose leaders are portrayed as a bunch of foulmouthed creeps, Forrest silences the crowd simply by saying he was there (a crowd that, needless to say, doesn't include Ron Kovic or any Vietnam Veterans Against the War). Forrest puts a bunch of similarly repellently depicted African American militants in their place by saying he didn't mean to spoil their "Black Panther party." Yuk yuk—was this movie really embraced by Hollywood liberals?

Yes it was, probably for one main reason: the music that utilized all the counterculture hits of the era. With all the sonic power the IMAX sound system will bring to that soundtrack, what will become painfully obvious is the tone-deafness with which those songs were used. They don't comment in any meaningful way on the sequences they're placed behind. They're cued in so heavy-handedly that you can almost hear the tone arm needle thunk into place on the vinyl record. They're basically dog-whistles to alert baby boom audiences: this is YOUR movie, the soundtrack of YOUR life.

And it all worked. They bought it. This despite the fact that no doubt couples influenced by the feminism of the '70s were among the movie's fans, and apparently didn't mind the most obnoxious aspect of the movie: the character of Forrest's lifelong love Jenny, played by Robin Wright.

Now that Ms. Wright has established herself as one of America's best actresses, and is hugely popular thanks to her role on *House of Cards*, I wouldn't blame her if she wanted to burn or erase every copy of the film. Jenny is a character that combines every negative stereotype of women of the Sixties and beyond: hippie pincushion of the commune, feckless idiot, heartless femme fatale bitch, and drug addict who of course gets her just deserts when she expires from a mystery illness whose name is never mentioned: you know, the illness that strikes only people who have too much sex of the wrong kind. She's basically just a character created to underscore how saintly Forrest is in wanting to save her no matter what (or wait a minute, she does give him one mercy fuck and a son, and then conveniently dies so only good old Forrest will raise the boy).

A clear message of the film is that thank God America got over the "Black Panther party" and every other party the awful, profligate, drug-and-sex-and-hate-ridden Sixties subjected us to. And we did it thanks to faith in God, shrimp (and ultimately Apple), and the dumb luck and good simple unlettered wisdom embodied in Forrest Gump. Is the movie ultimately a rueful comment on how lost Americans are without such simple faiths and maxims to live by? Well, a shrewder version of Gump was President from 2000 to 2008 (and as Sarah Palin, a Gumpessa, might have said, how did that simple wisdom thing work out for ya?).

So is this the vision of Gump's director Robert Zemeckis and screenwriter Eric Roth with regard to America and themes relating to the American '60s? Not at all. Zemeckis's films tend to side with eccentrics (of which Forrest Gump was one), but mainly anarchic and subversive ones. He directed *Who Framed Roger Rabbit?*,[2] a movie that had a very '60s/'70s theme (a battle against murderous corporate and political corruption), a still nonpareil blend of cartoons and live action, and a delightful but resonant story of the rebellious and creative Toons' battle with the forces trying to destroy Toontown and subject Los Angeles to the end of public transportation and the regimentation and despoliation of the freeway system.

Go figure—the guy who directed *Gump* also orchestrated the scene of private eye Eddie Valiant's entry into Toontown, a wild and wonderful sequence that suggests a blend of a Sixties Disneyland/World's Fair ride and acid trip.

As for Eric Roth, he went on to freely adapt an F. Scott Fitzgerald story into the screenplay for the marvelous film *The Curious Case Of Benjamin Button*[3] in a way that almost suggests he was trying to create an anti-Gump. The central character is a similarly mythic figure, a man aging in reverse, but he embraces the world with a wide-eyed, constantly developing intelligence. His lifelong love is a smart, brave, modern woman whose reaction to the cultural developments of the Fifties and Sixties is one of wholehearted affirmation, and their love is a mature and generous relationship of equals. The figure of Captain Mike, roughly similar to Lieutenant Dan, doesn't sink into despair before (with the help of Saint Forrest) finding God and Apple stock, but maintains his ornery free-spiritedness until he sacrifices his life in wartime. And the movie ends with images of a hummingbird and of Hurricane Katrina washing into New Orleans that are better reminders of the preciousness of Gump's feather of life than any Gumpish homily.

Button or *Rabbit* should've won the Oscar, not *Gump*. But movie and Oscar history is like a box of chocolates. Sometimes one pops out that's chocolate of the wrong kind.

War Is Hell Yeah

> *"Ideals are peaceful. History is violent."*
> – Don "Wardaddy" Collier in Fury[1]

In a touch that not even a comic like Jon Stewart or Stephen Colbert might have imagined, a videogame based on the movie *Fury* has been marketed under the slogan "Where the movie ends, the game begins."

Anyone who's seen the film, one of the most harrowing war movies since *Saving Private Ryan*, will realize the ghastly inappropriateness of linking the movie's end to that slogan's invitation to the thrill ride of tank warfare …

… except for those millions of gamers who believe that anyone who reacts to the ad campaign critically, who sees a problem with the continuation of a deeply serious war movie in a joint venture with the "World of Tanks" video franchise, is humorless and clueless. It's a game like any other war game, it's media synergy, and it's … awesome. And that attitude toward war entertainment, nurtured by hundreds of video war games, has become a backdoor way to changing Americans' attitude toward war itself.

Movies have always been a pretty good barometer of our country's beliefs about war and peace. So it may surprise young people to know that for most of the past sixty years, war films in America have been primarily antiwar films.

Even after America's victory in World War II, a war universally considered just and unavoidable, a dark view of postwar America and the scars of that conflict set in. In part that was because of an American tradition, at that point still fresh, of fear of a standing army, perfectly captured in James Jones' pre-Pearl Harbor novel set in Hawaii that became a postwar highly honored film, *From Here To Eternity*. There was also an honest reaction to the difficulties faced by veterans readjusting to home life: it wasn't called post-traumatic stress disorder back in the '50s and early '60s, but it was very much the topic, along with physical war wounds, in William Wyler's Academy Award-winning *The Best Years of Our Lives*, and in movies like *The Man in the Grey Flannel Suit* (which anticipated *Mad Men* in its story of an adman, played by Gregory Peck, suffering from horrific war memories).

By the time of the '60s and '70s, after Korea and during Vietnam, it was hard to find a movie that didn't have a jaundiced or outraged attitude toward war—all our wars. Films like *Soldier Blue* and *Little Big Man* recast the conquest of Indian tribes—once celebrated in cowboys vs. Indians westerns—as genocide. *Fail-Safe* and *Dr. Strangelove* were, respectively, terrifying and black comic portrayals of potential nuclear doomsday. M.A.S.H. saw the Korean War through the ironically detached but compassionate eyes of battlefield doctors cleaning up its bloody mess; it was later spun off into a classic television series.

Most Vietnam war movies of the '70s, while not mirroring anti-Vietnam-war politics, were still dark and tragic in tone. *The Deer Hunter* showed how the war devastated a group of working-class men, even if it turned on Robert DeNiro being a loyal warrior trying to rescue them both during and after the war. *Apocalypse Now* was a canvas of the war's epic madness, and *Coming Home* dealt with the anguish of a paralyzed vet's rehabilitation that led him to turn against all wars, not just Vietnam.

The overall pacifist attitude of the period was so pervasive that even the noble just war came in for a critical view. *Slaughterhouse Five*, based on novelist Kurt Vonnegut Jr.'s actual World War II service, portrayed the firebombing of the German city of Dresden, the Allied forces' worst atrocity. And *Catch-22*, while never attacking the mission of the soldiers in World War II, relentlessly satirized the military bureaucratic insanity that ensnared bomber crews in the midst of the Italian campaign.

It may be hard for anyone under thirty today to realize just how against war people under thirty were in the '60s. Antiwar demonstrations were a regular activity for young people. The slogan "War is not healthy for children and other living things" was on one of the most popular posters of the day. John Wayne was roundly attacked in the media for his pro-Vietnam war movie *The Green Berets*. Of course a huge chunk of the country shared Wayne's view for most of the '60s, but by 1969 a daylong Vietnam Moratorium to protest the war by not going to work or school virtually shut America down.

To go back to that quote from *Fury*, that might have been because, the Vietnam War and the military draft notwithstanding, the '60s were a peaceful time of ideals. America had won WWII, President Eisenhower had ended Korea, the Kennedy administration had averted nuclear war. The United Nations was troubled, but still young and hopeful. The Cold War's threat of nuclear apocalypse made even the smallest brushfire proxy war between "democracy" and "communism" seem insane. There seemed to be no reason why, if we couldn't just "stop the war in Vietnam, bring the troops home," that the whole loathsome, horrible, unnecessary business of war (and we knew it was a business) couldn't be brought to an end.

But, as the quote from *Fury* reminds us—and it's a good update of Albert Camus's observation that people think plagues and wars are surprising, but there are always plagues and always wars—history is violent. And men caught up in a war can only react to that violent history. But how do we explain the way in which the current American population, served by a volunteer army, untouched on the continental United States for almost sixteen years, seems to want to be caught up in that historical violence (without, of course, getting hurt)?

Part of that may be that we've had many years now of videogames that attempt to instill a suggestion of war fury in gamers. We've had almost as many years of a major television network and a dominant political party that constantly beat on the drums of fear and war, above all, war on terrorism, whatever that is, however long it takes.

One of the most touching and powerful aspects of the movie *Fury*—a movie which, shrouded in icy grey and muddy brown tones of dread, is an unending visual representation of "war is hell"—is how it shows that, within that hell, some of the potentially worst explosions of anger and sadism, the moments that can be most frightening and that will most haunt men afterwards, come when the shroud lifts. Those menacing moments come during the breaks between battles, when for a brief, precious time, normalcy, civility, even something like romance can resume. It's at that point that warriors can be so vulnerable to being emotionally devastated, or consumed by rage, or psychologically destroyed, that both for them and the movie audience the calls back to action and immersive battle sequences come as something of a relief.

And that seems to be part of the movie's theme. The tank the men ride in and that they've named "Fury" isn't just their home on the battlefield. The war the tank plunges them into becomes their spiritual home, in a strange way their refuge. War may terrify them, they may know they're going to die unless dumb luck saves them, but war is also when they're at one with their brothers, when they experience honor and something like love, when they're doing their job. Any more complicated thinking about what they're going through might drive them insane.

The other half of Camus's thought on plagues and wars has to do with "humanists," who believe plagues and wars are exceptional, becoming therefore the first victims, because they don't "take precautions." It's very possible that the pacifists of the '60s are now the humanists of the early 21st century in not taking precautions (except perhaps for President Obama, who has taken a political beating for that). Not taking seriously enough the desire for a great portion of the population, even while civility and safety still exist, to evade the awful looming problems of the day by escaping into war fantasies. Not educating them enough as to why that's a very bad idea.

It's one thing for a videogame entertainment machine to distill violence into the thrill of gamer combat and set that thrill in imaginary worlds where the difference between fantasy and reality is clear. But if a videogame can boil a truly thoughtful and frightening movie about the historical reality of an actual war into purely its components of ride the tank and kill the enemy, then we shouldn't be surprised if that adrenaline rush colors attitudes toward events unfolding in the present. Bomb-bomb-bomb-bomb-bomb Iran.

We shouldn't be surprised if, given the commercial impact of such entertainment, whole sectors of the population become so turned on by vicarious bloodlust and by jacking into war mania that, with no experience of its actual horrors, they want our nation not to seriously tackle global problems but to "cry havoc and let slip the dogs of war" whenever possible—until one day the fantasy becomes reality and comes back home.

Where the movie ends ...

Tomorrowland
Beauty and the BS

In the film *Tomorrowland*,[1] a lovely young woman who's also a young scientist is left with a pin that, when she touches it, gives her a vision of a magical refuge where all science's biggest and most hopeful dreams have come true.

It's not hard to get pulled in by that premise. For one thing, it counterpoints an initial sequence that depicts the chilling of a young boy's science dreams. And to have a girl anchor the story is a welcome response to the old misogynist view that women can't succeed at science.

Casey loves science so much—as well as her dad, a former NASA engineer—that she's willing to get into serious trouble in order to try and stop NASA from demolishing one of its gantries. Being, as it becomes clear, a genius, and drawing in the help of a figure who assists geniuses, the mysterious and childike Athena, she resists her clearly genius-averse world, and that leads her to her discovery of Tomorrowland.

Much was made of director Brad Bird's animated movie *The Incredibles* as some kind of Ayn Rand antigovernment screed, which struck me as over the top; there may have been some malicious barbs aimed at political correctness—and haven't we all aimed them?—but the movie was a witty, ornery, and fabulously done animated film. The idea of exceptional figures being put out to pasture (or worse) so that official mediocrity can triumph is hardly a conservative idea in any case, unless you consider Ray Bradbury's *Farenheit 451* or Kurt Vonnegut Jr.'s short story "Harrison Bergeron" right wing.

Bird's *Tomorrowland*, though, is a different kettle of robots. It recalls the kind of Walt Disney optimism and hope that made the endearingly creaky '60s-era Tomorrowland the boyhood corner of "the happiest place on earth." But beginning with the thought that "the future can be a scary place," the movie then goes down the story structure and philosophy path of saying that the future being scary stems from a kind of socially conditioned mass defeatism that's the main problem our heroine has to fight.

It reminds me of the one weirdly cranky scene in the otherwise captivating *Interstellar* where it's revealed that the space program, humankind's only hope, was shut down so that some Hillary Clinton-esque administration could put every last dollar into farming on a dying planet. *Tomorrowland* also shows the space program as neglected, to the great detriment of all mankind, but here it's not even so the money can be diverted into a last-ditch survival farming effort (as opposed to say, the sure thing of finding a wormhole). Here the implication is that we know what, in effect, the salvation wormhole is, it's our own can-do scientific efforts, but we just don't believe in that anymore.

Among other problems with *Tomorrowland* is that it miscalculates the visual and dramatic language used to put over that view. To see a young girl, however attractive and well-meaning, penetrate a NASA operation, even to stop the destruction of one of their own gantries, and then sabotage NASA's efforts with the help of her private drone, is not going to strike most Americans as positive. Similarly it's hard not to see Brad Bird's visions of *Tomorrowland*, however impressive and vertigo-inducing (why wasn't this film shot in 3D?) without thinking of Dubai or Abu Dhabi or those needle-like skyscrapers going up in New York that don't represent science and hope but hedge funds' and international oligarchs' investments. Bird turns a part of the real estate of the "happiest place on earth" into a version of 21st-century designer utopias for globotrash.

Visually the film is for the most part a treat, an excitingly filmed live-action cartoon with its share of fun surprises, like when the Eiffel Tower launches an interstellar rocket, or the frail and winsome young symbolic figure Athena suddenly turns into Hit Girl (but don't worry, parents of very young moviegoers, she's only smashing robots).

The film's invocation of the can-do spirit of the early '60's also works nicely. I could've easily spent more time in the film's charming evocation of my beloved 1964 World's Fair. That early sequence, where the George Clooney figure as a child arrives at an inventor's exposition at the Fair carrying his "Electrolux" jetpack (which still has a few bugs in it) did take me back to a mid-'60s world where belief in science was everything. Even if, like me, you were on your way to putting words or images together and not wires and gears, you tried to emulate your friend who was kit-building a radio. You had a chemistry set, you read *Life* Magazine and *Popular Science* or *Popular Mechanics* and daydreamed. You thought the underwater and Antarctic cities of the Futurama World's Fair exhibit would surely happen in your lifetime, along with your very own flying car.

And why not? Look at those heroic but regular American guys orbiting the earth and going to the moon. And more importantly, look at all the definitely regular guys with slide rules in their shirt pockets helping them do it.

And that's where *Tomorrowland* flies off the rails.

In *Tomorrowland*, there is no dedicated corps of regular men and women, either of the Mission Control variety or the Whole Earth Catalog variety (the late '60s ecological movement was hardly unfriendly to science). There's only a benign leadership at the "spaceport" serviced by a horde of sometimes very good-sometimes very bad robots, and they're recruiting "dreamers" and inventors from Earth, what have elsewhere been called the "talented tenth." In the pop poetry/mythology of this movie—and it does have one—these robots (called "audioanimatronics," referring to the lifelike Disney talking figures of the 1964 World's Fair) have been inviting such dreamers to an interstellar tech nirvana, Tomorrowland, for years, where they've been given free rein to construct a perfect future.

What have the rest of us been doing in Tomorrowland's universe? Basically languishing on Earth in a miserable torpor. As one character says "it's hard to have ideas, it's easy to give up."

So what's stopping us? What (in the storyline of the film) will destroy the planet? Our own pessimism and death-wishes? Spoiler alert ... literally that's where the film goes. A giant tachyonic projection computer program has been beaming what appears to be a prediction of the world's end that's actually conditioning us to cause our own destruction, and why? Because we want to believe it. It's sort of the opposite of how you revive Tinkerbell in *Peter Pan*—hey, kids, clap hard enough, and not only will she die, she'll die of cancer.

The film evokes the death of NASA and destructiveness of climate change, and pretty much links it to the sensibility that embraces dystopic novels. Thinking makes it so—if we thought differently, then we could do something about it.

At one point the heroine tries to get her dad past his despair that he's a NASA engineer "with nothing to launch," and shouts "I want my 'New Frontier' dad!" Well frontiers, whether the old west or President John F. Kennedy's New Frontier, were not conquered and settled merely by elites, and the 1960s effort that culminated in the moon landing was a collective triumph. What elites can do is seriously fuck things up, and this is where *Tomorrowland* ultimately becomes annoying in a way it wouldn't be if it had just kept to the robot-fighting and the sweet moments and didn't so loudly double down on the position that it's our defeatism that's blocking the progress of science.

The film has it ass-backwards. It's easy to have ideas, but if you really care about them, it's hard to give up on them once you have them. People are still fighting for science. What's blocking their progress, and the continuation of the great scientific promise of the mid-'60s, is a Congress that won't fund it. An American political elite (so to speak) that doesn't care enough about it. Congressmen from safe seats who say that evolution and climate change thinking are lies from the pit of hell. Religious beliefs that are driving stem cell research to Korea. Budget-cutting right after a lethal train crash that may prevent the latest in railroad safety science from being installed on Amtrak. Not flying cars, *Amtrak*.

Tomorrowland's incarnation of lovely young women (one still a child, one not) as beacons of hope, and its casting of George Clooney, every boomer male's vision of how he'd like to age out, as finally flying that young kid's jetpack before nobly passing the scientific torch to the next generation, is undercut by that willful ignorance of what really stands in the way of science, and the hollowness of the film's suggestion that an upper crust will save us all, instead of, more likely, planning a future that serves their needs and maybe will trickle down to the rest of us. The movie gives a nod to this when a bad guy named Governor Nix (get it?) turns out to have been showing civilization its doom not to warn it but to lull it into despair, so that Tomorrowland can shut its doors and no longer invite any "savages" from earth into its domain. Once Nix is defeated, Tomorrowland is once again open to dreamers.

But that hardly dispels the sourness of the story. The reason *Tomorrowland* not only doesn't come close to great popular sci fi like *Star Wars* or *ET*—whether you're talking about quality, appeal, or (as seems to be proving out catastrophically) box office—is that it turns the audience away rather than inviting them in. We can all, even the older ones among us, connect with that feeling of trying to save or vindicate your people and your world, whether on a horse or a Millennium Falcon. We've all had beloved nonhuman companions who've awakened in us love and whom we wanted to save at all costs, as in "Lassie" or *ET*. We didn't all get A+ at Stanford, nor are we all going to respond to a message that we're slaves to our own defeatism if we're not yet successfully defeating the obstacles of bureaucracy, student debt, flat wages, and the endless demands of special interests as we try to do what we feel we're meant to do.

Tomorrowland's vision of the future, in the words of Samuel Goldwyn, includes us out. And Mr. Bird, you're a hell of a filmmaker, but again quoting Mr. Goldwyn, next time you want to send a message about a super-talented elite saving us all, it might be cheaper to go Western Union.

Our Fair Lady

Ever wonder why we still love the Brits (from *Downton Abbey* to, inexplicably, the royals) given that (1) we severed our ties rather bloodily back when (2) the UK, as John Cleese and others have pointed out, is almost a wholly-owned subsidiary of Murdoch, Inc. (3) the music hasn't been John-Paul-Thom quality lately, and (4) we've all been stuck at some point or other with the bar tab?

Maybe it all goes back to the '60s, and, earlier than the Beatles, to a show that, until *A Chorus Line* in the '70s, was Broadway's all-time longest-running smash hit before it became equally successful as an Oscar-winning film: *My Fair Lady*.[1]

I have to admit I'm partial to this show since, as a precocious sixth grader, I convinced my class to let me direct a version as our class play and star as Henry Higgins. No doubt my parents were very proud to see their son prancing around pretending to be the original Higgins, Rex Harrison (while other parents were probably gritting their teeth), and whenever I remember my delight at that experience and the applause that followed, I wonder if I peaked when I was twelve.

I at least didn't succeed in chilling any of the other parents' love for the movie *My Fair Lady*, in which Henry Higgins, "confirmed bachelor" and linguistics professor, turns low-class flower girl Eliza Doolittle into a fake duchess by improving her speech in order to win a bet, only to find himself falling in love with the woman she's now become. *My Fair Lady* became one of the most beloved and successful films of the '60s, as the play had been when it opened in the '50s and played for seven years. Both were luminously designed and entertaining productions that, except for mid-'60s pacing (and even that isn't so bad), have held up just fine in their various revivals.

American audiences were primed to love this essentially British import. It wasn't just that Americans had been looking to England for cultural gravitas at least as far back as Henry James. It wasn't just that Americans had always had a sneaking attraction for British aristocratic elegance and the class system; during the '50s and '60s, when rotary phone numbers were part-numbers-part-names, Mayfair and Trafalgar were two of the names.

And World War II had left many soldiers literally in love with

England through memories of (or even successful marriages from) wartime romances, the kind of relationship captured in the John Schlesinger film *Yanks*. And in the midst of America's postwar memories of fighting and loving beside England Julie Andrews emerged as the perfect lovely and well-rescued British lass. She was embraced as Eliza Doolittle from the moment she stepped on stage in the original cast of *My Fair Lady*, later going on to another British-themed musical triumph, *Camelot*. During the '60s she would even make light of her appeal as the ultimate Brit damsel in the daring comedy *The Americanization of Emily*, where she played a woman with a reputation for giving "mercy fucks" to soldiers en route to the battlefield (Ms. Andrews always had more sass and acting ability than she was credited with, never more so than in the movies directed by her late husband Blake Edwards, especially *Victor Victoria*).

One reason for the success of *My Fair Lady* is that it was a truly witty, sophisticated, and faithful enough but also just softened enough adaptation of the source material, George Bernard Shaw's *Pygmalion*. That play builds to a much sharper conflict between Eliza and Higgins, with its last two acts devoted to a battle between them over her personal freedom versus his continued dominance over her. It's clear his work of transformation has made her into a kind of mechanical doll version of herself, and she reclaims her humanity only by rebelling against him. It's also clear they'll never marry. When the flower girl turned into a fake duchess becomes a fake duchess who turns herself into a real woman, she can have no place in Higgins's life.

There is also in the play a sense of the impermeability of the British class structure, never far from George Bernard Shaw's mind, that is at least somewhat toned down in the play and movie. That Eliza, during her tutelage by Higgins, in effect becomes a servant of his is soft-pedaled in *My Fair Lady*, whereas the sheer power of the dialog in *Pygmalion* throws that into starker relief.

But after all *My Fair Lady* was meant to be a romantic vision as much as a Shavian comedy. Here's a description from the movie program book of the time of the décor design (by Cecil Beaton). "The oriental carpets in Higgins's home were re-dyed to achieve color harmony; the lampshades, wallpaper, Edwardian bric-a-brac, and the Art Nouveau furnishings of Mrs. Higgins's home were hand-picked or handmade or in many cases imported from London... the cage for the mynah bird is a $1250 collectors' piece and the Ascot silver service is priceless."[2]

George Cukor, considered the one of the best "women's" directors and a superbly tasteful master of art direction and costumes, directed the film. Rex Harrison was a no-brainer to reprise his role on Broadway. But casting Audrey Hepburn instead of Julie Andrews was controversial enough that it played into Hepburn's not even being nominated for an Oscar, while Julie Andrews was awarded one for *Mary Poppins*.

It seems in retrospect a particularly unfair judgment: Hepburn was radiant as Eliza, and the decision to dub in another singing voice for "The Rain In Spain" and "I Could Have Danced All Night" was not hers and is the only part of the movie that now really clunks, especially since Ms. Hepburn sounds charming and natural in the numbers where she sings. Where Hepburn is at her best is the phase where Eliza, having rebelled against Higgins, is all alone and so betwixt-and-between the classes that she has no home anywhere and virtually no identity; perhaps Hepburn communicated the genuinely touching moments of despair in those scenes by drawing on her past as a starving young refugee in World War II. And because she so commits to those moments, her later finding of herself is all the more winning; Hepburn embodied a process of transformation in Eliza that, especially for female audiences, is equally captivating today.

Part of finding herself becomes finding a way to go back to Henry Higgins. For unlike in *Pygmalion* the movie strikes a balance for its audience—it's clear that Eliza has won Higgins's love, and she's beginning to domesticate him, but he's not going to give up very easily (and never completely) and she understands that. But even if she's back in his life, you know she's never going to be his doormat again.

It's about as fair an ending for Eliza as you could have hoped for back in the very un-feminist mid-'60s, and it definitely sent the audience out happy. Whatever the Academy bitchery about Ms. Hepburn, none of it stopped audiences from adoring the movie, especially the sheer London elegance so beautifully realized by Cukor, right down to using Eliza's background as a flower girl to surround every frame possible with flowers and even recreate the old Covent Garden flower market (I remember my mom was especially taken by that, and so am I to this day). It all worked, and *My Fair Lady* the movie, and also *Mary Poppins*, completed the '60s love affair with Britain before the Beatles sealed the deal.

And here's the secret sauce to that romance: the Brits brought us back our nonconformity, even before the Beatles' cheekiness and irreverence made that the way to be. In *Mary Poppins*, Julie Andrews, anything but a starchy British nanny, and joined by a goofy high-kicking Dick Van Dyke, liberates the two uptight children, and later their uptight father, who winds up singing "Let's Go Fly A Kite." (Andrews would play a similar role with the Von Trapp kids in *The Sound of Music*—was she actually the first and only G-rated hippie?). In *My Fair Lady* Rex Harrison as Higgins, for all his priggish insistence on fidelity to correct English, is very much the bull in the British mannerly china shop, showing up at one of his mother's elegant formal-dress soirees, for example, in his tweedy professorial work clothes.

Let's see: insistence on doing his work absolutely right, preferring the company of men above all else, raging against marriage, tall and handsome and dapper but in a gritty regular fellow way—perhaps one reason for *My Fair Lady*'s success with both men and women in America was because Rex Harrison as Higgins was, in his Brit way, an ideal American independent male. His Higgins incarnated every American '50s–'60s husband of the time's wish that he could be, at least for a little while, freed of the conventions and requirements of the nuclear family (this was the heyday of mother-in-law jokes) and be a sophisticated hail-fellow-well-met bachelor again. And of course Julie and Audrey were every American woman's wish that they could break free, at least for a little while, and find their inner princess. It was a match made in box office heaven, and behind it was the way Higgins made Eliza different and she accepted his differentness.

And we were all ready to be British-invaded afterwards, especially by four young men who, like Rex Harrison, were relatable blokes and sexily British while exuding a part of our independent American spirit and giving it back to us—in this case our early r & b and rock-and-roll.

So next time you find yourself enamored of the latest Brit pop tart, or turned down for a laddish guy from London, or, after a night of cheerful carousing, once again stuck with the bloody check, remember that England has been shaping our desires and stealing our hearts ever since Rex and Julie and Audrey, and it's a trade deficit no one seems to be able to do anything about.

Selma and the '60s
Tragedy and Redemption

In the mid-to-late 1960s, historical events spun so fiercely out of control that many people felt like saying, to quote the title of a popular musical of the time, *Stop The World, I Want To Get Off!*

And in 1965, that became true of the civil rights movement. Lyndon Baines Johnson, the President of the United States, realized that he'd lost control of the situation, and Martin Luther King, the greatest voice for civil rights in the country, feared that he'd lost his way.

Selma,[1] one of the best films of the year, captures a moment where King had won a Nobel Peace Prize, but neither he nor his movement could stop church bombings, state police shootings of protesters, and constant denial of legal and human rights to African Americans in the South, especially the denial of the right to vote, which guaranteed that, with only whites voting, repressive racist regimes would continue to run the southern states.

And when King sought help from President Johnson, he found a threatened leader worried about the legislative fate of his "war on poverty" if he came out too strongly for civil rights, and beholden to the governors of the "Democratic South" and the machinations of J. Edgar Hoover and his FBI.

Meanwhile other African-American activists challenged Dr. King and his philosophy of nonviolence. *Selma* captures in two hours plus one of the great themes of Taylor Branch's magisterial nonfiction trilogy on the civil rights movement, *Parting of the Waters/Pillar of Fire/At Canaan's Edge*: how centrifugal forces in King's movement threatened to tear it apart. The Student Nonviolent Coordinating Committee, which had been trying to register black voters in Alabama for years, saw King as an interloper. Malcolm X and his militant followers called him an "Uncle Tom."

At that historical moment, King was utterly frustrated by presidential inactivity and Alabama police brutality in his attempts to hold a protest march from Selma to Montgomery in support of voting rights, and so was plunged into some of the most uncertain and despairing moments of his life. And so at that moment the civil rights movement could have fallen prey to the tragedy that claimed so much of the political activity of the '60s. The incredible energy and passion it took to create and to fight for all the period's achievements in music, art, the ecology movement, the anti-Vietnam War movement, and civil rights were linked to a "too much ain't enough" all-or-nothing mania—or in the ancient Greeks' term "hubris," immoderation and unreasoning pride. Tied to episodes of destructive militance and radical violence, that lack of reason finally contributed to the great reform movement's breakdown.

There were many, many other factors that turned the ferment and hope of the '60s into the excesses of the '70s and the conservative crackdown of the '80s. But as Albert Camus wrote in his great historical and philosophical book *The Rebel*, speaking mainly of Stalinist Soviet Communism but also of violent and dictatorial revolutionary regimes in general, when rebellion becomes revolution, creative resistance turns into repressive control of one's own people in an attempt to transform society, and that point the movement becomes prone to violence and just another master-slave system.

Or as The Who sang, "Meet the new boss, same as the old boss."[2]

The civil rights movement, embroiled in bloodshed, misery, and hopelessness down south in 1965, torn by internal arguments (given an honest airing in *Selma*), could have succumbed to that dynamic. Anger and militancy could've defeated nonviolence and strategy, as it often did in later years, after Martin Luther King and Robert Kennedy's assassinations, only to drive urban ghettoes deeper into drugs, poverty, unemployment, and despair. And sadly there's a direct path from that decline to the way President Obama was unwilling for so long to fight harder for African-American causes so as not to look like the stereotypical angry black man; and to the split between the nonviolent and tactically thoughtful and the angry and unfocused protesters in the streets of Ferguson and New York; and to the victories, if you can call them that, of a do-worse-than-nothing Congress, whose bland smiles mask the latest reactionary measures: voter suppression, massive incarceration of young men of color, police shootings of unarmed black men. The new Jim Crow.

But that didn't happen in Selma in 1965. Instead King's commitment to patient, resourceful nonviolence, despite his followers' exposure to savage assaults and even murder, became the greatest weapon in his struggle to enlist the whole country in his cause. Like the movie *Lincoln*, *Selma* shows that the outcome of a long and bloody fight between the South and the federal government was climactic wrangling over the passage of a landmark piece of legislation, the Voting Rights Act. During that struggle either a recalcitrant or reluctant (depending on your interpretation of history) President Johnson came around, along with millions of other Americans.

And so Selma became a symbol of all that was redemptive and compassionate in the '60s, all that could unify the various voices of the movement: black, white, student, labor union, intellectuals, and community workers. Dr. King, so well-versed in the thoughts of Gandhi and Reinhold Niebuhr, was able to transmute them into both strategy and some of the most stirring oratory of the 20th century (the King estate, unfortunately true to form, forbade use of King's words in *Selma*, so the speeches were crafted by the writer and director of the film).

When the Voting Rights Act was passed, it exemplified Camus' hope that rebellion and resistance need not become revolution, that creativity and righteous anger, along with an acceptance of tension and limits and a resistance to the temptation of intolerance and violence on one's own side, could win a great victory.

Now a major part of the Voting Rights Act has been gutted by the Supreme Court, the rest of it is in clear and present danger, and African Americans are once again having to fight for basic human and civil rights. But you can't turn history back entirely. You can't recreate a world without an African American middle class, an African American educated class, an African American music empire, and for eight years a literally African American president who will retain a great deal of influence. All of these advantages can be used, following Dr. King's example and Camus' words, in a creative, patient, nonviolent, but unyielding resistance.

Segregation is forever illegal. There's a black caucus in Congress. The protests against police brutality and massive incarceration are coalescing into a new movement. And finally, the movie *Selma* was directed by a young African American woman, Ava DuVernay.

Jim Crow won't go quietly. But we've made a start on sending him packing.

Selma and the Dramatization of History

"Just gimme some truth."[1] – **John Lennon**

The question of whether the film *Selma* distorts '60s history in its depiction of President Lyndon Baines Johnson comes down to one's views on the roles and boundaries of historical fiction and docudrama.

When I wrote and published my book *Cats' Eyes*, I worried a great deal not so much about its depiction of famous public figures, shown in very brief scenes, but about characters that bore some relation to the people who are or were closest to me, my own family and friends, not to mention myself. I quickly realized the only way to ease my worries and enable myself to produce anything like quality fiction would be—and I would propose this as a rule to all young would-be fiction writers—to make sure the characters were composites.

To put that another way: no matter how closely a character resembles someone you know, you can only write them in an effective dramatic way if you make them a fictional character.

In the case of the characters in my book, that meant changing their ages, interests both athletic and creative, their degree of rebelliousness, their hair color, size, beliefs, and above all experiences (in a '60s novel, given how fast events moved, all I had to do was, for example, make the male adolescent character two years older than myself). I injected all the characters with aspects of other people I knew. I used incidents I remembered that the family shared, but once I created new characters, they were filtered through different points of view.

I faced a different problem in my one experience writing a docudrama in Hollywood that unfortunately was never produced. Many of the public figures were still around then, and were trial lawyers—so there was some very careful work involved in noting exactly who said what to me (or what fact from what book I used) during my research. I soon realized I would have to sort through conflicting points of view and perspectives to build a script, and that inevitably someone would be dissatisfied. Who would've torn me a new one, I'll never know.

These kinds of problems are the reason that these sorts of movies, although they may win awards, don't get made that often now—and given the North Korean Sony hack and the atrocities in Paris may get made even less in the future. In the case of *Zero Dark Thirty*,[2] for example, there were accusations that director Kathryn Bigelow and screenwriter Mark Boal bought into the CIA's justification of enhanced interrogation techniques (that is, torture) by depicting them in the film in relation to intelligence-gathering.

For why and how these kinds of accusations that major historical films got it wrong surface around Oscar campaign time, I recommend Jason Bailey's excellent article on *Flavorwire*.[3] If controversy was ginned up to bring down *Zero Dark Thirty*'s Oscar prospects, it certainly worked, denying an award to Kathryn Bigelow despite her magnificent job of direction, Mark Boal despite his masterful script, and above all Jessica Chastain, one of America's finest film actresses, in her finest performance. It also produced a spectacle that must have made arch antifeminist Rush Limbaugh split his giant gut: one of the Senate's greatest woman senators, Dianne Feinstein, attacking one of Hollywood's best veteran woman directors, Ms. Bigelow.

So how exactly did *Zero Dark Thirty* buy into the CIA's view of torture? By showing that it happened? In the movie Maya, the character played by Chastain, is clearly sickened both professionally and personally by the torture techniques she witnesses. She also has one objective in her life, to capture or kill Bin Laden, and will do anything it takes to achieve it—including go along to get along with her colleagues in the program.

So yes, she's shown participating in the torture program, and also countering it. When prolonged torture of one detainee mentally breaks him down but gets nowhere in obtaining useful information and preventing an attack, Maya comes up with the clever idea of lying to him that, because of short-term memory loss due to sleep deprivation, he forgot that he gave up information that actually prevented the attack, and now he's going to be rewarded. Given that lie and a decent meal, he gives up names.

The film gives a balanced view; yes Maya collaborated with CIA torturers on her watch rather than, say, objecting to it on her first week at work and getting thrown out of her life's goal. And yes, that clever tactic of hers does build on how torture softened up the detainee, a reasonable assessment of what might have actually taken place, right or wrong. But Maya's tactic proves how ineffective torture is compared to clever interrogation. It makes her a more complex character, builds in another personal dynamic to the film's intensification of conflict, and honors the truth of what happened. How did the real "Maya" feel about this? Well, because she's probably living more underground than any human on the planet, we'll never know. It was up to the screenwriter and director to utilize whatever information they got to create absorbing drama that also reflected the complicated nature of the situation.

But just because the movie showed torture as a reaction to the shock of 9/11 and a nightmarish prelude to the ultimate success of dedicated human intelligence work, just because the movie acknowledged the cruelty and horror of the War on Terror, just because it *showed it happened*, the media wolves came out (and again, I refer you to Bailey's article).

Selma now faces the same kind of brouhaha over its depiction of President Lyndon Baines Johnson, who, unlike the real Maya, is a towering historical figure about whom volumes have been written. But despite LBJ's historical prominence director Ava DuVernay still faced the same problem of docudrama and historical fiction creators everywhere: how do you dramatize an actual person? The "real" LBJ has been dead for so long that, despite the historical record, no one can recollect him for you that accurately, and even if they could, you still won't capture the real person. Screenwriter Jason Hall of *American Sniper* wrote that he spent months with the subject Chris Kyle before his murder, but still didn't feel he completed his portrait of the man until, after his death, he spoke extensively with his wife, Taya.[4]

So Ms. DuVernay was going to inevitably come up with her own vision of the encounters between LBJ and Dr. King, or, as John Lennon wisely sang, it's a matter of "gimme some truth" rather than an impossible delivery of all the truth. In this case the choice was to show LBJ as a kind of composite, a compassionate believer in human rights and a hard-ass cynical wrangler of other powerful men. He moves from being a wily Southern pol, cautious and calculating, whose main cause was poverty, not civil rights, and who always had to look over his shoulder at the then "Democratic South," to someone so outraged by the events of Selma and the way Governor Wallace of Alabama was refusing to enforce state voting laws on the books that he not only pushed through the federal Voting Rights Act but quoted the civil rights anthem "We Shall Overcome."

How accurate is that? Here's a complementary question; is it possible we're looking back and projecting rosy scenarios on the situation based on what we wanted to believe then and still believe now? One of the most popular movies of the '60s, *To Kill A Mockingbird*, showed a righteous white southern lawyer Atticus Finch, played with great warmth and rectitude by Gregory Peck, risking his livelihood to defend a black man unjustly accused of rape. The movie and book were beloved for their stands against prejudice and Peck won an Oscar, beating out Peter O'Toole in *Lawrence of Arabia*. But as we know from author Harper Lee's fifty-year-delayed sequel, *Go Set A Watchman*, *Mockingbird*'s story was originally meant to be part of an overall depiction of the breakdown of daughter Scout and Atticus Finch's relationship due to Finch's devolution into a reconstructed "polite" southern racist.

An editor wisely suggested that *Mockingbird* could stand on its own as a book, and the rest is literary history. But especially given what we know now both about Lee's work and about new-style racism, *To Kill A Mockingbird*, while still holding up powerfully at its best moments, seems also a little stiff and preachy, and noteworthy more for its black-and-white cinematography and performances by Peck and child actor Mary Badham than its authenticity.

Perhaps Ava DuVernay might have helped her cause by being more conciliatory about the contradictions in her portrait of LBJ, but (to her credit) she wasn't, and even insisted she wasn't trying to provide teachable history, but striving to create a work of art. And so she became part of a two-year snub of African American talent at the Oscars (in that year both Chad Boesman as James Brown and David Oyelowo as Martin Luther King Jr. also didn't receive nominations).

In fact the only truly disturbing depiction of LBJ comes when the President tells J. Edgar Hoover, head of the FBI and an avowed enemy of King, to keep tabs on him. But that scene also acknowledges that LBJ, knowing that with Hoover he had a particularly nasty and even deranged watchdog in the house, preferred to keep him on a leash rather than let him run free.[5] And from a dramatic point of view, if you want an audience to be moved by a character's evolution in the third act, take him down as far as possible in the first. By the end of *Schindler's List*, no one remembers that Oscar Schindler started out pretty much pimping for the SS.

LBJ is ultimately shown as a reluctant President coming to grips with a new reality—and after all it took President Obama and Attorney General Eric Holder, both African Americans, nearly that long to move decisively against voter suppression in the South of today. Is this the right portrayal of LBJ? Did *Zero Dark Thirty* get it exactly right with regard to the use of torture to produce actionable intelligence? Can any historical fiction novelist or filmmaker know how well his or her judgment is working in building characters that are both true to life and imaginary creations?

This essay was originally written as a blog post the week of the Charlie Hebdo massacre in Paris. It's being rewritten as Donald Trump, self-proclaimed enemy of the media, ascends to the presidency. Here's what should be paramount in our minds in the face of such circumstances: if readers, viewers, media pundits, nations, and religions insist that journalists, novelists, and screenwriters get the story absolutely right according to their points of view—forget about ever getting the story.

The '60s and the Films of 2014

Maybe it's a coincidence, but as we say goodbye to *Mad Men*, a show about post–World War II advertising business characters incidentally influenced by the transformations of the '60s, a cluster of movies has come out that deal far more directly with the period's history, lifestyle, and legacy.

There has been *Selma*, a landmark evocation of the 1965 civil rights struggle, which has been Oscar-nominated for Best Picture of the Year (though infuriatingly snubbed for Best Actor and Director). Another related film, which received no major nominations at all, is *Get On Up*, the biography of James Brown—not even a nomination for the incandescent lead performance of Chad Boseman.

The film looks at Brown as a pioneer who created the basis of the funk genre and his own brand of soul music—as well as ways to own that brand—over a volcano of personal demons. *Get On Up* explores the counterpoint between the joy and liberation Brown found in his work and the deep-rooted anger that sabotaged almost every aspect of his life; it's sadly ironic that the man who managed to single-handedly bring peace to a city on the verge of a race riot could never find peace himself. A daring departure from most biopics in its quick-changing structure and creative visualizations of Brown's musical process, *Get On Up* reveals how the music and nightmarish racial history of the '60s fed each other to create, in one genius's career, one of the era's musical legacies.

We usually think of '60s music as soul, funk, and rock, not jazz. But some of the greatest jazz came from that period: Miles Davis's quintets, Horace Silver and Art Blakey's "hard bop," and the John Coltrane Quartet. Some of the best rock music of the era was influenced by Coltrane—Roger McGuinn's lead guitar solo on The Byrds' "Eight Miles High," for example—and groups like Blood, Sweat and Tears and Jethro Tull wove jazz extensively into their songs.

That's why I wish this year's celebrated film set in the world of jazz, *Whiplash*, honored that legacy more. J.K. Simmons truly earned his Golden Globe and Oscar for his performance as Fletcher, the splenetically abusive jazz teacher, and writer-director Damien Chazelle's dialog writing and razor-sharp direction add up to one hell of a debut.

Too bad the film itself is bullshit. *Whiplash* turns the jazz world's combination of competitiveness but also collaboration and sharing of any number of hardships into a kind of all-American jazz boot camp, a "Survivor: Birdland" where only the toughest (and yes, whitest) musician gets the prize. As Fletcher whips, and at one point literally smacks, young drummer Andrew into jazz submission and perfection, he repeatedly exhorts him to shape up with the story of how young Charlie Parker, trying and failing in a "cutting" competition jam session, had a cymbal thrown at his head by disgusted drummer Philly Jo Jones. Leaving aside the fact that this story may be apocryphal (an elegant word for "bullshit"), *Whiplash*'s version is bullshit squared, for in the actual story the cymbal is thrown at Parker's feet, not his head. It's the gestural difference between "you're sad, come back when you've got it together," and "get off this bandstand before I kill you."

That's pretty much how Fletcher treats Andrew, literally almost getting him killed at one weirdly melodramatic point. Fletcher's outright abuse of Andrew in an academic setting in a top conservatory draws some consequences, but is ultimately an obstacle to be gotten past rather than the career-ender it would actually be. And in the film's most ridiculous touch, we're asked to believe that Fletcher, having presumably smacked around many young up-and-coming jazz musicians in New York, has a comfortable life as a respected jazz combo leader in the city's tight-knit musical world.

By the end of *Whiplash*, it's clear Fletcher has brought Andrew up to his exacting standards, and also created a fellow musical monster who turns his back on his family and his girlfriend to join but then surpass Fletcher's little cult. It's at least a sophisticated ending, and I don't pretend to know how jazz conservatories actually operate (although I suspect Wynton Marsalis doesn't beat his musicians). But in terms of the legacy of the jazz of the '60s, with its spirit of musical sharing and yes, caring underneath the "cutting," the movie is both a flat and sour note.

To go from dissonance to delight (as also in—addendum 2016— Chazelle's second film, the musical *La La Land*; through getting marvelously unreal he got far more real about love, showbiz, and jazz) *Inherent Vice* is not only a well-done adaptation of a Thomas Pynchon novel—and whoever thought that would happen?—but a witty evocation of L.A. '60s–'70s stonerdom. Writer-director Paul Thomas Anderson gets the look, the wardrobe, and the casting just right, but more importantly he navigates the book's loopy complexities with aplomb and authentic soul. Pynchon is a world-class author known not only for a Joycean level of worldplay but the creation of complicated mytho-poetic subterranean systems in his novels. His *Gravity's Rainbow* is a book to struggle through in college or when you have a lot of time on your hands. But *Inherent Vice*, though it also has its conspiratorial underground, is accessible and very funny, and Anderson and Joaquin Phoenix, dope-y/clever and sweetly big-hearted as private investigator Doc, sail through the storyline.

Inherent Vice may not make that much sense, but the point of this private eye comedy is not the plot but Doc's attempt to locate both a vanished millionaire and Doc's hippie chick love, a regular vanishing act in his own life. The movie's visuals and scenes are more colorful exaggerations than believable renderings of the period, but they're true to the era's spirit of wild dreams, sexual excess, paranoia, and genuine integrity about peaceful and loving goals and a spirit of live-and-let-live. The scene in which Doc watches his sometime ally/sometime nemesis, madman cop "Bigfoot" Bjornsen, played by Josh Brolin, order sushi in top-volume Japanese, is priceless; in Doc's eyes is a combination of bewilderment, open-mindedness, and even a bit of admiration for how bizarre the moment is and Bigfoot's ability to pull it off—hey, if you're going to be hounded and even beaten by an insane cop, it's better if it's one that you have a sneaking and reciprocated fondness for. That may be good vibrations Pynchon/Paul Thomas Anderson-style rather than Beach Boys-style, but it's good enough, and funnier.

So it seems that the films of 2014 touched on almost every aspect of the '60s except the antiwar movement—but as it turned out, indirectly, one major film did that as well. *American Sniper* may not be about the Vietnam War, but in its story and in some of the media reaction to the movie it brings back all those angry ghosts.

If you grew up a left-wing New York kid in the '60s and '70s, Clint Eastwood was not your friend. He was a typical shoot-'em-up tv cowboy who became the avenging vigilante Man With No Name and Dirty Harry, and almost simultaneously a right-wing pro-war icon—along with John Wayne, the man young baby boomers loved to hate.

But he then slowly became a great filmmaker, and in his focus on Westerns and his versatility with genres our truest successor to John Ford and Howard Hawks. And his best movies are steeped in the awareness of the terrible responsibility of the typical Eastwood heroes, the loner gunman and the enforcer. In *Unforgiven*, his greatest, where he plays western gunslinger William Munny, he tells a young boy who realizes he doesn't have what it takes to kill people that killing a man "takes away everything he has and everything he's gonna have," and the cost of living that kind of life is all over Munny's ravaged face.

The cost of being "America's most lethal sniper" is also all over Bradley Cooper's tightly wound performance as Chris Kyle, and is built into a story that shifts from battle scenes in Iraq to Kyle's growing post-traumatic stress disorder between tours of duty. For all Eastwood's right-of-center views, for all his bravura work directing *American Sniper's* battle scenes, which pulled in the box office all over the country, his movie is truly and disturbingly thoughtful about war and its aftermath.

One of the worst legacies of Vietnam is our ambiguous attitude about the men and women this country sends to war. The soldiers who were drafted to fight in Vietnam came back to not only crappy care at the VA (see *Born On The Fourth Of July*, book and movie) but insults like "baby-killer"; the ones who fought in Iraq came back to crappy care at the VA and thanks-for-your-service-and-good-luck. As a people, we may prefer to evade and look past the consequences of sending soldiers off to arrogant and horribly mistaken wars of choice, but as an artist, Eastwood shows us those consequences. This darkest of all legacies of the '60s—the lesson of Vietnam that Colin Powell remembered in the first Gulf War and chose to forget in the second—is felt in *American Sniper*, and makes the film, if not one of Eastwood's best, one that needs to be remembered in this year of recalling the legacies of the '60s.

Loved It Madly, But Not the History
Mad Men was great television, but hardly the last word on its era.

Now that *Mad Men* has passed into pop culture memory, it's worth considering the implications of the show having been the only view of '60s history that most living Americans have ever known.

Mad Men, which its creator, Matthew Weiner, once defined as a story of the World War II generation—*not* the baby boomers—facing the cultural disruptions of the '60s, has been appropriated by baby boomers as the iconic portrait of their era. Such is the alchemy of television's recasting of historical events that a show whose inspirations included John Cheever's caustically skewed visions of postwar suburbia; Gregory Peck's portrayal of a '50s adman with World War II PTSD in *The Man in the Grey Flannel Suit*; and Billy Wilder's acidic view of New York high-end business life and sexual mores in *The Apartment* has become a lens through which events that occurred many years and cultural leaps later have been examined and judged.

Mad Men's potency in reevaluating '60s history was directly connected to its allure as entertainment. It was different, it was powerful, it was high drama with a hint of mystery, and it was great fun. I was such a fan that I paid for a podcast of the JFK assassination show that I had missed, something I've never done for any show since.

The program was in some ways a traditional workplace show which, like a Steve Bochco-David Milch cop show or *Law and Order*, took you inside a vital occupation and showed you both its highs and lows. But it centered the action around a mysterious antihero—not a troubled straight-arrow like the '80s *Hill Street Blues*'s Frank Furillo, but a truly lost soul—and that made it a breakthrough that anticipated shows like *Breaking Bad* and *True Detective Season 1*. It also established a third tier of quality television beyond primetime and premium, with movie-level production values. And it trusted the audience to go with an allusive and ironical presentation of its characters' journeys through a morally compromising world in a way that was unprecedented.

One way the show seduced us into watching such a new and strange approach was through its sexy surfaces, a vision that stressed '60s high style more than journalistic reality. But it was a view that, however heightened, was dramatically valid because it reflected the point-of-view, the yearnings, the womanizing, and the life's labor and obsession of its major character.

Don Draper, as his name implied, was brilliant at laying beautiful illusions on both the public and his own life, as well as laying of the other kind (as in "Don Juan" complex).

As such, he was admirably suited to be master of a universe where, as Marshall McLuhan stated in his *Understanding Media*, American advertising stressed iconic and seductive images and the products themselves as part of larger social purposes and promises, embodied in the commercial storyboards that *Mad Men* so smartly mimicked.[1] The goal, according to McLuhan, was the "complex togetherness of the corporate posture" and a "programmed harmony of production and consumption…"[2] Don Draper was always giving the people what they wanted, namely consumer goods embracing and guiding almost every aspect of life (and, as far as women went, giving them Don Draper).

And in a show that reveled in ironies, it was a particularly delicious one, as well as a witty statement about the lies and delusions within the industry molding our dreams, that the man who was a master of programming that harmony was a shell of a human being quietly going nuts, trying to create collective identity while his own fell apart. The animated teaser for the show was an image of that classic Camus absurdist moment where a man looks around and his whole life falls away like a stage set. Down Don went past the floors of a New York skyscraper in a silhouette reminiscent of Saul Bass movie graphics of the '50s and '60s, as he plummeted past the glistening icons of his own making. Much of the tension of the show was in how Don was ultimately going to take that fall.

And so we watched Don Draper's seven-season dive down, and as we did our view of the time and place became Don's view, a fairly bleak and jaundiced one. But it's time to appreciate what sophisticated and juicy entertainment that was while not being persuaded by its perspective, separating the portrait lens from the wide-angle one.

From the beginning, the show gave short shrift to the counterculture of the era, and also laid a sleek/chic sangfroid over a predominant culture that, even at its WASPiest, roiled with discontents (the DeCaprio-Winslet movie *Revolutionary Road* caught that unrest better). After all, this was the period where the white picket fence suburbs, as in some David Lynch movie, never quite buried the film noir/ghetto/Rat Pack/wham-bam/Kennedy assassination pustulence under the flower beds, and with the Vietnam war, the outrages against African-Americans, and the buildup of sexual and artistic ferment, the body politic finally exploded.

But in fairness to Mr. Weiner, neither his budget nor his post–World War II angle on the '60s allowed for inclusion of the Columbia student strike or Newark riots or Woodstock or the whole hundred-flowers-bloom riotousness of the era. It's the aspects of the counterculture the show did attempt to capture that require a second look.

Not surprisingly, key developments of the '60s, viewed from the jaded sophisticate realms of Madison Avenue glamour professions, didn't come out very well—shabby, threatening, at best a distraction from affairs of the office and the heart. Artists and hippies living in the Village or on a commune came off as garbage-scroungers, parasites, morons, and, at worst, cultish brainwashers of Roger Sterling's daughter. New York Mayor John V. Lindsay's courageous walk through an African-American ghetto after the King assassination, where he went into agitated crowds and shared their grief and thus averted a riot in the city, was described by Betty Draper's second husband Henry Francis as Lindsay "smiling as if it were a pancake breakfast." Meanwhile those African Americans' struggles were hinted at on the show but at best tangentially explored.

Above all, the war in Vietnam was handled in the same terms as men (only men back then) enlisting would be handled today. It broke the hearts of the women left behind. It prompted confused feelings in another woman who wasn't sure if the young enlistee was doing it because he had a crush on her. The political context of the war was at least suggested by a bitter argument or two but then set aside, certainly by the time the show's 1968 period rolled around, when domestic fury over the war was at its height.

Perhaps that's because of Weiner's expressed view of the Vietnam War and the resistance to it by the baby boom generation, which he shared on an episode of the *Colbert Report*. "What really happened is there was a generation that was asked very little of, they got education, they got a lot of entertainment, a lot of spending money, they became the focus of the economy, of entertainment, everything. There was a war going on and they were supposed to fight, some of them didn't … the generation before them, all of them fought."[3]

Weiner quickly admitted he'd been a bit "judgmental." That's an understatement about ignoring that the Vietnam War, unlike

World War II, was not solemnly debated, followed by a constitutional declaration in Congress, and pursued with almost total national unity. Like George W. Bush's second Iraq war, the Vietnam War resulted from a grant of emergency powers to the President based on a provocation, the supposed firing on an American ship in the Tonkin Gulf, that turned out to be a lie. Most young men—including, for two years, college students—were faced with a draft lottery which, if they lost, would buy them a compulsory ticket to that controversial war, where they could see on television and *Life* Magazine how they might come back badly wounded or dead. Meanwhile many had adopted antiwar positions and believed the war in Vietnam was an immoral, illegal, undeclared war, wrong on every level. And they were led by members of the World War II generation, like Robert F. Kennedy and Dr. Benjamin Spock, and by protest and musical leaders of the Korean War "silent generation" who were silent no longer, like Tom Hayden and William Sloane Coffin and Bob Dylan and many of the great '60s rock musicians.

Given Weiner's view on Vietnam, and his views, also expressed on that Colbert show, that the baby boom generation had a "rosy version" view of the '60s, it's no wonder the show ended the cynical way it did. It was, to give Weiner credit, a genuinely open ending; Weiner did his mentor David Chase of *The Sopranos* one better in providing a conclusion that was ambiguous not because the camera was turned off, but because there really were different ways to interpret it.

Given all that suspense about how hard Don was going to hit bottom, it was kind of a soft landing: a sojourn among West Coast hippies that was fairly bland. And yet it was during a late-'60s style "encounter session" that Don received the blast of emotional truth that he needed to lose all the bullshit and finally shed the false identity with which he had shielded himself ...

... and turn the experience into one dynamite ad campaign when he came back to all the bullshit. Or not. Did major action happen offscreen in a massive time cut, with Don, after raising his consciousness '60s-style, going back to the Coca Cola account (don't you miss Coke, he'd been asked) and using his great revelation to create the post-hippie "I'd Like To Teach The World To Sing" campaign? Or was the commercial more like the song at the tail of the show, tangentially connected to the main action: Don Draper really did discover a new way of thinking and feeling and living, really did shed his skin and transform, but the next Don Draper found a way to turn that process into a cynical, meaningless sales pitch for the all-American soft drink.

Or did it matter? Isn't the point that Don-Draper-ness never stops? There's always someone coming up who, in the words of the David Bowie song, wants to be the man who sold the world, wants to program consumer desires harmoniously—just like *Mad Men*, in its way, shaped our reaction to the '60s. However you interpret the ending, it now appears part of a clever, funny, and basically conservative take on the era.

One thing *Mad Men* did get right, in terms of personal and historical truth and free of any conservatism, was the difficult climb of its female characters. Perhaps the most effective irony of *Mad Men* is that what held the show together and made it work were sane women. So much so that you could almost see the show as symbolically about the end of the dominant white male era, the passing of the torch at least in part to women both in the era it takes place in and the television of today.

But half the story remains to be told. When will the dissent and activism, both comic and tragic, of the '60s make it to the large or small screen? (It's been awhile since the largely overlooked films *Steal This Movie* and *Panthers*). When will we acknowledge in our media, in anything other than the occasional historical documentary, that women weren't the only ones fighting their way from beneath the shadows of the "mad men," who in our own time—no longer with a postwar sense of duty, ethical seriousness, openness to new ideas, and love of education—have become Michael Moore's "stupid white men" and have elected President Trump? Struggles over wars, voting rights, racial injustice, bad cops, censorship—all these very current battles were being enacted in Manhattan back when Roger Sterling, Don Draper, and their ilk were ruling their roost from the suburbs or their high-style ad-world bubble. There was a whole cast of African Americans, Latinos, gays, students, artists, intellectuals, musicians, and activists engaged in a very colorful battle with the oppressive establishment of the '60s, one which we're still sorting out.

The time is still ripe, with regard to looking at the '60s, for what psychoanalysis calls the return of the repressed. *Mad Men* was a great and groundbreaking show but to say, as one article did, that with its end the '60s are over—that's the maddest line of all.

The N-Word and Other Shocks to The System

Overall I agree with the Chris Rock rule that states "Can a white person say 'nigger'? Not...REALLY!" But I'll be using the word here for the purposes of historical recollection and making points about that history.

The '60s were, collectively, a time of conscious taboo- and boundary-shattering in all sorts of art and media: music, painting, novels, film, theater, video, and standup comedy. So naturally it was a time when the censors were very busy protecting "The System."

Television was their most successful stomping ground. Every so often an act broke through—as when Jim Morrison promised Ed Sullivan that the Doors would leave out the word "higher" when they performed their hit short version of "Light My Fire," and then, during the performance, he rushed up to shout that word directly at the camera. But on the CBS show that followed Sullivan, *The Smothers Brothers Comedy Hour*, which was considered a "with it" show, the gentlest attempts to allude to drugs, heavy-handed policing (anyone remember Officer Judy?), politics, and war were often met with the censor's axe.

The more Hollywood-attuned *Rowan and Martin's Laugh-In* was risqué silly and more censor-friendly (with its catchphrases like "Blow in my ear and I'll follow you anywhere," or mocking the conservative criminal justice system with "Here come da judge!"). But Tommy and Dick Smothers had come up performing their combination of music and comedy in the Greenwich Village folk scene, were politically aware, and kept the very civilized but censor-challenging material coming. Tommy Smothers took the issue of censorship directly to FCC commissioner Kenneth Cox at the National Association of Broadcasters.

They ultimately lost the battle and, as soon as CBS could get away with it, their program. Dick Cavett's smart and gutsy talk show of the era also faced such struggles, and Cavett once had a show featuring four of the Chicago 7 defendants—Tom Hayden, Abbie Hoffman, Jerry Rubin, and Rennie Davis—outright canceled on him.

Meanwhile, outside other medias' kingdoms, the barbarians were definitely at the gates. In the world of novels, many writers and booksellers had been defying censorship since the 1940s. Philip Roth, our great writer who has always had a streak of performance comedy in him—he revealed on a televised interview that *Portnoy's Complaint* grew in part out of a kind of schtick he enjoyed doing for his fellow writers[1]—published that book with its then shocking language and sexual passages to near-universal acclaim. And the country's best comics were busy dismantling the barriers between "clean" comedy and political awareness, sexuality, and obscenity, especially in the use of the word "nigger."

It wasn't called the "n-word" back then, and it was indulged in freely by bigots and racists, especially down south, where it was used as a part of denying basic rights and humanity to African Americans and was sometimes accompanied by beatings, shootings, and lynchings. As James Baldwin said in a 1960s public television interview, "We didn't invent the nigger. White people invented him."[2]

Our current strategy against the use of this hateful word in the world of the new Jim Crow of mass incarceration, resegregation of neighborhoods, and neglect of inner city schools is censorship. You're not supposed to say it, and Chris Rock has a point. But the other side of Baldwin's quote is that white people can conceivably uninvent the nigger, and the best way to do that is to not repress the word and sweep it under the rug but to confront it and all it means.

That's how African Americans and their white supporters opposed to everything that word stood for reacted during the '60s when the word represented a more brutal and pervasive and oppressive racist system. They took it over. Black activist leader Stokely Carmichael said, in response to Martin Luther King's assassination in 1968, that now was the time to find out "if all the scared niggers are dead."

So the use of the word in the '60s and especially in the '70s didn't represent black weakness, but in an indirect way black power. Richard Pryor, once he broke out of his Ed Sullivan "clean humor" performing shell, would use the word to bring his hilarious sketches of African American life and characters alive and subvert it in any number of ways. And growing up in the '60s as a sympathetic white kid joining African American kids in political activities, I saw any number of instances of the totally domesticated use of the word in the black community, robbing it of its evil, slyly making fun of it, a most recent example of which was Larry Wilmore daring to affectionately refer to President Obama that way (and he took it in good grace).

But there was one white comic who dared to use it to devastating effect. Lenny Bruce was all about robbing racial and sexual epithets of the power the censors gave them. He reclaimed those words' anger so that it could be tamed and their lust so it could be enjoyed. Above all he wanted people to face the truth, however nasty, inherent in those words. "What I want people to dig … is the lie."[3] And so he used uncensored language to break through the bullshit, much like his standup comic descendant George Carlin would later do in his "Seven Little Words" and "Soft Language" comedy pieces.

Lenny Bruce was, as they say, a little before my time (although YouTube fortunately is, within the video era, timeless). He was also a little before his own time, often falling into what he called the "semantic bear trap of bad taste" before he became outright obscene and addicted to heroin enough to be not just trapped but often arrested for his comedy and lifestyle. He would ultimately die of an overdose, the pictures of his corpse in the bathroom shamelessly circulated by the police.

When asked what offended him, Bruce listed, among other causes, "Governor [Orval] Faubus and segregation." Protests against Jim Crow down south had long been a subgenre of jazz, such as in "Strange Fruit," the classic Billie Holiday song about lynching. Jazz bassist and composer Charles Mingus made much of his music in the '60s a programmatically direct protest; there were no words in a piece like "Fables of Faubus," though sometimes Mingus chanted some on the spot, but the title said enough, along with the two parts of the melody, suggesting both a bumptious nasty clown and a combination of world-weariness but also fierce energy in fighting the offense of Governor Faubus's southern racist policies.

Lenny Bruce took that furious protest into his comedy. In a remarkable experimental theater biography of his life I did get to see, *Lenny*, the actor Cliff Gorman performed him doing a bit where President Johnson tries to say "Negro" but can't stop saying "nigger." It was an unfair sendup of our greatest African American civil rights president since Lincoln. But no one has ever accused comedy of being polite or fair, and besides, if the bit had been about arch-segregationists like Governors Faubus or George Wallace trying to not say the word, it wouldn't've worked because they wouldn't've tried. What Lenny Bruce was getting at was that race hatred was so comically persistent that even when it's of total political and personal benefit to get rid of it you can't.

Taking over the that word was a way of confronting that hatred and what we now call implicit bias and institutional racism head on, as opposed to censoring it and hoping it will go away. These days we make it "politically incorrect" and all the more tempting for the bigots among us. We give it its power back.

So what if, the next time an unarmed black man is shot, protesters parade with buttons and signs with his picture and the word "Nigger," next to pictures of black police officers and leaders with the same word? Or if a protest against mass incarceration featured protesters carrying signs, each with a picture of a different black man behind bars, and that word? Would it be disrespecting the leaders and prisoners and victims? Or would it be telling every white person who saw those photos, and who think of themselves as "post-racist," that they're part of a system and country that treats African Americans in the way the word symbolizes? That they may not use that word, but (as Lenny Bruce often tried to tell us) they think it and believe it and live within its shadow?

Race hate words weren't the only taboo language taken on in the '60s. Obscenity in general was gleefully adopted in the service of sexual liberation and not being "uptight" and "boo-zhwah" in general. Here's a small example of rhetoric of the time, from *Rat* magazine: "Jesus Talked Dirty" and "I hereby offer my thanks to all the fucking aluminum companies—Reynolds, Alcoa, etc.—for this particular variety of shit (pull tabs) that fucks up our environment." Spraying obscenity around was the easiest way to offend the Establishment. It was part of a lot of other assaults on "uptight" sensibilities: dressing down (or up in convention-defying ways), even sitting down at a "rug concert" at Lincoln Center (infuriating some conductors) or even on a New York sidewalk, an unimaginable breach of protocol back then.

And also getting down—along with scatological language taboos, sexual taboos were also smashed. In the early '60s, in left-wing periodicals like *The Village Voice*, nudity showed up not just in porn but in movies we'd now call soft-core porn: *Sex in Sweden*, or *Heaven and Hell*, narrated by aging-out-of-Hollywood British actor Edmund Purdom, all gleefully X-rated (it used to be a boast at times). By the late '60s, an X-rated movie, *Midnight Cowboy*, won the Best Picture Oscar. Nudity in movies went from outrage to fad, constantly present in adult movies from 1967 on, especially in sexually explicit foreign imports like *I Am Curious (Yellow)* but also in Anglo-American comedies like the young Brian DePalma's *Greetings*.

Yes, kids, this sort of stuff percolated in the back of your grandparents' and parents' dawning consciousnesses (in case they ever get too angry at you for your lifestyle). Even *Life* Magazine had pictures of bare-assed models and a VW van ad that said "You'll never lose it in a parking lot."

Movies also, while slathering on the nudity and sex, took aim at every target from the war machine—depicted often with taboo-busting horrific violence that pioneered the violent effects of today—to racism, to advertising (and in the case of Robert Downey Sr.'s ferociously funny and subversive film, *Putney Swope*, the last two at the same time). Theater was even more outrageous. Live tableau of any kind inevitably attracts more daring and physically "out there" forms of expression. That kind of performance art had roots in the '60s in everything from the sexually and politically confrontational plays of Jean Genet to the street theater and "happenings," public art events often of a destructive variety, staged in New York neighborhoods.

A lot of theater of the time reveled in horniness and anger, but also sought pure shock, jolting people out of their comfort zone sexually and politically. In the case of the Broadway revue *Oh Calcutta!* the nudity was mainly for titillation and laughs. But in an off-off-Broadway theater piece like *CHE!* the point was to explore the boundary between revolutionary sex and politics, the oppressions of both kinds, as when Che Guevara is taunted, sexually confronted, and terrorized by a Castro played by a naked cigar-smoking woman. Whatever you thought of the play—many didn't think much of it and the cast was arrested at one performance for obscenity, public lewdness, and consensual sodomy (for what appeared to be live sex)—it was certainly true that, as one reviewer wrote, it "tests the limits of sex on stage."[4]

And then there was theater that actually tried to make viewers feel in the moment some sort of political outrage and empathy with rebels or even tried to share visionary experience with its viewers. Such theater drew on experience the show's creators had had out on the streets, or on drugs—especially LSD trips—or, most profoundly, attempts to live an alternative lifestyle and share its benefits with the public.

What we'd now call "immersion theater" was utilized in the '60s to make people feel what it might like to be in an inner city neighborhood at moments of maximum crisis. In one particularly provocative example of such "gut-theater," *RIOT* at Boston's OM Theater Workshop,[5] whites battled blacks with real bayonets and karate chops hovering near the audience. Out of the darkness came beer cans and bodies flying, shots and explosions, writhing figures, smoke from something burning, moments all culled from the Newark riots in a church basement (the lone critic there did get a cut from some flying object). The involuntary audience participation was justified by the statement "Lifestyle and performing style are not separate." (Such pronouncements and attempts to induce white guilt in frightened but determinedly *au courant* theatergoers of course attracted satire, especially in a segment of the early Brian DePalma film *Hi, Mom!*)

Drug experience informed the explosions of colors and distorted sounds of "psychedelic" art and music and made its way into theater as well. The era was marked, as has been told ad infinitum, with much "experimenting" with marijuana, but also more intensely with psychedelic drugs like mescaline and LSD/acid for "consciousness expanding" purposes—and that was not to be scoffed at. Acid was a bit like playing Russian Roulette with your sanity: in the fifth chamber was the potential bad trip from which (as in the case of one friend of mine) you might never come back. But many reported ravishing hallucinations and visions of the oceanic oneness of life, and before it became a controlled substance, the drug was used to ameliorate conditions such as frigidity, alcoholism, and end-of-life depression, and both LSD and "magic mushrooms" are coming back into use for these limited purposes today.

In fact, members of the elite of the media and the arts of the 1950s like Claire Booth Luce and Cary Grant discovered it first (described in a lyric by the postpunk band The Godfathers: "Things ain't what they used to be/Cary Grant's on LSD"[6]). Grant memorably described LSD experiences as "controlled dreams" that freed him from the shackles of his subconscious fears and demons and allowed him to really "connect with himself." In one such experience he imagined himself as a "giant penis launching off from Earth like a spaceship ... I seemed to be in a world of healthy, chubby little babies' legs and diapers, smeared blood, a sort of general menstrual activity taking place."[7]

Other than causing us never to look at *North By Northwest* or *Bringing Up Baby* quite the same way again, such descriptions help us to see where some of the more outrageous and primal visions of '60s theater, as well as similar scenes in movies like *Easy Rider* and *The Trip*, came from. But whether drug-induced or not, productions found inspiration in the combination of visions and ecstasy, drunkenness and music, and appetites of the infantile id and adult lusts for violence, creation, and destruction that all combined in the myths of Dionysus/ Bacchus the wine god. In *Dinoysus in 1969*[8] (a.k.a. *Dionysos '69*) Richard Schechner's performance group mixed modern re-creation of ancient rites, nudity, improv, chanting, and a simulated birth of Dionysus through the naked spread legs of the young women of the company. To see it on film is to see a group trying to reach back to some sort of raw and primitive emotional state, mixing in confessional personal stories, all the while depicting modern theatrical versions of ancient rituals while stating "there's only one ritual in the country now, it's killing."[8] The hope was that the other rituals and a submergence in their visions and states of mind could liberate us and counter that mechanical route to death.

No such hope was present in the so-called "hippie" version of Euripides' *The Bacchae* put on at the Yale Repertory Theater. Critics may have made reference to its ancient versions of love-ins, drug trips, and freak-outs, but there was no way to make more relevantly enjoyable for '60s theatergoers the tragedy's message of the ghastly consequences of divine madness, illustrating Euripides' counsel that we must find a balance, responsibility, and restraint against the great and dangerous powers of Dionysus.

That was not a popular message in the Dionysiac '60s. But it at least was implicit in disciplined art that tried to disorient and wake up the senses and the subconscious, possibly even providing a near-equivalent to a drug trip, without use of any drugs—whether it was abstract art, scientifically precise but intriguingly disorienting "op" art, art that tried to jar us into new ways of thinking about how the nimbus of advertising and consumerism affects/effects us (Andy Warhol and James Rosenquist), or multimedia that ranged from the Joshua Light Show that played behind rock acts in the Fillmore East to the video art provocations of Nam June Paik to conceptual art exhibits that tricked or bombarded your senses with all sorts of images, words, and loud sounds. Disarranging and jolting the senses to get beyond conventional oppressive assumptions of politics, of society, of sex, of our very perceptions, to free us into a world of greater equality, joy, peace, and love—it was all a part of this intriguing strange brew.

Perhaps the ultimate expression of all this, at least the most "mind-blowing" one for me, was the Living Theater.[9] The show was presented by the Open Theater at Hunter College Assembly Hall at 68th Street and Park Avenue (where I'd previously, if you can believe this, seen

Cream) and produced by the Radical Theater Repertory. This 1968 cooperative group, which included the Open Theater and Bread and Puppet Theater, had among its other goals sustaining and extending the radical community, sharing voluntary poverty, and making experimental "collective creations" dedicated to "exploring space, time, minds, and bodies"[9] in new ways.

The Living Theater was led by Julian Beck, who was partially bald but long-tressed and looked like a Hindu mystic, and his wife Judith Malina. "Le Living," as it was known in Europe, had become famous for productions that had roused the wonder of audiences and the ire of authorities worldwide.

I knew we were in for the proverbial heavy shit when we were presented with a chart at the beginning of the show. There were sketches of what looked like a Swami and a Queequeg-like figure, kabbalistic lettering on one hand, religious symbols on the other. Reading from bottom up on the chart, one progressed through all sorts of ascending rows amounting to a reconfiguration of society and human life, in little boxes that looked like what would now be sketches for Power Point presentations. They were labeled with titles like "The Sexual Revolution: The Exorcism of Violence," and moved up through "Revolution!" of Action, Transformation, and Being (which included, for all NASA fans, and we all were, "The Vision of Landing on Mars") through Love and Heaven, to the topmost rungs, the ultimate goals of "Abundance. Fullness. The Permanent Revolution. Change!" and "The Rung of God and Man."

There would be eight sections to *Paradise Now*, each with a rite and a vision. "Paradise" would be a process, the revolution itself, getting past "ego ethics" and "authority power" and changing without violence the hearts of men. *Paradise Now* would confront and invite the spectator into action.

That confrontation started with the Living Theater members, skinny, half-starved looking, dressed in skin tight leotards, moving through the audience screaming things like "I cannot travel without a passport", "I can't stop the war!" "I can't save the earth!" Pretty soon audience members were either screaming along or screaming arguments at them. When they at last gathered on the stage, faced the audience, and screamed "I'm not allowed to take my clothes off!" the crowd laughed, anticipating some nudity, but none was provided. Instead they were soon leading theatergoers in a chant of

"Paradise Now!", which Jim Morrison talked about joining in the production he saw.

The rest is a mostly forgotten blur, but I do remember that they enacted "The Rite of Universal Intercourse" as a group of writhing bodies on the floor which theatergoers could join if they wished. I also remember a Ring of Prayer, and that I was touched in my youthful and still very hopeful being by the experience, for that's what it was and what it was meant to be. The exhortations spilled out into the street (the show didn't end so much as dissolve and overflow). There was a lot of animated discussion about everything from getting rid of the money system to ending outworn models of marriage to not just a power shift but an end to power. There were also people yelling that the Living Theater had created a situation, but didn't deal with it, and had no idea of how to truly change the power structure represented by the Park Avenue they were standing on.

That void at the heart of sociopolitically minded art and media confronts us more than ever in the present day. One way for artists and media workers to dismiss that void is to stick to decorative art, installation art, art for art's sake (which has inevitably devolved to art for art collector's sake).

The other way is to do what the Chinese artist Ai Weiwei did in February of 2016. He attached 14,000 lifejackets from migrants who had crossed the Aegean to the pillars of the Berlin Konnzerthaus, commemorating refugees drowned at sea. Having previously (and very controversially) created a photo of himself replicating the photo of the little Syrian boy whose drowned body was found on the shore, he then one-upped that act of artistic subversion at the red carpet ceremony of the Berlin Cinema for Peace gala. The celebrity and wealthy guests walked past a rubber lifeboat, and once inside were asked to don thermal heat-preserving emergency jackets that had been placed on the nearly drowned migrants for a photo op the German press described as particularly outrageous.

One can understand the Berlin response. After all, Germany has admitted more refugees than any other country and might interpret the gesture as incredibly ungrateful and unfair. But after all, in the '60s the angriest and longest-lasting protests took place in the United States and France, the countries with the longest-established traditions of democracy and freedom of expression. And the starkness of the contrast Weiwei's actions set up between ultimate wealth and security and poverty shadowed by utter insecurity was a devastating artistic and political statement.

It reminded me of one last group of provocative '60s "shocks to the system," the creating of not just art but actual events with politically, mentally, and spiritually transformational goals. Yippies throwing dollar bills onto the floor of the stock exchange. Ken Kesey and his Merry Pranksters, carrying plenty of LSD, riding their bus Furthur across the country in search of visionary experiences, the subject of Tom Wolfe's *Electric Kool-Aid Acid Test*. Street theater with mock Vietnamese massacres. Demonstrators placing flowers in the guns of national guardsmen. And the nomination by Abbie Hoffman and other counterculture provocateurs of Pigasus the Pig for President, including a (flagrantly tasteless for the '60s) mock-assassination attempt. Such stunts, whether you call them art or not, really made onlookers and participants feel something about the injustices, inequalities, and horrors being dramatized. If an extremely wealthy person dons a thermal jacket at the Cinema for Peace gala, maybe he or she will be more provoked to use that influence they have to make peace a reality.

Can we bring a lot of those '60s shocks to the system back? Probably not in major cities where even the most politically unchallenging theatrical and dance groups can't afford theaters—though 2016's *Party People* at the Public Theater in New York, with its "new counterculture" provocations of the audience and its harking back to the Black Panthers and Young Lords, is a welcome exception that found a home in a long-established venue. Certainly a production like *RIOT*, with all the signing of releases in the world, would probably, on a bad night, run afoul of liability laws. The hard sophisticated ironical shell developed by most consumers (the right word to use now) of art would probably inure them against the kind of emotional appeals made by the Living Theater.

Obscene and raunchy comedy is now second nature and rarely shocks effectively anymore, although in the hands of raunchy women it seems to be getting a second life. Television has moved far beyond the censorship of the '60s, and it's become a little tiresome how on premium cable and YouTube just about anything goes. Nudity in the movies is permanent, while nudity onstage, at least on Broadway, might have just met its end after *Game of Thrones* star Emilia Clarke's run in a production of *Breakfast At Tiffany's*, where a nude scene practically stopped the show as the men in the audience defied theater policy and whipped out one of their favorite sex substitutes, their smartphone cameras.

The main problem now in the arts is, first of all, conformity, apathy, and philistine stupidity across generations, whether in the trivial app-driven pleasures of the young or the "guilty pleasures" of the old. While support for genuine, let alone experimental art, falls away, gentrification in major cities eats up up arts-supporting neighborhoods. More and more art is manufactured for the consumption of and private exhibitions by the mega-rich.

But somehow artists, musicians, moviemakers confronted equal apathy and philistinism in the '50s and got through to the '60s renaissance with, at first, very little financial wherewithal, and during the Trump presidency, I suspect a whole new wave of such efforts will be made. For example, an oral history documentary play of 1963, Martin Duberman's *In White America*, powerfully drew on songs, journals, historical letters, and recordings of former slaves to depict the historical injustices perpetrated on African Americans (and was quite cheap to produce). There are one-person shows and short YouTube pieces that venture into this territory, as in the work of Anna Deavere Smith and Sarah Jones, but it seems the time is right to update this sort of production with the voices of incarcerated African Americans, kids recovering from gunshot wounds in hospitals, bereaved relatives of unarmed black men shot by police, maybe even the police themselves, and unless a theatergoer can sue for getting angry or heartbroken, there would be no liability problems. One could even go further and have the theatergoer experience (if they signed onto it) what it's like to face the kind of police questions and tactics and arrests young black men encounter at the hands of police.

In the new medium of "screendance," there are combinations of nonverbal action and video or even virtual reality that dramatize the effects of our new media on human thought and emotions, and they could definitely be given more of a political or even spiritual edge; they're already being used to disorient and awaken people's senses and kinesthetic reality. And amid all the art installations that are the latest and lucrative craze, one can read about many that prod our awareness, in sometimes beautiful but sometimes painful and frightening fashion, over what we're doing to the planet. The Endangered Species Mural Project nationwide and the Manhattan Audubon Mural Project to create murals of climate-threatened birds are family-friendly art projects of this sort, while during the climate change negotiations in Paris, far more disturbing installations were created, including, when a People's Climate March was canceled due to terrorism fears, the placement of 20,000 pairs of shoes in the Place de la Republique, linking the two global threats of terrorism and human-caused climate cancer.

The shocks to the system are more oblique now, less emotionally transparent, more caught up in interaction with cyberspace, and superficially gentler, but they're nonetheless stinging and will probably start to sting a lot harder. If we can keep censorship and potential expanded libel or anti-dissent laws and the end of net neutrality from happening, it's a good start for a return to disturbing the peace in order to create more of it.

Marshall McLuhan: Medium of the Media

Just over fifty years ago, a cultural sage warned us about what worldwide media might become.

In 1964 Marshall McLuhan, a Canadian professor and Director of the Center for Culture and Technology at the University of Toronto—about as far from the '60s "what's happening" scene as could be imagined—published a book entitled *Understanding Media: The Extensions of Man*, and became an international sensation.

His book flew off the shelves, the subject of numerous interviews, newspaper articles, and endless bull sessions—the equivalent of hitting the best-seller lists and going viral at the same time. He became the subject of an NBC television show, "This Is Marshall McLuhan." John Lennon and Yoko Ono went to Canada to meet him. McLuhan eventually became so famous that he made a cameo appearance as the punchline of a joke in Woody Allen's Academy Award-winning film *Annie Hall*.

What the hell was all the fuss about?

In his first teaching post McLuhan wondered why his students, only a few years younger than he, might as well have been from another planet, operating under a whole different set of influences. At a time when the "generation gap" was becoming a hot subject, McLuhan figured out what some of those perceptual influences were: the very media through which we extend our bodies (the wheel, the railroads, jet travel) and above all through which we project our thoughts and communicate (print and electronic) which then, in a form of feedback, create a new environment and change the way we conduct our affairs. In effect new media had changed his students, the new-media-users, into different kinds of people.

McLuhan's stunningly ambitious book, *Understanding Media: The Extensions of Man*, covered just about every kind of "media," from roads to typewriters to photographs, but he had the most impact talking about books, movies, radio, television, and what was then called "automation"—computers and their potential to link all human consciousnesses in truly global communication. His most famous saying proclaimed "the medium is the message" because it is the "medium that shapes and controls the scale and form of human association and action ... Our human senses, of which media are extensions, utilize our energies and thus in the way they are applied change our awareness."[1]

Why, for example, were the youth of the '60s so different from their parents? To boil down some wildly complex ideas, for McLuhan books and the printed word, the main media of the older generation, were a mechanical age linear form of communication molding the reader's thoughts, driving and promoting specialized ideas and work. Print helped to create individualized Western man with his fixed point of view, detachment, information absorption, and noninvolvement in the tribalism of earlier history. That, and the fact that print extended a single sense, the visual, in high definition and filled it with data, made print and books a "hot" medium (movies, a narrative byproduct of literacy, were also hot).

But with television and electronic computing we enter the '60s electronic age, the age of the "cool" medium when we're not molded by our media, but participate and interact, because "our [entire] central nervous system is technologically extended to involve us in the whole of mankind and incorporate the whole of mankind in us ..."[2] No longer linear and ultra-specialized, we join with the world and many forms of human endeavor on many levels, and want deeper work roles and commitment to society. And in one of McLuhan's most important insights, the inclusivity of cool media was based on the near-simultaneous speed of electronic communication. First radio, then television and computers, would draw the world together so completely as to tribalize it and create a "global village."

McLuhan came up with all this in 1964—in videos he gives the impression of a man amused by his own intellectual fireworks. But isn't this all a little goofy? Doesn't the "cool" medium also involve words? Well, yes, but it subsumes the medium of print and creates a change in the whole form of environment and communication. New media take over, even "oppress" old media. And secondly, a "cool" medium, even if it contains words, doesn't compel us to certain individualized reactions, but instead draws in our involvement and participation on both an individual and, because it reaches back to more oral forms of communication, a tribal level.

McLuhan landed on rock music as the perfect example of how the media times were indeed a-changing. He wrote that "literacy is still officially the educational establishment, but unofficially oral forms are coming up very fast. ... Rock is a kind of education based on oral tradition, an acoustic experience..." So rock could be "... a central oral form of education" for the new counterculture tribe. "If Homer was wiped out by literacy, literacy can be wiped out by rock."[3]

Such aphorisms, or, as they came to be known, McLuhanisms, had plenty of sloganeering hype; sometimes with McLuhan, as with Timothy Leary, you get the feeling of a madman who could've been a very good "Mad Man." But McLuhan was intellectually rigorous—the sourcing and footnoting of *Understanding Media* saturates the book— and the culture of the '60s proved out some of McLuhan's points.

For McLuhan, "cool" media placed a premium on art in which more information was filled in by the receiver. It seemed to follow his suggestion that movies became more ambiguous, less narrative-dependent creations (*Blow-Up, 2001*) and rock lyrics became aphoristic and mysterious (Jim Morrison's "weird scenes inside the gold mine").[4] Meanwhile the counterculture reached for the tribal and mythical, seeking, for example, Native American earth consciousness and modes of dress, while also, in accordance with McLuhan's descriptions of the effects of new media, seeking greater global roles in, for example, the international ecology and peace movements.

Of course, the Vietnam War, marijuana and LSD use, and non-Western religions influenced a lot of these above-mentioned developments—McLuhan's theory was not all-inclusive—but if a theory enables a great deal of prediction, then his is pretty effective. Here are just some predictions McLuhan made in 1964:

He predicted hot media, for example, the movies, would not die but, under pressure of cool media like television, enter into a portable and accessible phase playing on a cartridge as if on a tv screen. Perhaps Apple should name an iPhone app after him.

He stated that "all media that mix ads with other programming are a form of paid learning ..." since "processing and moving of information is ... easily the dominant means of wealth in the electric world"[5] and advertisers would gladly pay the reader or listener directly for his time or attention. That part came out a little differently—free Internet and data mining—but one thinks of McLuhan when one recalls one of the great statements about digital media: if you don't pay for the product, you are the product.[6]

"Men are suddenly nomadic gatherers of knowledge," he stated. Electric energy creates "patterns of decentralization and diversity in the work to be done" including "self-employment and artistic autonomy" paradoxically "individualizing rather than controlling humankind."[7] It's a fair description of what's become of much of the post-Internet workplace.

In the greater scheme of things, interlinked computers would create new patterns of association that could not only eliminate many specialized jobs (he predicted back in 1964) but also create for people "depth of involvement in their work and human association that our preceding mechanical (substitute something like 'print and the assembly line') technology had destroyed."[8] If you think about all the means of communication and more multifaceted involvement in our work that software programs and the Web have opened up to us, and the huge scale of information and interactions (regardless of their quality, content, and pay scale—a whole other issue) you can grasp McLuhan's point.

To quote one of McLuhan's other book titles, *The Medium Is The Massage*—and yes, he meant "message", but as a Joycean scholar he enjoyed the accidental wordplay, "Mass-Age," in the misprint and let it stand—we have "extended our senses and nerves by various media," he wrote, leading toward "the final phase ... the technological simulation of consciousness."[9] In the mid-'60s, when computers had achieved a few startling innovations—managing offices, writing abstract symphonic music—but still lacked a universal language whereby they could even talk to each other, McLuhan was already envisaging a future where they would become so powerful and pervasive that they would not only become (even if he didn't specifically name it) the Internet, but also change the entire way people thought and behaved. At some points, he sounded positively apocalyptic. "We extend our central nervous system globally, instantly interrelating every human experience ..." and "Might not current translation of our entire lives into the spiritual form of information seem to make of the entire globe, and of the human family, a single consciousness?"[10]

McLuhan by no means enthusiastically embraced this possibility. He once told an interviewer that he never said the global village would be nice. When the medium massages us, sometimes its touch is deeply painful.

McLuhan reached for the myth of Narcissus to define those hypnotized by the power of the media, seeing in it the image of themselves, and who as a result serve what is supposed to serve them.

Using electronic technology we are controlled by it; we become its slaves in exchange for the wealth it provides us. Think about our belief that technology can grow without restraint: what can possibly go wrong with endless data mining by social media or drones over cities or limitless NSA surveillance?

McLuhan predicted accurately that an explosion of information from seen and unseen worlds would drive people into reactionary shells. He wisely foresaw a "spectre of joblessness and propertylessness" when "wealth and work become information factors."[11] Once the world contracted to village size the global media would showcase "village tastes for gossip, rumor and personal malice"[12]—a pretty solid forecast of online shaming and cyberbullying.

And here was an amazing insight: in the electric age small and "backward countries" could effectively combat us by understanding oral propaganda and persuasion; think of ISIS' grasp of the tribalizing power of the Internet. Political power and mastery of new media would go hand in hand; think of Donald Trump mastering social media, specifically Twitter, more than any candidate before him and using it to help catapult himself to the Presidency.[13]

One of McLuhan's most frightening observations deserves to be quoted in full:

> Archimedes once said "Give me a place to stand and I will move the world." Today he would point to our electric media and say "I will stand on your eyes, your ears, your nerves, and your brain, and the world will move in any tempo or pattern I choose." We have leased these "places to stand" to private corporations.[14]

So how does one resist the negative effects of the new media? For one thing, realizing that, as McLuhan stated, new media take over the old. So how do you combat ISIS' use of the Internet? Not with well-written pleas and lectures to misguided young people, but the Internet itself. The federal government has at least made a start with positive outreach online to Muslim youth, but perhaps more direct messages could be tried, the verbal equivalent of Anonymous hackers flat-out taking down ISIS sites: videos like "What It's Like To Be A Sex Slave," testimonies as to what it's like living in a city where people are hung and beheaded in the streets. Gruesome, yes, but as McLuhan teaches us, fight fire with fire, not paper.[15]

McLuhan also felt that "media fallout," both corporate and private, could be combated by education as a kind of "civil defense," such as anti-cyberbullying efforts.[16] And he stated that "when the technology of a time ... powerfully thrusts in one direction, wisdom may call for a countervailing thrust ... the implosion of the electric age can be met with decentralization and flexibility of small centers."[17] Specifically he meant the dissolution of the power of large central universities (already beginning to happen thanks to the growth of MOOC on the Web and, for example, efforts by President Obama to elevate the role of community colleges). But it's a rule that could also be applied to all sorts of smaller social units, perhaps somewhat reminiscent of the communes of the '60s.

Because for McLuhan, electronic media could become so powerfully disorienting on a global scale as to extend both a great promise and a terrible threat to civilization. As author W. Terrence Gordon pointed out "When [McLuhan] published *Understanding Media* in 1964, he was disturbed about mankind's shuffling toward the twenty-first century in the shackles of nineteenth-century perceptions."[18]

McLuhan's prescience came primarily in the form of a warning. In his "Challenge and Collapse" chapter of *Understanding Media* McLuhan quoted Arnold Toynbee in pointing out that times of trouble or rapid change produce militarism and other global nightmares. He later stated, "The stakes are civilization versus tribalism and groupism, private identity versus corporate identity, and private responsiblity versus the group or tribal mandate."[19]

Back in the '60s, when McLuhan defined that challenge, it was hard to see where the defense of the individual, the responsible, the noncorporate would come from. It still is.

198 | FIFTY YEARS AGO TODAY

THE ISSUES

"You know something, people, I'm not black, but there's a whole lots of times I wish I could say I'm not white."

"Trouble Comin' Every Day," from the album *Freak Out!* — **Frank Zappa and the Mothers of Invention**

FIFTY YEARS AGO TODAY – THE ISSUES

JFK: 1963, 1991, and the Twenty-First Century

In 1964 Richard Hofstadter, alarmed by the speeches of Barry Goldwater and the policy ideas of his supporters, published an article in *Harper's* entitled "The Paranoid Style in American Politics." Focusing on "angry minds at work mainly among extreme right-wingers, who have now demonstrated ... how much political leverage can be got out of the animosities and passions of a small minority,"[1] the essay described a syndrome, going back to the early years of the Republic, in which large groups of people come to believe the government has been infiltrated by dangerous outsiders turning the system against ordinary Americans. The "paranoid style" was neither left- nor right-wing, and often rose up at a time of challenges to the status quo racial and religious majority. Hostadter cited as examples 19th-century populists who believed an internationalist (mainly Jewish) "gold ring" was out to destroy America, anti-Masonic movements, nativist anti-Catholicism in the big cities, and in the 20th century Senator Joseph McCarthy's 1950s harangues claiming Communists had infiltrated every branch of the American media and government, which built to a crackpot crusade that destroyed hundreds of careers in Hollywood and Washington, DC and was only stopped (barely) when McCarthy took on the US Army.

As Hofstadter stressed, these movements were more a matter of overheated imagery and rhetoric than clinical insanity. But as he demonstrated, despite the fact they were based on the wildest and most inaccurate "conspiratorial fantasy" theories and factual distortions, they regularly swept the country and catalyzed acts of political and personal destruction.

When Hofstadter wrote the article, the oldest members of the baby boom generation were just entering their college years. They were about to become beneficiaries of the greatest surge of American higher education in history, already set in motion by the post–World War II GI Bill's provisions for college education for returning veterans. They would grow up in an age of a prosperous middle class with unparalleled access to civics texts, philosophy, literature, and quality domestic and international films. They would have an intellectual and cultural experience of the world and the country that no pre-jet-age and television-age Americans could even dream of.

And yet, as the boomers enter old age, many of these "older voters" turned to and helped elect Donald Trump, who gained notoriety claiming President Obama was not a legal American (birth certificate notwithstanding), and who stated, among other paranoid scenarios, that all American Muslims are potentially radicalized, that murderous Latino illegal immigrants were overrunning the country, that secret forces under Hillary Clinton were out to abolish the Second Amendment and give those illegals massive social benefits, and that the media and the government were rigged against not only ordinary Americans but himself. The rhetoric was nasty and, in the case of suggesting "Second Amendment people" do something about Hillary Clinton, just short of a lethal threat.

And the boomers bought it. And that contributed to the greatest triumph of Hofstadter's paranoid style in American history. Of course there were legitimate economic reasons for people's rage, particularly in the job-stripped Rust Belt. But if they'd wanted to vote for a blue-collar-aware candidate who was dyed-in-the-wool conservative, who'd actually created jobs, and was a reasonable politician and Governor, they would've voted for John Kasich. No, they responded to Trump's bellow that America was in one of its darkest hours, and "only I can fix it."

The deep well of resentments against what Hofstadter called "cosmopolitans and intellectuals," not to mention Washington bureaucrats, has always been there to be exploited by politicians who use the believers without subscribing to the beliefs. Trump is the successful culmination of a long line of cynical inflamers of subgroups like the "alt-right." He cleverly exploited classic racial and religious fears against the demographic rise of people of color and Muslims in American life.

Still, what led mature adults living in a stable period of reasonable economic recovery—even given awful but rare terrorist attacks that everyone nonetheless realizes are hard for any government to shut down completely—to distrust the federal government so much and join a movement fueled by conspiracy theories? Why are especially voters of mature baby boomer age continuing to believe not only these conspiracies but even crazier and more toxic ones spread by so-called "fake news" on the Internet, like the belief the the Sandy Hook massacre was an act to promote gun control, with the parents pretending their children died, and the delusion that Hillary Clinton was running a child sex ring out of a pizza restaurant?

JFK: 1963, 1991, and the Twenty-First Century | 203

Alongside the sociopolitical reasons spelled out by Hofstadter, there is one event that can help explain it, perhaps the formative event of older baby boomers' consciousness of the machinations of government and younger baby boomers' awareness of the outside world: the assassination of President John F. Kennedy. In part that was because the reaction of many shocked Americans, especially after two more assassinations in 1968, grew more and more paranoid. But it was also the deep distrust of the way the investigation into this most crucial and awful event of the whole decade was handled that lodged a germ of fear and loathing of government in the dawning consciousness of an entire generation.

That distrust was stoked in the 1960s as much by liberals building conspiracy theories as by the right-wing conspiratorial underground that existed at the time, and (no matter what your views of the film) they found their fullest and most successful expression thirty years later in Oliver Stone's *JFK*. The nation's response to and handling of the Kennedy assassination aftermath could certainly background the anti-Washington hatred of the boomers who, fifty-three years later, found common cause with Donald Trump.

***

It's the one day in history where those who were above the age of five can remember all the details; I still remember the face of the girl who brought the news from the principal's office to our public school class. Then came the early exit from school, the dismal shutdown of a whole city, the three days of doing nothing but watching President Kennedy's funeral, with all three major stations (only three back then) broadcasting the first 24/7 news coverage of a major event: the funeral cortège, JFK Jr. saluting his father's coffin, the whole heartbreaking procession. And then one major interruption, which was supposed to showcase the reassuring power of swift justice, the perp walk of the President's alleged killer, but which instead became the end of any possibility of a trial: the murder of Lee Harvey Oswald by Jack Ruby, live in front of the whole country, as those strong silent Texas lawmen screamed in rage and bewilderment—an event almost as searing to the national consciousness as the assassination itself.

Afterwards the United States, which had just been steered through the Cuban missile crisis by President Kennedy, and now viewed the international Communist threat with deepening dread, was gripped in the wake of losing its brave, smart, and well-loved leader by more immediate and even deeper fears. The new president, Lyndon Baines Johnson, and the Congress quickly established a commission led by the Chief Justice of the Supreme Court, Earl Warren, to investigate the assassination. The Warren Commission would amass two-dozen 500-page volumes of work summarized into a 296,000 page report, backed by 20,000 pages of testimony, which it would boil down to a very thick book for public consumption.

Johnson would confidently state "that the truth is known as far as it can be discovered": Lee Harvey Oswald alone killed the president. And as part of that conclusion, as *Life* Magazine would summarize, the report would "lay to rest the lurid rumors and wild speculation that had spread after the assassinations."[2] Congressman and future president Gerald R. Ford, who would later pardon his predecessor Richard Nixon and refer to the same need to calm a wounded and frightened nation, would state "there is not a scintilla of credible evidence to suggest a conspiracy to kill President Kennedy."[3]

But that was hardly the end of it—not in a country that was so uneasy about government intrigue and potential right-wing or military takeovers that conspiracy-oriented tales like *The Manchurian Candidate* and *Seven Days In May* were extremely popular both as books and movies. There were numerous counterinvestigatory books from left-wing sources, most famously Mark Lane's *Rush to Judgment* and *Inquest* by Richard J. Epstein, while southern Senator Richard Russell, no left-winger, stated "reasonable disturbing doubt remains."

Most significantly (and most forgotten), in America's iconic *Life* Magazine Texas Governor John Connally, who had been in the car with President Kennedy and had been shot himself, disputed the Warren Commission Report. One of the bulwarks of the Warren Commission's case was that a single bullet struck both the president and the governor, the "single bullet theory." But Connally insisted he heard a shot, turned around, and felt a second shot hit him, and that he and the President were hit almost simultaneously by two separate bullets, indicating two assassins.

Arlen Specter, who handled the Commission's investigation of the shooting, disagreed with Connally's "sensory perceptions." Specter's strongest point was that no part of the car was struck by an entire bullet, backed by a thorough and apparently honest and precise reenactment of the crime staged by the FBI that supported the single-bullet case. Meanwhile Gerald Ford said "sometimes a wounded man doesn't exactly know when he's been hit."[4] That may be true in a wartime scenario, a fierce battle where shrapnel and debris are exploding everywhere along with the bullets, but on a sunny day after waving to a happy crowd?

Connally selected from the Zapruder film the frame where he thought he was hit, 1.3 seconds after Kennedy. Oswald's rifle, it had been shown, could not be fired faster than once every 2.3 seconds. Specter interpreted the film differently from Connally (and it seems strange, given how these ghosts continue to haunt us, the man's name). But *Life's* photointerpreters disagreed with Specter.

The *Life* section also examined how the medical evidence was confused: doctors at Dallas's Parkland hospital first thought the wound in front of Kennedy's throat looked like an entrance wound, supported by all the witnesses who said they'd heard the first shot from the infamous "grassy knoll" ahead of the motorcade. But doctors at Bethesda naval hospital apparently never saw a front entrance wound. *Life* claimed the autopsy was a "remembrance and reinterpretation."

And so the article in *Life* pushed for a new investigation. "The case should be reopened."[5]

It of course never officially was. And so people continued to rehash and argue the case all through the '60s, looking for high-level conspiracies, especially after the horror of the dual Martin Luther King and Robert Kennedy assassinations, where the most plausible explanations turned out to be perhaps a low-level group of racist killers (though no conspiracy behind James Earl Ray, King's assassin, was ever proven), and Sirhan Sirhan's managing to get to his perch in that hotel kitchen at a time decades before security cameras, metal detectors, and smartphones.

Still, some argued, how did Sirhan get there, and why was Robert Kennedy led out through there? This kind of argument has haunted the lives of baby boomers. The conspiratorial faking of the moon landing has been seriously proposed, including in two films, *Capricorn One*, and in one segment of the documentary *Room 227*, where a commentator actually suggested the film *The Shining* was Kubrick's coded apology for filming the fake moon landing for NASA.

I remember the arguments of friends of mine who believed O.J. Simpson (who had been in the cast of *Capricorn One*) had been set up by the L.A.P.D., the detail in which they made their case over and over. Of course, that kind of argument also goes back to the way police departments, starting in the '60s, would go after civil rights leaders and black militants using broad applications of "conspiracy" charges to drag in as many suspects as possible. And of course one of the greatest 1990s television shows beloved of baby boomers, *The X-Files*, was built on the concept of government conspiracies to either hide or secretly make use of alien arrivals and activity on Earth, a conspiracy many Americans seriously believe to be reality.

It all leads back to the way the conspiracy theories regarding JFK's assassination were hardly laid to rest, to the point where "conspiracy" almost became a meme lodged in the baby boomer brain. And while *Life* would never see the government reopen the case, almost thirty years later, a brilliant unofficial investigation put the JFK conspiracy argument right back in the headlines.

***

Oliver Stone is our greatest film chronicler of the 1960s. In his Vietnam trilogy (*Platoon, Born on the Fourth of July, Heaven and Earth*), and his biopics of *The Doors* and *Nixon*, he explored the great subjects of the period with incandescent cinematic flair, intensity, and authority. His points of view have always been controversial: some felt his complex portrait of Nixon, especially as portrayed by Anthony Hopkins in one of his best performances, was almost too sympathetic, and the late Ray Manzarek, who led The Doors along with Jim Morrison, blasted Stone's downbeat portrayal of Morrison and what he felt was Stone's giving short shrift to the music they made together.

But no one has ever doubted Stone's ability to immerse himself in his subject matter, unearth a wealth of ideas and details, and shoot and edit them in a style that reflects the hallucinatory explosiveness of the '60s—especially in his Vietnam films, given that Stone himself served in an infantry platoon. And no film of his was richer in ideas, more detailed, more vivid, and more controversial than his 1991 *JFK*.[6]

Stone's film, based on Jim Garrison's *On The Trail of the Assassins* and Jim Marrs's *Crossfire: The Plot That Killed Kennedy*, is in its Director's Cut almost four hours long, but it's worth watching twice, first because it's a terrific and engrossing film where many of the details just might slip by you, and second to hear Oliver Stone's thoughtful and wily commentary on his work. Stone knew what he was doing in terms of both its effectiveness and its limitations. He called the film a "countermyth" opposed to what he considers the myth of the Warren Commission Report.

The basic structure of the countermyth begins right in the orchestration of the film's first few minutes. The movie begins with documentary footage of Eisenhower's warning about the "military-industrial complex" and the high points of Kennedy's three-year presidency, into which is suddenly and seamlessly cut footage of a hooker, Rose Sharamie, being thrown from a car by Jack Ruby's mob buddies. The prostitute is played by Sally Kirkland, one of the most outrageously sexy actresses of her day; her breasts hanging out, she's beaten bloody and crying out in the road and in the hospital about how "they're going to kill the President... serious ... fucking guys... " In two shots we're wrenched from the march of history into a sleazy and horrific forecast of the disaster to come, and (by extension) the countermyth: how America's nobility, dignity, law, and order, up to the highest levels of government, is about to be pitted against the cesspool of the American political underground.

The second aspect of the countermyth is Stone's creation of the hero. The storyline is based on New Orleans district attorney Jim Garrison's hunt for what he believed to be a cadre of assassins who killed the President. Garrison himself was a canny Louisiana politician who had risen through one of the most corrupt shark pool governments in America, but Stone transformed him with his script and his casting of Kevin Costner into a 1990s version of Atticus Finch, the pillar of rectitude from the film *To Kill A Mockingbird*. Costner was not only one of the male hearthrobs of the 1990s but the latest incarnation of the kind of strong, silent type, shrewd but morally upright, that had been the standard American hero since Gary Cooper and John Wayne. And so Stone in effect created a Disneyfied portrait of Garrison and fesses up to it, at one point calling a scene with Garrison and his family on the front porch his "Norman Rockwell moment."[7]

JFK and Garrison's quest to smoke out, arrest, and try the president's killers thus becomes, to use the old single-logline Hollywood trope, Atticus Finch in Hell. That investigation of the hell of what Stone called "the underground Bund" is portrayed in nightmarish detail, using a variety of film techniques Stone bombards the viewer with in the first ten minutes: contrasting film stocks and colors, fast-motion subliminal editing to points yet to be fully revealed. One example is how the movie starts with the echoes of only three shots—echoing the official interpretation—and blurred visuals of the assassination. Clarity will come three-and-a-half hours later.

JFK emerges as an amazing work of sheer stamina and conviction, nowhere more than in its marshaling and direction of its huge cast of characters: cryptofascists, depraved gay prostitutes (the film has a retrograde view of homosexuality), foreign killers for hire, bagmen, mobsters, rogue generals. They're played by the kind of cast—Kevin Bacon, the late Jack Lemmon, the late Walter Matthau, Tommy Lee Jones, Joe Pesci, on and on—that would soon no longer be budgetarily possible to assemble.

And it's worth playing the entire film over again to listen to Stone's commentary, which is sometimes learned, sometimes slyly self-exculpating, sometimes candid about the shortcomings of certain scenes. He delivers his case with the sureness of a d.a., both the legal and storytelling beats crisply established, but when events are an absolute mystery to him, such as how Jack Ruby got into the Dallas police station, he's very un-d.a.-like in admitting it.

His editing as "deconstructed reality and layers of life"[7] seems to suggest that yes, of course it can all be manipulated, along with the conditioning effects of using colors that Stone at one point calls "solid blue" versus "corrupt yellow." Is Stone a paranoia-inflamer at times in *JFK*, not to mention some of his other work? Fair enough criticism. But again, very unlike a conspiracist fanatically insisting on the infallibility of his case, Stone's commentary and film cops to the weaknesses of many of Garrison's witnesses, who are often either alcoholic or crazy or participate in New Orleans's lawless politics. Stone admits to many moments of dramatic license, especially in the simultaneous appearances at various places of conspirators in the film (like Clay Shaw and Oswald) that are only hinted at on record.

The strengths of the movie include all Stone's techniques. His use of editing and pacing as well as those different colored film stocks and fogging and grain levels of film to illustrate the piecing together of the case is a fascinating re-forensicization of the assassination. His use of documentary footage to background his case, involving the escalation in Vietnam and the secret war against Castro, works beautifully.

The Director's Cut fills out the portrait of Lee Harvey Oswald and a carefully calculated process by the conspirators of framing him as the sole killer. Again, however you feel about Stone's handling of this

JFK: 1963, 1991, and the Twenty-First Century | 209

portion of the drama, it allows us the full wattage of an extraordinary and underrated performance by Gary Oldman (perhaps Oldman should've trademarked "extraordinary" and "underrated" for his film acting).

Stone shows how Garrison gleans clues by investigating the stories of various witnesses to the assassination, their memories shown in brutally staccato vignettes of panic. He smokes out the histories of international businessman Clay Shaw (played by a surprisingly fey Tommy Lee Jones) and mercenary pilot David Ferrie (a hotwired but very un-Italian Joe Pesci). He teases out links between CIA cold warriors and the dregs of the right-wing movement ready to be guns for hire. Ferrie is found dead in a truly awful scene, and Garrison's assistant Bob Broussard is gradually traduced by the FBI who tell him, yes, there's been disinformation, they know it was Castro behind JFK's killing, but don't want to provoke another potential nuclear war crisis. Stone admits this is a lucid argument—after all, the government had tried to use the Mob to get to Castro and was prepared for payback.

But meanwhile Stone does a great job (again, however you feel about his case) of showing what he views as only putatively "real" events to contradict them with what he considers the actual events: the movement of people toward the grassy knoll as shots were fired, the superficial wound sustained by an onlooker through the ricochet of an unexplained bullet, "blips of consciousness" as Stone called them. It's semi-subliminal, it doesn't allow time for careful consideration, its borrowed from fast-motion commercial editing, but the technique absolutely pulls the viewer along.

It all builds to the most disturbing encounter in the film, Garrison's meeting with "Mr. X", the movie's "Deep Throat," played by Donald Sutherland, and, according to Stone, a composite character based largely on career Cold Warrior Colonel Fletcher Prouty. This is the film's most chillingly persuasive scene. I defy anyone to listen to this passage, including the revelation a New Zealand paper had the story about Oswald's being Kennedy's assassin four hours (due to the time difference) before he was actually charged, without at least considering Oswald's assertion he was the "patsy" in a conspiracy.

It's Mr. X who most directly buttresses Stone's position that the assassination was military black ops planned at very high levels (and Stone, as he underscores in his commentary, does not make the mistake of charging LBJ with collusion in the crime). Mr. X, played with icy and sardonic precision by Donald Sutherland, narrates how he would have been normally responsible for security during JFK's Dallas visit but was yanked away from that detail, allowing for all sorts of sloppiness and havoc to follow, including a changing of the parade route to allow for what Stone calls, in military terminology, an L-shaped ambush. In a "tight little cell" as Stone put it, triangulated fire by multiple assassins was planned and executed.

Ultimately Garrison tries Clay Shaw, the only surviving provable culprit, for a conspiracy to assemble Oswald and other killers and assassinate the president. There are certainly weaknesses in the case, some of which Stone admits, some of which he doesn't. Kennedy's desire to withdraw from Vietnam as a reason for his killing never seems a sufficient one, especially given that the condensed *Pentagon Papers* would later reveal Kennedy as troubled and looking for a way out, but hardly "going rogue" over his generals (Kennedy's resistance to the CIA after the Bay of Pigs fiasco, however, is well known).

Stone admits that his impressions from his meetings with Garrison were that he "made many mistakes. He trusted a lot of weirdos and followed a lot of fake leads. But he went out on a limb, way out. And he kept going, even when he knew he was facing long odds."[8] Garrison also (not surprisingly) could never finger specific high-level black ops people, and Stone's making the CIA an all-powerful bogeyman seems a little old-hat now. There are weaknesses in the film itself, especially domestic scenes with Sissy Spacek as Garrison's wife highlighting Stone's biggest weakness: actresses. And when she shows up at the trial and beams at him, Stone undercuts one of the harshest truths of Garrison's story: he really did lose his family over the case.

But all that fades away in Garrison's closing argument, strong and silent Costner giving an old-style oration that's one of the high points of American movies in the '90s, culminating in the "back ... and to the left" repetition accompanied by the most gruesome portion of the Zapruder film. As Garrison outlines a theory of a coup d'etat to keep the war machine and Vietnam war in action, with FBI Director J. Edgar Hoover and LBJ acting not within the conspiracy but potentially as part of a coverup, it's all undeniably effective. You can't dismiss it, only realize that it's either a brilliant crescendo of that old "paranoid style" or a genuine secret history Stone would follow up on and expand decades later with his *Untold History of the United States*.

What we can't doubt is the subsequent history of the "disappearing" or classifying of assassination-related material, from CIA documents

JFK: 1963, 1991, and the Twenty-First Century | 211

to supporting documents of the Warren Commission to even the President's brain; the revelation of the dual autopsies in the film, which include actual photos of the slain president, are truly unnerving. If this is how the LBJ administration and the Warren Commission meant to lay to rest lingering suspicions, they did us no favors.

***

The film was a major hit in 1991, reigniting the whole debate, and Stone was as angrily disparaged as celebrated. But the passage of time has not exactly trashed his point of view.

Stone released versions of his "Director's Cut" between 1999 and 2001. Since then we've seen the Bin Laden family flown out of the country after 9-11, while all other US flights were grounded, despite the obvious contributions they could have made to the investigation of the terrorist attack. We've seen the cooking of intelligence and the deliberate reliance on an untrustworthy source planting all sorts of false rumors to justify the Second War in Iraq. We've seen a ginned-up case for Saddam Hussein having weapons of mass destruction planted in the *New York Times* and advanced at the UN by the Secretary of State. We've seen George W. Bush's election influenced by corrupt electoral practices in Florida and a Supreme Court decision so nakedly political that the Court took pains to establish it should never be used as a precedent. We've seen a Vice President conduct both a secret war and energy policy that, among other goals, so advanced his own private interests that even his favored companies' supplying of insufficiently armored vehicles and shower stalls that electrocuted soldiers couldn't deter their contracts. We've seen Congress completely abdicate its responsibilities (including a request by the President to authorize military action in Syria) in order to block President Obama every step of the way, responding as anyone could see to the influence of fossil fuel industry chieftains, megacorporations, right-wing ideologues, and campaign donors. And we're surprised that Donald Trump can claim the entire system is rigged and become the next President of the United States?

***

So how do we put the increasingly dangerous paranoid strain to rest? Stone has always been partially blamed for it, but at least with *JFK* he was too smart to buy into it. As he ultimately concludes, Garrison knew he didn't have a solid legal case so much as a solid appeal to the court of public opinion, and Stone knew he was putting forward that same appeal. Ultimately *JFK* is a thrilling film about the journalistic aspect of the law, as much as *All The President's Men* was about the legal (or law-influencing) aspect of journalism. And as Stone quips, "Darrow lost the Scopes trial but who remembers that?"

I'm one of those who believes that Stone, despite subsequent misfires as a filmmaker (*Savages*, *W*) and overreaches as a documentarian in his *Untold History*, essentially made his public appeal and lost his case very well with *JFK*, in just the same way he did recently with the more restrained and thus very effective *Snowden*. It's unfortunate that Stone's film might have contributed to American baby boomer paranoia; in my opinion, it's just as unfortunate that he's at least partially right. Ex-CIA chief Richard Helms would later admit Clay Shaw was CIA, and, as a result of the film, Congress would in 1992 pass legislation to review and possibly release many of the classified Warren Commission files.

Stone would later say that the assassination and its aftermath led to a "deeper and more significant erosion of trust" and the beginning of his generation's betrayal as Americans. Or, in the word's of Stone's Garrison, "the ghost of JFK confronts us with the question of the secret murder at the heart of the American dream."[9] Those questions alone stand ready to contribute to any inflammation of the paranoid tendencies always lurking behind American politics.

There's no doubt that the men of the Warren Commission were motivated by solid American ideals, service to a panicked public and the Constitution. But perhaps with their staunchly patriotic postwar attitudes they respected boundaries they no longer should have, leaving private citizens to take the search further, with predictable out-of-control and paranoid but not necessarily wrong results. One step to counter that may be to finally reopen the JFK assassination case with all relevant documents and photographs declassified, with every lead followed, the assassination finally, if not solved, at least addressed the way it should have been (but maybe couldn't have been) decades ago. Certainly if 9/11 families can now sue Saudi Arabia in an attempt to reveal possible Saudi support of the 9-11 attacks, why can't a member of the Kennedy family, or someone else with some kind of standing, sue relevant government agencies to reopen the case?

If South Africa could have a Truth and Reconciliation Commission dealing with the countless crimes of generations of apartheid so soon after its overthrow, perhaps, fifty-four years later, we can set the record straight about one president's assassination. If only symbolically, it would replace with some light the shadows of the past, so that they don't grow even darker in the future.

Addendum 2016

In *Jackie*, the best film of the year, the many levels of revelation in the script by Noah Oppenheim, direction by Pablo Larraín, music score by Mica Levi, and above all Natalie Portman's amazing performance build to what Jacqueline Kennedy endured, both in her planning in the midst of a near-breakdown and her ultimate participation, to give the nation a funeral and personal example that truly helped it to heal. In light of that one can almost become angry at Oliver Stone for peeling off those scabs. But *Jackie* also dramatizes how Mrs. Kennedy, in her righteous anger, was skeptical about all official reassurances and platitudes and often wanted to confront the nation with the brutal truth of what happened—and incidentally how all the officials around her were worried about other assassins coming out of the shadows. What is most poignant from the perspective of 2016, both in *JFK* and *Jackie*, is the lament about whether John F. Kennedy's ideals and unfinished achievements would be able to continue.

Ferguson Won, Occupy Nothing

When I visited the Occupy Wall Street encampment back in the fall of 2011 (yes, it's really been that long ago), it was a powerful reminder of demonstrations I'd been a part of in the '60s. There were the dedicated young people, arguing, carrying signs, looking a lot worse for wear than I did back in the '60s because they'd stayed in the same place for days in the cold, which I admired. There were the older activists backing them up.

But there was one thing missing—a microphone.

To secure permission for their occupation, Occupy had bargained away the use of a public address system, and resorted to the communication process that would become known the world over as "Mike check!" Crowds of people repeated the words of a speaker loud enough to be heard clearly…

… how far? A couple of hundred feet? Would that be an efficient means of communication in the event activities quickly needed to be reorganized (like if the police were charging)? And in terms of speeches reminding the crowd of the fairly complex sociopolitical and economic conditions they were attacking, how could that possibly be effective?

And that's when I was reminded that, while it might be true that life is 90% showing up, unfortunately demonstrations, even large attention-grabbing ones, need a little more than that. In part because of the inability to circulate complex ideas and instructions while dealing with complex logistics and protesting a very complex situation, Occupy became a well-intentioned protracted flash mob. And it was a mob that was increasingly unpersuasive as it became infiltrated by the homeless and the mentally disturbed looking for free food and a platform to rant to the press.

What the Occupy movement was missing was just about any of the civil disobedience strategies honed in the '60s anti-Vietnam and pro-civil rights struggles. Give Occupy credit for first highlighting the issue of economic equality in its home base on Wall Street. But it's too bad Occupy didn't effectively reach back to some of the tactics used back in the '60s both here and abroad to try and force governments to change their policies.

For example, teach-ins, loosely defined as extended meetings involving lectures, debates, and discussions to raise awareness of or express a position on a social or political issue. If Occupy even held such discussions—and I'm not saying they didn't—somehow they missed all sorts of key facts relating to effective resistance to the big Wall Street banks.

For example, Occupy called for depositors to withdraw their accounts from the big banks and put them in credit unions. I expressed my willingness to do that and was emailed a map of walkable credit unions near my address. So far so good. There was only one problem: None of the credit unions would have me as a member, not even one accepting deposits from Writers Guild of America East members (I'm still a member of WGA West, and, in a development reminiscent of Monty Python's *Life of Brian*'s epic battle between the Judaean People's Republic and the People's Republic of Judaea, the East and West Guilds hate each other).

Had the Occupy movement investigated some basic facts about the narrowly defined memberships of credit unions, they might have come up with a more long-term but effective counter-big bank effort, such as organizing to pressure the government to grant the postal service the limited banking powers it had years ago, or to charter more state, public, and infrastructure banks. There would have been no immediate gratification there, but it would've been a far better way to channel the anti-"bankster" effort when they had the public's attention.

There was also the problem of the way the Occupiers presented themselves. I read with horror and sympathy about Cecily McMillan's brutal arrest during Occupy and her three-month sentence for resisting that arrest, during which, if the officers truly fondled her breasts, she was responding instinctively to a thuggish sexual assault.

But the images of her arrest in a tight blouse and microskirt were jarring. Something we all knew in the '60s was that you do not dress provocatively during a demonstration: first, the event is supposed to draw attention to the cause and not the individual demonstrators; second, jeans and denim clothes stand up much better to running or falling; and finally, given that the police may pick you up and throw you into a paddy wagon, you do not want to be wearing a tattered American flag cape or hot pants.

But that was only a misjudgment for which Ms. McMillan endured unjust and unmerited suffering. Far worse was an inherent flaw in any movement that depends on simply remaining in place to make its point—it will deteriorate, and very publicly. The growing presence of disorderly homeless people at Occupy reminded me of the Poor People's March and creation of Resurrection City in Washington DC in 1968. Dr. Martin Luther King had actually planned that event before his assassination, and his closest aide Ralph Abernathy carried it out. For weeks the City maintained food and daycare facilities and organized demonstrations. But its indefiniteness proved its undoing. The movement ultimately got two hundred more US counties to qualify for surplus food distribution. But Congress recalcitrantly (no surprise) waited out the City's demands for economic justice until heat, rain, and the angry confrontations among different factions aggravated by the weather gradually broke the City down even before it was forced to close by the Department of the Interior.

In the words of Reverend Walter Fauntroy, who was present at Resurrection City, "when you've got a muddy spirit and muddy eyes and a muddy future, you turn on one another instead of to one another."[1]

When Michael Brown was shot by police officers in Ferguson, Missouri, at first it appeared the demonstrations that ensued would follow the same protracted, ignominious, and divisive scenario. People who just wanted to provoke the militarized police showed up. The summer heat frayed tempers as the demonstrations went on without any specific results.

But then real organizing began. That started with the reining in of the police response by Captain Ron Johnson, who also reached out to the aggrieved community. Alderman Antonio French was constantly out in the streets, telling would-be troublemakers to go home. People with experience in either catalyzing or structuring effective protests, like activist Philip Agnew of the Dream Defenders and Trayvon Martin's parents, spoke to crowds in Ferguson and St. Louis. The basic message: don't be violent, don't hang around a town whose parents want their kids to be able to go back to school safely, and prepare for the long haul.

In Agnew's words, "I came here as a young person who knows all too well what it's like to live on the second rung of society. I came here to be a part of resistance. We have not seen a reaction of nonviolent civil disobedience to officers of the state like this in my lifetime. And I came here to stand side by side with folks and to learn how we can help."[2]

Help soon began as specific groups with long-term aims sprang up, such as French's Heal STL—with its focus on multiracially unified political engagement, education, and community development—and

Peace Fest 2014. I can't think of one such group that was generated by the slogan "We are the 99%," which is catchy but means what? Resist the 1%? Like the doctor who treats you at the hospital or the filmmaker whose movies you love? That's the 1%. It's the .1% or maybe even .01% that's the problem, for which Occupy had no proposed solutions.[3]

But "Hands up, don't shoot!" is quickly becoming the seed of a new civil rights movement to resist police brutality and the for-profit prison system at the root of mass incarceration of people of color (not to mention poor white people for increasing categories of minor crimes). One can easily imagine such groups coalescing into larger efforts, such as a one-day economically damaging moratorium similar to the one held by immigrant groups a couple of years ago, or to the 1969 Vietnam Moratorium against the war that virtually shut down the country. Sit-ins, teach-ins, and demonstrations can keep the issues alive all over America, even in the face of a Trump presidency.

In the long run, such groups are well suited to teaching a new generation the old lessons of '60s civil rights protest, resistance, and reaching for alternative ways of organizing communities. It's not about showing up, sticking around, "branding" and calling attention to the problem in the brave but unfruitful fashion of Occupy—or worse, in the showy, empty fashion of Global Citizen or the idiotic catch-Joseph-Kony awareness campaign. It's about the hard work of structuring cooperative organizations, building links between different arenas of protest and civil disobedience, and figuring out how such groups can support themselves while they pressure lawmakers and institutions and, in the words of Antonio French, "turn a moment into a movement."[4,5]

The New York PBA: Bringing Back the Ghetto

In the wake of the horrific assassination of two police officers in New York, the president of the Patrolmen's Benevolent Association Patrick Lynch declared that there was "blood on many hands,"[1] and clearly implicated those protesting the Eric Garner grand jury decision and the Mayor, Bill de Blasio, in collective guilt for the officers' deaths.

Granted emotions were running high after the deaths of two cops, it was still a wretchedly inflammatory thing to say. And it didn't come out of a vacuum. That sort of sentiment goes way back to the most racially tense period in modern New York history, the '60s and the '70s.

It was a time when Mayor John Lindsay was dealing with black and Hispanic ghetto neighborhoods—and they truly were ghettos back then, the only neighborhoods where people of color could live and have businesses—which were always on the brink of an explosion. Meanwhile, compared to slogans used in the current totally nonviolent protests, which Lynch accuses of "demonizing" the police, in the '60s the names poverty-stricken people of color and students protesting the war in Vietnam directed at police included bulls, heat, fuzz, and above all, pigs, as in the cry heard at demonstrations of "Off the pigs!"—kill the cops—and as in the Black Panthers urging armed self-defense against the police. Lindsay's greatest achievement as Mayor was to reach out to those neighborhoods during that bitterly angry period so many times, and so effectively, that New York was one of the only major cities during that period not to have had a full-scale race riot, not even after the assassination of Martin Luther King Jr.

Many of us cooperated in that effort, including in a small way teenagers like myself who joined Lindsay Volunteers to participate in slum cleanup projects. Definitely weekend activism, but better than nothing, and appreciated by ghetto neighborhoods as just that.

But the group that almost never cooperated in those attempts to keep the urban peace was the ironically named Patrolmen's Benevolent Association. They attacked the Lindsay administration in the sympathetic press. At a funeral ceremony for a city commissioner, the head of the police guard refused to shake Lindsay's hand.

So to any New Yorker my age the battle between the police union

The New York PBA: Bringing Back the Ghetto | 219

and the protesters of the Eric Garner grand jury's refusal to indict the police who killed Garner; the cops who turned their backs on the Mayor; the disinvitations to police funerals; and Patrick Lynch's pronouncements on City Hall blood guilt for officers slain by an out-of-state deranged career criminal—all of it sounds nastily familiar.

Back in the '60s and '70s, there may have been a more consciously bigoted slant to such police actions and statements. But as ghetto neighborhoods like Harlem, BedStuy, and Ocean Hill-Brownsville sank further into poverty over the next twenty years, the harsh police presence wasn't just about racism. It was about how crime-ridden those neighborhoods had become, and there were many African Americans who tolerated, even welcomed, police crackdowns for that reason.

Then came the first tenure of Commissioner Benjamin Bratton, and the beginning of a policy of "broken windows" policing that by the late '90s was proving effective. Add the fact that the tragedy of 9-11 pulled the city together in an unprecedented way, and New York became one of the safest cities in America.

So given that success, why are the police so at odds with African American protesters and their supporters now, raising the specter of '60s-redux racial civil unrest? Is it the reining in of stop-and-frisk excesses? Is it really Reverend Al Sharpton, with his appearances on MSNBC and (despite what the *New York Post* says) no real power with the Mayor except an ability to bend his ear?

Or is it more likely Patrick Lynch's demonization of the Mayor, insults of peaceful demonstrators, and even thinly veiled attacks on the police commissioner, which are inflaming his fellow police into even more of an us-against-them mentality?

When New Yorkers engaged in a series of remarkably peaceful demonstrations, Lynch's response was to say that was wrong because it was the police who protected their right to protest. Against whom? African Americans? And it's the First Amendment that protects that right, not the PBA. When police officers were assaulted by a few thugs, Lynch of course blamed the whole movement. And now in the wake of the cop killings, Lynch has made truly disgraceful statements and, despite all the pleas for moderation, doesn't seem to be backing down from them.

Follow the logic here, and it's straight out of the bad cop bad old days of the '60s: if you allow "the element" (read African Americans) in the ghetto and their liberal supporters to get away with their anti-police demands inevitably crime and anarchy follow, and no matter what the circumstances, you're responsible. Only "law and order" can then take care of the problem, and that law and order must be unquestioned (and Nixon's The One).

Thanks largely to the *New York Post*, Lynch has a voice so far out of proportion to his actual authority that he's even put Police Commissioner Bratton on the defensive. And here's what's scary about this. It was Bratton who turned the tide against crime with his "broken windows" policing, whose basic doctrine is that if you stop the little crimes (for example, illegally not lighting hallways, which is one reason a jumpy rookie cop accidentally shot and killed one of the recent African American police victims) then you can make progress against the major crimes. It worked—but now it's under attack from an incensed African American community, made all the angrier by Lynch's confrontationist remarks.

No New Yorker who lived through the "Kojak era," the *Midnight Cowboy-Superfly* days (and who thus by definition can no longer run or kick like in those days), wants to see Bratton's successful policies reversed. I certainly don't. As someone who, as a former police story writer for network television, has talked to and known many cops, as someone who's always been sympathetic to cops and what they endure on a regular basis, I want them as safe and as able to do their jobs as possible, even when that has to include lethal force.

And what I most remember from interviewing and riding around with cops is one cop proudly calling himself a "peace officer," and the good cops (and, while maintaining necessary skepticism, I'm convinced they were mostly good cops) being proud of all the times they completed an arrest without drawing their gun. They might have been confronting an EDP (emotionally disturbed person) on PCP, the deadliest acronymic combination on the street—and they brought the EDP in alive. They might have been grappling on the sidewalk with a violent offender swiping at them with spiked brass knuckles—and they brought him in alive.

Such ethical cops also cultivated community cooperation over the past thirty-plus years, and that's all now seriously threatened. You think "no snitching" is counterproductive—how about no neighborhood cooperation with the police at all? If Bratton doesn't want that to happen, he has to defend his legacy. As part of speaking to the grief and fears of New Yorkers, he has to confront the confrontationist head of the PBA. It really is a "who's the boss?" moment in New York. If Bratton can't stand up to Patrick Lynch he should step aside for someone who can.[2]

Because ultimately the Garner case is not just about racism. In part those cops killed Garner because cops all over the country seem to be more careless and extreme with African American offenders (even minor offenders), and that speaks not so much to racial bias (given black cops have also shot unarmed black men) as a reflexive institutional bias that needs a great deal of retraining. But mainly they killed him because they were bad-boys-bad-boys-whatcha-gonna-do bad cops. And what's true about bad cops is what's true about bad union members in general—they bring the whole union down, and in the case of the police union, the consequences can become not just paycheck-threatening but life-threatening.

It's incomprehensible that these Staten Island cops who violated the biggest rule in the book about illegal use of deadly force, killed an unarmed man with a banned chokehold, exposed the city to civil unrest and huge financial damage, and exposed their fellow cops to potential additional violence, have turned the citywide PBA into their protection society. These cops violated a rule that's essential because, in limiting certain kinds of use of force, it helps safeguard cops when they use other kinds of force. They violated a rule that helps their fellow officers do their job and come home safe, and their union unbelievably weighed in on their side.

Sometimes the police have to use violence or even shoot to kill to protect themselves and others. But as the wrong kinds of police actions toward citizens are allowed to continue, we're on a 'back to the future' trip to those '60s racist days (almost all the victims have been people of color)—thuggish and corrupt days where good cops were forced to follow the bad cops' lead, uniting behind their police comrades against the press and politicians even as they were made uneasy by everything from traffic ticket quotas to using fines to shake down neighborhoods of color (like in Ferguson) to beatings or even shootings on the street that were violations of their training and their code.

Because when bad cops are allowed to rule the roost, as they were, for example, during periods of New York's crime-plagued decades from the '70s to the early '90s—just look up the Knapp Commission, or watch the great Sidney Lumet movies *Serpico* and *Prince of the City*— it isn't just community relations that get poisoned, but the morale of the police force itself. Good cops, publicly paid professionals with families who want to make it to the end of their careers and their pensions, don't like the bad conscience, let alone the risk to life and limb, that bad cops subject them to.

That suggests a rethink and a remedy. It's not that all cops are racist because they're cops, nor is the problem as small as a few bad cops. The main problem may be cadres of police unions like the PBA that inflame their memberships, who are already being militarized and taught to look at crime-ridden neighborhoods as occupied territories, into a complete us-against-them mentality. That suggests a remedy that's difficult but not impossible: slates of newer more reformist officers pushing to take over police unions and the equivalents of the PBA, throw the hardliners out, and work with cities toward retraining and demilitarization of their departments.

For if in New York (and all across the country), the cops no longer protect and serve, but search and destroy, the neighborhoods they occupy may respond in kind: they may not only decide that drugs and crime are all they've got, they might battle the police in more direct ways. And these neighborhoods are no longer ghettos. Young white people seeking cheaper rentals have been moving into neighborhoods like Harlem, East Harlem, Bushwick, and Bedford-Stuyvesant for years, while Los Angeles neighborhoods, at a lesser pace, are seeing the same demographic change. Maybe in the '60s the thin blue line was able to protect the old white line from the consequences of police violence. But this time if police action drives neighborhoods in major cities like New York and Los Angeles to explode, the victims won't all be people of color.

Police brutality and lethal violence in New York, in Ferguson, and all over the country is indefensible, and if the good cops are going to keep on keeping the peace in multiracial cities, the bad cops have to be prosecuted to the fullest extent of the law they're supposed to enforce. And here in New York, younger cops, who are diverse as the neighborhoods they serve, who came up under Bratton, who hopefully don't share the views of cops like Patrick Lynch and his blowhard troglodytes, should take note: If an episode of police overreaction or brutality becomes the spark that lights the tinderbox, and '60s-era rioting or fighting ever recurs, Patrick Lynch and his ilk won't be on the front lines. They remember, like me, how scary the "Kojak era" could get. They can't run and kick like they used to either. They'll tell themselves they fought their fight, and inevitably leave the new fighting and the bad old/new New York to you.

99 Homes and America Ain't One

The best movies can be windows into America's heart and mind, just with a one-to-five-year delay.

At a certain point the movie *99 Homes*[1] began to feel like a movie from the '60s, not so much in its subject matter but in the way it kindles so much uneasiness and anger that you almost want to turn away.

Scenes in '60s and '70s movies could be like that, whether a particularly fraught emotional confrontation in a John Cassavetes movie or an up until that point unprecedented bit of goriness in an antiwar film or Western like *The Wild Bunch*, or the famous last bullet-ridden scene of *Bonnie and Clyde*. The idea was to try to make the audience really squirm, really feel the moment in an authentic, no-escape way.

In *99 Homes*, Dennis Nash, played by Adam Garfield, a construction worker who's lost his home and must take work of any kind, gets deeper into doing dirty work for real estate speculator Ray Carver, played by Michael Shannon, and participates in massively evicting people just like himself. These scenes are done in long takes that frame Nash so he's surrounded by the suffering and social breakdown he's causing. During one sequence of him pushing out a series of families from their homes it's easy to think okay, point made, let's advance the story—and then you realize that what you're reacting to is not slowness but the intensity, and the intense wrongdoing, as Nash has to perform the task over and over again.

It's '60s-style protest filmmaking set in the "oughts"—or maybe, given what happened to the country politically and economically back then, the naughts.

Orlando and the rest of Florida were one of the centers of devastation of the Great Recession. And so *99 Homes*' subject matter is also reminiscent of all those anticorruption films of the '60s and '70s (many of which were developed in the '60s), all those films about the urban and suburban darkness of the time, or about the misery and violence of the '30s Great Depression that resonated with increasingly stressed '70s audiences.

There's one thing those old films though, for the most part, weren't about, and that was 99 *Homes*' theme: the destruction and impoverishment of the American middle class. Because back then, for the most part, it wasn't happening.

There are two myths about the '50s and '60s promulgated since the Reagan era. The first was that the '50s were a golden age. That may have been true if you weren't a person of color, or a woman with ambitions beyond housewifery, or a left-wing student or artist, or a blacklisted writer, or a vet with at that time totally misunderstood PTSD (as in the film *The Best Years of Our Lives*), or a commuter adman hating his suburb and his job (*Revolutionary Road*), or average Americans so economically precarious amid plenty (*Death of A Salesman*) or so fearful about what was beyond the picket fence that the McCarthy hearings and *Invasion of the Body Snatchers* and film noir movies accurately shadowgraphed their states of mind. Other than for those people, it was Shangri-La.

The other myth was that the '60s was a time of chaos and destruction and hatred (*Forrest Gump*) leading to the moral and physical deterioration of the '70s from which the Gipper rescued us all. In this case, I personally can attest that my dad did complain loudly about '60s and '70s New York taxes and economic mismanagement, and that there was way too much crime along with intermittent acts of violence by extreme radical groups. Drug use and misuse took its toll as well.

But, as this book is dedicated to showing, so many new and thrilling elements of art and music and political thought were injected into the national spirit, along with so much courageous use of freedom of assembly and petition in the antiwar movement, and so much nonviolent and productive civil disobedience in the civil rights movement, that the '60s were an unprecedented period of growth and mental and spiritual enlargement and change.

Here's the paradox: what allowed all that to happen was that the fundamental middle-class economic security of the '50s (which we should give the '50s credit for) remained unchanged. There was an economy, loosely defined as an earning of sufficient income to allow the production and exchange of goods and services, a fundamental economic scope of action that, at just about all income levels except intractable poverty, was safe. It was safe enough so that President Lyndon Baines Johnson thought he could have wars both on North Vietnam and that intractable poverty (a terrible era-defining mistake). And what anchored that safety? Safety in one's home.

No matter what was happening, people could be reasonably secure in their homes, and not just in the Constitutional sense. In New York, due to much more widespread rent control and stabilization, most people could live in their apartments indefinitely—and the poorest could live in single-resident-occupancy (s.r.o.) apartments. Meanwhile Brooklyn was known as "the borough of homes" because of all its homeowners. Beyond the cities, safer bank mortgage regulations and practices as well as a stable, if not fantastic economy guaranteed long-term homeowner residency and faith in one's home not just as a place to live but an investment.

And that meant that with all the fracas of the dissent of the '60s, certain basic middle-class values were adhered to and acknowledged. The Port Huron Statement, which launched the Students for a Democratic Society and all the disruptive protest it caused, begins "We are people of this generation, bred to at least modest comfort, housed now in universities, looking uncomfortably to the world we inherit."[2] For a defiant statement of purpose, it begins as modestly as the comfort it describes. It basically says: we're bourgeois kids who have the safety to think hard about what's going on. And the main thought behind the statement is: we're comfortable. We're "housed."

Of course the '60s were divisive, but there were boundaries based on that "housed"ness. How could white people sympathize with Dr. King's struggle down south if they couldn't see it and feel sorrow about it watching television in their homes? How could they feel for the pain of nonviolence if they weren't comfortable themselves? How could students protest if they didn't look at universities at temporary homes and enclaves of learning and not ten-to-thirty-year loan agreements? Above all, how could basic norms of conduct be observed by the great mass of people during a time of repeated political assassinations and urban rioting if they weren't secure? Even Woodstock worked because, basically, amid all that rain and mud and disorder and drug use, people were well-behaved, waiting to hear great music for which many had had the money to buy tickets (though never collected), and had safe homes to go back to.

No, it was the Reagan era that, for all its economic growth, opened the door to the real disruption and chaos through the gambling with the nation's economy during the savings and loan scandal and, here in New York and in many communities, the destruction of s.r.o.'s (whose "housed" became homeless), the erosion of limits on rents, and the massive flipping of small-business spaces (the so-called "store wars") that ruined so many storeowners. And that was of course just a warmup to the ruinous wave of bad loans followed by foreclosures and real estate flippings through all sorts of dubious methods (touched on smartly in *99 Homes*) that most characterized the terrible anguish and losses of the Great Recession.

Was there *any* punishment for those who so financially and psychologically damaged large sectors of our population, who burned out not just their middle-class lives but middle-class values and left rage and hopelessness in their wake, while they caused the nationwide destruction of the basic security a home once represented? As *99 Homes'* Carver tells Nash, in a speech reminiscent of the rant of Jordan Delfort (Leonardo DiCaprio) to the FBI in *The Wolf of Wall Street*, I'm nothing compared to the ones at the top and what they get away with. His basic message: winners get bailed out, not losers, and America is "of the winners, by the winners, and for the winners." And that's a lot of what the populist rage of Donald Trump's supporters was all about—although by now, with the appointments of Trump's cabinet, they must know that they've elected just what and whom they most feared and despised.

In a final turn of the screw, the winners pushing people out of their homes and stores now, taking advantage of American late capitalism's speculation and also competing with those speculators, are often not American. In New York, funds of mysterious origin are investing in "ghost condos," driving up real estate prices and rents so that previous occupants are driven out and spaces go empty for months. Similar well-heeled investors are now also trying to "collapse co-ops" by buying up shares (buying out residents) until they own the majority of the shares and the remaining previous shareholders have to become tenants or even leave. Now even the well-off are insecure. The global big banks are of course happy to take fees on all this activity.

Here in New York, given Goldman Sachs's prominence in the Trump cabinet and that cabinet's ties to the Russians, those of us, renters or coop owners, who have lucrative "air rights" above our heads face the possibility of mass purchases of the ground beneath our feet. It could be the greatest land grab since Crimea, with the possibility of lease terminations and evictions on an unprecedented scale.

If there's any way to stop this—along with restrictions on property purchases by noncitizens and non-permanent-residents, as is done in Australia—it's not by (except through tax reform) trying to stop economic inequality, part of the bargain we accept as Americans, or even tinkering at the edges with highly complicated bank rules, but by a real "back to the future" move to re-regulate the housing market and free it from speculation as it was in the '60s. Protect and increase affordable housing. Strictly regulate all mortgage-related rules and documents. Forbid as many speculative practices as possible. Be prepared to suspend mass foreclosures in the event of another crash, and make homeowners and renters whole before big banks. Above all reinstate the separation between investment banking and savings, pensions, and home lending, so that big banks have to gamble with house money and not houses.

As *99 Homes* so blisteringly dramatizes, communities and basic social norms throughout America fall apart when people are no longer secure in their homes from search and seizure by a government seized by banks and real estate interests. Defending the homeland will mean nothing if America doesn't defend the homes within it.

Black Mass for Citizens

The movie *Black Mass*[1] has so much colorful attention to detail, such remarkable acting (Johnny Depp in the zone, the others right behind him), and such a searing and multileveled true story, that I was almost grateful for the garden-variety straight-line screenplay.

It's not as if co-writer Jez Butterworth, who also co-wrote *Edge Of Tomorrow* and *Get On Up* with his brother John Henry, doesn't know how to write a structurally inventive script. The linear flow seems in part a deliberate choice by the writers and director Scott Cooper to make sure the audience realizes every nasty step of the way how the FBI, in the person of Agent John Connolly, attempted to use Whitey Bulger as an informant against the Mafia, only to slowly sink to criminal depths itself once Whitey Bulger played Connolly in the most shameful ways possible. Perhaps that makes for a less poetic movie, but it certainly delivers a journalistically powerful one.

And so perhaps this movie will wake a lot of people up to the fact that the FBI has broken the law in pursuit of its targets for a long time. To give the Bureau some credit, its war against its main enemy, the Mafia, was largely a success. During the 1960s the Mob was so powerful it controlled Las Vegas, much of New York's waterfront, and labor unions like the Teamsters. Now its entertainment value is more significant than its balance sheet, and it's a far smaller threat to the economy and security of the country.

But during the height of its 1960s battle with the Mob, the FBI conducted at the same time an equally intense war against the political left wing of the United States. They used against nonviolent protest and civil disobedience the same tactics they justified using against gangsters and communist saboteurs. In the process they violated the constitutionally protected liberties and privacy of not just civil rights leaders like Martin Luther King, Jr., but all sorts of ordinary citizens, especially college students, involved in legitimate political dissent. Consequences for the victims included harassment, job loss, even murder.

The Bureau's major weapons against these Americans, as in *Black Mass*, were wiretaps and informants, along with the kind of dirty tricks and subversion practiced by the CIA and the Nixon Administration. They fell back on these tactics no matter how often they blew up in their faces and put the Bureau itself on the wrong side of the law.

Bulger wasn't the only FBI informant who went rogue between the 1960s and 1990s, just the most horrific one. You can Google many such stories. One involves Michael Raymond, whose undercover informant work for the FBI and other law enforcement groups busted many of the corrupt officials in New York's Parking Violations Bureau during the 1980s, but who also during that period "… traveled widely under a dozen aliases, carrying out swindles, embezzlements, thefts and, Florida authorities suspect, at least one murder…"[2]

The 1960s were a field day for such loose cannon agents and their informants and infiltrators, all grouped together by FBI Director J. Edgar Hoover under a program dubbed COINTELPRO, as in "counterintelligence program" against domestic political activity. As shown in *The COINTELPRO Papers: Documents from the FBI's Secret Wars Against Dissent in the United States* by Ward Churchill and Jim Vander Wall,[3] local FBI offices were showered with a blizzard of letters emanating from "Director" suggesting all sorts of tactics to be employed against "New Left" groups and especially "Black Nationalist" organizations. Hoover even wrote a letter excoriating the San Francisco office for objecting to such programs aimed at the Black Panthers' "Breakfasts for Children."

The push for local offices to take the initiative on such tactics not only opened the door to rogue operatives, but also pushed those offices toward campaigns that reflected J. Edgar Hoover's racism and reactionary politics. COINTELPRO was in part driven by the same old-style nativism and bigotry that crops up in *Black Mass*. In the film Agent Connolly argues for making Bulger an informant by appealing to ethnic hatred: use beloved "southie" Boston Irish to bring down the loathed Italians. Similarly, in COINTELPRO the Bureau cast itself in a war against "black nationalist hate-type organizations" as compared to, in Hoover's phrase, "responsible Negroes."

How do we know all this? Ironically, through a bunch of criminals who got away clean. A group of burglars calling themselves the "Citizen's Committee to Investigate the FBI" stole documents relating to COINTELPRO from an FBI office in a Philadelphia suburb in 1972. They mailed the stolen documents to newspaper reporters in Boston and New York. That started a long flood of disclosures over decades, especially regarding FBI activities, which included many Freedom of Information Act requests and the post-Watergate Senate Church

Committee's investigation of domestic intelligence.[4] The "Citizens Committee" only revealed their identities forty-five years later, when they could no longer be punished for their actions.[5]

The documents revealed by the group make for some very uneasy reading. Even given the fact that some radical groups did engage in bomb attacks on buildings during the 1960s; even though in 1967 one branch of the Black Panthers did march upon the California state Capitol carrying guns, ironically to protest an anti-open-carry gun-control bill, which equally ironically turned then Governor Ronald Reagan into a gun control advocate; nonetheless it's appalling to read how the FBI conducted itself like some sort of *Minority Report* pre-crime squad, targeting individuals and groups because they felt they would commit crimes in the future if the Bureau didn't get to them first.

The tactics stemmed from a long campaign, beginning in the 1950s, against civil rights leaders, political organizers, and suspected communists that sometimes sank to ludicrous depths: the FBI once sent an extortionate letter to Martin Luther King threatening to expose his adultery if he didn't commit suicide. As the movie *Selma* showed, the FBI constantly shadowed and wiretapped Dr. King.

Why? In a letter headed "Counterintelligence Program/Black Nationalist-Hate Groups" a goal was set to "prevent the coalition of black nationalist groups" (such as the Black Panthers and the Nation of Islam) because "an effective coalition of black nationalist groups might be the first step toward a real 'Mau Mau' in America," referring to a racist term derived from a Kenyan revolutionary movement of the era.

A second goal was to "prevent the rise of a 'Messiah' who could unify, and electrify, the black nationalist movement," and that was where Dr. King figured in. The FBI believed that he might "abandon his supposed 'obedience' to 'white liberal doctrines' (nonviolence) and embrace black nationalism."

But the Bureau's worst tactics were reserved for the Black Panther Party and similar groups, tactics often lumped together under the heading "Racial Intelligence." The Ghetto Informant Program, also called "Ghetto Listening Post," employed some 3,248 snitches; by this point, J. Edgar Hoover had put several times more FBI agents into domestic spying and internal security infiltration than he threw at organized crime. Hoover informed his agents that the purpose was disruption and "it is immaterial whether facts exist to substantiate the charge."[6]

Some actions had devastating effects. "Snitch jackets," or

accusations of informancy, forged by the Bureau, caused violence among various groups. An FBI informant's drawing of a floor plan of Illinois Black Panther Party Chairman Fred Hampton's apartment (a space also used by the Party itself) was turned over to the Chicago police and prepared the groundwork for a police attack on that apartment that killed Hampton.

Meanwhile, the "Counterintelligence Program/Internal Security/Disruption of the New Left" was created to neutralize the New Left from within, based on the erroneous view that the SDS was allied with older hardline communists (thus ignoring the phrase "New Left") and that opposition to the Vietnam War was anti-American.

From 1964 to 1968, an unknown number of informants, provocateurs (to try and turn demonstrations violent), and infiltrators were utilized in "non-criminal investigations." Some informants naturally went off the reservation. One of them, after burglarizing Socialist Worker Party files for the FBI Watergate-style, was arrested for non-Bureau burglaries in Denver. Another, in the case of the "Camden Twenty-Eight," infiltrated an activist group and then actually led a raid on a New Jersey draft board and destroyed Selective Service files in order to implicate the rest of the group—and revelation of the informant's involvement led to the acquittal of the entire group on all charges.

Meanwhile more than 800 wiretaps were installed and 700 bugs through over one hundred "surreptitious entries," and, in a final grace note, letters with messages like "Beware the Siberian Beetle!" were mailed to dissenting organizations in the hope they would freak out the acidheads in those groups.

In *Black Mass*, Ken Weeks, Whitey Bulger's driver, about to give evidence to the government, declares "I am not a rat." Of course they were all rats, whether becoming informants while they disclaimed their rattiness, whether calling it an "alliance" like Bulger, or whether, as Connolly did, overlooking Bulger's murders and narcotics racket and taking Bulger's money to keep up a "business" relationship to try to catch Mafia kingpins.

One doesn't want to tar with this brush all the Bureau's dogged and sometimes heroic ground-level agents and counterterrorist experts. And there was hope that after decades of modest reform, especially after the 1975 Church Committee hearings, and with an enhanced focus on international criminals like terrorists and cyberhackers, that the FBI had reformed. They do appear to be out of the business of letting loose informants on regular citizens, whether to suppress their domestic civil liberties, or, in the case of cooperation with Bulger, to bury them in a river.

But the recent election showed the FBI's rogue side has not been suppressed. The Bureau seems to have careened from having a dictatorial Director running roughshod over individual agents to having a weak Director manipulated by unscrupulous agents from below, forced to cry wolf about a spurious pending investigation of then candidate Hillary Clinton to get ahead of potential leaks. It seems of a piece with the '60s history of rogue agents, rogue informants, and rogue operations. Director James Comey's having made his second and bogus announcement of investigating Hillary Clinton was unethical, marginally illegal, and put a big thumb on the scales of the election; if so one news release may have done as much damage as all of Cointelpro.

The credibility of the FBI has been so damaged that it's even suspected by some of its critics of an alliance with Vladimir Putin, and as of this writing the department of Justice's Inspector General is investigating Comey himself. To restore that credibility, the current or future Director needs to remember the history of the former Director, how badly external and internal security measures can be misused and abused, and what a rat's nest once existed within the corridors of the FBI.

Fury Road Lingo and American Ecospeak

Summer's almost gone, as Jim Morrison once sang, and with it the silly season of comic book and action movies. But this year's serial- and-special effects bounty, as in the year of *The Dark Knight*, has seen one true masterpiece: George Miller's *Mad Max: Fury Road*.[1]

There's no need for me to add to all the critical praise for the film itself. What grabs me as a writer is the invented language of the film and how it reflects the film's ecological nightmare: it's the lingo of humans adapting to an environment they've utterly destroyed and a dictatorship that wants them to choose such death over any resumption of life. That language and the movie's imagery deliver the themes of the film with a speed that matches the action, and also (and this is truly spooky) suggest the kind of doublespeak being used right now to help us shrug off warnings of disaster while blunting our desire to do much about it. *Fury Road*'s slang is a grotesque version of language being used today by climate-change deniers, industrial agriculture food producers, corporate polluters, and the politicians who serve them.

Mad Max: Fury Road has many movie antecedents, including silent movies, which George Miller has said are his ideal of pure cinema, and of course westerns; Miller's original Mad Max trilogy was called an "armagestern." But *Fury Road* also harks back to unabashed "message" movies of the '60s.

The '60s were a very serious-minded time, and there were apocalyptic films and books about impending nuclear and ecological destruction that delivered their messages head on. *Seven Days In May* about a military takeover of the country, *Silent Spring* about a natural world devastated by pesticides. *Fail-Safe* about nuclear war started by accident—they all included speeches and scenes we'd call 'didactic' today. In Rachel Carson's original nonfiction book *Silent Spring*, there was even a fictional passage, "A Fable For Tomorrow," mirroring the nonfiction in its depiction of a town where nature had been destroyed by DDT—talk about letting fiction be utterly didactic in order to prove its point.[2]

These late '50's–'60s books and movies may seem a little preachy now, but they reflected a desire of a newly king-of-the-world but not exactly feeling top-of-the-world America to hear what it felt it needed to hear and to hope such warnings could be effective if they could be acted upon by responsible men and women. This was, after all, the post–World War II generation, beneficiaries of actual experience in saving the world, not to mention GI Bill educations and socially progressive government programs. Such newly sophisticated audiences took their messages straight, no chaser.

The even more well-educated and socially concerned baby boom generation of the '60s also responded to such message-ing within films; a little bit of verbiage was tolerated when seriousness was taken seriously. Movies did, however, in response to attention spans modified by television, start to move faster. 1962's *The Manchurian Candidate* delivered its message about the dangers of McCarthyite right-wing lies and fearmongering within a tightly plotted thriller, which also, in its final twist, equated such right-wing politics with any and all dictatorships (a timely warning then and especially now). The film used an ingenious flashbacking structure and adopted the (back then) quick-cut pacing borrowed from TV news and commercials to speed the action along and slip in the lies and schemes of its politician villains almost parenthetically.

But the best serious-themed and most popular political movie of the '60s turned the whole approach on its head by making it a comedy. And in so doing, *Dr. Strangelove* also supplied its own comically inverted language to reflect the absurdity of impending nuclear war ("Gentlemen, you can't fight in here, this is the war room!"). Stanley Kubrick often explored language distorted for the purposes of masking savagery: in *A Clockwork Orange* the vicious thugs have their playful and courtly Nadsat argot, in *Barry Lyndon* the savage duels have an exquisitely formal code, and in *Strangelove* the technical and military language has gone completely nuts in its inverted, Bizarro-world way to allow people to persuade themselves into mass murder.

Kubrick's use of such language is a major prototype of *Fury Road*, but of course Kubrick got that in part from the literary master of such perverted language, George Orwell. Orwell's main proclamation in his novel *Animal Farm*, an allegorical condemnation of Communism, was "All animals are equal, but some animals are more equal than others."[3] and in his *1984* the slogans for the thought-controlling dictatorship of Big Brother were War is Peace, Freedom is Slavery, and Ignorance is Strength.[4] Orwell's great 1946 essay, "Politics and the English

Language,"[5] deals with how sloppy or deliberately distorted or inverted language leads to widespread acceptance of dictatorial and destructive political systems, and no movie better conveys that thinking than *Mad Max: Fury Road*.

Like *Strangelove*, *Fury Road is* in many ways a black comedy, even if the movie asks the question "who killed the world?" with utter seriousness. George Miller, a learned film master in his seventies, probably knows his Orwell, Kubrick, and other '60s films well, but also has known since his '80s Mad Max trilogy that today audiences won't go for too much 'speechifying'; his movies move faster than any Marvel franchise. With the exception of a pause in the middle where Furiosa and her band of women share their goals with Max and the audience, Miller, in order to propel the action at lightning speed, layers the darker aspects of the film's ecological protest with life-into-death inverted language and imagery and the very sound of dehumanization in a way that replaces explanatory dialog.

On the soundtrack the groans or grunts of people are mixed with the roar of cars. The oil that destroyed them becomes an object of worship, their vicious aged rotting-away leader is called Immortan Joe, and since he controls the water supply, he warns them "My friends, don't get addicted to water" (an inversion and parody of George W. Bush's hypocritical warning about not being addicted to oil). Life is death. The war boys embrace their "half lives" (they are radioactively and chemically decaying) and chant "I live I die I live again" believing in some automotive Valhalla; they even spray themselves with what looks like liquid chrome on their way to battle. Oil is mother's milk. What kills them makes them well: healthy babies are sneered at by one character as an impossible and worthless goal. The most determined young soldier is called Nux (as in null) and rides into an apocalyptic dust storm screaming "What a lovely day!" The steering wheels of their beloved cars are carved with skulls and their ruler wears one on his crotch, the very act of generation becoming death.

Even Max, the titular hero, is so literally buried in the rot and dirt of this land that in one brilliant bit of imagery a dusty mountain is revealed to be him rising out of the earth. It will take women to stir him back toward action, sanity, and decency, and women (literal seed-carriers) turn out to be the salvation of Mad Max's world.

It doesn't give too much away to say that Miller thus leaves the audience at the end with at least some hope, although the two times

I saw the film in the theater the applause and cheering that normally follow a successful action film were absent. The film has too much impact for that.

Such movies back in the '60s were sometimes, believe it or not, followed by government action. Protesting the effect of out-of-control technology on the environment has a long history, and the consciousness stirred up by books and movies on that theme led to, in the case of *Silent Spring*, the banning of DDT, despite the pushback led by (of course) Monsanto. Later years saw the Clean Air Act and conscientious and effective action to curb acid rain and modify the effects of ozone on the atmosphere.

Unfortunately seriousness at the movies is no longer taken as seriously as it once was, even in the case of a movie as entertaining and—not even prescient—plain old accurate as *Fury Road*. It's not just that there are parts of the world where the Mad Max scenario is literally playing out. In cities like Delhi children are living in an environment so polluted that often their lungs don't develop or are permanently damaged. In territories ruled by ISIS, jihad is defined as death leading to eternal life, and oil, stolen and smuggled, is indeed the life's blood of all this death.

And in a much subtler way, the *1984/Mad Max* language of doublespeak is being employed in more sophisticated countries like the United States to numb our concerns and frustrate and turn back our attempts at conservation and environmental energy source reform. Here are three examples I happened to find as a journalist and researcher; not an investigative journalist, just as someone on various assignments who can't ignore other information grasped along the way.

Florida Forever:[6] I've been to Florida many (i.e., enough) times, and so learned about "Florida Forever," a program Governor Rick Scott claims is part of his having "invested record funding in protecting the environment." For years before Scott's regime the Florida Legislature invested up to $300 million annually in this program to buy land with money from a tax on real estate transactions for environmental preservation. But as both Nature Conservatory and PolitiFact have pointed out, Governor Rick Scott once tried to cut it completely, then the next year upped it to a princely eight million, and since then has alternately cut it back and raised it in a way that Frank Jackalone, Sierra Club's Senior Organizing Manager in Florida, has called "disconcerting."

Scott and Republican lawmakers also forced state water management districts to slash property tax collections, which inevitably curtailed their activities in water resources and wetlands protection. And the state government has famously forbidden the phrase "climate change" to be even uttered in its administration, much less acted upon; the preferred/mandated term is "sea level rise." Which come to think of it doesn't negate the term "Florida forever"; it just means that, given the refusal to acknowledge climate crisis, there's a good chance that parts of Florida on the edge of the ocean, particularly in the Miami area, will eventually "forever" be a part of the continental shelf.

Affordable Food:[7] Ah yes, "affordable"—as in sometimes fruits and vegetables are out of reach for poor people, but thankfully there's plenty of corn-related food coming out of the heartland. Especially from the agribusiness giant Cargill, a major producer of high-fructose corn syrup, which shows up in so many foods implicated in obesity. Certainly smaller family farms do exist and they can choose to grow fruits and vegetables (even though, unlike corn farming, such farming is less subsidized and thus it's difficult for it to compete with cheap corn-based food in the marketplace). This is especially true given that when you drive by acres and acres of Midwestern cornfields, much of which is devoted to bioplastics and cattle feed and ethanol, you wonder what entities other than huge "king corn" agribusinesses can afford large-scale farming at all. Farming is still important in this country, but if cheap food rules, you get what you pay for, and you may eventually lose what you can't afford.

Concentrated Animal Feeding Operations (CAFOs): A largely neutral but nonetheless slightly sinister phrase that describes giant cattle confinement areas where thousands of beef cattle's stomachs are re-engineered to eat corn, which also requires large doses of antibiotics, thus posing a threat to public health. The manure and methane produced by such factory farms is a constant threat to the air and water quality where they're situated. There's still meat in this country that comes from ranches who do business in a more ecologically sane way. But such ranches face severe economic competition from the CAFOs: a former rancher I talked to, now a banker who gives ecotours on his land, told me he would have to be a millionaire to ranch now. But again, this keeps meat more "affordable." The same "size does matter" rules also apply to massive pig and chicken farms, along with the inhumanity and health threats.

Community Efforts And The Latest Technology:[8] A perfectly innocuous phrase, except when it's proposed as a way to deal with oil spill cleanups and regularly appears in publicity-related materials in the wake of the Deepwater Horizon disaster. While I don't know what the latest technology is, it seems every oil spill is still dealt with by the same booms that have come out over decades, and there's only so much bucket brigades can do in the face of a massive oil spill. It's fairly easy to go on the Web and find out that BP has provided $6,107,180 to the state of Alabama as part of their Deepwater Horizon Economic Settlement in what they're (charitably) allowed to call "Gulf Seafood And Tourism Promotional Fund Grant Proposals," another choice manipulation of language, and the mention of efforts at oil spill remediation in, for example, a film at Mobile's new Gulf Quest museum is never accompanied by any reference to any kind of public-private regulation and oversight.

This corporate doublespeak hardly rises to the intensity of the inverted language that hypnotizes the war boys into an appetite for self-destruction in *Fury Road*. But George Miller, who was a doctor before he was a director, isn't diagnosing our current condition, just pointing out where it might go if we don't heed the warning indicators, and this kind of soft language, keeping us complacent and inactive about what needs to be done to even just manage the climate crisis, is definitely unhealthy.

Miller has sounded ecological warnings not only in his Mad Max movies but also his *Happy Feet* animated films. It all percolates in the background, and hopefully, in the case of the *Happy Feet* films, promotes new ways of thinking in children. There have been many documentaries, above all *An Inconvenient Truth*, which did finally create awareness of the climate crisis, which has led, gradually, to a deal with China, the Paris accord, and President Obama's executive actions (time will tell how many of these survive). But unlike in the '60s, it seems that sustained serious-minded media can't catalyze much national support for, for example, more repurchasing of land for environmental purposes, protection of and directing of subsidies toward small family ranches and farms, and enforcing of government regulation and oversight against oil companies.

The actions of one enlightened president can be all too easily undone, as we will no doubt find out. And when it comes to the kind of books or movies that, in the '60s, created a sense of urgency, and energized significant and lasting antiwar or environmental change, we now seem to prefer our entertainment (unmad)maxed, our seriousness diluted, and our inverted language straight, with no chaser except a ticking clock.

Punch the Hippie, Kill the Planet

I still remember my first trip to the health food section of the Freshman Commons at college. The food itself struck me as some of the most godawful slop I'd ever had; this was decades before the excellent natural foods and recipes of today. But what was more off-putting were the glances I got from what was clearly the hippie contingent of the class, as if I were an interloper in a very exclusive clique.

That kind of snootiness was a bit reminiscent of the line in the tune from *Hair* "Easy To Be Hard," about the thoughtlessness of "'specially people who care about strangers/Who care about evil and social injustice."[1] 'Specially since it was pretty clear there was a moneyed element in prep school and college hippiedom, since if you worked summer jobs and kicked in for your own education and then worked a dining hall job in college and studied afterwards it wasn't exactly on the program to drift into an off-campus or summer vacation alternative lifestyle world.

As a Hawaii journalist decades later I certainly got to cover and occasionally participate in my share of back to the earth (and the sea) activities as part of my stories. I also got to meet and admire plenty of people, Hawaiians and transplanted *haoles* (whites), who were achieving impressive feats of ecology-related art or renewable energy implementation and living genuine countercultural off-the-grid lifestyles. But I was also occasionally reminded of the superiority and self-righteousness I'd spotted way back when I was a kid. You're still living like they are, they'd tell me, amidst all the materialism and consumer goods and greed and pollution and false values in a too-developed part of Maui (and by the way, I'm a great source for your story on dolphins, because they speak to me).

It sometimes seems as if the resistance to climate policies in the present day is in part a transplantation of resentment against that kind of '60s and '70s era hippie-ism. Many "straight"—as, in '60s parlance, drug-free or more conservative—kids did not see counterculture behavior as a genuine desire to adopt simpler ways of life and to choose sustainable agriculture and artisanship and music over materialism and support for military-industrial war policies (which in fact it could be). They saw it as an arrogant, phony spoiled rich and/or drugged-out stunt (which it could also be), and they've matured with that bias intact. The popular phrase for this attitude is "punch the hippie," and its manifestations can be relied upon to rally right-wing crowds everywhere.

But it wasn't always so. In fact, the early Earth Day rallies and demonstrations that grew out of the hippie-influenced ecology movements were pretty much the most noncontroversial demonstrations you could attend back in the late '60s and early '70s. Smog was awful in L.A., the Hudson River was filthy, the Cuyahoga River in Cleveland had caught fire—it was pretty obvious something needed to be done. Most Americans happily jumped on the ecology bandwagon, just as most Americans wholeheartedly supported, during the Nixon years, the creation of the EPA and the Clean Water and Air Acts. The Reagan Administration and its infamous Secretary of the Interior James Watt were a definite step back, but the first Bush administration saw action to curb acid rain and international efforts to repair the fraying ozone layer of the upper atmosphere.

Of course none of these required the kind of sacrifices from ordinary Americans that dealing with the climate crisis will demand. Except for complying with smog tests and other emissions controls on cars, and various degrees of recycling, most Americans don't factor improving the environment, and especially trying to avert rising sea levels and violent weather systems and more harm to the very air we breathe, into their daily lives. That will not be the case in the future, and understandably that fills people with a dread they counter with denial.

Do I "believe" that manmade greenhouse gas emissions are causing disastrous climate cancer? Yes, just like I "believe" the sun will rise tomorrow. And I prefer the term "climate cancer" to climate change, first because it makes the stakes clearer, second because, if you submit human lungs to huge doses of pollutants, that's what you're going to get, and that cancer sited in the lungs will destroy the rest of the body as surely as the polluting greenhouse gases are leading to violent storms, worsening droughts and fire seasons, acidifying oceans, dying coral reefs, and rising sea levels. As former President Obama stated in a recent *New York Times* article, there is no greater challenge to not only planetary civilization, but what Bob Dylan called "the sanctity of the earth."

In the face of such necessities it's trivial to allow dislike of the priggish snobbery of the "tree-huggers and granola-eaters" to get in the way of the absolute necessity of a transformation of our energy program.

But on the left-wing end, the environmental cause and ethic needs to be stripped of any and all taints of self-righteousness. This isn't the first time it's happened; the Sierra Club itself was originally wealthy and privileged, which impeded its popular acceptance. But gradually the Club democratized and came up with stronger tactics on various environmental issues, now including staunch support for a phase-out of fossil fuels.

So given the need for Americans to join the world in addressing the climate cancer problem in as strong a manner as possible, and recognizing time is running out, let's go back to that "punch the hippie" perception problem. Today's climate change deniers are trying to build a mass movement to equate environmentalism with hatred of regular people and job destruction. So let's see how that anger by many Americans toward that leftist '60s stereotype of hippie environmental advocates can be decoupled from the desperate need to try and save as much of the planet as possible from the ravages of client cancer.

See the Danger: People need to be urged to process (to use the cliché) not the dangers alluded to abstractly on a global level by experts they may distrust or environmentalists they resent but the perils right before them. The incredible frequency of floods and fires. Increased tornados and hurricanes. The growing incidence of earthquakes in Oklahoma, a center of the fracking industry, which is finally impelling this reddest of red states to curb fracking activity. Perpetual intermittent flooding along the Florida coastline. Don't think about global movements against climate change, think about your own backyard, as the Gulf Coast thinks about BP, or people living near aquifer areas think about oil pipelines.

Think About Pollution As Pollution: People who truly reject climate cancer's relation to greenhouse gases should think about what will happen worldwide if the United States (as it may very well as of this writing) backs out of global climate agreements. It's very possible that China and India will follow suit and continue with fossil-fuel based development. It's also possible that they won't, given that Indian and Chinese major cities are becoming air pollution hellholes. But we will have lost the ability to influence China and India because we will have backed out of what are, no matter their long-term goals, curbing-of-air-pollution agreements. And if global air pollution problems worsen, we will wind up breathing them in the western United States and beyond, and feeling their effects in all our oceans.

There's another way to look at it: Pascal's wager. The French philosopher Blaise Pascal professed belief in God through reasoning that, if God did not exist, he would merely be wrong, but if God did exist and he asserted he didn't believe in God, he would go to Hell for eternity. Similarly if you believe in taking action against climate cancer, in the highly unlikely case the greenhouse gas theory is wrong, at least you'll in some small way strengthen the effort to curb carbon-based air pollution in the world. If you deny climate cancer and join the efforts against it, and the greenhouse gas theory is right, you and your descendants will live in hell on earth.

Follow the Money: The resistance to legalization of marijuana was once the greatest of "punch the hippie" reactions. What's changed that? The results of the legalization in marijuana in Colorado: a tidal wave of revenue. In fact, so many capitalists now want to get in on it that recently voters in Ohio had to reject a legalization proposal because it was so clearly also an attempt by a group of investors to monopolize that potential industry. It's such a runaway success there's probably no way the new federal government can stop it; one hopes instead some kind of sanity will prevail and marijuana will be taxed and its content more controlled (for example, the lack of regulation on edibles potentially given to children, or on the kind of marijuana ingredients that can cause anxiety, should quickly be addressed).

Money can also be corrective as well as persuasive. The Nature Conservatory has taken flak over the years for working with wealthy corporations and individuals to essentially buy off tracts of land or have them turned into easements that can continue to return tax benefits for their owners as long as development is forbidden. But their efforts to preserve beautiful stretches of coastline and vital watersheds (especially in Hawaii) have been quite successful, and one can see how that tactic can be applied to stop oil and gas drilling and fracking on other tracts of land. Could even more massive amounts of money be utilized to save other stretches of land from mountaintop mining, while simultaneously (a) teaching coal miners that such mountaintop mining and related automated mining techniques are killing their jobs anyway and (b) retraining them for jobs in the new renewable energy environment? It may take many years, but why not?

Ditch Clean vs. Dirty: And while we're at it, how about the environmental movement no longer telling those coal miners and their bosses that they're in the "dirty" as opposed to the "clean" energy business. In New York we've recently been subjected to a commercial where a prissy girlish voice talks about how a well-known fast casual food franchise will soon have nothing but "clean food." Personally I don't like the insinuation that all other food—that is, everything I've eaten before and will eat if I don't patronize this franchise—is dirty food (not to mention I won't patronize any company whose girly-girl spokeswoman pronounces "food" as "fuuud"). This sort of arrogance of "clean food" or "clean energy" advocates is particularly annoying when you consider that they wouldn't think of curbing their jet-fuel-propelled flights to business meetings or exotic destinations, nor would they think of denying the energy usage of the new dome at the Arthur Ashe Stadium at the US Open, or restricting their computer use, despite the fact that computers need servers and servers need coolers and those coolers need, as of this point, oil. They would certainly not accept rolling energy blackouts in major cities combined with conservation-related brakes on the growth of those computer network servers, all of which may be needed in the future.

So for now, no more hypocritical "clean" versus "dirty" dichotomies.

Less (But Not No) Red Meat: Concede this one to the vegetarians, but don't necessarily feel you have to follow the injunction to eat no meat at all. Just use a little moderation. Cattle farts are a major source of greenhouse gases, plain and simple (think of it as in the millions, every day). Cutting down forests for grazing land is a major contributor to rainforest destruction, which deprives the earth of a major engine of carbon reabsorption. So before you buy that fast food burger, or buy more than, say, two pounds of red meat a month, think about how restraining yourself may offset the environmental damage of your far more necessary car commutes to work. And on that note, "granola eaters"…

Stop Hassling People Who Drive Ordinary Cars: They can't live in expensive cities like you do, or afford Priuses or Teslas. Just push for—or maybe, billionaires, pool your money for—encouraging production of cheap electric cars. Maybe Elon Musk should be awarded however many billions he needs to build a fleet of mini-Teslas.

Most importantly environmentalists, vegetarians, and latter-day hippies:

You Also Need To Support Science More (Beyond Climate Crisis Policies): So it's time to consider revised attitudes to some of the usual targets of environmentalists.

The "no nukes" movement was around throughout the late '60s and '70s, but it really gained traction due to two incidents. There was the mysterious death of Karen Silkwood in 1974, a nuclear plant worker attempting to provide evidence to the *New York Times* that the Kerr McGee corporation was manufacturing defective nuclear fuel rods, which became a cause célèbre and a long series of legal cases ultimately won by Karen Silkwood's family. Then in 1979 came the near-catastrophe at the Three Mile Island nuclear power plant. I lived in New York then, and still remember the fear that caused.

But I also remember growing up in the '60s when peaceful use of nuclear energy was promulgated and taught to us in texts such as "Our Friend The Atom." Was this propaganda to take the edge off everyone's horror of nuclear bombs and save a fledgling industry? Probably. But nuclear science produced results, everything from use of radiation in medicine to nuclear submarines. Under the strict control and safety procedures of Admiral Hyman Rickover and his successors, that fleet has not sustained a single accident.[2] For nuclear power plants, especially when one considers Three-Mile Island and the Fukushima reactor in Japan, the record is obviously more mixed, but at least in America catastrophe has been averted.

So perhaps its time to modify that "no nukes" resistance; the very phrase conflated peaceful use of nuclear power with nuclear weapons in a way that foreclosed any progress on the former with authentic horror of the latter. Some kind of transition to a renewable energy world is necessary, and so it's time to consider a public-private consortium, like the '60s space program turned out to be, which will build a small number of cutting-edge nuclear power plants and shut down and replace older designs, which will site the new plants far away from population centers and earthquake zones, which will transmit power through a far "smarter" grid, and which will be patrolled by top-of-the-line security forces and procedures. Power companies who join the consortium will be allowed to keep whatever profits they make, but will have to also diversify into renewable energies and contribute to all public expenses of the nuclear plant upkeep, including disposal of nuclear waste. That remains nuclear energy's biggest drawback, but perhaps we can consult with, for example, French experts, given their country's massive reliance of nuclear power.

In the same way the environmental left wing needs to consider that genetic engineering is not to be taken lightly, but there can be exceptions.³ About a year ago, an article appeared in the *New York Times* about how successful experiments to create genetically modified, pest-resistant crops in ways not toxic to humans were meeting fierce resistance in Bangladesh, India, and Africa, despite massive problems with malnutrition, crop diseases, and pesticide poisoning of farmers. As international exports, these crops face increasing boycotts in Europe and the United States.

The creation of pest-resistant crops is *not* the work of Monsanto, which is engineering crops to work *with* massive doses of their chemicals, one of Monsanto's many crimes against humanity and the planet. But creating pest-resistant crops is the sort of scientific work that can be carefully monitored, and that may be necessary to avert more massive famines in numerous countries. It will also help to avert the pesticide runoff that is a major cause of dying patches of ocean and, in turn, the slow death of the coral reefs that provide not only so much of the sea's beauty but so much of the support system for the world's fisheries.

All that being said, to reverse sanctimonious anti-science left-wing attitudes is the least of our problems in dealing with climate cancer. We may still have to suffer incalculable consequences for the delay and denial of at least twenty years, and the election of Donald Trump as president will now, as we know, be a damaging blow to climate-crisis-related efforts. Who knows how much we can save of the beauty of the earth, the many wonderful animals of the earth, or even the "sanctity of the earth," but we're still working for the future of humanity and life on earth. They may not thank us for what we did a hundred years for now, but at least they may be around to spit on our graves.

Still we can hope we're already on the way to rebuilding the environmental consensus of the '60s and '70s that led to the cleanup of large sections of the Hudson River by organizations including the Clearwater project and successful smog curbs in L.A. We've seen a climate cancer agreement signed by over 120 nations in Paris. We've seen the People's Climate March of 2015, organized by 350.org and other 21st-century environmental groups. We've recently had an agreement in Kigali, Rwanda to phase out coolants releasing HFC, dubbed a "super-greenhouse-gas," in air conditioners. The market for renewables is growing, auto emissions are being curbed, and there's the beginnings of a coalition to make the movement toward renewable energy a movement that can lead to better jobs and a better society, with economic justice and climate change remediation action combined.

Even Congressional and presidential repression and inaction driven by climate-change deniers will not stop alliances between Indian tribes and imperiled ranchers, hedge fund billionaires and ground-level anti-coal-infrastructure activists. So those deniers will no longer punch the hippie. They'll punch the upper-class doctor, the middle-class knowledge professional, the Native American, the business magnate, the working family. And millions of people will hit back.

Helluva Good Country Once

What a great '60s film does and doesn't tell us about contemporary America.

In 1969 a microbudgeted movie, starring two very good young actors who were as of that point known for nothing more than a family name (Peter Fonda) and a bad boy reputation (Dennis Hopper) became a monster sleeper hit, brought small-crew-and-portable-camera filming to the Hollywood mainstream, and became an icon of the era's youth culture.

Easy Rider's[1] logline read "A man went looking for America and couldn't find it anywhere." That pretty much captured the disillusionment and anger of young Americans at what was happening to their country in the '60s. But at the time this particular young American was disillusioned and angry with the movie. Wasn't it a little self-righteous and self-indulgent, this martyrdom of the motorbikers? Didn't director/actor Hopper realize his heroes started the movie scoring on a drug deal and that their big poetic goal was to party at the Mardi Gras?

Of course he did. Hopper not only brought to the film a photographer's eye for the American landscape—eliciting the first major work from his cinematographer, the great Laszlo Kovacs—but also a cynical take on the drug culture/counterculture he knew firsthand; one of the slang meanings of "easy rider" is a prostitute or her john. But Hopper still empathized with the desire of his two renegades, who named themselves Captain America and Billy (the Kid), to find a better life in an America that lived up to its myths, even if those myths were dying away. That slow death was summed up by the character George Hanson, an alcoholically adrift lawyer played by the film's breakout star Jack Nicholson: "You know, this used to be a helluva good country. I can't understand what's gone wrong with it."

That tension between the ill-fated sleaziness of Captain America and Billy's enterprise and their longing for redemption in a country gone somehow right again—along with views of an American road that, in the late '60s, still had some authentic openness—are what make *Easy Rider*[1] a helluva film. When the two men are killed and the Byrds sing "All he wanted was to be free … " we're not supposed to see Captain

America and Billy as martyrs—in Captain America's own words "we blew it"—but feel for them as men who went in a misguided way on a uniquely American quest.

Perhaps the one negative of *Easy Rider* is that it froze in time for the baby boomer generation a view of the South and the heartland, or as Hollywood might put it, "flyover country," as a land of utter ignorance where violence and lethal bigotry from redneck cops and thugs stalk the roads everywhere.

Forty-seven years later, we've seen that that's not a complete lie, but that the truth about flyover country is a lot more complicated. That region no longer sits immured in violent backwoods or sleepy hamlet ignorance in the shadow of New York, Los Angeles, Boston, San Francisco, and other major coastal cities. It has its own set of concerns both economic and political, it's become the center of a populist wave, and it elected President Trump.

Along with that astonishing political earthquake has come a lot of hand-wringing from the so-called northern and east coast elites. Why didn't we listen to them more? How can we reach out to them?

It would be a very good idea going forward for Democrats and the professional and financial classes they represent to connect more with the grievances of the part of the country that voted for Donald Trump, especially the poverty-stricken regions of West Virginia or the the dying towns of the Rust Belt. It would be an excellent idea for that party to choose new officials dedicated to rebuilding its alliance with American labor, and to meditate on what lower cost overseas goods for big city shopaholics have done to the middle Americans in the heartland who used to make them. Remembering as I do how the walks of Mayor Lindsay through New York's then black ghetto neighborhoods created real rapport, I wish Secretary Clinton had taken the same kind of walks through cities in Wisconsin or Michigan.

But let's also remember that, at the end of *Easy Rider*, Captain America and Billy are blown off their bikes by sadistic rednecks. That's part of the story too: they're shot dead because of the way they look and their different culture and their long hair. These days a modern Captain America and Billy riding through the heartland or the South on motorbikes, no matter what their hair length, are as likely to be greeted by high fives as hatred, and that's in part because *Easy Rider* and '60s music and counterculture are now a big part of the regular culture there. In Nashville it's literally at the heart of that city's renaissance.

But you'd better not be even walking down many of those streets in Trumperica "looking Muslim," a cloudy distinction for such a multiracial community, but it generally means brown Asian. And let's face it—the economically left-behind might have voted for the promise of jobs in Trump, but they also voted for the reality of a point of view that could create immediate peril for many other Americans.

So let's address George Hanson's question: what's gone wrong with this helluva country? Racism and religious bigotry are back with a vengeance. But there's also a deep and vengeful cultural antipathy. The Trump vote was equally about the big paycheck and, to quote James Brown's proto-hip-hop tune, "The Payback"—as in Brown's lyric "I don't know karate, but I know ka-RA-zy!"[2] They were told Trump was ka-ra-zy, certainly by Constitutional politics standards, but they voted for him with that in mind as a weapon against not just Hillary Clinton but everyone behind her. The Trump election may have been in part a legitimate cry for a redress of grievances, but it was also an angry, spiteful, and potentially deeply injurious blow struck by one half of the country against the other. It was blowing Captain America and Billy off the road.

You need gun control because in major cities crime and terrorism is a problem? Too bad. You're worried our attitudes about Muslims are not only cruel but may radicalize them in your communities? Also too bad.

You have thriving media organizations? We want to take them down or sue them out of existence, so that the territory is ruled by right-wing and Christian media. You have productive immigrant populations? We want to demonize them, uproot them, get rid of them. You're worried about the climate crisis? What climate crisis? You feel anyone should be able to marry whom they love? Our religion trumps your love. You believe women should have access to birth control and reproductive choice? We want women victimized by rape or incest or caught in an unfortunate accident to be adoption breeders. You believe women should be paid as much as men? We think they should be put in their place. You believe those women should also no longer judged solely by their looks or bullied or sexually abused, even become national leaders? We want to grab them by the pussy.

Of course, what you encounter in the heartland and the South, especially southern cities, is hardly so politically cut-and-dry. Ardent environmentalists protect the Platte River in Nebraska, and cultural preservationists have kept the town of Red Cloud, Nebraska pretty much the way it was a century ago as a tribute to Willa Cather. Kids in Mobile or

Atlanta dress and act like they're from Bushwick. Miami has an incredible mix of food, pleasure, and immigrant culture, Austin keeps weird, and New Orleans is … New Orleans. Above all, Nashville, America's music city, is building a museum that pays homage to African-American music, and is the mecca for musicians who, while playing mainly country music, have a whole range of attitudes and races and faiths (and which had a large anti-Trump demonstration after the election).

But don't delude yourself it's changed totally since the '60s—not just the 1960s, the 1860s. You can also find, in a very hip museum in one major southern city, the years 1861–1865 described as the "War of Northern Aggression." In a house museum a lithograph from the Civil War is described as one of the most touching pictures of "the Lost Cause." In tourist emporiums in various spots you can buy a Confederate flag right along with your American one. The African American female journalist I met on one of my assignments told me she'd had encounters on other southern travel junkets with folks who had tried to convince her, with all the goodwill in the world, that slavery was better for blacks.

So let's face it, these old and cruel and discredited truths combine with new bigotry against Muslims and Latinos and are part of the new flyover country flexing its muscles. And how is it the "new" flyover country? What are some of the differences between the rural backwaters of *Easy Rider*'s day and the angrily assertive Trump-voting bloc states of today? How about Charlotte and Omaha being financial centers? How about the poor farmers in the Midwest that we're supposed to be so concerned about having in many cases been the ones who survived the destruction of family farms during the Reagan era, so maybe they're not so dispossessed and disenfranchised as we think? How about major sports teams? Empires of Christian and talk radio with hosts like Rush Limbaugh and the incessantly paranoid Alex Jones? Labor unions destroyed in the original heart of progressivism, Wisconsin?

One of the reasons *Easy Rider* holds up is that it's a much more complex and resonant movie than first appears. The promise of open sky and earth and sunlight is squandered in an acid trip that goes nowhere. The hippie good faith and desire for a better, simpler life on the land is balanced by the sheer hucksterism and wooly-mindedness and greed of the drug culture. It's not like Captain America and Billy are heroes, and it's not at all that the liberal-leaning Hollywood that created them, then and now, is without excess and abuse.

But the pain and anger at those thugs striking back at Captain America and Billy just because of what they were, longhaired hippies—or, in the case of George Hanson, just a sympathetic fellow voyager on the wrong journey at the wrong time—was very legitimate and very real back then. Or as Jimi Hendrix sang "They're hoping soon my kind will drop and die/But I'm gonna wave my freak flag high."[3] It's certainly legitimate now for immigrants, African Americans, Latinos, pro-Hillary women (or as they're now typed by some Trumpoids, "Hillary bitches"), and artists and intellectuals of east and west coast cities to feel like Hendrix without his brio and with that freak flag as a target on their backs.

If the red-state elites, led by Trump, go after those groups and the institutions that represent them, one response available is simply to accept it. But another response could be the one North Carolina has received in the wake of its transgender bathroom law: economic boycott. A product comes from a Trump state so far as you can tell? Don't buy it. Want to see Wisconsin fall foliage? Minnesota's just as good. That trip to do the "literary tour" of the South or to casinos in Biloxi? Cancel it. Major music stars going down south? Follow Springsteen's example in North Carolina and don't go there. Sports prospects of color signing with Trump state teams? Choose other options.

But that kind of pushback against whole regions should be very much a last resort. Remember how complicated the new "flyover country" is. There's absolutely no reason for conflict, politically or otherwise, with Nashville, Atlanta, Austin, New Orleans, Savannah, or Virginia. Not to mention the fact that red-state-non-elites will probably soon learn the validity of Trump's promises, when trade wars destroy jobs instead of creating them, when tax incentives amount to endlessly expensive bribes that only save some of the jobs, when instead of higher wages there are higher prices at franchise stores and credit card interest crunches—and at that point they'll be receptive to outreach from the other side once it starts listening as well as talking to them.

There are still ties that bind. The Constitution. Support for our veterans (well, not back in the '60s, and wrongly so, but certainly now). Sports—there was genuine national unity about 2016's amazing World Series, which now seems an eon ago. Above all American music, like the rock songs so prominently featured in *Easy Rider*.

But let's face it, Jack was right. This was a helluva country *once*. Now, if we don't watch out, it's heading, in practice if not in blue versus grey secession, toward being a hell of two countries—in fact, given California's muscle, the long-simmering Washington/Oregon movement to confederate in some way with British Columbia in "Cascadia," and Alaska/Hawaii's separatist impulses, maybe even three or four.

A post-2016 coming together must be earned, and that "malice toward none, charity toward all" effort, as Lincoln said, is mainly up to the winners. Nixon after 1968 at first worked to earn it successfully, then in his second term went ka-ra-zy and forgot his own lessons, with the infamous results we all know. If *all* Americans can't have unity, earned unity, if President Trump and his most intolerant backers, which now seem to include much of his new cabinet, can't learn to compromise (perhaps to the tune of the '60s song that played out Trump's rallies, "You Can't Always Get What You Want"), if that's the way *they* want to play, then the blue states have to do whatever can be done to resist: from causing pain in the pocketbook to Trumperica to obstruction in Congress, from fighting bigoted mob rule channeled by the Trump organization to demanding respect and a backing off from *our* American way of life. Not burn the American flag, but keep our own flags flying.

The winners should take note of the enormous anti-Trump demonstrations in the wake of the election victory, and the hate crime increases all over the country. When Captain America and Billy not only can no longer hit the road looking for America, but won't even want to, a helluva lot will be lost. And payback is a bitch that grabs back.

Peace Then
Finding our religion

The only group I was ever an early adopter of was REM. I heard the album *Murmur* in Tower Records, was told by the clerk the company had just shipped it in, bought it and practically played the grooves off of it. It was little frustrating that you could barely understand any of the lyrics, a deliberately blurry (and "murmur"ous) vocal style that Michael Stipe would get past in his later singing. But the music was, to my '60s-honed ears, a lush and pastoral and otherworldly evocation of the Byrds that somehow or other also had a touch of the edge and grit of the Velvet Underground. It was fantastic '80s folk-rock.

Soon after I saw their first show at a little L.A. club, the Music Machine, the band just a few feet away from me, and I would follow them through the rest of their long career. There would be a range of beautiful and adventurous songs, along with evocations of the '60s in memory songs like "Shiny Happy People" or political protest songs like "Auctioneer." In the early Reagan '80s they were among the only great carriers of that '60s legacy along with neo-folk performers like Billy Bragg and Springsteen with his "Born in the U.S.A.," a song President Reagan memorably misunderstood as suitable for his campaign anthem until the Boss explained it was an angry song about a veteran suffering the aftermath of the Vietnam war and ordered Reagan to stop.

Many of REM's songs alluded to a seeking for an evanescent peace and beauty ("Nightswimming") or the desire for some kind of spiritual comfort, sometimes out of a growing madness and agony ("Everybody Hurts"), but sometimes out of pure yearning, and never more so than in their most popular song, "Losing My Religion." It's hard to tell what turns a popular song into an out-and-out megahit. Usually it's a tune that's silly or joyous: "Wooly Bully," "Walk Like an Egyptian," or "Happy." In this case it was a deadly serious song with a melancholy refrain and deliberately fragmented, inchoate expressions of halting confusion and aching loneliness. "Losing My Religion" seems to hint at the pain of feeling love and not being able to express it or be sure of it or even know it when it's there:

I thought that I heard you laughing
I thought that I heard you sing
I think I thought I saw you smile.
That was just a dream...[1]

Not the cheeriest sentiment. But the way the song reaches out to listeners and listeners reach back is uncanny. I've twice experienced being with younger people, once in a car, once in a Starbucks, a couple of us singing along impromptu with that tune. Listen to the live version—without Stipe ever abandoning the microphone and aiming it at the crowd as so many frontmen do today, the crowd sings along loud enough to be heard above the band. The melody and the desire and the sadness in the lyrics (as well as the pauses in the music, giving you time to prepare to sing) just do that to you.

Perhaps it's also the title, even though it's true meaning may be a kind of slang for "going nuts" and being "at the end of your rope." That alone would make it an object of devotion for troubled teens in the same way so many related to early James Taylor songs as the '60s became the '70s. But the song also suggests a desire for faith, a desire for some positive sign from a loved one and thus from the universe ("I think I thought I saw you smile"). That makes it a '60s sort of song, for that was a time of losing faiths and trying to discover new ones.

First of all was the embrace of love itself as a religion. That, however unformed, was enough for some. But it led many others down new spiritual paths, especially toward Asia. The embrace of eastern religions in the '60s, from transcendental meditation to Buddhism to all sorts of gurus, is well known; one unusual offshoot of it was Vietnam War veterans who discovered Buddhism in Vietnam and found in it a way to achieve equilibrium and peace in the midst of their postwar traumas. In the cases of, for example, Allen Ginsberg and George Harrison, Eastern religion became a permanent part of their poetry and music and their lives, and they brought along thousands of other genuine converts to Buddhism and aspects of Hinduism as well.

Many sought enlightenment and visions through LSD, which, in a comedy of errors and terrors, got away from CIA "psyche war" experiments and brought "trips" wondrous and visionary and sometimes nightmarishly awful to thousands. The embrace of "New Age" faiths in the '60s, an equal combination of sincerity and hucksterism, seemed to come along with the drugs.

But a lot also happened on the traditional Judaeo-Christian side. In a nation that had been on a war footing for so long (and was destined to be on one much later for even longer) you could say that for the America of the '60s the triad of peace, equality, and justice became a new religion, imbued with a holy spirit in which the best of the older religions played their part.

The '60s were at first a time of massive withdrawal from conventional Jewish and Christian faiths. Reform Judaism was very much on the ascendancy; some called it "godless Judaism," which was inaccurate, but it certainly was a far less strict form of worship than Conservative or Orthodox Judaism. Oppressive aspects of the Catholic Church, from Cardinal Spellman's power grabs and excessive anti-pornography campaigns in New York to the exclusionary obsolescence of the Latin Mass came under fire (and this was way before the pedophilia scandals), after which encyclicals from Pope John XXIII liberalized many of the practices and views of the Church, particularly on social progress. Churches in general came under withering attack as being a front for "Establishment" political views and morality. And atheism was on the rise, so much so that on April 15, 1966, oddly enough on tax day, *Time Magazine* put out its cover asking "Is God Dead?"

As with Mark Twain, reports of His death turned out to be greatly exaggerated. And many reacted with angry criticism, even from some unexpected quarters. Bob Dylan, with characteristic wryness and unimpeachable common sense, stated "If you were God, how would you like to see that written about yourself?"

But behind that rejection of the conventional God was much severe questioning. In the '60s, it wasn't so easy for Americans to believe that a beneficent God was actively steering the lives of humankind. After years spent battling evil abroad, after the horror of the Holocaust, American Christians watched as "godless Communism" drew its sinister curtain across the world. "As always, faith is something of an irrational leap in the dark, a gift of God," the *Time* article explained back then. "And unlike in earlier centuries, there is no way today for churches to threaten or compel men to face that leap; after Dachau's mass sadism and Hiroshima's instant death, there are all too many real possibilities of hell on earth."[2]

Those "atrocities of the 20th century" weren't the only ingredients in the mix, said Peter Manseau, author of the history of American spirituality *One Nation, Under Gods*.[3] There were also events such as Muhammad Ali's joining the nation of Islam and claiming he was minister of Islam and thus would not fight in America's war, shocks that forced Americans to think about religions other than Christianity, and a counterculture that encouraged questioning religious assumptions.

Finally, Western spirituality in the '60s came from so many other sources. Existentialist philosophy that ranged from Albert Camus, who was a total atheist, to Jean Paul-Sartre, who left some room for a Supreme Being in his work (both men having had their worldviews steeped in the fires of the French Resistance); Martin Buber with his more Jewish existential approach; Thoreau's *Walden* inspiring a worship of nature; Ethical Culture, a spiritual path based on ethical achievement instead of God; and folk and folk-rock music that echoed the Bible and its themes in many of Dylan's songs and in the Pete Seeger song setting of Ecclesiastes, "Turn, Turn, Turn," made into a hit single by the Byrds.

But within the antiwar movement and the civil rights movement traditional American religion found its new voice. Much of the leadership of the civil rights movement down south came from the black Church; Martin Luther King's teachings and speeches also drew on sources from the Old Testament to the theologian Ronald Niebuhr and his concept of the human drive for divine justice faced with implacable societal evil. King also studied Mahatma Gandhi's *satyagraha*, or "holding on to truth," and doctrines of nonviolence that Gandhi had learned from Leo Tolstoy's pacifist Christian *The Kingdom of God is Within You*—above all, its injunction, from the Sermon on the Mount, to "resist not evil," as well as Tolstoy's own injunction "never to do anything contrary to the Law of Love."[4]

The core message of the new movement was to get to the "promised land" of equality, justice, and the end of racism through peace and nonviolence, and to accept Christlike agony if necessary on the way. Jesus's sayings were invoked in the midst of events where the crosses to bear and the physical suffering in the name of love and justice were all too real. There were few atheists in the foxholes of the battle for African American equal citizenship down south.

For white Americans, religion wasn't a response to a challenge to their human rights and to their very existence so much as, for young men, their basic freedom. The military draft loomed as the equivalent of a prison sentence that would also force many men to violate cherished beliefs about the sanctity of life and the commandment "Thou shalt not kill" before possibly being led to their own deaths. Lt. General Lewis

B. Hershey, who ran the nation's Selective Service, was unsympathetic to students who might become his "sad sacks" in basic training and his casualties overseas. As he told *Life* Magazine "A society that hasn't got the guts to make people do what they don't want to do doesn't deserve to survive. A democracy has to make people do things for their own good. The presumption is that the citizen is responsible for his government. That means defending it."[5]

But what if you firmly believed your country and the killing in Vietnam in its name was wrong?

"Draft dodging" techniques included marriage, early enlistment in the Reserves, and the easier options of keeping a draft deferment by staying in college and graduate schools. But once the draft was doubled in 1965 to support increasing escalation of the Vietnam War—influenced by the mentality that the war on Communism, like the war on terror, was what we had to do, anytime, anywhere—the grad school deferments went away, and ultimately even the college ones. People who could not get "conscientious objector" status (followers of a religion that would not allow them to be in combat) went to prison, or fled to Canada, where they would not be pardoned and allowed to return home until a decade later.

In the midst of the agony and the fears brought about by such struggles, religion provided guidance and comfort, especially Quakerism and the American Friends Service Committee. This branch of Christianity was the original source of the conscientious objection doctrine and sanctioned totally committed pacifism and refusal of combat, and played a big part in antiwar demonstrations of the time. Christian Science also played a part; Daniel Ellsberg, the son of Jews who converted to that faith, would ultimately leak the "Pentagon Papers" detailing the secrets and secret official doubts behind the Vietnam war strategy to the *New York Times*.

Jewish antiwar expression more often came from secular sources: distinguished thinkers, activists, musicians, comics like Lenny Bruce and Mort Sahl, and filmmakers like, above all, Stanley Kubrick, who refused to accept what novelist E.L. Doctorow called "our Bomb culture." The movements of the '60s included Jewish student leaders on college campuses; Jewish followers and helpers of the civil rights movement; the brilliant clown prince of protest, Abbie Hoffman; folk-rock bards like Leonard Cohen and Bob Dylan; and the poet Allen Ginsberg.

But there was also the work of Abraham Joshua Heschel, a major

Jewish theologian of the twentieth century. Heschel moved from basic political opposition to backing South Vietnam and its corrupt puppet governments to believing that the U.S. assault on North Vietnam was "an evil act."

Citing the Old Testament, "Thou shalt not stand idly by the blood of thy neighbor," he declared that public opposition to the Vietnam War was a religious duty, a protest against immorality that rose above even the requirement to obey one's country's laws, very much taking Niebuhr's view that it was part of institutional social evil. He also felt, as Martin Luther King Jr. later would, that the war was injuring America's soul and sapping its resources. At a time when Jewish writers and thinkers like Elie Wiesel were conducting what would be lifelong teachings on the lessons of the Holocaust, Heschel applied some of that same thinking to the Vietnam war effort.[6]

But it was from mainstream American Christianity that some of the most prominent antiwar religious figures came. Yale chaplain William Sloane Coffin had been a member of Skull and Bones, Yale's elite secret society, and a CIA agent, but changed all his views out of his rejection of the Vietnam War and awareness of civil rights injustice. His organization of busloads of Freedom Riders to go down south won him the name "the bus-riding chaplain." He would go on to lead SANE (now Peace Action), then one of the nation's largest peace and justice advocacy organizations, and eventually the Riverside Church of New York.

And then there were the priests Philip and Daniel Berrigan. As the *New York Times* pointed out in its obituary of Daniel Berrigan, who lived to be ninety-four, his long life, based on his reading of the Scriptures, was focused on calling attention to racism, poverty, militarism, and financial greed as facets of the problem of an unjust society. He and his brother took their battle out of their pulpits and into the streets, and in the defining event of their career as activists, they burned Selective Service draft records in Catonsville, Maryland. "We destroy these draft records not only because they exploit our young men but because they represent misplaced power concentrated in the ruling class of America," they stated, adding "We confront the Catholic Church, other Christian bodies, and the synagogues of America with their silence and cowardice in the face of our country's crimes."[7]

The trial of the "Catonsville Nine" catalyzed increasing antiwar protest throughout the country. The Berrigans ultimately went underground when they were convicted but later served prison terms for their civil disobedience, and Daniel Berrigan would write that only a stubborn and rigorous belief in God got him through it. Much of his later work was devoted to helping AIDS patients and protests like Occupy Wall Street, as well as studying Biblical figures like the prophet Jeremiah, who warned his ruling society of impending disaster for forty years.

So now that we've lost that warning voice, among many others, and now that we're fighting the new Jim Crow and war seems an endless preoccupation of the United States, what, if anything, was achieved by the '60s flowering of alternative religion? We do remember that we live in a country influenced by the civil rights progress that, however endangered, is a huge factor in American life, from the black middle class to the Black Caucus in Congress. But we've almost forgotten one of the greatest demonstrations of protest in American history, which took the form of a holiday but nonetheless evinced genuine spirituality: the 1969 Vietnam Moratorium.

Life Magazine called it the "Day of Dissent," and it just about shut down the country on October 15, 1969.[8] There were readings of names of dead soldiers in ceremonies across America. Colleges and high schools closed except for teach-ins. I remember I went with my friend to a very crowded screening of the antiwar period film *Oh What a Lovely War*, whose cast included John Lennon; the Moratorium was such a hugely supported event that it was equally leisure and protest time. But beneath the 'school's out' feeling was seriousness of purpose. Peter, Paul and Mary sang and antiwar Senator Eugene McCarthy spoke to a crowd of 40,000 at Bryant Park in New York; planes skywrote peace signs. In Washington, DC there was a demonstration on the Mall and a nighttime candlelight memorial rally of 30,000 at the Washington Monument. Participants included many of the middle-aged, including a Dallas businessman now rejecting his hawkish views, and cops who wore black armbands.

Quite a result for an effort that began with Moratorium organizer Sam Brown and his small band of student activists, in a period when "social media" was leaflets and people yelling "let's have a Moratorium against the war!" It was so powerful that afterwards President Nixon would brood on why he didn't get more credit for reversing the course of the War and drawing down the draft (perhaps because he also bombed Cambodia and ended student draft deferments). In a scene dramatized in Oliver Stone's *Nixon*, a year after the Moratorium and soon after the killing of antiwar students by the National Guard at Kent State, the president, who was raised a Quaker, even made a surprise visit to an overnight antiwar demonstration at the Lincoln Memorial to plead his point of view.[9]

Beyond giving Richard Nixon brief twinges of conscience, what did the Moratorium achieve? Not the war's conclusion; that would come in 1975 at the hands of the victorious North Vietnamese. But according to former Secretary of State Henry Kissinger, the massive protest played a part in dissuading Nixon from using tactical nuclear weapons against North Vietnam. If that is the case, then this collective spiritual expression of the American people achieved an enormous goal.

Can this kind of spiritually inspired protest on a mass scale happen again? A large sector of Americans that have adhered to conventional religion have become more hardline. They include ultra-Orthodox Jewish communities and those extreme Christian groups that are becoming involved in supporting a more warlike posture in Israel, fighting gun laws, and arming themselves against what they view as oppressive elements in the federal government. And of course radical Islamic jihad (whatever you choose to call it) and its "lone wolf" or banded-together followers are a worldwide scourge, although less of a problem in America than anywhere else, thanks to a grateful Muslim community that so far peacefully practices their faith.

But given that increasingly militant behavior by the intensely religious, one wonders what's the status of the old Judaeo-Christian antiwar voices? Perhaps we're in an "Onward Christian Soldiers" phase, with the election of Donald Trump and exhortations about the defense of Israel and the rise of ISIS muting those voices. If so, then one can also worry that only the pro-war voices will grow. Will religion once again put the brakes on war and on the world's becoming, in Pope Francis's words, an "immense pile of filth"? Or will the three desert religions only be satisfied when the world's a desert? Is religion what Arthur Koestler meant by "the ghost in the machine" that will destroy humankind?

One thing we know: the yearning expressed in that REM song will not go away. We also know, from groups like Reverend Barber and his Moral Mondays, that religion still has its place in the new civil rights movement. Music also has had its spiritual influence way beyond the '60s, in the anthems, to name the most prominent examples, of U2, Bob Marley, and Bruce Springsteen. U2's most memorable songs heartbreakingly protested the Irish "troubles," and Bono has become a voice for charitable ngo's, including his own, around the world. Marley's songs of redemption are international. Many of Springsteen's best songs have had a spiritual bent, and his "The Ghost of Tom Joad" almost word-for-word echoes the movie and book *Grapes of Wrath*'s evocation of a collective people's soul in resistance to oppression.

That kind of perspective and evocation of true American spirituality suggests that an alternative religious resistance is not yet dead. As someone who considers himself an agnostic, but is also intrigued by doctrines such as Martin Buber's I-thou concept and his belief that everyone is sometimes addressed by the universe, I find myself reaching for the atheist's prayer, "O Lord, help thou my unbelief." I remember the Dylan line "If God's on our side, he'll stop the next war." I hope that especially when it comes to the greatest battles that began in the '60s, the antiwar movement, the battle against racism and for civil and human rights, and the efforts to save the Earth, not to mention the '60s spirit of peace and love, that religion old and new, instead of disastrously dividing us, will help all of us to journey to some kind of promised land.

Hiroshima

I got up very early in the morning on May 27 to watch President Obama's remarks at Hiroshima in part because of two related developments in cultural history.

The first was the 1959 film *Hiroshima Mon Amour*,[1] a favorite film of my mother's back when I was way too young to see it; it had been a founding film of the French New Wave of the 1950s and 1960s, which was so influential when I was a film student in New York in the late '70s; at that point, it became one of my favorite films as well. A couple known only as He and She, Japanese and French respectively, have an intense affair and conversation in which memories of his suffering in the aftermath of the bombing of Hiroshima and hers at the end of World War II in France continually surge into the narrative. The film is as much about the universal omnipresence of memory and trauma as it is about the events it discusses, but its documentary passages on Hiroshima, representing the Japanese ex-soldier's story, are devastating. *Hiroshima Mon Amour* also expanded the vocabulary of film, not just with its blending of drama and documentary, but with its techniques of mutable, contradictory narration and visual flashbacks—developed by screenwriter Marguerite Duras and director Alain Resnais—that are used to this day.

The second cultural event was the book *Hiroshima*[2] by the journalist and author John Hersey, which intriguingly also used multiple narrations with shifting points of view and techniques of both fiction and nonfiction (perhaps because such techniques were the only way to encompass the enormity of the event). I was fortunate enough to have had a class at Yale with Hersey, whose initial coverage of the aftermath of Hiroshima was the first journalistic treatment to ever take up an entire magazine, the August 31, 1946 issue of the *New Yorker*.

When that issue later became the classic book *Hiroshima*, the boundaries between novels, nonfiction books, and journalism were dissolved, preparing the way for the then-called New Journalism of writers like Tom Wolfe, Norman Mailer, and Gay Talese. The '60s had many great novels and novelistic autobiographies in many genres: comical and devastating portrayals of Jewish-American experience in works by Philip Roth and Saul Bellow; Harper Lee's *To Kill A*

Mockingbird and Claude Brown's *Manchild in the Promised Land*; the immortal *One Hundred Years of Solitude* by Gabriel Garcia Marquez; and speculative/science fiction by Kurt Vonnegut, Jr., Ursula Le Guin, and Philp K. Dick. But there was something particularly relevant to the era about the work of the "new journalists." It was through their eyes and their styles that some of the major political and cultural developments of the '60s were perceived, in books like Wolfe's *The Electric Kool-Aid Acid Test* and *The Right Stuff*, Mailer's *Armies of the Night* and *Miami and the Siege of Chicago*, and Talese's *Thy Neighbor's Wife*.

The way in which the bombing of Hiroshima shaped the culture of the '50s and '60s, and brought out the best in the writers and filmmakers of the time (including films like Sidney Lumet's *Fail-Safe* and Stanley Kubrick's *Dr. Strangelove*), is intriguing and memorable. But it's Hiroshima's effect on human history that's far more important. The rightness of whether to drop the atomic bomb on Hiroshima (and especially the second one on Nagasaki) will be debated forever. What is not debatable is that those events confronted all of us, especially people living in New York or Moscow in the 1960s, with the threat of nuclear annihilation. What is not at issue is that the event proved a boundary line for the human race, a line of transgression that, if crossed again, could lead to the extinction of humanity. We thought that line had been erased with the end of the Cold War. With the warmongering of North Korea and Russia, the bellicose rhetoric of Donald Trump, the growing tensions in Asia, and the new threat of terrorist groups trying to acquire weapons of mass destruction, it confronts us now once again.

President Obama's speech at Hiroshima rises both to the occasion of his visit—the 71st anniversary of the dropping of the atom bomb on that city—and the stern lesson Hiroshima teaches us. It's simply one of the most beautiful Presidential speeches I've ever heard or read, the remarks of not just a leader of America but the entire planet.[3] With its reminder of how man's first tools were also weapons, the President's speech recalled Kubrick's *2001*, whose rising monolith was with terrible irony realized in that very year as a crumbling one. His words were a reminder that humanity is now enshrined with the task of preserving not only its civilization but the survival of life on earth. The speech makes the simple and profound point that the world must forever guard against not just the use of nuclear weapons but humankind's own tendencies toward war and destruction. If in America, eternal vigilance is the price of liberty, in the world it's now the price of survival.

Sticking to Our Guns

We the People of the NRA, in Order to form a more perfect NRA, establish the NRA, insure the domestic NRA, provide for the common NRA, promote the general NRA, and secure the blessings of the NRA to ourselves and our Posterity, do ordain and establish this Second Amendment for the United NRA of America.

In the '50s and '60s, every American boy had a cap pistol. It was a toy gun that actually fired something that smoked and smelled of sulfur. I still remember me and my cousin "shooting" my dad, who would then shout "You got me," and collapse into a chair.

Our favorite TV shows were westerns. Even the more well-written ones weren't exactly *High Noon* or John Ford or Anthony Mann. The formula was simple. Lawman vs. Badman. Cowboys vs. Indians. *Have Gun, Will Travel.*

In summer camp, there were only two activities I was any good at: swimming and riflery. One reason was that neither had any psyche-out trash-talking during the competitions, in the first case because your mouth was in the water, in the second because riflery was performed in total silence, and with ritualistic respect for the rules and procedures of picking up a potentially deadly weapon and shooting it

For it was a National Rifle Association program, with a total emphasis on gun safety. The counselor slowly and with unnerving intensity described to us all the terrible things that could happen if we played with the guns, and laid out the rules and the series of commands—when to pick up the rifle, when to click on the safety—which, he swore, if we ever broke, if we ever deviated from by so much as a twitch, we would be banned from riflery for the rest of the summer. Orders to target-shoot were given step by step with great deliberateness and military precision. I loved the program, competed on the camp's team, and got to Sharpshooter Bar 2 level.

Then one year that counselor was gone, replaced by a hoodlumish new guy who didn't mind if we clipped toads we found in the forest to the target frames and shot them to pieces. My early introduction to the two sides of American gun culture.

It's a culture that one must respect, like it or not, for it has its roots in the founding of American society: the shooting of game to survive, the need to protect the farm on the edge of the wilderness, the American Revolution. But that reliance on the gun could also be a profoundly destabilizing force. In the chaotic pre-Constitutional period of the Articles of the Confederation Shays Rebellion had shown the power of local groups arming themselves and rising up to at least stymie the central government, as did the Whiskey Rebellion later during George Washington's presidency. It had to be on the Founders' minds that those sorts of citizens had to be placated and their skills rendered utilizable to the new republic, especially given that the militarily superior British "redcoats" had been defeated by just those sorts of guerilla forces.

And so the Second Amendment states: "A well-regulated militia, being necessary to the security of a free State, the right of the People to keep and bear arms shall not be infringed." Right away as a proofreader I notice that unnecessary comma that seems to have the effect of putting those first three words on the sidelines. Perhaps the Founders should've spent a little more time on copy editing to connect those three words more strongly to that "security of a free State" phrase, because the devil has been in that detail all our lives. How do you square the initial precondition of a *"well-regulated* militia" with what the current NRA, very much in the spirit not of my first riflery counselor but the toad-shooter, defends as the individual's unlimited right to own and wield any weapon of any kind in any way desired? And with no precondition of military service, except maybe freelance *posse comitatus* vigilante bands?

In June 2008, in *District of Columbia v. Heller*, the Supreme Court voted 5-4 to strike down Washington DC's tough gun laws. In what was viewed as a victory for the NRA, the Court ruled that Americans have an individual right to possess firearms, irrespective of membership in a militia, "for traditionally lawful purposes, such as self-defense within the home." But here's what Justice Antonin Scalia, beloved icon of conservatives everywhere, wrote in the majority opinion:

> Like most rights, the Second Amendment right is not unlimited. It is not a right to keep and carry any weapon whatsoever in any manner whatsoever and for whatever purpose: For example, concealed weapons prohibitions have been upheld under the Amendment or state analogues. The Court's opinion should not be taken to cast doubt on longstanding prohibitions on the possession of firearms by felons and the mentally ill, or laws forbidding the carrying of firearms in sensitive places such as schools and government buildings, or laws imposing conditions and qualifications on the commercial sale of arms.[1]

So even Justice Scalia held out a role for regulation. In so doing, while also writing the opinion on the side of less regulation, he manifested a debate that's been going on throughout American history. The NRA was originally established in 1871 in order to take that "well-regulated militia" part of the Second Amendment very seriously; its primary goal was improving American civilians' marksmanship in preparation for war (but not black citizens, forbidden by several "black codes" down south from owning guns).

The '60s was the peak of the gun debate up to now. Following the assassinations of a beloved president, the greatest of all African American civil rights leaders, and the most promising presidential contender of 1968 who was also the slain president's brother—all within five years—the nation was gripped by the sheer horror of it all, the despising of the rampant gun violence (which also included the near-assassinations of Andy Warhol and George Wallace), the desire to do anything to stop the madness of the bullet ballot. The Gun Control Act of 1968 was passed for the purpose of "keeping firearms out of the hands of those not legally entitled to possess them because of age, criminal background, or incompetence." The Act regulated imported guns, expanded gun-dealer licensing and record-keeping requirements, and placed specific limitations on the sale of handguns, the infamous "Mr. Saturday Night Special" of the Lynyrd Skynyrd song.

It was nowhere near as strong as the measures that could've been passed; particularly poignant in that regard is a videotape of the soon-to-be-assassinated Senator and presidential candidate Robert Kennedy arguing for stricter gun control and arguing against the wrong kind of person getting his hands on ... a rifle.

Over the decades it seemed to take major consciousness-searing events to create any kind of gun control efforts in this country. Because we nearly lost President Reagan and his press secretary James Brady to an assassin's bullets in 1981, we had, *thirteen years later*, the 1994 Brady Law and Assault Weapon Ban. The Brady Handgun Violence Prevention Act, still loathed by many gun dealers, imposed a five-day waiting period on the purchase of a handgun and required that local law enforcement agencies conduct background checks on purchasers of handguns. The Violent Crime Control and Law Enforcement Act of 1994 prohibited the sale, manufacture, importation, or possession of a number of specific types of assault weapons for a ten-year period.

But starting in the 1990s came a hardening of "Second Amendment" positions by the NRA and consolidation of their position as the group with a stranglehold on potential gun control legislation in the United States. The U.S. Supreme Court, in the case of *Printz v. United States*, declared the interim background check requirement of the Brady Handgun Violence Prevention Act unconstitutional. At this point some compromises were possible; major American gun manufacturers voluntarily agreed to include child safety trigger devices on all new handguns, but in 1998 an amendment requiring that trigger lock mechanism to be included with every handgun sold in the United States was defeated in the Senate; they could only be optional.

The law prohibiting certain classes of assault weapons expired on September 13, 2004, after Congress failed to reauthorize it. In 2004 President Bush also signed the Protection of Lawful Commerce in Arms Act limiting the ability of victims of crimes in which guns were used to sue firearms manufacturers and dealers.

And this is pretty much the status quo despite all the horrific school and terrorist shootings since then. There can be no compromise even on universal background checks, closing gun show and online loopholes regarding the Brady laws, and fitting guns with "smart" controls so that only the legal owner can fire the gun. There can't even be a nationwide ban on sales of ivory between states, which would help protect endangered elephants and also help curb ISIS's lucrative trade in poached ivory, because the NRA claims such guidelines would be an attack on gun owners wishing to sell firearms that contain ornamental ivory, and also infringe on the rights of Americans to legally kill elephants for their tusks. That's right, the NRA is anti-elephants and not particularly anti-ISIS; given how their opposition to banning sales of assault weapons facilitates terrorists' acquisition of such weapons in America, as ISIS has boasted, that should come as no surprise.

The NRA has become one of the most feared and the most politically and financially powerful advocacy organizations in the United States. It's unashamedly the lobby not just for gun-owners but gun-sellers. Its ideological position has hardened to the point where no compromise seems possible. But it didn't get way through some sort of minority cabal support.

For as much as the '60s assassinations stimulated gun-control advocacy, other key '60s events spurred the backlash to that. *In Cold Blood*,[2] Truman Capote's great novelistic nonfiction work published in 1966, described the murders of four members of the Cutter family in the town of Holcomb, Kansas; after that there was no way any isolated farmhouse in that region would not arm itself as much as possible. And in countercultural California, the 1969 Manson murders pretty much chilled out any kind of figurative or literal "open door" policy of peace and love and increased private gun ownership among that blue-state population. In fact, things got so weird about guns in California that after the Black Panthers declared their right to openly carry firearms to the Sacramento state legislature, Governor Ronald Reagan briefly became an anti-open-carry gun control advocate.

And in a classic case of racist backlash and overreaction the actions of the Panthers and the riots in Watts, Newark, Detroit and other ghetto neighborhoods in the '60s sent white people rushing to gun stores. Firearms were a billion-dollar industry within which, until 1968, handguns, rifles, shotguns, and ammunition were commonly sold over-the-counter and through mail-order catalogs and magazines to just about any adult anywhere in the nation. And after the '60s urban riots the pitch was clear: one gun store advertised "Nigger Getters" and "This gun carries a nigger-back guarantee."[3,4] Meanwhile the growth of urban crime and the appeal of vigilantism espoused in any number of popular films through the late '60s and '70s (*Dirty Harry, Death Wish*) fostered a new gun culture that pitted itself against any kind of gun control.

At a time of worsening race relations and more polarized divisions between North and South and rural and urban areas, this is where we are today. A little understanding is needed on both sides. Gun owners in the south and the heartland who support the NRA unconditionally have to learn how intolerable the free movement of guns and assault weapons sales allowed in or near major cities can make life for that other half of the country so responsible for generating much of the revenue, the media, the sports, the entertainment, and the technological products that are a big part of their way of life. If southerners and heartlanders don't give a damn about mass deaths of both adults and children north of the Mason-Dixon line, they should consider not only that mass terrorist attacks with killing-machine weapons can also strike them in their cities, but also that opposition to gun regulations that northern cities need could have reverberations that could deeply vex the heartland, especially (see "Helluva Good Country Once," this volume) when it comes to their states' economies.

But pro-gun-control advocates make a grave mistake attacking what they view as antediluvian opposition to gun control. First of all they call it by the euphemism "gun safety," which is bullshit. Gun-owners know all about gun safety. The instructors who don't make sure of safety can pay for it with their lives, as in the "Bullets and Burgers" shooting range incident a year or two ago, where one instructor was shot and killed accidentally by a girl not yet in her teens. What we're talking about is gun control, and the people who oppose it don't become any more placated when you don't call it what it is.

Secondly, if you've been to the Midwest, the south, or Texas, as I have, and seen all that empty space around isolated houses (not to mention if you've read *In Cold Blood*) you know why they have those guns and are almost paranoid about the possibility of losing them. There's still game to hunt and in the event of a home invasion, the first responders are far away. And once you've conceded that people should be able to have guns for hunting and self-defense, it's logically impossible to deny them extra guns for fun and games, any more than in L.A., where you almost have to drive, you can tell wealthy people they can't buy high-polluting older Porsches and other performance cars.

Perhaps it was especially in the '60s when we realized that the role of guns and the myths behind them were a burden and a paradox we accepted as Americans as surely as our counterculture musical heroes dressed simultaneously with native American "Indian" feathers and headbands along with cowboy hats and buckskin.

Still, given it has been estimated that US civilians own 270 million to 310 million firearms, and that 37% to 42% of the households in the country have at least one gun, what the hell has happened to that "well-regulated" part of the Second Amendment? The current uncompromising stance on gun regulation is influenced by antigovernment "hard" and "alt" right forces who have believed, ever since the battles of extremists with the ATF in Ruby Ridge and Waco, that the government is out to confiscate all firearms. It's a belief that was most ridiculously summed up in the Trump line that Hillary will take away their guns (her and what Emily's List army, Mr. President?). But by protection of a "free State" the Founders meant our country, not the free "state" of mind of a gun-owner who hates and fears the country—especially given that individuals now possess arms that have the power of what the Founders would have considered the thunderbolt of Zeus or Satan's hellfire.

Is no "well-regulating" compromise possible? Recall what Justice Scalia said about regulation. Just as you can impose regular smog checks and mandate higher fuel efficiency for most cars, you can mandate sales of "smart" guns that only the owner can fire (which is the only kind of regulation that might have stopped the Newtown shooter from using his mom's guns to kill her and all those children). If you can't legislate the licensing of guns, or at least handguns, as was tried in the wake of JFK's assassination, you can certainly tighten Brady Bill and gun show loophole-related restrictions, and create faster and more thorough procedures in background checks (which might conceivably have stopped the hate-killer who murdered churchgoers in Charleston).

If you can't forbid the sale of military grade assault weapons and ammo, why can't you mandate that, in the spirit of the Second Amendment, they be registered with our "militia," the National Guard, with record-keeping that might limit people accumulating terrorist-group-grade arsenals, and with strict laws and procedures to track those weapons potential resale and theft?

No of course you can't, because of the NRA, right? But guess what? Back in the '60s, you could barely ship goods in and out of our waterfronts or have them moved by truck without dealing with the Cosa Nostra. People could smoke in hospital waiting rooms. Things can change, starting with perhaps that ivory ban to slow the killing of elephants and take some money from ISIS. There may yet be new leadership in the NRA, some reform, perhaps even an alternate group of gun owners formed to reflect what seems to be the will of the American majority on minimal gun regulation.

For some final wisdom on guns let's turn to the '60s and one of the greatest of all American film directors, John Ford, the father of the American western.

Ford, among all his other achievements, basically created John Wayne's position in the pantheon of American heroes in films like *Stagecoach* and *She Wore A Yellow Ribbon*, but by the end of the '50s and the '60s he and (to his credit) Wayne were already enriching and subverting that persona. In what many consider one of Ford's greatest films, *The Searchers*, a film that had an incredible influence on every filmmaker coming up in the '60s from George Lucas to Martin Scorsese and on films like *Star Wars* and *Taxi Driver*, Wayne plays Ethan Edwards, a former Confederate soldier and outlaw looking across the West for a girl kidnapped by Indians, and a man who is darkly consumed by racism and a lust for revenge.

As Joseph McBride pointed out in his massive biography of Ford, "*The Searchers* subversively turns the concept of Western heroism inside out, showing the lone gunman who acts in the name of nascent civilization as a warped, destructive force."[5] It's the film's other less vengeful characters who bring the quest to a just and merciful conclusion, not Edwards; the best that can be said for him in the end is that, in one of American film's great moments, he spares the young woman the death he'd been planning for her for having assimilated with the Comanches.

And in perhaps his last great film, 1962's *The Man Who Shot Liberty Valance*, Ford explores the idea that the West was the creation of both the gunman and the legislator, that both the civilizing and protective impulses were emblems of the American spirit; John Wayne's calling Jimmy Stewart "pilgrim" is both mockery and an awareness that his quest to bring knowledge to the hinterlands links to one of the founding principles of the country. The wrath of the gunman must be contained, whether it pours out from a psychopathic villain like the very ambiguously named "Liberty" Valance, or flares up in a fit of rage from John Wayne's Tom Doniphon when he burns down his own house after the loss of the woman he loves. But as the ending of the film so touchingly evokes, Doniphon's heroic contribution can never be forgotten, even though publicly there will be a reaffirmation of the glory of the politician celebrated for killing Valance, not the revelation of the gunman, Doniphon, who, hiding in the shadows, actually pulled it off.

And that killing, however necessary, forever corrupts Stewart's Ransom Stoddard's political career and triumph with the burden of a lie, as well as rendering obsolete Doniphon's noble and self-reliant frontier ethic as the town built around that killing ultimately negates his values. Doniphon secretly shot Valance, and conferred glory on Ranse Stoddard, from a dark alleyway, and that darkness will now capture Doniphon. As for Ranse Stoddard, whose whole narration has been an attempt to tell the truth to the press, he receives the reply "When the legend becomes fact, print the legend." His false virtue, his false gunplay, despite all his efforts, will be lionized as before. The bond between the two men, privately affirmed by both of them during the film, will not be taught to the public.

There's a balance here that needs to be recognized and respected. In this valedictory classic Ford shows us the kind of gunman who tamed the west, so lauded in our mythology and in his films, as worthy of that glory, but also a tragic figure, wedded to the kind of lawless violence he tamed, and needing, even at his best encouraging, the however compromised lawmaker to step ahead of him.

One wonders what Ford, and even John Wayne, would've made of a culture where guns are fetishized, where stand-your-ground laws give Tom Doniphon's power to George Zimmerman, where open-carry laws are triumphing everywhere, where possession of mass-killing machines unimaginable to the old West and strictly controlled during military drills are considered the right of anyone over the age of fourteen. The myth that any good guy with a gun can stop any bad guy with a gun lives on. And as we've known ever since the '60s, the fact of the heroism of the western gunman is in our history and his tragic legend is in the movies. It's insanity that's on the streets.

Generation Gapped

> *"Don't trust anyone over thirty."* – **Jack Weinberg**,
> activist, Free Speech Movement, Berkeley, California

It was one of the most famous slogans of the '60s, summing up the "generation gap" that was proclaimed to be, as a title to a *Life* Magazine article put it, "The Gulf Between Parents and Children."[1] It could take the form of political arguments, deep divides in musical and literary taste, or, more viscerally, parent-child battles over drugs and sex.

Marshall McLuhan theorized that the generation gap was an effect of the explosion of new media on young people's consciousnesses. Any number of political figures tied it to the civil rights struggle and the protests against the war in Vietnam. However you explained it, in most families in America you couldn't escape it.

The *Life* article, naturally, focused on angry kids, alienated kids, kids on the streets. A 14½-year-old Sunset Strip groupie talked about taking marijuana, diet pills, and LSD; her combined age and drug and sexual experience made her every parent's most extreme nightmare. But even her words revealed the Gap (yes, the company did get the name from that) was not unbridgeable when she simply and sadly stated, "My parents, they can't do anything with me."[2] She represented a host of young people who thought parents didn't care what they did, and one or two kids said they missed discipline and being grounded. One young interviewee actually lamented "It seems that everybody's childhood is getting shorter and shorter."[3]

On the other side, a sympathetic parent suggested that "Now there is a real confusion for the kids about where they are going and how to get there. And there is this war in Vietnam with no end in sight." Another kindly professional voice, a psychiatrist, pointed out that, especially in relation to the war, kids were smart enough to "criticize and be impaling parents on their own expressed ideals." But countering such opinions were angrier parents accusing less stringent parents of being afraid of the kids, or "being ostriches. They can't cope with them, can't understand them, so they ignore them."[4]

Part of the parental fear and anger stemmed not just from the orneriness of their individual children but the sheer size of the baby boom generation, as manifested in antiwar demonstrations and rock festivals. This would clearly be a force to be reckoned with. Part came from the radically different political views shared by many of the kids. Part came from their liberated sexual practices, made possible not just by new thinking but by use of "the Pill" for birth control. And there was also the need to understand the young baby boomers by understanding their new media: rock music above all, but also film and theatre that was obscene or nakedly sexual (often as in just plain naked), the first underground 'zines out of the East Village and Haight Ashbury, and a whole new way of responding to television.

Much of this should now be sounding familiar. For in the millennial generation, loosely defined as individuals born between 1982 and 2004, we see all the characteristics of the '60s "youthquake." The sheer size, even greater than the baby boom. The brand new musical tastes. The different politics from their parents. Sexual practices and views of the morality of sex that prompt amazement or aversion even in a generation that came through the "sexual revolution." Different and scarier drugs of choice. And above all a whole new way of perceptually interacting with the world through the new media of smartphones, social networks, and the Internet.

Not surprisingly, as a result the '60s-style "generation gap" is back; it might not be as loud and out front and sloganized as it was in the '60s, but its definitely prompting a lot of unease and even dismay on both sides.

If there's anything the '60s have to tell us about this generational difference, it's obvious; please consider your youthful experiences, baby boomers, before you in any way judge or condemn youthful millennials. And baby boomer parents deserve credit for having in some cases bent over backwards to understand their children's changing tastes and practices, although the best parents have underscored or, with younger millennials, are still underscoring, that there will be consequences for unacceptable behavior.

But before praising the millennial generation, it's necessary to bury them a little. To criticize—with I hope some understanding—out of a duty to warn. Younger readers can dismiss this as a "get off my lawn" passage, but I promise there will be more empathetic paragraphs in this essay and a second essay addressing, per '60s history and thinking, some affirmative possibilities for millennials, especially college students, and how they can improve their lives. But first…

If I had a millennial daughter, I'd be terrified.

There's an epidemic of sexual abuse and assault going on in the American millennial generation. From the rise in reports of incidents of sexual assault on college campuses to the nauseating incidence of sexual assault in the military—about 12,000 incidents reported in the 2012 documentary *The Invisible War*[5] and significantly greater since then—this is a very serious problem (and not confined to women either). Even in its lesser manifestations, like young men in a group at Yale chanting "No means yes! Yes means anal!" it's pretty rank. It's grown severe enough that there are now organizations such as *Know Your IX: Empowering Students to Stop Sexual Assault,* where students are guided on websites through reporting and pursuing a sexual assault case per Title IX and the Clery Act.

Sociologists and psychologists, I'm sure, are debating the reasons for this extensively. Perhaps it includes all the warrior myths, idiot hypermachoism (what Don DeLillo once described in his novel *White Noise* as the "great dark lake of male rage"),[6] and sexual aggression and brutalism that underscores so much mass entertainment, and that now reaches all the way to the White House.

But in comparing boomers and millennials, part of the phenomenon is also a rise in both the incidence of reporting and the ways of dealing with the problem. During that sexual revolution of the '60s–'70s, it was probably true that more of the sex, influenced by the youthful values of the time, was more peaceful and consensual (and mellowed due to mellower recreational highs)—but there was also less informed awareness about defining what wasn't consensual, and much more of a reluctance to report it.

I learned a few years ago something that I'd never known at the time; that during the late '60s to early '70s and beyond my then all-male high school, Horace Mann, was in the grip of sexual abuse perpetrated by certain teachers, at least one of whom preyed on my classmates. But back then, especially in an all-boys school, and long before Title IX or sexual abuse survivor procedures or confessional TV shows, the forums for and the willingness to reveal such traumas were far less than they are now. Given that at least one of my classmates may have committed suicide because of a combination of possible sexual abuse and definite teacher-to-student mindfucking, I wish it had been otherwise.[7]

And it's also true that there was what used to be called "male chauvinism" and outright sexual abuse among not just *Mad Men*-type executives but within the "free love" counterculture, where women were regularly expected to cook for the commune, be giving and forgiving sexual mamas, and generally take a secondary and pleasure-providing position. In its wicked satire on the counterculture, *Neil's Book of The Dead* referenced the cry of "Chicks up front" that was heard at demonstrations. The idea was that cops would be less willing to beat women with their nightsticks, and if that weren't the case ... well, chicks up front.[8]

In fact, I know some parents of millennials who are amazed at how "good," how relatively chaste or monogamous, they seem to be, compared to the sexual mores of young people of the '60s, heterosexual and gay, which were pretty unconstrained all the way until the 1980s AIDS epidemic. In a witty and thoughtful *Time* Magazine article, Joel Stein (no relation) makes the point that millennals are, if perhaps a narcissistic generation, polite and thoughtful, definitely on the herbivorous side.[9]

But in my neighborhood their inner carnivore comes out. That would be Kips Bay/Murray Hill in Manhattan, sometimes known as "Murray Hell" for, among other events, truly disgusting "Santacom" revelry and general prowling of bars and restaurants where all the manifestations of bros-before-hos sexism can be glimpsed, the kind of behavior where a guy drinks too much on a flight and gets aggressive and they have to divert the plane.

And it seems to me the young women aren't exactly rushing away from all that. In a great *Saturday Night Live* sketch, Tina Fey played an Eastern European woman temporarily moving in with Lena Dunham's *Girls*. When Jessa says she recently slept with three men, the Tina Fey character says she understands, she's a prostitute. When Jessa laughingly says she didn't take money, she replies, oh, you're a failed prostitute.

Increasingly young millennial women are deciding not to fail. As recent articles in *Vanity Fair* and Manhattan's *Village Voice* have pointed out they're "sugaring" with rich clients, whom they meet via websites such as Special Arrangements, to exchange sex for rent or college costs. According to the articles, many of these young women feel they're entirely in control in these sorts of relationships, a concept of sexual empowerment that dates back not to the '60s, and its prostitutes in the often violent grip of "the man," but to an '80s concept of sexuality as power wielded by material girls, and, more recently, networking that has made it very hard out there for a pimp.[10]

One can feel ambivalent about self-employed here-and-there prostitution (and of course it's not just women)—it's between consenting adults and it's not hugely different from some one-night stands, but there's also the fact that, like any vice, you can take it up and it can eventually take up you. But it's hard to have the same tolerance for what's in effect unregulated concubinage—"unregulated" as in not even tempered by the unspoken rules, courtesies, and standards of, say, consorting with the Parisian Belle Epoque courtesans of Colette's time. To those young men and women who say that "sugaring" is no different than a series of hookups via Tinder, or what was for my generation singles bars—well, how about how a Tinder night could become either "just one of those things" or a real relationship, as opposed to constantly being the good play-wife or the constantly up-for-it girlfriend/boyfriend "experience"? How that poisons one's outlook on life and the world could be devastating.

So there definitely seems to be a contemporary boomer-millennial generation gap in sexual behavior. That goes along with differing political views; my female contemporaries don't understand why many female millennials feel the feminism associated with Hillary Clinton is old-hat and unnecessary. It's very troubling that Harvard lecturer Yascha Mounk and Roberto Stefan Foa, a political scientist at the University of Melbourne in Australia, have put out a study, showcased in the *New York Times*, that shows how the millennial generation all over the western world for the past thirty years has basically lost faith in democracy, and views with indifference possibilities such as military takeover of their governments.[11] Even the fact that millennials strongly reject discrimination against gays and other minorities didn't seem to translate in sufficient numbers to voting for a candidate who espoused their point of view. Millennials in the wake of Trump's election might want to reconsider such (in)actions. A wall of little therapeutic post-its in New York's Union Square subway station wall is touching, but *it would have been better had you voted.*

Fear and loathing over millennial drugs—MDNA, synthetic marijuana, Adderall, opioids, and heroin—seems justified; we're beyond gateway drugs, we're fully past the barrier, and the hospital statistics prove it out. Again, '60s youth had their bad LSD trips and heroin overdoses, so no judgment here, but fatal opioid o.d's, especially when mixed with fentanyl, have become epidemic.

And then there's the generation gap Marshall McLuhan observed and predicted accurately would be caused by the onset of new media. The deVIces (as Frank Zappa used to pronounce it, referring to other kinds of toys) and their use by millennials, puzzle and rankle even my more tech-savvy friends. The almost sleepwalker obsession with Pokemon Go; the conformity of speech ("trending words"), tastes, and behavior that constantly being online seems to induce; the downward-facing focus on the small screen that's almost constant on the streets of New York, where it really does pay to be more alert; the need to have your matches made in compatibility cyberheaven—all of which inevitably leads to the corporations behind the deVIces having a captive audience for their messages and products, and for complex cultural and political thinking being reduced to 140 characters per tweet—one wonders if a great portion of the millennials have become app sock puppets.

But now let's look at the other side of the modern generation gap, the side that, for many millennials, is looking more and more like a gap that's becoming an abyss.

That military rife with sexual assaults was swelled by millennials responding to 9/11 by unselfishly enlisting to serve their country. Our baby boom President George W. Bush's administration sent them into one near-endless and a second seemingly endless war—the first of which was driven by blunders and lies—then put them through horrific repeated deployments, then welcomed them back with delayed/denied medical care, especially negligent with regard to their mental health.

Is this, many veteran millennials now ask, the reward for their service, and what they can expect in the future? Talk about, as that '60s parent said, a real confusion, and a war with no end in sight.

We also didn't make a sufficient effort to provide employment for veterans. Of course maybe that's in part because employers didn't have the nerve to cajole and compel young veterans to work for nothing. Many millennial college graduates are now expected to work in internships that are sold as training for *almost* certain jobs in the future, for which the pay is exactly $7.25 less than the federal minimum wage, or zero. This is especially true for many of the glamour professions of the cities of New York and Los Angeles, two of the most expensive cities in the country. Many of these interns still live with their parents or three-to-a-one-bedroom in Soho or in what remains of affordable Brooklyn or Ridgewood, Queens, where a landlord may demand three months or more rent as security.

The whole internship practice is unconscionable, even if just for a summer; summer jobs for adolescents used to be a combination of grunt work plus potential training, and we used to get paid for them. There should be mandatory minimum wages for interns on Wall Street as well as workers at McDonald's, especially if the internship goes on for more than a couple of months. Until then, it's understandable that a percentage of young men and women have taken up "sugaring." They're already free sugar for their employers.

And there's a price to be paid for those de-VI-ces and the immersion in cyberspace they bring, and it's not the costs of constantly upgrading your iPhone, or dousing your Samsung, or even vulnerability to hacking, phishing, and other cyber-mischief.

McLuhan was one of the first to point out the effect of the impingement of new media on ways of communication and expression, the intense perceptual and cognitive modification involved. In the case of the Internet it really can pull you into a secret invisible world, a cyberspace collective unconscious in a way Jung never imagined. And that unconscious has its monsters of the id. Two years ago *The New York Times* told the story of "Obnoxious" and his "swatting" of women online: Twitch, a site where people can watch other people play videogames, was gradually infiltrated by this depressive little fiend, who subjected women to ddos attacks and slowed down their Internet until they did what he said (like sending him nude pictures), and who then progressed to "swatting" the ones he didn't like (as in faking calls that sent SWAT teams to their residences).[12] And there have been many suicides due the kind of cyberbullying that brands you as pathetic or repulsive and makes that image of you universally available to the online world, including the suicide of a married young woman strong enough to become a firefighter.

For millennials, the Web is indeed that, an all-surrounding entity, an extension of personal space that can become a frightening ensnarement. It's much easier for those of us who remember a world without the Internet to detach from it when it's contaminated by the mental semen of evil morons. For those for whom cyberspace is every bit as important as "irl" (in real life) there needs to be more rigorous patrolling, but megacorporations such as Twitter have complied at best reluctantly and incompletely with that imperative.

And consider all the existential threats millennials face: nuclear war, climate cancer, new diseases (one that strikes at pregnancy), and global terrorism. In the '60s, except for a very immediate possibility of nuclear war, we only had one such immediately pressing threat for young men: the draft. Any young man at the time, including college students in the early '70s, could be subject to compulsory call-up and forced service in feared and hated combat in Vietnam. Many fled to Canada, or even chose prison. Others swelled the antiwar movement by the thousands.

Yet college-age millennials face the same kind of big D threat to, if not life and limb, at least a productive and sustainable future existence, and they don't seem to be uniting against it yet … The debt. College-related fees and costs are saddling many young men and women with, in effect, twenty- to thirty-year mortgages: $30,000, $80,000, for the dental student who last year deep-cleaned my teeth $125,000.

Seen the commercial where the financial planner says to a woman barely in her twenties "let's talk about your long-term goals," and she replies, "you mean paying them back?" and there's good-natured laughter all around? It's the kind of ad that makes you wonder if your television screen will blush with shame. I was in debt for several years, and not nearly as much as many college grads, and kids, fasten your seatbelts, it's going to be a bumpy couple of decades. Constantly deferred choices to buy a house, or even move out of your old house. No cars, no luxuries, few investments in the future since you're so tied to the past, and possibly insufficient healthcare, all so you can have the kind of liberal arts education designed for a middle class with some leisure time … which you're not going to have. All so that, unless you're a doctor or engineer or business school grad, you can have that required accreditation for a job that might be there, or might be far in the future or already gone. Meanwhile, according to recent Pew surveys, many millennials are afraid to even get married because of the fragility of their economic situation.

As the song says, you better believe "bright college years" are "the shortest gladdest years" of life if that's what comes after.

But here's where the generation that passed through the '60s has the most to offer millenials, mainly through traditions of protest and resistance on college campuses. For the youthful stage of boomers and that of millennials may have more in common than first suspected. My guess is that millennials also sense that however much they're now dominating public taste and are being catered to by parents and corporations (as were we) because they're such a large generation (as were we) the future will be harshly, even brutally competitive (as we found out when the peace-and-love of the '60s became the dog-eat-dog of the '80s). And unlike us, millennials will be competing for dwindling economic and planetary resources. Repression of fear and anger stimulated by such abysmal intuitions could very well be another reason for a retreat into app-induced conformity punctuated by episodes of hostility.

But there's some good news in that actions taken by student rebels on college campuses in the '60s can serve as a guide for millennial students seeking a way to liberate themselves from those shadows and channel righteous anger not into sexual or online or other kinds of aggression but into some form of resistance. There are whole new sets of problems, many originating on the college campuses themselves. But there may also be solutions found in new incarnations of fifty-year-old movements toward unity and reform.

When Students Struck and Won
And how to bring it all back home

It was called "the politics of confrontation" and "the Movement." Its rhetoric heralded "The System must be overthrown." It featured the burning of draft cards and flags. It was an American Spring.

On many college campuses it was led by the "New Left" Students for a Democratic Society (SDS), so defiantly nonorganizational they boasted that old-style Communists couldn't take them over because they wouldn't know where to find them. In reality they were at least loosely organized toward local activity. They often expressed how the "System" was broken and deeply unequal in Marxian terms. But in many other senses, they were an American reformist group seeking nonviolent change.

1968 saw demonstrations at or near Columbia University against the war and the draft, which took place against the background of Reserve Officers' Training Corps (ROTC) drills on Columbia's South Field, military and CIA recruiters on campus, and classified military research in university labs. The campus was roiled by the Black Panthers, the Puerto Rican Young Lords, teach-ins and rallies against the war, and shouting matches with military recruiters. But the spark for the major resistance action was an attempt to tear down a construction fence in Morningside Drive around a gym Columbia was building that planned to let black community residents in only through a back door—a so-called "Apartheid Gym." That vandalism of the fence was followed by the arrests of some student demonstrators.[1]

That sparked a Columbia Sundial rally and an all-night seizure of Hamilton Hall by the Students for an Afro-American Society. Due to fissures between that group and the local white-dominated SDS led by Mark Rudd (no one's saying there was ebony-and-ivory harmony here) the SDS, while expressing solidarity, split off from the black students and took over Low Library and a cluster of other buildings.

It was carnivalesque for awhile, with the students making sure to keep the buildings clean while proclaiming their activism and also enjoying themselves. "Pukes" fought jocks as they tried to send up food; the guy with the best arm for hurling bags of food past the jocks turned out to be John Taylor, son of Telford Taylor, a sympathetic faculty manner and the prosecutor at the Nuremburg trials. In a constructive endeavor, however dicey, files were "liberated" and published in the counterculture magazine *Rat*, revealing Columbia's covert links to the war machine and defense contractors.

Students for an Afro-American Society peacefully withdrew from Hamilton Hall once promised future negotiations, with the city overseeing the agreement. But the other occupations ended when police broke through the doors of the occupied buildings and hauled the students out. Tom Hayden pledged the students to nonviolence and took the brutal consequences with them. In what was later called a "police riot" the cops picked off and beat up many bystanders and sent them to the Tombs prison along with the students who actually occupied the buildings.

The Columbia administration got their real estate back for what they hoped would be a normal conclusion to the school year, but that was not going to happen. They utterly lost public support. There would be subsequent building seizures in the neighborhood, no grades that year, and visits from progressive labor unions and participants in the French student-worker revolt. Most of the class of '68 walked out of graduation for a counter-Commencement.

At Columbia classified war research was halted, the gym was canceled, ROTC left campus, military and CIA recruiting stopped. In the aftermath, the faculty united to support dropping of charges against students, the court cases against seven hundred people were gradually dismissed, Columbia President Grayson Kirk resigned (calling it "retirement"), and the Civilian Review Board ultimately ruled the police used "excessive force."

To sum up, Tom Hayden, the SDS, and the students flat-out won.

There was damage, and not just to property; it took Columbia about a year to recover. But recover it did, because the strike was not against Columbia, which was revered by many students and had a great deal of left-wing faculty, as well as students who were already involved in Harlem Community Action projects. Nor was it meant to be student against student, although it became that at times. It was about national causes: stopping the Vietnam War, which cost 2000 southeast Asian lives and at the very least several American ones every day, and about fighting racism. The IDA (Institute for Defense Analysis) had indeed been conducting classified war and weapons research for the Pentagon regarding the "automated battlefield" and defoliation. The attempts to evict the CIA dated back to 1965. Opposition to the gym and its takeover of Harlem property had been going on for two years.

This was no campus flare-up with an ad hoc response that was heedless of potential consequences. This was a well-prepared combination of principled belief, strategy, and tactics involving everything from teach-ins, to long sit-ins that became occupations, to demonstrations and calls for activism elsewhere, all organized through word-of-mouth and mimeographed leaflets.

And because of not only how events went down at Columbia but because they happened in the first place, another Ivy League campus was better prepared to handle its own day of crisis.

***

In the '60s racism and racial discrimination was at a level that, current problems notwithstanding, would be inconceivable today. Racial intermarriage had only recently become legal, as shown in the excellent film *Loving*. Schools were still desegregating. Ghettoes really were that: the only places most blacks and Latinos could live or get any kinds of money for businesses.

The African American self-help and self-defense group The Black Panthers had long been trying to fight racial discrimination and oppression with their breakfast and self-help programs. But because of more controversial programs like firearms training, because of the deep and ultimately megalomaniacal personal problems of founders like Huey Newton and Eldridge Cleaver, and because of harassment by J. Edgar Hoover's FBI, the Panthers reeled with internal discord. The murder of young Alex Rackley in the mistaken belief he was an FBI informant (one of the FBI's favorite tactics was to fake "snitch jackets" on black activists) led to the FBI charging Ericka Huggins and Bobby Seale with conspiracy to commit murder.

So the Panthers were falling apart, criminalized, and desperate when they decided to mount a May Day demonstration at Yale and on the New Haven Green. Kingman Brewster, a (then) liberal-moderate Republican and President of Yale, spoke out in favor of the acts of dissent and tried to become an intermediary, but certainly was aware of the threat of violence from Panther chief of staff David Hilliard; Panther leaders actually invited Yale students to burn down Beinecke Library as part of getting Bobby Seale out of jail. Another more sensible leader, Doug Miranda, called for a nonviolent student strike.

Brewster, perhaps realizing what obdurate resistance to student demands did at Columbia, took a gamble some kind of reason would prevail against the continually provocative Hilliard. He expressed skepticism that "black revolutionaries could achieve a fair trial anywhere in the United States."[2] But meanwhile he said Yale could not contribute to a Black Panther defense fund due to not-for-profit-university-related rules. He gave students the option of participating in the strike and completing required papers over the summer. It was a clever but principled response, and it worked, hailed as an effective compromise by the *Washington Post* and other newspapers.

May Day there were thousands of National Guard and other law enforcement officials in the city. At Yale, the Panthers gave speeches which at one point angered the largely white crowd with police-killing and reverse-racist rhetoric. But later, even with Hilliard among them, the Panthers actually calmed another crowd, urging them toward dialog not confrontation, along with Tom Hayden, who continually emphasized the value of teach-ins and what he called, per a line of Castro's, cultural guerilas. Even the usually fiery Jerry Rubin tried to deter people from marching into the streets.

Meanwhile Brewster entertained counterculture defense lawyer William Kunstler and Rubin while working with the police chief to keep Yale gates open and keep cops and guardsmen from interfering with the rallies. Even during one ill-considered march to the Green, peace was kept.

At both Columbia and Yale forces that had united in the nonviolent advance of their chosen causes and the activism necessary to sustain further programs carried the day, and in the case of Yale, had full college administration cooperation. So what do these examples have to teach students who want to fight institutional racism and other forms of societal oppression today?

The first part of such a consideration is to see not what those '60s demonstrations were about, but what they weren't about. For that, it's instructive to remember when Mr. Zappa went to Washington.

***

Frank Zappa, who led the band The Mothers of Invention in the '60s, was such a fierce advocate for freedom of speech and expression that in 1985, in the midst of a post-'60s career that was still thriving and would until his death eight years later, he testified in Congress against putting "parental advisory labels" on rock music albums to warn about obscenity and sexual references, because he believed rightly that such labeling was implicit censorship in the marketplace (and he was joined in Washington by Dee Snider of Twisted Sister, and, though he would never ever have run into any parental advisory censorship, John Denver).

One wonders what Zappa would have thought about students at Columbia who demanded a similar form of advisory label, "trigger warnings"—messages sometimes posted on campus publications, assignments, and other material noting that they might be upsetting for people who have had traumatic experiences—for Ovid's *Metamorphoses*, because, after all, there are scenes in this classic where gods come down from heaven and rape mortal women.

One wonders also how Mario Savio would have felt about such labeling of speech. Implicit in all the student protest activities of the '60s was an insistence on students' freedom of expression in making those demands. Led by Mr. Savio, the 1964–1965 protest campaign at Berkeley called itself the Free Speech Movement.

Unfortunately this was anything but the case in the 2015 student protest demonstrations at Yale. These students were totally concerned with their own university environment and with making it "safer" and more acceptable for themselves by fighting and excluding speech they disliked. They indulged in the kind of labeling of themselves and others and restricting of expression that inevitably chilled freedom of thought on campus.

And this had nothing to do with issues of, say, institutional racism, or even censorship of literature. This had to do with the burning issue of potentially offensive Halloween costumes—actually the *possibility* of potentially offensive Halloween costumes. That's what brought out a cadre of students, in one case in a shrieking video that went viral, to curtail the careers of two professors, march against free speech on campus, and commit the university to major budget items to redress their grievances.

To recap (and it's amusing to step-by-step contrast this timeline with the timeline of the '60s Columbia and Yale demonstrations), on October 28, 2015, the Intercultural Affairs Council of Yale sent out a warning against such offensive Halloween costumes. Two days later Erika Christakis, associate master of Silliman College (one of the residential "colleges" within Yale), replied with an email in which she suggested the Council had tried to exert too much control over students on "a day of subversion" for young people. "Is there no room anymore," she mused, "for a child or young person to be a little bit obnoxious ... a little bit inappropriate or provocative or, yes, offensive?"[3]

She soon learned there wasn't. Christakis received an open letter signed by one thousand students and spearheaded by a group called Next Yale consisting of about two hundred students protesting that her suggestions invited ridicule upon student minority communities.

Things snowballed from there. The campus remained quiet—no sit-ins, no occupations—but there were three large outdoor gatherings (one of which became a massive dance party). There were also genuine intense, painful discussions spurred on in part by rumors of previous racist incidents on campus, and certainly sexist ones, as in the "No means yes, yes means anal!" crowd described in the previous essay.

But it became clear that this conflict would not be about issues on the level of the kind of discrimination, from police violence to deep economic equality, that faced the African American community in the '60s and still do now. This would be about "What do we take away from our time at Yale?" It should be "thousands of unique and shiny moments bursting with significance, strung together over the course of four years. Bright college years filled with light and truth." But for students of color "those moments often include much darkness ... differential treatment ... casual racism."[4] Racial jokes, slurs, misperceptions, costumes that were never worn.

The students demanded "relevant and respectful" learning experiences—relevant, why not, but not at the expense of more sophisticated historical perspectives ("relevance," for all its virtue, was used as an attack word that way in the '60s too). And respectful? Since when should the lessons of history, from whatever political point of view, be respectful? An overemphasis on respect for LBGTQ issues can easily engender demands for more respect for a new historical perspective on slavery. Unless you're willing to be respectful of, for example, the Dolly Parton Dixie Stampede's celebration of the antebellum South in one of its musical numbers, don't try to ward off "hurtful" criticism of your own point of view.

What did the students win? Erika Christakis, stating "the current climate at Yale is not in my view conductive to the civil dialogue and open inquiry required to solve our urgent societal problems,"[5] stepped down as associate head of Silliman. Nicholas Christakis also resigned as head of Silliman college, and they both decided to "return full time to our respective fields of public health and early childhood education,"[6] though Erika Christakis wound up saying she would not be teaching at Yale in the future.

Yale did promise its current coterie of proclaimers of cultural insensitivity a university-wide plan for a "multidisciplinary center for study of race, ethnicity, and other aspects of social identity."[7] Adding teaching staff and faculty and courses representing underrepresented communities. A fifty-million-dollar plan for faculty diversity. Doubling of the budgets for cultural centers.

But that remains to be seen, along with how and by whom it will be paid for if it happens. In the immediate future, the aftermath of the Great Halloween Costume Contretemps has been far less affirmative. Next Yale and their adherents won a nationwide backlash, fed by righteous indignation over their attack on First Amendment principles. It started on campus. As third-generation Mexican American senior mocked, "It offends me, therefore I'm right. You're wrong, because I don't feel safe."[8] Alumni announced cancellation of their contributions.

The group came under fire for anti-intellectualism and immaturity. After trigger warnings on Ovid, what comes next? Banning *Moby Dick* because of animal cruelty, racism against Queequeg, and the antireligious attitudes of Captain Ahab?

The University of Chicago took the unprecedented step of sending out a letter to incoming freshmen that stated "our commitment to academic freedom means that we do not support so-called trigger warnings, we do not cancel invited speakers because their topics might prove controversial, and we do not condone the creation of intellectual 'safe spaces' where individuals can retreat from ideas and perspectives at odds with their own."[9] Other universities made similar statements, but the message from Chicago was "clearer and more direct than I've seen," stated Greg Lukianoff, president of the Foundation for Individual Rights in Education (FIRE), an organization that attacks destructive speech restrictions at many campuses through supporting legal cases, education, and outreach programs.[10]

FIRE is acting against university speech codes put in place by college administrators and works to publicize their most ridiculous consequences and worst abuses of free speech rights. To that activist who claimed FIRE was speaking for "a specific kind of lost voice" that was "racist and probably immoral," Lukianoff replied that that's precisely the kind of lost voice the American Civil Liberties Union (ACLU) spoke for; he's a former ACLU worker who also worked in refugee camps.

The ACLU during the '60s was perhaps the most significant nongovernmental organization defending the First Amendment, and in the wake of President Trump's election it's growing again. The ACLU was behind the lawsuit of atheist Madalyn O'Hair that ended officially sanctioned Christian prayer in schools. Labor organizers and war protesters—they too were initially reviled, and the ACLU took their cases. Most outrageously and courageously, it defended the right of Nazis to march in Skokie, Illinois. Back in the '60s one of the most famous musical and comedy stars was Danny Kaye, who was also decidedly pro-Israel since back in the years he'd helped the United Jewish Appeal raise money for the then fledgling country. In one of his last roles, on the television movie *Skokie*, Kaye played a Jewish Holocaust survivor protesting the Nazi march who ultimately comes to accept, however grudgingly (as Kaye did himself) the primacy of the First Amendment.[11]

That's the kind of spirit that "identity" and "warning: collegiate advisory censorship" labels violate.

***

It's time for students to take a hard look at the damage such cultural insensitivity campaigns are doing not just to campus morale and the quality of their education. Such divisive issues may also block any chance students have of joining together in efforts toward meaningful change in issues that directly impact all their lives, both in college and beyond. Ironically these "political correctness" campaigns are in many ways a mis-aimed outgrowth of justified '60s left-wing demands for minority rights and the teaching of minority voices, and "identity" politics and courses remain one of the few domains of American intellectual life the Left can control. Nonetheless they need to be rejected not only because they're destructive in and of themselves, but they impair the progress toward greater goals.

And the American Left, whether on campus or in Congress, must be absolutist about free speech, particularly because, for example, Trump ally and billionaire Peter Thiel's suit against Gawker, forcing it out of business, has previewed how the Right is going to move against free speech: everything from ruinous lawsuits to ending net neutrality to possible McCarthy-era-esque witch-hunts in Congress. If the Left, especially left-wing college students, doesn't stand for the opposite, starting on college campuses, what does it stand for?

Students by a healthy margin seem to support cultural insensitivity–related policies, even though such support brings potential self-censorship to course materials and potential threats to faculty careers. All part of a hotel mentality: I want my college education perfect. Meanwhile teachers, backed by FIRE and other groups, are filing lawsuits claiming that they've been unjustly terminated for violating sexual harassment and other policies simply due to the manner in which they teach. Students, this will bleed money from your hotel.

And then there's the old conundrum of how groups who should be fighting against common oppressors instead split the focus and fight among themselves. Identity political groups on campus focus only on their identity cores, which means that just at a point where they should be learning about a wider world they're narrowing their focus, and defining themselves against rather than for or with.

No question that racism and the genocides that have come from it—the Native American slaughter and the Middle Passage of slavery—are America's original sin and we haven't been purged of it. No question the treatment of gay and transgender Americans up to and past Stonewall has often been shameful. All this can and should be taught. But is the answer to problems in student and American life really to retreat into identity shells: I am white, I am nonwhite, I am gay, I am Latino, African American, a woman? Or, in the words of Mel Brooks's two-thousand-year-old-man on the beginning of civilization, "let 'em all go to hell except Cave 76"?[12]

Students must not forget, to use one of the old '60s slogans, that "the people *united* can never be defeated." Each separate group, in drawing inward, loses their ability to persuade everyone else on campus. The sideshow destroys any potential for a unified Big Show that could enlist a majority of the student body to fight for programs and policies that might create, to use '60s parlance, not only effective resistance on campus but a new New Left for millennials and Generation Z to face all sorts of crises in the future.

****

These crises, in campus life and beyond, will be at least '60s level in perniciousness and scope. All the old problems of racism and quite possibly new wars and deepening economic inequality, combined with a whole new series of offerings from Pandora's box (that's as in free horrors, not music). If you're asking: how do I protest, within my pristinely isolated college environment, real-world problems such as gross economic inequality and the corporate and financial worlds' roles in that nightmare—stop kidding yourself that all that isn't already connected to your on-campus world. The goal of the Columbia strike was a "free university," as in free of secret government grants, corporate investment, influence on educational process, and takeover of adjacent real estate that could be used for affordable housing. All of this has returned worse than ever.

Meanwhile, no surprise, there's also backlash against left-wing students that's now becoming excessive. It's possible to take this condemnation of the "crybullies" to such a punitive level that it will depress and marginalize the kind of students who could become the core of a new and more effective redirected activism.

So how does the Left on campus fight such a backlash and fight for worthier causes?

Anchoring demonstrations to massive problems outside the campus would be a good start. Teach-ins that show how identity politics, whatever its downside, is a reaction to societal pathologies that include mass incarceration, violations of Native American rights (as at Standing Rock), and immigration injustice against people of color, all might be useful.

Tactics in support of such positions could certainly include sit-ins on campus real estate, perhaps greatly inconveniencing ones. They must be nonviolent and need not, and must not, spread to attacks on fellow students and teachers (a huge mistake of the old New Left).

But student protests should also focus on the problem of corporate incursion into student university life. As Natasha Singer showed in her article "On Campus, It's One Big Commercial," on one college move-in day students happily worked for a youth clothing chain American Eagle as "brand ambassadors" or "campus evangelists," handing out American Eagle coupons, American Eagle water canisters, and American Eagle pens.[13] Such workers, whether interning or paid, number in the thousands. Major corporations seek out popular students to spread the word about them on social media as "influencers." Meanwhile universities increasingly embrace corporate sponsorships.

It's understandable that students who desperately need money go where the money is, but not so understandable in the case of their college administrators. It seems hardly an accident that schools with the highest presidential salaries also had the fastest-growing student debt, which now exceeds $1 trillion.[14]

Again, it's understandable (barely) that universities, no longer receiving the support from state and federal government that they used to, now charge upwards of $26,000 for room and board—and that's the relatively cheaper rate at state universities like UCLA or SUNY Stony Brook, which, to their credit, try to keep fees as low as possible given a short-sighted electorate's preference for low taxes over education. But new buildings, not just science labs or classroom buildings, but swanky recreation centers and dorms with nearby swimming pools, are being built with that money to attract more money. Sometimes these projects are financed by endowments, sometimes though taking on debt (raising the specter of a higher education "bubble"), while corporate-style administrators replace full-time faculty with low-paid adjunct professors.

It's University Megabusiness pulling in Student Consumer. As Frederick DeBoer wrote in "Why We Should Fear University Inc." "Enrolling at a university today means setting yourself up in a vast array of for-profit systems that each take a little slice along the way: student loans distributed on fee-laden A.T.M. cards ... ludicrously expensive athletic apparel brought to you by Nike."[15] And such corporations bring with their influences all the biases of their corporate cultures.

More insidiously, as DeBoer points out, "what could be more corporate or bureaucratic than the increasingly tight control on language and culture ... Those efforts ... contribute to a deepening cultural disrespect for student activism"—all of which is receiving buy-in from the "cultural insensitivity"-addled left wing of the campus.

DeBoer even points out how justifiable Title IX complaints and procedures against sexual abuse are being corporatized and used more to protect the reputation of the institution from bad publicity and lawsuits rather than to help sexually abused students themselves. Meanwhile at the nodded-and-winked-at major fraternities, which boost universities' reps as "party havens," homophobia and sexually aggressive behavior persist.

No university more exemplifies the callousness, the arrogance, and the greed of the new academic-industrial complex than, unfortunately, the institution where I spent three terrific years in the graduate film and television school, New York University. Perks like a game day at Yankee Stadium while students, who after all have to live in Manhattan, struggle under such a debt load that a group of them taking jobs as sex workers became a lead story in the *Village Voice*. Countless local real-estate grabs in the once cultural and intellectual haven of Greenwich Village, whose brilliance long contributed to NYU's luster. And a history of being subject to investigations over inhumane working conditions at the campus NYU is building in that great center of learning and intellectual and political freedom, Abu Dhabi.

To sum up, whatever the university, the issue that should unite all students of all races, colors, and creeds, that replaces the draft of the '60s, is the debt. College students need to start thinking of themselves by another name: college stakeholders. After all, they're incurring a twenty-year debt to invest in four years of education, in the hope that the value of that education over twenty years will grow in a way that justifies the massive initial investment. For those who feel that's a cold way to describe the proverbial bright college years, perhaps they should consider, given how much of the curriculum is influenced by "politically correct" or "identity" criteria and learned under truly awful financial pressures, that it's a bit of a misnomer now to call colleges "liberal arts" or "humanist." Especially since, setting aside young humans, you wouldn't put a dog through behavior school if you knew it would forfeit 15% of its dog food the rest of its life to complete the classes.

That now enormously greater expense for their educations should give students the right that at least stockholders have to receive financial statements and have annual meetings where they can vote on the course of the company/university, and protest with some clout issues such as not divesting from fossil fuel companies or economically cutthroat corporations' presence on campus. Students pretty much claimed that right unofficially in the '60s, when they were nowhere near as much on the hook financially. In case it isn't clear, this sort of resistance will not receive administration support. Students will have to unite and organize for these rights on their own, and be willing to reduce some of their own "perks" in the process.

For it may be true that colleges now have great education-abroad opportunities, not to mention great shopping opportunities, not to mention their own Starbuckses. But they also have all those new building projects and higher salaries for administrators. Kids graduating colleges (and not necessarily good ones) thousands and thousands in debt on the one hand, princely administrative salaries and real estate on the other hand—it's a sweet racket, the academic-industrial complex. Students have to have that degree, loan officers know they'll borrow whatever it takes, and so college administrators charge whatever they can get away with: supposedly liberal college bosses and conservative "banksters" and corrupt and avaricious lenders like Navient (Sallie Mae) never shaking hands but in a very productive long-distance financial arrangement. Meanwhile the (many) less fortunate among millennials and the oncoming Generation Z are guided toward an educational system that, to paraphrase a line from Clint Eastwood's *Unforgiven*, takes all the money they have and just about all the money they're ever gonna have.

If students want to strike, unite, organize to improve the world, why not start with their own universities and lives? Why not start with actions challenging and blocking all that new construction and excessive amenities that (Next Yale take note) the administrators will probably put on their or successor students' tab, one way or another? Why not start with the fact that their own futures are at risk because of the debt they're assuming to get their college education, not to mention the country's future, with a whole generation hampered from making home purchases and other investments? Why not organize, do student walkouts, shut down campuses over that?

For one thing, the possibility that college administrations might call on militarized campus police who are far more likely to, for example, pepper spray peaceful demonstrators than they were in the past (demonstrators take note: be sure to wear goggles). Also students lose part of the value of the education they pay for with every day of such a protest. So here's a suggestion that would never have been even conceivable in the '60s: parent-student strikes. For baby-boomer parents, it might be particularly appropriate to support their kids in this way, forming ad hoc organizations that vow to sue any university that allows police violence on any peacefully demonstrating students, and pledging support for their sons and daughters with regard to the issue of economic justice on campus. Perhaps even putting their bodies on the line with their kids.

Or if private colleges are going to be turned into ludicrously expensive protocol minefields where all sorts of education and educational discussion is off limits, why bother going to them? Except in the case of scientific fields like engineering and medicine, other specialized pursuits like law or political science, or for would-be PhDs trying to teach in colleges themselves, it's certainly possible to combine Marshall McLuhan's '60s vision of a "campus without walls" (facilitated by Massive Open Online Courses [MOOC])[16]; Senator Bernie Sanders' ideas for cordoning off public colleges for '60s-era tax-supported cheap or free tuition; and California's idea for a Virtual Online Campus whose courses could serve to shorten the time and expense required for a college degree. Expand that to credit-equivalent courses taken online a la carte, so to speak, and students won't have to go into crippling debt moving into those shiny new buildings, especially those built by near-slave-labor in Abu Dhabi. And as millennials more and more take over hiring positions at major firms, perhaps they'll put less stress on an official college degree than before, and be open to different kinds of educational credentials.

But let's assume for now that the American university system is worth saving. Only when college campuses stop becoming shakedown operations on their own students can they be restored to what the late Tom Hayden wanted them to be: places where students can get a good education and organize to improve society. Until then what students presumably came to college for, a mind-broadening education, will be slowly sacrificed to restrictions on all sorts of speech and study, out of both political and corporately self-protective correctness, while the potential economic promise of their degree will be overwhelmed by debt as they face a future of (no matter how many brand loyalties they've developed) virtual indentured servitude.

So try this identity: American students. And as a part of that new unity break down once and for all the worst barrier of all: between men and women. Millennial males need to get this once and for all: Title IX, otherwise known as the Patsy Mink Act (here's to my old Hawaiian Congresswoman) has first of all changed the physical performance level of women in America, resulting in female athletes whose strength and speed would've been unimaginable a decade ago (i.e., they can kick your ass). Meanwhile younger women's other achievements are truly startling, from a woman who can front a jazz orchestra playing her own complex jazz songs while singing and playing jazz bass (Esperanza Spalding); an opera singer with an incredible vocal range and near-Olympic-fitness-level choreography in her roles who can also conduct an orchestra while singing (Barbara Hannigan); and any number of female authors, scientists, inventors, heads of tech companies, and at least one world leader at the age of eighteen, Malala Yousafsai. Young men must learn to view women as equal comrades and potential leaders in the tough fights to come.

Perhaps students can get past college programs and politics increasingly based on their identity—in a nation supposedly founded on the idea of unity of different races, sexes, religions, and nationalities—and can move toward unity against economic and corporate oppression in the name of true education and social progress. It can happen here. It happened before.

When Teachers Struck and Won —and Lost

Not all '60s developments and their repercussions were positive, especially those where there were clear winners and losers that would have to then live with each other and their uncompromising victory or defeat for years to come: the kind of protracted aftermath where the invitation to bitterness and backlash and disfunctionality would lurk in every debate on the subject for decades. No event from the '60s illustrates that more than the New York City teachers' strikes of 1968.

Beginning in 1965, Mayor John Lindsay had been wrestling with the demands of municipal unions and trying to limit them, enduring many labor reprisals, right from the giant transit strike that had taken place at the very beginning of his administration. Even those of us who admired (in my case damn near idolized) Mayor Lindsay had to admit this was not an arena where he was very skilled or successful. And the stage was set for his most damaging city vs. labor confrontation when an experimental school decentralization project in the ghetto neighborhood of Ocean-Hill Brownsville took radical actions over the issue of community control of teachers and schools.

This was in a neighborhood where 95 percent of public school students were black or Latino, while two-thirds of the teachers were white. By any standards its public schools would've been judged as overcrowded, segregated, and "failing" in grades for reading and math today, and parents not only knew this but knew they had no say with the teachers; the school was controlled by the bureaucratically centralized Board of Education, which ran all of the city's schools, and its teachers were provided by one of the most powerful unions in the city.

In an attempt to answer parents' and activists' demands, the Ford Foundation funded, and Lindsay granted, experimental "community control" to the school, pretty much in line with a vision of African American control of community organizations advocated by activists like Stokely Carmichael. Principal Rhody McCoy was suspected to have ties with the Black Power movement.

It was an ethnic, racial, and educational flashpoint waiting to happen, and it was primed once the parents demanded more control over not just the curriculum but the teachers. No doubt at least some of them knew that in other whiter neighborhoods and districts, you had programs like the "i.g." (intellectually gifted) public school acceleration programs; I was fortunate enough to be a part of one in Manhattan's then premier public school, P.S.6, and the stability of sticking with the same class and getting that kind of education had lifelong benefits for me. The Ocean Hill-Brownsville parents probably also knew that New York public schools were at least capable of achievements on the level of Bronx High School of Science. But none of those possibilities were available to their kids. For them, the record showed that the Board of Education and the United Federation of Teachers, the teachers union, simply weren't delivering the educational goods.

But public school teacher tenure had existed in New York since 1917, even before the union. What was considered "due process" was a virtual trial if you wanted to terminate a teacher for poor performance. So as part of the decentralization experiment McCoy utilized the method of transferring out a teacher, allowed by the Board if a teacher proved mediocre. But his demand was startling: the transfer of thirteen teachers and six administrators, all of whom were Jewish. Even Lindsay, who had seen community control as a possible source of social stability, was horrified, and demanded the action be rescinded. The teachers tried to return to the school, but black parents blockaded the school until police were called to break the blockade. That ultimately led to the temporary closure of the schools and a protest walkout by 350 other UFT teachers, who were then also suspended.

At this point it was time for cooler heads to prevail, especially in the teachers' union. The problem was that the UFT was led by Albert Shanker, a smart, tenacious union leader not without a tolerant side (his union had permitted some local control of schools), but also a man as militant as Rhody McCoy. His conduct was so bellicose and rude it was lampooned in the Woody Allen movie *Sleeper*, where Woody, having been asleep for decades, wakes up in the future and is told by his minders that the world as he knew it ended when a man named Albert Shanker got ahold of a nuclear bomb.

Shanker called the transfers "arbitrary firings."[1] Blacks accused Lindsay, trying to mediate the crisis and also not lose Jewish supporters, of the old anti-Semitic canard of caving in to Jewish financiers; as Roy Innis said at the time, it was an example of "black demands activate white racism which activates black reaction which activates racial confrontation."[2] Jews and blacks, allies all through the civil rights movement, became bitterly divided; a woman in my family who was teaching at the time was cut off by a dear African American friend, and the pain of that transformed her previous liberal political views forever. Meanwhile, for all Lindsay's valuable tours of the ghettos and peacemaking efforts, the poverty program, in terms of concrete results, was falling short due to the city's worsening financial squeeze, and with the school crisis he began losing not only Jewish support, but African American support as well.

Looking back, there was room for compromise. The UFT was aware of neighborhoods like Ocean-Hill Brownsville's problems; they'd been behind More Effective Schools, which had improved academic outcomes in part by hiring more teachers for poor children, and providing those teachers with extra training for leading multiracial classrooms. And among the black parents' demands were perfectly middle-of-the-road ones like more discipline and a longer school day.

Meanwhile McCoy had instituted programs like bilingual education and Montessori-style elementary classrooms and built up the school library, and the radical teachings that one of his teachers, Les Campbell, was assailed for, like telling kids they could give up their "slave names," were based on events already in the news (as in Malcolm X and Muhammad Ali). And teachers in Ocean Hill–Brownsville had sought professional help in order to better serve their students, but were ignored by administrators, while McCoy had stated quite honestly: "Everyone else has failed. We want the right to fail for ourselves."

But Shanker was having none of it, and he led his union into a citywide walkout to try and stop the teacher transfers and bring down the decentralized school administration. 93 percent of New York City teachers chose to honor the picket line, almost 60,000 teachers, and the strikes, which came in a series right in the first two months of the school year, were timed to be particularly disruptive. There would be one that would be apparently settled, and then Shanker would infuriatingly put his teachers back on the picket lines, while over one million children were kept out of school. And he kept up his angry rhetoric, which stemmed in part from the extremism of the times, but also the arrogance of power of yet another municipal union leader sensing Mayor Lindsay's weakness in labor union negotiations.

Still in Ocean Hill–Brownsville, 60 percent of students continued to attend schools, and replacement teachers came from the African-American Teachers Association, a black separatist group; white liberal supporters of community control; and young New Left activist teachers. Students had to enter school through police barricades, with heavily armed rooftop police watching them. Anti-Semitism raged in the neighborhood; a flyer was placed in the mailboxes of some Ocean Hill–Brownsville teachers calling them "Blood-sucking Exploiters and Murderers" who taught black children "Self-Hatred." And then a fifteen-year-old read a poem on a radio station that began:

> Hey Jew Boy with that yarmulke on your head
> You pale-faced Jew boy – I wish you were dead.[3]

What was particularly sad was that 70 percent of the replacement teachers that McCoy hired were white, and half of them were Jewish. There was no proof at all that the school decentralization supporters as a whole were anti-Semitic. But Shanker put out 500,000 copies of the anti-Semitic flyer with the statement, "Is this what you want for your children? The UFT says NO!"[4]

The impasse was finally resolved in late November, when the New York State Board of Regents placed Ocean Hill–Brownsville under state management, a de facto termination of the decentralization of the school. The attempt to give low-income and minority parents more control over the budgets and programs of their schools had failed. The Board of Education and the UFT had won.

But it proved to be the classic Pyrrhic victory, one that would come with terrible costs that would stretch far into the future. It's most direct consequence was a lost year for students, for which the UFT would primarily be blamed, especially after Shanker gave a lecture at Oberlin College where he stated about the strikes "Listen, I don't represent children. I represent the teachers."[5] It was a statement that was met with almost universal disgust. The series of strikes would poison city, state, and national views of teacher unions for decades to come. It would also impair African American–Jewish relations at a grave cost to the American left and left-center voting blocs, and slow contemporary school reform.

By the 1980s what had been a minority black view of the deterioration and general undesirability of the public schools would also be adopted by white conservatives as part of a view of a free-choice educational marketplace of charter schools which, in their version, could also hire nonunion teachers and weaken teachers' unions. The record on these charter schools has been mixed; some, especially in lower income neighborhoods, have gained the reputation of "magnet" schools so prized that students have to join lotteries to try and get into them, and New York Mayor DeBlasio's attempts to protect charter schools from 'poaching' on public school facilities handed him a defeat that forced him to some painful compromises on his program for universal pre-K. But some charter schools have seen a third of their teachers choosing to leave, are racially and economically segregated, and do no better than the better public schools.

The ultimate irony is how much modern school reformers have as their precedent Rhody McCoy and Ocean-Hill Brownsville. Just as the Ford Foundation funded parent activists in Brooklyn, Bill Gates now contributes to "parent-trigger" efforts in California, where school reformers help low-income parents petition of behalf of transforming the management and staffing of their children's schools, sometimes turning them into charter schools that block out teachers' unions. What's considered to be the greatest impediment to quality schools? Then as now: tenured union teachers. From militant African Americans to the liberal elite to the right wing, the attack on the teachers' unions has been passed down, with often the only dissent being the fading memories of teachers like the woman in my family who asserted that teaching in the public schools was misery until the union came along.

As someone whose initial education was in a terrific public school, I certainly understand that there are other students who were and are less fortunate than I was, and there should be alternatives to failing or sclerotic schools and educational systems. But I wish these experiments in education (and every charter school is by nature a local experiment) were not still being conducted under the shadow of '60s events that forever darkened the reputation of unionized teachers and public schools.

For the two branches of education could learn from each other, and especially from educators who have a foot in both camps. Like the would-be educational reformer who, before his death in 1988, suggested a thoroughly reformed public school, pretty much a charter school within the public school system, where teachers could experiment with new and innovative teaching ideas. In such a school teachers could create "high-performing educational laboratories" which could serve as an example to traditional public schools (a little like my old "i.g." class). He got the idea from a 1987 trip to a public school in Cologne,

Germany, where teams of teachers pretty much controlled the school and stayed with students for six years. There was a mix of incomes and intellectual abilities, just like in '60s P.S.6, and students did forty percent better in getting into four-year colleges. In the American reformer's vision, these schools would be unionized, but parents and students would be more involved and watch them closely. A good public-charter school compromise.[6]

Conservatives like William Kristol, then chief of staff to Ronald Reagan's Secretary of Education William Bennett, would take that kind of vision and run with it in their own more free-market nonunion way. But this particular reformer didn't get too far pursuing his vision, perhaps because he'd lost some credibility due to actions in his past. His name? Albert Shanker.

Tom Hayden and American Freedom

"The intellectual should constantly disturb, should bear witness to the misery of the world, should be provocative by being independent, should rebel against all hidden and open pressure and manipulations, should be the chief doubter of systems, of power and its incantations, should be witness to their mendacity." — **Václav Havel**[1]

Havel's words could certainly stand as a tribute to Tom Hayden, who passed away last year. But they don't quite embrace a remarkable career that traversed the realms of radical activism, within-the-system public service, and in his final years, to quote William Blake, "mental fight" in his work of teaching and writing to preserve the integrity of the history of the era that defined him.[2]

Hayden's life and career combined fierce idealism and effective resistance: a resourceful framing of ideas to protect and extend American democracy; the courage to fight for them; and the grit and wisdom to try and join the prevailing system and change it in a more evolutionary fashion. As an antiwar, civil rights, and counterculture activist, as well as a California assemblyman, state senator, and influential writer and advisor, no other figure from the 1960s did more to try to make its noblest dreams a reality.

Born in 1939, he attended the University of Michigan, and was in the audience at Ann Arbor when President John F. Kennedy announced the formation of the Peace Corps. He soon began to raise his own voice as one of the initiators of the influential leftist student group Students for a Democratic Society (SDS). But he also took his beliefs to more dangerous ground, to Georgia and points South, getting jailed for attempting to desegregate a railroad station.

As a co-founder of the SDS, he was one of the main drafters of the 1962 Port Huron Statement, which emphasized the concept of "participatory democracy," seeking the creation of a "radically new democratic political movement" in the United States that would reject the hierarchy and bureaucracy of old-style Communism; hence the later term "the New Left."

For a supposedly radical document, it begins quite temperately: "We are people of this generation, bred to at least modest comfort, housed now in universities, looking uncomfortably to the world we inherit."[3] Reading the Statement, one is constantly surprised by its inclusiveness, its common sense, and its affirmative belief in President John F. Kennedy's liberal doctrine of social change. Its main moral support is reserved for the civil rights movement, and as part of that, Hayden's SDS initiated Economic Research and Action Projects in poor urban areas. They were motivated by the belief, encouraged by the civil rights Student Nonviolent Coordinating Committee, that privileged students needed to get involved in such underserved ghetto poverty pockets.

The goal of life, Hayden and his co-writers argued, should be the development of the potential of individual men (back then "women" were subsumed in that generic gender) and their courage, reason, independence, and ability to authentically oppose an oppressive system. It's a youthfully hopeful, wholeheartedly liberal-radical vision reminiscent of Albert Camus' vision in his book *The Rebel* of multiplied individual resistance which avoids collectivization and Soviet communism. And the main tools to achieve its goals would be participatory democracy involving individuals in decision-making public groups and democratic social regulation—not top-down committee or cadre rule, and most definitely not what would become known as the "free market" system manipulated by megacorporations, campaign donors, and big banks.

SDS's goal in its own university world would be to contend against student apathy and involve students in fighting for social change, including against "elite rule and minority control" by the university administration itself. The New Left, in Hayden's view, would need American universities as bases for its own learning, arguments, recruitment, and consolidation of a nonviolently militant left wing to "give form to the feelings of helplessness and indifference, so that people may see the political, social, and economic sources of their private troubles, and organize to change society."[4] Liberals, socialists, and other allies made in the fight for peace, civil rights, and the rights of labor would be welcome.

From 1964 to 1968, Hayden lived in Newark, New Jersey, where he worked with impoverished inner-city residents as part of the Newark Community Union Project, helping with daily problems and a battle to stop an urban renewal plan that would have evicted thousands of families. In his "The Politics of 'The Movement'" in 1966, he argued that a coalition of the poor, students, and middle-class insurgents and intellectuals was the best way to form a new society. Hayden would try in his own work to create "community unions" of resistance through tactics like rent strikes involving both poor and working-class people.[5]

But by 1968, Hayden and much of his movement, spurred on by fury at the Vietnam War and the military draft, had decided such incremental progress was not enough. At New York's Columbia University, activist students, led by Hayden and local SDS activist Mark Rudd, occupied buildings in order to force the university to stop building an "apartheid gym" in the Harlem community and disassociate itself from the Institute of Defense Analysis and its pro-Vietnam War activities. Interviews at the time show that Hayden still believed in creative and critical thinking as part of achieving Movement goals, and that some of the "heavy shit" bothered him, but his rhetoric leading the student strike went in another direction:

"Morale in the liberated areas is high! … The barricades are built firmly and strongly. We will achieve our demands. Vietnam has come to America, and if those who claim to be the Administration call in the police to protect them from their own people, we will resist until the end!"[6]

Paraphrasing Che Guevara's statement on Vietnam, Hayden wrote "Create Two, Three, Many Columbias." It was a militant manifesto daring America either to change its policies or send its troops to occupy America's campuses. He naively proclaimed that Columbia showed an evolution of student groups from "mill-ins to the creation of revolutionary committees" and "permanent occupation of buildings." He saw students as organizing to oppose the "imperialism of the very institutions in which they had been groomed and educated."[7]

He caught the bug of extremism.

And yet, in leading the students to noviolently resist a violent police seizure of the Columbia buildings, Hayden effectively provoked a smaller-scale version of the kind of shame and revulsion that Martin Luther King created at Selma, and it brought down the University administration. Hayden and other student leaders' tactics, though they threatened property destruction, went no farther than break-ins "liberating" files that revealed Columbia's cooperation with the Institute for Defense Analysis to the underground press, as Daniel Ellsberg would later do in bringing the "Pentagon Papers" to the *New York Times*. And SDS cooperated with Afro-American (the term back then) student organizations and community groups and helped them achieve their goals of stopping Columbia's expansion into their community.

In short, in an era of "moral victories," Hayden and the Columbia students achieved a real one.

Hayden went on to help lead protests demonstrating against the 1968 Chicago Democratic National Convention. Mocking Vice President Hubert Humphrey's campaign motto, he declared "we're going to Chicago to vomit on the politics of joy!" He and other protest leaders, including Abbie Hoffman and Jerry Rubin, were indicted on federal charges of conspiracy and incitement to riot as part of the "Chicago Seven." Hayden and his "co-conspirators" not only ultimately got the charges reversed but turned the trial into effective theatrical nonviolent resistance. They cast light on the vicious tactics of the Chicago administration, fueling the clear condemnation of the police in the federal government's *Rights In Conflict* Walker Report, and, through Hayden's very effective writing, further advanced the New Left's values and goals.

Hayden kept up the struggle for those goals after the dissolution of his Movement in the midst of the chaos and violence of the end of the '60s. He endured his own bitter disappointments; it couldn't have pleased him to see Mark Rudd's Weather Underground turn to domestic terrorism, or to watch labor unions (an original teaching ground for SDS) grow to hate the New Left, move ever rightward, and ultimately be rewarded for their embrace of "law and order" and President Nixon by their near-destruction in the administration of President Reagan.

But Hayden went where he was needed. His Indochina Peace Campaign mobilized antiwar dissent from 1972 to 1975 and kept up the pressure for amnesty for draft evaders that President Carter ultimately granted. He married Jane Fonda and together they raised more money for anti-Vietnam war efforts than anyone except John Lennon and Yoko Ono.

He then decided to meet the system halfway and got involved in Santa Monica city politics: the state Assembly from 1982 to 1992, and the state Senate for two terms afterwards. But he lost his bids for mayor of Los Angeles against Richard Riordan in 1997 and for the Los Angeles City Council in 2001, as well as runs for governor and US Senate.

Much of this phase of his life was tough for him, plagued by up-and-down electoral fortunes, divorce, and personal turmoil, while he was constantly under fire from both left- and right-wing groups. But he still managed to remain productive. His Campaign for Economic Democracy, allied with then-and-now Governor Jerry Brown, promoted solar energy, environmental protection, and renters' rights policies. When and where he managed to win he helped to pass more than one hundred measures during his time in office, tackling issues ranging from small-business tax relief to the reduction of gang and domestic violence.

Tom Hayden wrote nineteen books, served as a member of the advisory board for the Progressive Democrats of America, taught numerous courses on social movements, and was director of the Peace and Justice Resource Center in Culver City, California. In his final years he became a supportive presence for what he called "the young people of Occupy" and all Americans still trying to steer America from the grip of corporate and financial power and, in President Eisenhower's words, "the military-industrial complex." In his tireless attempts to reform the Establishment he once set himself against, and to build on the achievements of the '60s like farm workers' unionization and African American voting rights, Hayden exemplified Camus' call to be a rebel and not a revolutionary, and to accept, rather than dictatorial enforcement of an attempted utopia, "tension and limits" and inevitable compromise.

Hayden stated about his years trying to change the policies of California:

"When you go from the margins to the mainstream, you get caught in the muck of the middle. And you fight the fight as far as you can go, until you achieve all you can achieve. You leave nobody on the battlefield, but you use up all the energy at your disposal, knowing that the final phase will be memory, looking back to see what was achieved and what can be built upon...."[8]

One of his last battles was to protect those memories from censorship, from distortion, and from repression. In particular he took aim at official efforts to commemorate the Vietnam war that would leave out, in his words "Vietnamese nationalism, sacrifice, casualties or ultimate success—not to mention the ongoing deprivation, Agent Orange poisonings, cluster bombs left behind as signs of inhumanity ... mention of the peace movement, the historic rallies, the unity across racial lines, the GI revolts inside the armed forces, the unconstitutional domestic spying and indictments, the McGovern campaign, or the Pentagon Papers..."[9]

Hayden called this battle for historical interpretation of the Vietnam war a "legacy to the next generation ... The warmakers could win on the battlefield of memory what they lost on the battlefields of war. We must not let that happen."[10]

Throughout his long hard-fighting career, Hayden managed to combine affirmative belief in the possibility of radical reform—through "citizen action and strong advocacy from within"—with a streak of wry and sometimes purely bleak pessimism. "There may be no way to change this country. At least there is no way we can bank on. Both technological change and social reform seem to rationalize the power of the system to drain the heart of protest." But "The Movement at least suggests that we bank on our own consciousness, what there is of our own humanity, and begin to work."[11]

And devote some of that work to bearing witness to and remembering the legacy of Tom Hayden.

THE COUNTERCULTURE: BACK-AND-FORWARD

"All I maintain is that on this earth there are pestilences and there are victims, and it's up to us, so far as possible, not to join forces with the pestilences."

— *The Plague*, **Albert Camus**

"Nobody expects the Spanish Inquisition!"

— **Monty Python**

Bad Xanadus

"In Xanadu did Kubla Khan
A stately pleasure dome decree..."
– "Kubla Khan," **Samuel Taylor Coleridge**

If you're a baby boom child of a certain age, it's hard to overestimate how bright a star you were born under, at least according to the official Eisenhower/Kennedy era worldview. The feeling of the times was captured in an early 1960s *Life* Magazine series, "Portrait Of Our Planet," a beautifully illustrated and photographed summation of scientific investigations in fields like oceanography and astronomy during the 1957–1958 "International Geophysical Year" (I.G.Y.). The sheer optimism of this period, the belief in a technological utopia inspired by these investigations of earth and especially outer space, was both celebrated and spoofed by Donald Fagen in his song "I.G.Y." from his album *The Nightfly*, a concept album, somehow both satirical and romantic, on life and music in the '50s and early '60s:

> *Standing tough under stars and stripes*
> *We can tell*
> *This dream's in sight*
> *You've got to admit it*
> *At this point in time that it's clear*
> *The future looks bright*
> *On that train all graphite and glitter*
> *Undersea by rail*
> *Ninety minutes from New York to Paris*
> *Well by seventy-six we'll be A.O.K.*
> *What a beautiful world this will be*
> *What a glorious time to be free*

The song goes on like this, with a breezy and luminously polished shuffle of a melody, until the trademark Fagen barbs stick in. First the line "More leisure time for artists everywhere ... " and then:

> *A just machine to make big decisions*

Programmed by fellas with compassion and vision
We'll be clean when their work is done
We'll be eternally free yes and eternally young.
Ooooooooh....[1]

Fagen, like many children of the '60s, grew up bathed in utopian postwar hopes, which nurtured a generational rebellion against a barbaric Jim Crow regime down south and an undeclared disastrous war in Vietnam. The youth of the '60s resisted and protested and tried to create their own utopian manifestations that went under many names: communes, be-ins and love-ins, consciousness-raising, Woodstock Nation. But Fagen discerned the underside of that utopia, which he described in his memoir and musicological tribute to his influences, *Eminent Hipsters*. After giving due credit to the novelty of the Haight-Ashbury San Francisco counterculture scene, its "dazzling young girls," and some of the music:

> It was fascinating, for about a week, anyway. Then you started to notice that a lot of the kids looked waxy and wild-eyed and that they were talking much too slow or much too fast, and then you got that *Oh shit* feeling ... On the corner, you'd spot the hustling [drug-dealer] predator (whose consciousness hadn't been raised yet) looking to score off the middle-class kids who'd walked right onto their turf. It was over, bro, before it even hit *Life* Magazine.[2]

By the time of the Manson murders, the alternative community was broken, no longer bedazzled and beloved but bewildered and torn apart. So the '70s became a period of quasi-religious personal-growth-and-repair utopias (Meher Baba, Sun Myung Moon, Scientology, encounter groups, EST) that all climaxed very very badly with 1978's mass suicides in Jonestown.

The utopian impulse mixed with a pleasure-loving binge on sex, drugs, and rock and roll, which in itself became a kind of too-much-ain't-enough pseudo-creed. For all but the diehards, the balance of saving the planet while enjoying the consumer culture pretty tipped to the smiley-face side. The Me Decade entered into its full self-indulgent glory, captured in a movie called *Xanadu*, in which the Greek muses incarnate themselves on Earth to inspire heavily chest-haired men; one of the goddesses, a beautiful roller-skating sylph named Kira (Olivia Newton-John), encounters an artist named Sonny Malone, who's frustrated with being a commercial sellout—but with the help of Danny McGuire, a man Kira had inspired forty years earlier, Sonny builds a huge pleasure-dome disco roller rink where dreams can come true.

As the '80s would say, gag me with a spoon.

But it's not as if baby boomers in the '80s got smarter and abandoned their utopian/Xanadu impulses. They went on to the oldest American dream in the book: easy money. Thanks in part to lower taxes and a lessening of regulations, the 1980s, as William Greider pointed out in his history of the Federal Reserve, *Secrets of The Temple*,[3] became the '60s for bankers. There was a herd movement toward conspicuous consumption and questionable investments and transactions like junk bonds and flipping houses and business properties—all moving at a "white lines" pace—and the music on almost every baby boomer's turntable (not to impugn the lovely Linda) was Ms. Ronstadt's *What's New?* with its standards that evoked the glamour and prosperity of the upper class of the '50s.

The Reagan era economic expansion did legitimately create new wealth and companies. But it also fueled a growing deficit and a savings and loan crash that, unfortunately, taught the financial/political sector nothing (especially Democrat baby-boomer god President Bill Clinton, arch-deregulator of banking). And the '80s ended in a brutal recession that pointed toward a far worse one to come.

What bred such three-decade Xanadu-addled credulity among such an educated generation? Those gleaming auspices of boomer birth that led them to look for A-O-K all-systems-go everywhere? Their education in the all-embracing ideologies that dominated the 20th century—capitalism, the New Deal, Communism—which kept them looking for grandiose solutions to the world's problems? The fact that utopianism has always been a strong thread in American thought? The fact that advertising got more and more powerful in selling such ideas?

As Tom Waits used to answer when people shouted requests at him in his concerts, "all possibilities ..." At least by the '90s that utopianism and pleasure-seeking seemed to abate. That decade's music, Seattle's grunge and New York and L.A.'s rap, was fiercely specific in its visions of American pain, sleaze, poverty, and violence. But meanwhile the biggest source of utopian delusion for the aging baby boom generation and its children was soon to emerge: the digital revolution. The ultimate Xanadu loomed, a worldwide delivery system of wealth (at first often profitless) and information (later often corrupted).

What Leon Weseltier called "idolatry of data" in his *New York Times Book Review* article "Among the Disrupted" he summed up as "the bankruptcy of utopia."[4] Imagining ourselves spiders happily sated in the Web, we learn we're actually the flies, losing our marketplace of ideas to the conformity of "likes"-minded media, losing our privacy, losing the security that used to routinely protect bank accounts, perhaps even losing, in the future, much of our free agency to software that does the thinking for us. Sure a lot of it is gratis, no fault, seemingly limitless—but to quote a great line about the software industry: If you don't pay for the product, you are the product.[5]

One of the root problems here is the blurring of utopian dreams (which after all can involve hard work and shared sacrifice) with the excesses of Xanadu, doubling the delusion, adding up to wanting everything for nothing—music, drugs, real estate, information—from some giving daddy system, whether it's Scientology, "morning in America," or the Internet. Unfortunately there's a megatrend coming that will be neither giving nor forgiving: environmental crisis. And there will be no pleasure-dome shelter or utopian way out of that one. In books such as *Does Capitalism Have A Future?*—written by five distinguished scholars of varying political beliefs—and Naomi Klein's intensely liberal *This Changes Everything: Capitalism Vs. The Climate*, the authors argue that the engine that directly or indirectly fueled all our attempts at utopias and Xanadus, capitalism itself, because it degrades the environment and never attempts to restore it, may simply not be able to continue in the face of the growing climate crisis.

One hopes that solutions will found in the coming decades so that it won't be necessary to dismantle an economic system that is at least built on fruitful creativity and competition. But if we persist in the most dangerous utopian belief of all—a belief that a late-stage capitalist "free market" system, programmed by fellas like Lloyd Blankfein and the Kochs, will regulate itself to the benefit of all of us—it was belief in an economic system's neutral wisdom (despite Ukrainian genocide, purges, and gulags) that destroyed the Soviet Union society we beat in the Cold War, and wrought incredible environmental damage as well.

Here's a possible answer: the beliefs of the '60s that have most stubbornly held on have, thankfully, been the ecological communitarian ones. The communes of the '60s might have been motivated by naively utopian beliefs of living off the land, but they fashioned ways of living lightly off that land.

Having spent five years in Hawaii as a journalist, I saw, whether it was local biofuel stations in Maui (remember the video of Willie Nelson fueling his truck with fuel made from Thanksgiving turkey grease?), or individual solar homes, people getting off the energy grid and applying local renewable energy solutions to energy problems. Is it possible to knit together a mosaic of small, self-contained solutions like that not just in rural areas in Hawaii, but in towns and hamlets and even big cities across the planet? Can agriculture networks, solar building clusters, verticulture towers serving parts of cities, smarter and more decentralized grids, population control drives, and local biofuel stations everywhere all unite in a successful effort to save the world? That by itself is an absurdly utopian idea; there will have to be large-scale investment, new energy facility and seawall construction, and regulation of a type we haven't seen yet to salvage whatever we can of the environment we still have. But a gritty alternative backup of hands-on responsible communities, each protecting and nurturing their individual enterprises, could very well approach the somewhat utopian vision of President George H.W. Bush's "thousand points of light."

Just as long as we don't start believing those thousand points will somehow light up an easy way out, or some version of the good times we thought would last forever. Especially given our recent election, there will be no more pleasure domes for our g-g-g-generation.

Moon Age Daydreams and TV Reality

Stop me if you've heard this one before. "Surely, the nation that put a man on the moon can…"

Now fill in the blank. Repair our crumbling bridges. Transition to renewable energy. Reform the immigration system.

Yes, the nation that put a man on the moon could be capable of all these things, and so it's too bad that nation couldn't have foreseen the need to do them fifty years ago. But I'd no sooner bet on Trump's America completing such an endeavor than I'd bet on an angry speed freak doing his homework.

As someone who, as a wide-eyed boy, watched NASA and the astronauts year by year, step by step, despite some awful reversals, reach for and attain that walk on the moon, it seems to me that, first of all, the difference between that enormous venture and the space program of today is painfully clear: there barely is a space program. NASA's manned space effort is all but grounded. We still send probes to Mars and beyond, but we need the Russians for rides to the space station, and if it weren't for Elon Musk and SpaceX we'd need them for cargo transport as well.

So what factors may have contributed to the loss of the ability to do large-scale enterprises—like, for example, not just the space program but trying to avert climate catastrophe—in the supposedly most advanced superpower on earth?

In the '60s we were the preeminent nation militarily and scientifically … maybe. The Soviet Union launched the Sputnik satellite first, put a man in space first, and was virtually our equal in nuclear arms—"virtually" as in our slight edge was negligible given we could both destroy each other several times over. So basically through a combination of paranoia and patriotism we decided to beat the Commies to the moon.

But there was also a genuine desire to expand our scientific horizons no matter how much effort and money that took. President Kennedy said that we want to go to the moon not because it's easy but because it's hard, and America responded out of both inspiration and self-interest. NASA's funding was a lock, and the spinoffs in terms of scientific progress and job creation were unparalleled. The military of course benefited from almost perfect synergy, especially aeronautics, but all sorts of products—"space age" plastics, lasers, the beginnings of digital technology—were developed by companies like DuPont and Bell Telephone (AT&T).

And for all the dissension of the period, every space launch was an occasion for optimism and instilled in conservatives and hippies alike a spirit of adventure, inquiry, and almost mystical faith; you can feel that in the film *2001*. Then finally, in the same year as two other triumphs, Woodstock and the Mets winning the World Series (I'm a New Yorker), Armstrong, Aldrin, and Collins, as the Byrds celebrated in song, stuck that landing.

Here's what also fueled that effort: an ethos of teamwork. First among equals is what you strove for, as the team counted above all. And with that concept of the team came the concept of accountability to the team, the squad, the nation. If you messed up, or as the astronauts said, as quoted in Tom Wolfe's *The Right Stuff*,[1] if you "screwed the pooch," you suffered for it. Maybe you'd get a second chance, maybe you wouldn't, but you were totally responsible for the consequences of your actions. The team depended on it.

Those are some of the reasons why the United States put a man on the moon rather than the Soviet Union, or China, or Brazil. No amount of top-down corrupt military and bureaucratic control, while individual initiative was destroyed and the basic economy was botched, could keep the Soviet space effort alive, or indeed its entire system. China was going through self-purging-and-destroying Maoism back then. Brazil was a promising large country; they even had a truly space-age capital, Brasilia, for rent as a location for futuristic movies. But they also had entrenched massive poverty and hopelessly corrupt megabusiness classes jockeying for power under a dictatorial regime.

Any of this strike you as familiar? The shrunken middle class? The paralyzed government? The megabusinesses? The ideological craziness? The huge military and the corruption at the top? Try selling today's America on a massive government effort at doing something hard. Try mounting a major scientific effort (let alone reviving the space program) at a time when a significant portion of Congress hates the federal government, denies scientific evidence of climate change, and believes the 19th-century totally accepted theory of evolution is "lies from the pit of Hell."

And as for the kind of private-public cooperation that maintained the space program—government taking the lead and channeling tax revenue while private business provided creativity and investment—how can that happen in the midst of a top-down bureaucratic paralysis that allows a host of megabusinesses to carve up the public sphere for their own personal gain? Here's an interesting word: anocracy. It's the midway point between democracy and dictatorship, where various elites contend for power. It's a system where there can be no cooperation on major tasks that need to be done because, for example, the government, big energy, and the military-industrial and national security complex all fight each other for the greatest share of influence and treasure.

You couldn't even get an infrastructure bank, as former President Clinton suggested—a bank, where various parties could invest and receive interest—through a Congress and a system like this one, let alone a national climate change policy.

We're now being told under a Trump administration huge triumphant infrastructure projects may happen. But unless those are totally private business projects financed in part by public money (or tax breaks), that takes accountability and teamwork, and if you believe in that in contemporary America, buy a Chia pet for consolation. Congress got away for years with total obstruction and corruption. Wall Street banks wrecked the economy with patently illegal actions (by their own admissions and settlements) and no one went to jail. Thousands of servicewomen are raped and nothing's done; thousands of wounded vets face terrible waiting times for care, it becomes a national scandal, but very little happens.

And there's one other previously subtle, but now not subtle at all, influence undermining the whole concept of team unity, team dedication, team accountability, and team effort.

In the '60s even TV game shows manifested a good-natured "it doesn't matter if you win or lose it's how you play the game" team quality. Teams played *Concentration, Password, To Tell The Truth* (in the sense that the real person and the impostors were a team trying to fool the panel). Even shows where individuals competed, like *Jeopardy*, had a polite and pleasant feeling, and if Monty Hall on *Let's Make A Deal* got a little mean when a housewife dreaming of a Chevy Vega traded in the washer-drier for Door Number 3 and a donkey cart, there was an easygoing spirit about it all. None of the disappointed, if they weren't too oversensitive, went home traumatized.

When I first watched *Survivor*, I got a chuckle out of how it dressed itself up as a solemn tribal ritual—until I realized after a couple of episodes that a ritual was indeed what I was watching. As in a ritual being a theatrical space where a society's passages and deepest underlying rules are symbolically enacted and taught to the tribe.

And what ritualistic truth does almost every one of these immensely popular reality shows enact in the totally *not*-good-natured pressure-cooker trials they put the contestants through? There is no team in I. Teams are temporary alliances until a betrayer-in-chief emerges. Everyone else is an inferior, a castoff; the tribe has spoken, loser, it's Number One or nothing.

Reality tv began by putting "us" in front of "us"—remember the reasonably normal-looking-and-acting people that populated its first couple of years? But "reality" has now become hot bods and even hotter tempers (either already or provoked to get there) in physical or psychological cage matches, and this fakery can stand in for "real people" because so much of previously acknowledged real life, from 9-to-5 work to basic middle-class comforts and family rituals, has been eroded.

These unreal real folks go down to humiliating defeat, are chewed out by the MC, or literally fight each other, as the show unleashes, per Guns N' Roses, our appetite for destruction. Then "the tribe (us) has spoken": their torches are snuffed out and off they go into obscurity. So we vicariously participate in the destruction of "us"; even for the person who becomes Number One, their personality and individuality has sacrificially and gladiatorially gone through the wringer and barely survived to win the plaudits of the crowd. Who emerges unscathed and on top? The all-important MC.

Which brings us inevitably to the ultimate Master of unceremonious Ceremonies—and now of the executive branch of the United States government and its armed forces and nuclear weapons—President Donald J. Trump.

How did he do it? Yes his anger spoke to those betrayed and left jobless or even homeless by an elitist economy; the fact is, over more acceptable alternatives, the enraged chose him. Why? First of all, his candidacy in many ways was prepared way back in the 1960s. One can look at his candidacy through an historical lens and, since he's a baby boomer, a '60s historical lens, especially the *anno incredibili* and *horribilis* of the '60s, 1968.

That year saw the King and Robert Kennedy assassinations and the police riots of Columbia and the Chicago Convention, and it predictably yielded a tumultuous Presidential race that was the first one to have all the gonzo, third-party, and squeaker vote-total aspects that have characterized the elections of this millennium. Before anyone knew the phrase, it was very much a reality show election; indeed a terrific and unusual 1969 movie, *Medium Cool*,[2] blended its fictional story with the documentary reality of 1968 Chicago Convention demonstrations and the police response in ways that would be familiar to reality show watchers today.

On the gonzo end was candidate Pigasus the Pig, nominated by Abbie Hoffman, Jerry Rubin, and the Youth International Party (Yippies). Granted he was a boss-selected candidate who pretty much did what his backers told him to (their slogan being "If we can't have him as President we can have him for breakfast"). But as Hoffman pointed out, he was the only candidate who said the same thing in every state, and he bravely endured both an attempted (if theatrical) assassination and a riotous simultaneous nomination and arrest at the Chicago Civic Center, part of the clampdown on dissent that infamously went on that whole Convention week. On the more genteel side, comedian Pat Paulsen of *The Smothers Brothers Comedy Hour* ran for President. The injection of tv satire and attack comedy into the electoral process began.

On the less freaky and far less funny right-wing side was George Wallace, the former segregationist governor of Alabama, and his American Independent Party run for President. Wallace had an implicit and sometimes explicit "white America" message, demonized protesters and hippies and the press, shouted over and over again for "law and order," and stated that "there's not a dime's worth of difference" between the Republican and Democratic parties.

The Republican and Democratic candidates, Richard Nixon and Hubert Humphrey, fought it out in a nasty down-to-the-wire election with Nixon winning by one of the narrowest margins in history. Among the elements of his victory were a slightly more moderate "law and order" campaign, an appeal to the "silent majority," and a plan to end the Vietnam War that he claimed had to stay a secret so he wouldn't interfere with President Johnson and the Paris peace talks (while his people were not only interfering with but sabotaging the Paris peace talks).

Outrageous gonzo-ness and successful exploitation of a panicked public, skullduggery and conmanship, hidden forces manipulating events … it all figured in then and now.

Trump began his campaign with the kind of outrageous statements Abbie Hoffman used to pull all the time, with the exception that

Hoffman did it for laughs, civil disobedience, and shocking the public into a more acute awareness of the Vietnam War and related causes. Trump instead made an awful accusation that Mexican immigrants were rapists and criminals sent here by the Mexican government. That lost him some business, but won him his following.

Like all good cons, it had a grain of truth in it. The Mexican *narcotraficantes* do regularly penetrate the border to maintain their American market, from marijuana in L.A. to meth in the Midwest. Not that the Mexican government sends them, not that they're immigrants, and the immigrants now are from Central America anyway, not Mexico, but what the hell. His grotesque accusation, just like his "birther" claims that President Obama wasn't a native-born American, got him the attention and support he needed from a core of right-wingers on a hot-button issue.

Then he played the third-party insurgent threat—brilliantly—to cow the Republican Party, already fragmented by separate billionaires supporting many separate candidates, into not unifying against his candidacy, while he ran, in effect, a third-party insurgency campaign from within the party. And it had a lot of the Wallace points. "Not a dime's worth of difference" became that both of the principal candidates, then Jeb Bush and Hillary Clinton, were terrible, *terrible*. Law and order resurfaced. Implicit racism became the anti-immigrant rhetoric, pushing those old political panic buttons about macro- and micro-home invaders. The media were branded dishonest and corrupt.

Finally came all the Nixon elements, the use of the term "silent majority" (which Trump wisely did not associate with its user), the secret plan to stop ISIS, the hypercontrolled campaign stops, complete with evictions of protesters. All of this was somehow in Trump the salesman's phenomenal working memory, and it all worked.

But the big difference? His biggest strength? Yes he was the entertainer-in-chief, the Reality Show Candidate, but not in the way the pundits say.

As part of reality shows, as previously mentioned, any teamwork or alliances are preludes to betrayals. Team spirit is an absurdity. Winning rises above any other value, the one who betrays best wins, and there can be only one winner. The thought that you could, to use Trump's slogan, "make America great again" with that philosophy is an obscenity; it's a prescription for anarchy and chaos.

Yet people love it on tv to the point they embrace it in political life, with Trump as both Number One and the boss. And with that they'll also embrace that the game is rigged, both so that they can show contempt for the game, and to feel good when the boss rigs it himself in the name of their entertainment, while unleashing their most destructive urges ("I love war," said Trump).

In year two of *The Apprentice* it came down to a serviceman and a young woman from Harvard. Trump discarded all pretense of a fair competition to celebrate war and the armed forces and used everything but an RPG to blast the young woman off the stage. No big news here: reality show fans know that reality shows are part contest part con—and love it anyway. All that matters ultimately is the *schadenfreude*, the enjoyment of people's humiliation. Briefly, for one episode, they can vicariously share in the victory of the temporary Number One, but the main story is the ongoing victory of the entertainment system and its MC boss. Those who are about to die on television salute you.

And that kind of false "reality" unfortunately feeds into the basic cynicism of: it might as well all be a Big Show. There are no "facts" you can trust, the whole "reality" game is rigged, so it goes. American society is a corrupt winner-take-all cheating slugfest you can't beat, so while the system rapes your life and its media rape your brain, relax and enjoy it. Don't fight it '60s-style. Sit back, munch some popcorn, and then don't vote for hopelessly naïve reformers, vote for a real-life MC mainly out of despair and rage. That's where the power is, and that's entertainment. And that can/may be a prelude to a "reality show" government of real life cruelty, lies, and violence. Or at least W Redux: a secret cabal planning energy, business, and international policy, and a Number One President who wants it all simplified so that he in the most simple and one-man terms can be the decider.

Of course, it's worth remembering Trump lost the popular vote (by more than Nixon won it) and won the Presidency with about 46 percent of the vote; that's only 6 percent more than didn't vote at all. Still he won despite all the attempts to, as '60s novelist William Burroughs once said, "wise up the marks": point out all his frauds, his scams, his disgusting remarks about women and people of color and even captured or dead soldiers. Despite all of that Trumpism, not just in its right-wing nativist ideology but its spell of reality TV, its desocializing influence, and its exalting of a godlike mc who'll suspend not just disbelief but our thinking, triumphed. And it was prepared for by the trashing of the teamwork and cooperative checks-and-balances of the America we grew up with even in the turmoil-plagued '60s, leading, fifty years later, to a paralysis of government and a pervading sense of hopelessness and fury. As Napoleon said of his acquisition of the French crown, the United States Constitutional government was lying in the gutter, and Donald Trump and his minions picked it up.

There may be a way to get back to where we once belonged, as the Beatles sang, a long hard slog, four years, ten years, maybe more, but a possibility coming from the same place reform came from in the '60s: a righteously angry and honest desire for change stimulated by a back-from-the-wilderness revivified "new New Left," as the next chapter will propose. There's also a possibility that Americans can regain the class, heart, and professionalism that instils high values and good conduct that outlasts temporary conflicts and rises above the desire to betray everyone and win at all costs. In an event that may seem smaller in scale now but is worth remembering, the Cubs–Indians World Series, the way both teams played and took the victory and a crushing loss, was an inspiration.

For now, for all the sloganeering about making America as great as it once was, this can never be the moon-shot America of the '60s. The next time we see great public-private enterprise in a major country may be when China calls Elon Musk and offers him billions of dollars and millions of workers to create a Tesla-based electric car industry to corner the future transportation market. At that point, given our military style of policing, our for-profit prisons, our extremes of wealth and poverty, and our new administration, we may start to achieve the ultimate goal of 2017 America: 1965 Brazil.

The Left Is Senator Goldwater Now
Some immodest proposals

Watching Bernie Sanders in the election just past, I couldn't help thinking of another rebel political movement that was also led by a stern-looking, horn-rimmed-eyeglassed Jew.

Half-Jew actually, but conservative Senator Barry Goldwater anticipated Bernie Sanders's campaign for drastic change within a major party and went one better. In 1964 he led a right-wing movement that actually took over the Republican national convention, beat the moderate candidate Governor Nelson Rockefeller, and won the Republican nomination for the Presidency.

The result was a landslide victory by President Lyndon Baines Johnson and the Democrats. The Republican conservative movement was cast into the political wilderness; even Republican Richard Nixon's presidency would shape policies pretty much in the mold of a moderate-liberal post-FDR tradition.

That sixteen-year conservative exile began with a memorable 1964 Democratic convention speech from Democratic Senator and soon-to-be Vice President Hubert Humphrey with an equally memorable refrain:

> Most Democrats and Republicans in the Senate voted for an eleven-and-one-half-billion dollar tax cut for American citizens and American business—*but not Senator Goldwater.*
> Most Democrats and Republicans in the Senate, in fact four-fifths of the members of his own Party, voted for the Civil Rights Act—*but not Senator Goldwater.*
> Most Democrats and Republicans in the Senate voted for the establishment of the United States Arms Control and Disarmament Agency that seeks to slow down the nuclear arms race among the nations—*but not the temporary Republican spokesman.*
> Most Democrats and most Republicans in the Senate voted last year for an expanded medical education program—*but not Senator Goldwater.*

Other than the line about the "temporary Republican spokesman" (which it's too bad the Clinton campaign never copped) Humphrey stuck to the oldest rhetorical trick in the book: repeating that "not Senator Goldwater" refrain until the whole convention was roaring along and, eventually, most of the nation—for sixteen years. But the pendulum would swing in 1980 to President Reagan's "morning in America," and it would be a very long day: twenty years before Barack Obama and anything approaching the progressive liberal tradition of the Democratic Party would ascend to the Presidency again, only to be forced by Obama's second term into gridlock with a Republican right wing Congress.

Now we face the reality of a completely Republican-right-wing-controlled federal government under President Trump. The left is in the wilderness like never before in my lifetime. But thinking of Senators Goldwater and Sanders, I can't help but also think that while you can state about many American positions now and for some time to come "not the American left," nonetheless, we may yet see a return to power of the current progressive left wing, very much a descendant of the politics and philosophies of the '60s, within my lifetime; a return from that wilderness could be twelve, eight years away, maybe less. So it's worth thinking, especially in a book about the '60s, what such a left-wing governance approach might be when that political pendulum swings again in America. Admittedly an act of faith at this point, but let's try it.

Such a movement will have to manage the trick of being nonideological and "American constitutional" while adhering to core principles: not those of the communist revolution, the way right-wing commentators love to blather about, but a new 60's-style "New Left" awake to both current realities and past traditions.

Back in the late '60s when France was moving toward a more equitable and socialist system after the DeGaulle regime, author Jacques Servan-Schreiber stressed such a system had to avoid the old Soviet communist ideas.[1] In the same way the "new New Left" needs to steer clear of both the old-style New Left's outdated Marxism and puerile identity politics, along with old-style big government micromanagement, and repair its split with the working and middle classes. But it must also ditch the conservative philosophy that government is best that governs least. We've certainly seen an example of governing least in the last Congress. The new American left has to have the guts to say that government is best that *governs*. And that means regulation, now a dirty word, but if Retrumplican right wing barely controlled chaos or violation of basic American rights keeps running the table, it won't be always. So say it again. Regulation. Government of laws not men. National goals and standards, which mean national rules. *Regulation.*

Not the kind of picayune and enterprise-stifling regulation detailed in books like Philip Howard's *The Death of Common Sense*,[2] and which, in states and cities (especially New York lately) destroys restaurants and other small businesses. No, we're speaking of major regulation on major and global issues. No more trickle-down, the market self-corrects, growth unlimited, laws destroy jobs (as if the federal government can whistle up jobs in the first place, or businesses don't have enough state tax incentives). After four years, or maybe eight years, the Left will have a lot of ground to make up. It will need strong principles to do that, and regulation should be first and foremost.

And such regulation won't restrict democracy. As the '60s tell us, it's within the realm of a strong federal government that participatory democracy via advocacy groups—nongovernmental organization charities, Black Lives Matter, reformers of every stripe—can make its most effective appeals and can, as both FDR and Obama have said, push the executive branch (always remember: we're talking history and four to eight years from now). In the '60s, the antiwar movement might not have stopped the Vietnam war, but it helped bring about the Paris peace talks (however abortive, in part due to Nixonian sabotage); Nixon's subsequent quicker pullout of American troops; and ultimately, according to Henry Kissinger, Nixon's decision not to use tactical nuclear weapons on North Vietnam.

And it's from the federal government that we got the New Deal, antipoverty programs, and school desegregation. Despite states rights advocates wishing otherwise, such change might come from towns, cities, small businesses, and NGOs, but almost never from the states. A states' rights philosophy will now trap democratic movements in the gerrymandered and corrupt political satrapies that many states have become, and given states have to balance their budgets, there's only a very limited extent that they can be laboratories of democracy. Some states might work that way, but for every California there's a Kansas. In a United States with a weak central government, we know where the power would (or maybe will) flow: not to states or "the people," per the now outdated Tenth Amendment, but to the anocracy of unregulated financial centers and megacorporations. To give only two examples:

regulation foe Rupert Murdoch's relentless propagandizing to grow the power of his media and its political backers, and the Koch brothers' machine reaching out to influence the smallest local elections. It's not that state legislatures aren't worth fighting for, of course they are, but the '60s tell us that only with strong federal regulations can any kind of democracy be safeguarded against the economic mafiocracies and plutocracies of America 2017.

So in the hope that that "new New Left" may be gradually able to make such programs a reality, whenever such an opportunity presents itself, let's sum up some of the previous chapters of this book and riff a little (okay, more like a guitar solo) and see what new regulations might have to offer, 60s-style, in some of the realms discussed in this book.

The Economy

Before Trump's election, there was serious discussion about economic inequality by both parties, and Walmart raised its wages. For even big business has begun to realize that a continual flow of financial gains solely to the financial sector and the resulting gross inequality for a huge majority of Americans could cripple the country economically. Peter Georgescu, chairman emeritus of Young and Rubicam, wrote an article entitled "Capitalists Arise!"[3] in which he warned that failure to address such inequality would lead to social unrest or potentially much higher taxes, and stated that the economic disparities impose an economic "caste system" that will destroy the "capitalist engine," especially due to an increasingly impoverished population's unwillingness to invest and spend.

His proposed remedy: businesses must invest in their own operations and higher wages. But what if they won't? Governments can offer tax incentives to businesses who pay their employees more. Good idea, but what if they decide it's still not in their interest to do so? The article didn't have much of an answer for that.

One answer (and remember, we're talking about four years from now) is going back to '60s-style higher taxes, just not that high: a more equitable tax structure, where the super-rich pay a fairer share on all their economic activities, including income, capital gains, and shipping jobs overseas. How crazy a suggestion is that? Well, what if their taxes could be placed by the government in an infrastructure bank, where they could earn as high a rate of interest possible through investment in projects such as repairing roads and bridges, improving Amtrak, a smarter electric grid, and renewable energy? In effect the tax becomes partially a draft of their money for the national interest and their own interest payments.

Meanwhile how doomed is any kind of social insurance for the rest of us? Supposedly Social Security is off limits. The Ryan Congress is itching to privatize Medicare—like Senator Schumer said, "make my day," but this is frighteningly a matter of 'we'll see.' What about an increase at the federal level in the minimum wage? Wait 'til next decade.

It may be that all we can do is save Social Security. Contrary to conservative propaganda, social security is not an entitlement scheme but social insurance into which all Americans pay as soon as they start working, and social insurance has a long history in the United States. How does this sound as a scheme to address systematic poverty and inequality: a universal social insurance system comprising old-age pensions and disability support and universal stakeholder grants for young adults, funded by a 10% inheritance tax focused on land? The man who created this "agrarian justice" defended the private property system, while also branding large-scale poverty as preventable injustice and conceiving of universal entitlements to limit poverty caused by property-holding inequality. His name was Thomas Paine, and his "Common Sense" was one of the founding documents of the American Revolution.[4]

What are the other possibilities? The "sharing economy"? As we're learning from the battle with Airbnb in New York and as we've all learned from Facebook, the sharing/cybereconomy is often a cover for the most power-hungry megacybercorporations. Call it what it is: barter and the black market. It will have its app-assisted place, just don't misuse the term "economy."

Or how about breaking up the big banks, which will now get even bigger? Leaving aside the fact that will be impossible anytime soon, as Barney Frank, co-sponsor of the Dodd-Frank Act, stated: break them up into what, and how? To break up the big banks is to propagate, as Oliver Stone might say, a "countermyth" of restored financial purity. It doesn't touch, as Hillary Clinton pointed out, shadow banking and dark money. It will force countless complex financial deals to be unwound and delayed, with unforeseen consequences. Finally, given the big banks, as interest rates now probably rise, may squeeze credit card debtors (whose minimum payments and credit terms are not locked in) to the point we have a consumer-driven recession, now is not the time to make that worse, and that will probably be true through the 2020s.

Still, there's no way we can have a safe, sustained economic recovery and get back to even a semblance of an inclusive middle-class '60s-style economy without some regulations on the banks. The recent Wells Fargo scandal teaches us they will not give up their excesses voluntarily. Besides enforcing against them rules that remain on the books with much stiffer punishments, the Left, whenever it comes back to power, must compel them not to engage in speculation with individual depositors' or pension funds and be blocked from the housing market. And yes there should be taxes on the banks, especially on micro-transactions and speculative activity in general, which won't impair the activities of more conservative bankers, but the gamblers, the dopamine junkies, the debt-taker-onners, the blow-and-ho contingent, the Libor rate manipulators. The only way to stop them … is to stop them.

What could be the potential practical manifestation of all this (as in get real)? Members of Congress on both sides may be more amenable to such measures some time in the future because of the unanticipated results of the Citizens United decision. The supposed benefits of the Supreme Court taking the lid off political donations did not help the original Republican establishment; it destroyed it when a huge bunch of candidates each found their own well of money and kept running until Trump took over a thoroughly disunited Republican party and turned it into a Retrumplican party (with the solid traditional principled Republicans who refused to support Trump turned into Relicans). Meanwhile Hillary Clinton was defeated (minus that popular vote bit) by everything but the unlimited money.

And unlimited money may soon mean something very different and very un-American: the next couple of years may present the spectacle of foreign interests being steered toward increasingly hostile takeovers of American businesses and real estate, with hefty fees to Goldman-Sachs, but worsening consequences for everyone else, especially in big cities, and for the country. And the Trump Administration's tactical error of favoring Goldman-Sachs so heavily in their government may create some unexpected allies: big bank honchos are ultra-competitive types, and they don't like it when the playing field is so de-leveled.

So it may be possible at a later date to harness the kind of political pressure that could persuade non-Goldman-Sachs banks and megacorporations to withdraw from their occupied territories of the former middle class economy to avoid greater financial and political damage in the future, accepting campaign finance reform, infrastructure banking with interest, and a more inclusive economy.

Citizen Media

This section, unfortunately, does not have to do with four years from now, but as of the day after Inauguration Day, and it's where not alarms (not yet) but warnings should be sounded.

As of this writing, a deportation force rounding up millions of undocumented largely Latino immigrants, a Muslim registry, and a slow but relentless increase in for-profit prison-building and Incarceration Nation may gradually become a reality. The ground for this, unfortunately, was prepared by communities of color not coming out to vote or, in the case of Latinos, twenty to thirty percent of the voters casting their ballots for Trump. This despite the fact that Trump's first public utterances as President demonized Latino immigrants. This despite the fact that the outgoing African American president and his eloquent first lady begged African Americans to turn out at the polling places and warned them of the consequences if they didn't.

These communities will now suffer those consequences. The Left, looking toward future battles, can marshal some resources to nonviolently block such consequences, but it's more important to accept that this may very well happen and to publicize it in all its agony and not just human but economic dislocation. In the '60s all we had was mimeograph machines and 16-millimeter film groups if the national media didn't cover events. Now of course we have social media. And it's up to the main media (who are now having an Admiral Stockdale "Who am I? Why am I here?" moment) and Facebook to make up for a multitude of sins, from free publicity for Trump to fake news on Facebook pages, by giving as wide a dissemination as possible to the video that may come out of any mass deportations or attacks against dissent; if they don't, this is where Twitter, as it has in resistance movements throughout the world, can truly serve a social purpose for a change, and if not Twitter, apps like Periscope. Similarly, any attempt to "register" Muslims, and what that really will look like, has to be broadcast to all those American who maybe didn't quite think through, for example, what it will mean to "register" a Muslim

American soldier or cop.[5]

For it's certainly possible that the resistance will, after this first flush of dissent, not be televised. The pleasantly implacable Kellyanne Conway has recently commented on Chris Wallace's Fox show that reporters who talk "smack" about President Trump should be fired to protect their company's stockholders from the effects of the President's anger. One can hope that Trump's tweet-attacks will eventually becomes so wearisome that they'll no longer move bored markets against individual media companies. But another possibility is the chilling expectation of or actual engineering of attempted hostile takeovers against supposedly unfriendly media, not to mention expanded libel suits and the potential loss of net neutrality.

That's when we need to remember we all have smaller screens.

The People United

There should also be, to meet all Retrumplican repressions, a relentless continuation of protest and nonviolent resistance. Every aggressive act against human rights in this country should be a tripwire to set this off, but protest should always be considered self-defense. For example, it was only when President Johnson significantly increased the draft for the Vietnam War that the antiwar movement really became a force. Protest is not an aggressive complaint, it's prodded to life by heinous events. And neither civility nor appeals to patriotic unity override the right to organized nonviolent self-defense.

There will probably be repressive countermeasures, just as in the '60s, though quite possibly much worse, and so the Left also has to rediscover the '60s-era efficacy of bail funds and philanthropy contributing to legal defense. If Deportation and Incarceration Nation grows, its victims can't be simply left to overwhelmed public defenders and shipped off to endure the hideous cruelty of prisons like Rikers Island to await trial, or convinced to plead guilty to avoid that. It will cost a lot more money now than in the '60s, but it's an absolute necessity that civil liberties defense and bail fund NGOs mushroom in the face of this threat. In another arena, media-libel-defense funds need to be marshaled.

An even greater and frankly terrifying threat is Trump's insistence on a private security force along with the Secret Service, which presumably he could expand, and which he has previously used against protesters exercising their rights to free speech. Combined with Trump's penchant for identifying people he particularly disapproves of in his tweets, thus signaling their identity to his followers, this presents an out-and-out threat to loyal dissent in America, both politically and personally. Trump's threats to mount actions like, for example, send "the Feds" into Chicago will only be funny until they're not.

The Left will need a massive legal fund to, if all political attempts to deter such antidemocratic aggression fail, hold any and all private agents of Trump (including Twitter) legally responsible in criminal or civil court for any damages sustained by nonviolent legitimate dissenters. It would be the ultimate anti-Constitutional conflict of interest: the head of the executive branch which is supposed to impartially enforce the law having a security force answerable only to him and carrying out his private commands. Could it lead to or in itself amount to high crimes and misdemeanors that could become an impeachable offense? While the courts are still not dominated by Trump employees, a strategy has to be prepared to vigorously contest the legality of such potential executive branch private security actions.

And *if* Trump-supporting states and their Retrumplican Congresspeople support repressive actions in a larger way, economic boycotts against those states and moratoriums or outright strikes against Trump-supporting organizations and firms need to be considered. Both sides will suffer, but the non-Trump side contains most of the big cities, California, and the economic muscle that implies.

The building of more for-profit prisons needs to be stopped and delayed by any nonviolent means necessary. If such prison-building is federally driven, that would certainly be the time for those who believe in states rights to put their money and efforts where their mouths are and try to stop them if at all possible. As a further incentive to such efforts, the Left should consider the possibility that new crimes in the future to populate such prisons may include dissent being construed as aiding and abetting the country's enemies. This country has a long history of such repression, from the Alien and Sedition Acts in the Adams administration to the HUAC hearings, the Hollywood Blacklist and the McCarthy hearings, and the FBI Cointelpro in the '60s (generally in the second terms of Presidents like Adams or Eisenhower, but history moves faster now). No need to ask for whom the for-profit-prison bell may toll.

As Higher Education Goes Lower

With apologies to the great Roger Waters and Pink Floyd, we do need that education, and the Left needs to organize to reform it, first of all, in the same way it resisted the draft, by resisting the debt.

This is perhaps one of the most unjust and harmful economic developments for our future: the subjecting of our students, our "best and brightest," to the kind of crushing financial burden that will severely restrict their scope of economic and productive action in the future. This book has already suggested ways students can organize '60s-style against the academic-industrial complex, especially college administrators constantly raising tuition while awarding themselves huge salaries and engaging in construction boondoggles and real estate grabs.

On the national level, the Left needs to continue to fight to regulate student loans and curb crippling interest rates, while, in colleges themselves, as mentioned in "When Students Struck and Won," Constitutional free speech must be guaranteed and enforced and identity politics and courses contested. Bernie Sanders's vision of competitive free or low-priced state colleges, plans to expand MOOC's and community colleges, and regulations that allow students to take less courses on college campuses and more online and combine them into legitimate college degrees should all be implemented.

And as also previously mentioned, parents need to back their kids in on-campus demonstrations, even to the extent of parent-student strikes. As someone who's not a parent, I nonetheless sympathize with stressed-out parents my age who never expected, with all their other problems, the need to 'relitigate' with their discouraged and cynical kids democracy, the Constitution, and the Bill of Rights. But until the basic civics lessons come from a reformed educational system, they need to begin at home, and support for what college sons and daughters may have to do to assert their needs and their rights is a very good place to start.

And speaking of civics, here's one more contra-intuitive but pro-student '60s idea:

National Service

Yes, bring back the draft. Only make it a noncombatant one, unless strictly in the case of national emergency (which will have the added effect of making the government much more careful about national emergencies). A minimum term of national service, with opportunities to expand that, will make young people more aware of civics and what it takes to build and maintain a nation, combining education and useful out-in-the-field activities to help address national problems. Among many of the lessons students could learn from such service: our military, as many have stated, is one of the greenest organizations in the country, and the last and best resort in the world in disaster relief.

And a national service branch could eventually produce alternatives to colleges, a kind of GI Bill while students are still in the armed/national services that would stress educational centers both on- and offline with a more practical curriculum (more ecology and political science and humanitarianism courses, less identity politics–related courses), and with equivalents to college credits that will enable students to shorten their incredibly expensive private college educations, and even do the equivalent of postgraduate work in the national service system. It will inevitably lead to political associations and networks. These will help elect a solid group of veterans of either military or noncombatant national services, who will have a much better idea of the possibilities of government than either hacks out to make money out of the system or plutocrats out to dismantle it.

Immigration and Population Control

At what was supposed to be a Hillary Clinton victory rally, Bruce Springsteen at one point broke off from his songs to speak about the purpose of the election, and mentioned "compassionate immigration reform." From a man who's sung so often in defense of Latino immigrants, it seemed true wisdom that perhaps the Left can follow up on.

Paul Ehrlich's 1968 work *The Population Bomb* warned us all about the looming overpopulation problem for the planet almost fifty years ago, and it's been a slow-motion detonation since then. And what makes it a particularly touchy problem in America and Europe is that, in terms of the most effective and humane means of population control, education of young women and girls, America and Europe are doing well, but other societies not as far along in this way, and they're sending millions of immigrants to this country. That will create much greater competition for shrinking resources and jobs and the rental and home real estate market, with wages going down and prices going up. Barbara

Jordan, a civil rights activist and Congresswoman of the '60s and early '70s, warned back then about the threat to jobs for African Americans from mass immigration.

All this while America is suffering all the consequences of climate crisis we've already seen: more hurricanes on the coasts where most immigrants settle, a possible major earthquake on the west coast, and fires and droughts in the entire western half of the country. The result will be loss of habitable land, especially in coastal cities, with even more stresses on a burgeoning population.

The Left should never stop fighting for achieving a path to citizenship for the undocumented, even in the face of family breakups and deportations. But at that point we will be creating eleven million new citizens, and we will finally have to realize, as compassionately as possible, that our country's capacity to absorb new citizens has, to quote an ecology term, a "carrying capacity." Perhaps the fairest way to address this is an across-the-board cut of immigration by, say, 40%, with proportional cuts depending on how countries sent immigration to this country previously (if they sent 20% of the immigrants, they absorb 20% of the cut).

Meanwhile, the Left should also support or foster population control and girls and women's education programs abroad. Finally new restrictions on immigration should affect not just the poor, but the wealthy or super-rich. One way to establish this is restrictions on immigrants' abilities to purchase property, as is the case in Australia. The kind of visas that also admit "aliens of extraordinary skills" to take high-end jobs in this country should be curtailed in favor of more opportunity for, for example, the first-generation citizens currently graduating from our universities. And if we want to maintain American control of American businesses against incursions from all over the globe, we might want to consider restrictions on super-rich immigrants' activities in that sphere as well. There's now the strong possibility that new policies will result in an America far less desirable to the masses yearning to breathe free, but all the more a target for the moguls yearning to buy real estate.

Healthcare, Gun Control, Science, and the Environment

These are the heartbreakers now. These are the "hope we can catch up and we're not too late but probably not" issues. These evoke all the elephants and tigers extinct, coral reefs dead, floods and fires, people dying en masse in emergency rooms, endless school shootout scenarios. Is there any hope?

Short-term for healthcare, no—except maybe preserving no-preconditions and children-on-parents-plans in healthcare. Long term, prospects may be surprising. As even a couple of my friends who are conservatives have admitted to me, they believe single-payer healthcare, or "Medicare for all," (or at the very least a public option) is inevitable. This is anything but free socialized medicine, as Medicare provides for free or very low cost hospital services but requires at least modest premiums and copayments for everything else. But it's of course based on an extension of '60s social insurance thinking.

Any carrot of such a healthcare plan will also this time have to carry a big stick of cost control, regulating hospital pricing and allowing Medicare to negotiate down the price of drugs (which supposedly President Trump, as a dealmaker, supports). As for regulating competition among insurance companies—forget it, they'll rig prices whenever they can. (Hospitals are better on this score; many have financial aid programs.) There could be an upper tier of high-priced insurance and high-priced medical specialists, just as there was in the '60s, for those who wish to use them and can afford them. For unlike in the '60s, but buoyed by '60s-era thinking, by now we've learned that expensive tests ordered by specialists often return false positives, that "watch and wait" can be the best strategy for potential prostate cancer, that overmedication is a huge problem, that orthopedists are not necessarily better for your back pain than yoga or acupuncture, and that nurse practitioners and walk-in clinics can take up a lot of the slack.

And there should be community and local agitation on the healthcare front. Coops importing drugs from Canada; if we do go the way of some kind of health savings vouchers, we should have the right to spend our money this way. Similar networks making sure there are plenty of contraceptive "morning after" drugs in the United States, especially since access to abortion, for all practical purposes, will probably die out in this country.

Short-term on gun-control, no hope except state-by-state, where it's already happening. Long-term, as discussed in "Sticking to Our Guns," basic gun control measures, including getting military killing machine weapons off our streets through everything from buybacks to registration to regulation, while respecting the rights of gun owners, should definitely be on the new New Left's agenda. Part of that whole "*well-regulated* militia" Second Amendment thing.

As for climate cancer, the question is not whether in twenty years our planet will be the same—the engines of devastation have been set in motion—but whether we can sustain and save enough of it, starting now, to keep it from becoming, in Pope Francis's words, "an immense pile of filth." That involves all hands on deck, including the bad deckhands that have to be forced and also enticed to help save the planetary ship before the whole voyage goes to hell.

What's the possible enticement for '60s-style controls on megacorporate polluters, especially now that they can *get whatever they want*? Infrastructure-bank-related investment strategies as mentioned before, and public-private partnerships (more on that later). But long-term the regulatory stick will have to come down hard; this will be the new New Left's biggest battle.

The only way to stop them is to stop them. Voting out Congressional climate-change deniers. Getting out of fossil fuel company investments if they won't diversify into renewable energy; stockholders may be able to help this along. Nonviolent resistance mobilizing in the streets and in the courts against the polluters and climate-change deniers; those who think that's naive should consider that a bunch of "kayaktivists" blocking its way was the final straw that stopped Shell from moving a drilling platform to the Arctic, and that concerted native American demonstrations have possibly blocked a pipeline at Standing Rock, North Dakota (as of this writing, it remains to be seen what will happen post-Obama). Massive negative publicity can also be a factor. Koch Industries is already beginning to feel that and trying to show its kinder, gentler, more cooperative side. A recent Koch tv commercial I saw actually showed a '60s-era peace sign scrawled on a wall, which made me glad I had a cumbersome television wired up to a sound system or I might have thrown it out the window.

But nothing substitutes for direct application of the force of law, and that can now only be achieved in enlightened (or scared straight) states. Those who think that's ineffective should reflect on the fact that, under fairly tough regulations during a drought, California saved 29% more water and, last I checked, life in L.A. is not yet hell on earth. The state pulled together and achieved genuine conservation.

Looking long-term, there may be a possibility for public-private cooperation on conservation and renewable energy conversion (not to mention reform of current animal mass-slaughtering procedures which potentially breed antibiotic-resistant disease). Such partnerships could put some infrastructure money into, for example, improved solar storage batteries and fleets of electric cars, as Elon Musk is already working on.

But there's another side to that: as mentioned in the essay "Punch The Hippie, Kill The Planet" the "new New Left" must return to a '60s-era faith in science and at least be willing to try public-private energy company-government development of some nuclear power plants and *some* highly regulated genetic engineering to create fruits and vegetables that will require less pesticide use. Here's where the New Left truly is as ideologically sclerotic as the communists of old. There can be only one ideology when it comes to saving the planet: solutionism.

Conclusion

If you compare the achievements of the "big government" period of the 1960s with the achievements of the laissez-faire more limited government period of today, you can list the space program, Medicare, antipoverty reform, the civil rights program, etc., on the one hand, and insane consumption by the super-rich, recovering from self-inflicted wounds like the war in Iraq, and denying climate cancer on the other. Much of this is in service to a concept of smaller government that's an endless myth, since conservative-backed 'smaller government' gave us the second Iraq war and the bailout of the big banks via the Federal Reserve.

What have we reaped with this kind of sowing? How have the high-finance heedlessness, insane competition for overleveraged deals, and disgraceful 2008 Great Recession and mortgage crisis chickens come home to roost? President Donald Trump and a right wing-driven Congress.

At least '60s dissenters had respect for the Constitution and its federal institutions enough to want to reform them, even, in the case of the hated Selective Service (the draft), directing their ire not so much at the draft itself, although there was vandalism of draft boards, as the war it was meant to serve. It's Retrumplicans that have the rage to sweep it all away.

The new New Left must fight not capitalism itself, with its resources of creativity and competition, but the whole Retrumplican *free market late capitalist* establishment that unfortunately the Democratic candidate never spoke up against enough. The Left must become the champions of curbing "free market" abuses and excesses. "Free market" is one of those phrases that destroys itself in its very utterance with its total absurdity (try to bring goods to the free market as in, for example, bringing a new food product to major grocery store chains, and see how free you are to sell it on their shelves). "Free market" is on a par with, for those who remember, the Soviet Communist phrases "workers' state" or, better yet, "dictatorship of the proletariat." Yes, according to the Marxist-Leninist philosophy, the cadre running the armies and gulags would ultimately "wither away" when workers owned the means of production, which somehow never happened. Instead the Russian state has "withered away" into Putinism, the KGB without communists.

As many of us know from our varying personal experiences, free-market late-stage capitalism is an interconnected mafiocracy where distorting middlemen levy restrictions and fees that amount to unofficial taxes on every form of economic activity or seeking of goods and services, from health insurance premiums and deductibles to monopolistic cable carrier costs to grotesquely inflated college costs to the big banks' control and sabotage of the real estate market. Adam Smith's invisible hand has become a very tangible hand in your pocket. Let's call "free market" capitalism what it is: corruption—especially as in the rotting away of the earth as late-stage capitalism buys off or suppresses those who want to legislate against carbon pollution so they can keep free-riding on the environment and damaging it with impunity. There is only one answer for free-market privateering corruption and "pro-growth" policies that increase corporate control of our economic and political life and destruction of our planet: public government pushback in the form of federal, state, and city regulation.

The Left, in arguing for such a return to regulation, for forcing people to confront that, could lead the country in ethical education, and quite possibly win back that sector of Trump voters who voted for redress of their economic grievances but will soon learn just how much they've been shortchanged and deceived. It will make the Left unpopular for a good long while: think about how much Barry Goldwater, William F. Buckley, Jr., and other stalwart small c conservatives had to endure in the early days of their movement. But if the Retrumplican right now represents the "monsters of the id," the Left has to be the regulatory superego. Otherwise, they're not doing their job—they're just a lamer greyer id in a pantsuit.

While the Left sits on the backbenches, as the Brits would say, they can keep putting out ideas, winning more and more people over to the concept of, as both Presidents Kennedy and Obama have said, doing what's hard. We may yet escape total destruction and be able to have a livable world, but one precondition is that a courageous but more flexible American left chastens and limits out-of-control capitalism but then works with it for the sake of the country and the planet.

We can hope that enlightened corporations will back beneficial regulations, and more philanthropic and reasonable billionaires like Warren Buffet and Michael Bloomberg will come to the fore. But, for rich and poor alike, that's not enough. The only way to stop them is to stop them.

How to do all this? Being willing to nudge the new administration here and there a little bit and then compromise with it? Here's a matching question: Has the Trump administration shown any indication of being willing to compromise in any way? The Left's imperative should be the line from Radiohead's "The Numbers," a song reminiscent of Jefferson Airplane/CSNY's "Wooden Ships" in its structure and rhythm and anthemic planetary consciousness: "We'll take back what is ours." And there can be no compromise, whether over a Supreme Court justice or the healthcare system, when it comes to taking back our popular vote-backed will of the people, our system of government, our Constitution, our rights, and our planet.

The best hope for that seems to be the ingeniously decentralized yet unified in its purpose Indivisible movement. There's a process contained there that may very well lead to coalescences of many different groups across state lines (finding out and utilizing, for example, what issues grass roots forces in Retrumplican states need to dethrone "safe seat" Congresspeople). There could be Venn diagram intersections of issues like healthcare-environment-worker retraining in renewable energy skills. The Indivisible movement could not only prompt political but artistic and musical networking that could start to resurrect a '60s-style counterculture, and finally combine the politics and the popular art. And what we now have, which we didn't have in the '60s, is the fundraising megaconcert.

One can even imagine an Indivisible convention, both "irl" and intensely networked online, which could ultimately present Congresspeople, Senators, governors, and presidential candidates seeking its support with a hierarchy of demands, the top rungs of which, to borrow a '60s phrase, would be nonnegotiable. Maybe even an Indivisible party, if the Democrats don't measure up to this historic challenge. And the Indivisible movement, as befits its source in the Pledge of Allegiance, suggests a '60s-style new New Left rallying cry to beat "America First."

"America for All."

Woodstock and All After

> "Did you ever see a dream walking? Well I did."
> — Harry Revel and Mack Gordon, sung by Bing Crosby[1]

> "Stand!
> Don't you know that you are free?
> Well at least in your mind if you want to be."
> — Sly and the Family Stone[2]

During the film *Woodstock* Max Yasgur is introduced from the stage as "the man whose farm we're on," and receives thunderous applause and cheers. He greets the crowd with equal warmth, and gives them a benediction. "You've proved to the world that a half million kids can get together for three days of fun and music, and have nothing but fun and music, and I God bless you for it!"[3]

He could be forgiven the slip. He had after all won a lottery of popular culture godhood. He was hosting what had instantly become the third largest city in New York on its way to becoming a world history cultural and musical milestone. And the crowd, not to mention feeling pretty exalted themselves, was in a precarious enough situation that they needed all the blessings they could get.

They got them, and not just because "nothing but fun and music" meant they had avoided any violence. Woodstock was a potential colossal fuckup and (as predicted by the *New York Times*) disaster area that became instead a sublime accident displaying everything that was best in the '60s. It was meant to be exhibit A of successful American rock music festivals. Once it lost just about all its initial investment, it failed at that.

But it more than lived up to its almost-forgotten billing as an Aquarian Exposition. From August 15 through August 17—and, as it turned out, the morning of August 18, 1969—there was not only peace and love and great music, but an experimental space and testing ground for living the new counterculture. If you wanted three days of pleasure and consciousness investigation smoking weed and taking acid instead of the music, or along with the music, it was there for you. Yoga and other Eastern disciplines were constantly practiced or at one point led from the stage. You could briefly live off the land and pick up agrarianism tips in the encampments. You could join the nudist colony by the lake. There were no cops or guards able or even willing to stop it. On display and available to everyone, in the genuinely free spirit in which they were offered and in the for once appropriate word used back then, were all the "cosmic" values of the era.

Yes, Woodstock Nation was very much a "world's fair" of that music and those values, very brief, but very real, as I well know, because I was in that crowd. It was the greatest example in my life of *I vass dere, Cholly*, and I was also one of the few among the 300,000 or so who did not take a lick off a tab or a hit off a joint or a swig of alcohol stronger than Boone's Farm Apple Wine. So after I came back to New York and slept for sixteen hours, with all those images and sounds and memories echoing in my brain, I wondered if I could write about that as opposed to another adolescent poem or short story. And would my high school paper be even interested? They were interested, as would later be two other outerborough papers in New York, and so Woodstock became the occasion of my first writing ever seen outside the circle of my school and family.

For all these reasons, it's appropriate to make it the last essay of this book.

The Show

By the time we got to Woodstock, as the song goes, we never did—appropriate for a festival that bent many minds in many ways. The actual Woodstock, legendary in rock history (Dylan and the Band had lived there), never worked out as a location, so the new location became Walkill, New York. But as the festival's dates neared that fell through as well. So as the promoters of the "Aquarian Exposition" wrote: "To insure three days of peace and music, we left Walkill and are now in White Lake, NY, on Yasgur's farm."[3]

This as it turned out was a cue not all would go as planned. My group became aware of that when we piled into a van, and took the drive to the Catskills via the New York State Thruway and a "quickway" to Bethel, the nearest town to White Lake. That usually two-to-three-hour drive became a day-and-night-long hegira. What we were expecting with our three six-dollar tickets (standard for concerts back then), and with camping food as a supplement for what we figured would be plenty of concessions, melted away when we joined the traffic jam pilgrimage. Locals sat on their beach chairs in the grass and stared in amazement or snapped pictures as cars and VW vans and day-glo painted buses went by carrying young people dressed in everything from standard denims and aviator glasses to saris and djellabas, African headdresses, American flags, and amulets and beads and almost nothing else. The cars moved no faster than one could walk, which is why many put the cars, radiators merrily hissing, on the side of the road, further slowing the caravan (given, as I later found out, our driver was often on acid, the crawl was probably just as well).

During the all-night traffic jam, we shared food and music with fellow delighted teenagers and freaks from all over the world. People stepped or leaped across roofs of cars to say hello, or break out guitars and jam a little on top of adjacent stalled vans, which I would occasionally join, having brought my trusty blues harp. There were exchanges of food with people in the road and leaning out car windows: wine traded for peaches; generous sharing of cigarettes of all kinds, Hershey bars, gum, and of course "gorp," granola-based trail food. As night fell, tunneling headlights and a long comet trail of red taillights outlined a road that was like nothing anyone had ever seen, while out of the country darkness whenever we saw porch lights we saw people cheerfully waving us on.

There was a neverending raucous chorus of guitars and fellow bad blues harpists and loud-well-wishing on the level of "Where you from? …Good luck… You're beautiful, man!" and also a remarkable feeling of goodwill and unity on that waking dream road. Welcome school-and-homework-oriented sixteen-year-old to a gigantic, spontaneous, harmoniously loving community. Dig on your others in this benign apocalypse. No guarantee of seating, no guarantee we'd even get there, but there was almost a "Journey to the East" feeling that this road was now a part of the event we'd come to see, and if we never get to see it because of the fucking traffic, well, the roadmap has indeed become the territory.

We did finally get to an Aquarian Age Parking Area where sleepy staffers in red peace-symbol shirts waved us into a jumble of vehicles from which we hoped we'd be able to locate and extract our van at festival's end. We wandered through a forest where, along with the usual political leaflets and buttons and handcrafted hippie clothing accessories, drugs were openly sold from the tables. Psilocybin, mushrooms, hash, downers, grass, acid. Looking for the entry points where tickets would be collected and expecting a long wait on an entrance line, we instead stepped through a gap in the fence and took our seats in the famous pasture in Yasgur's farm. Gradually I began to see what 20,000, 50,000, 100,000 people and beyond looked like, while still wondering: how were they ever going to collect my ticket?

And just what schedule was this running on? The enormous wooden stage still appeared to be under construction. There was really nothing to do but munch the gorp and stare at the stage and the crew and the eighty-foot p.a. system towers while the crowd massed behind us, a Sargasso Sea of humanity, flags and balloons and Frisbees, but largely a spectacle of glorious brown of already slept-in-the dust mufti and blankets and jeans caked with mud below the knees. In an eerie foreshadowing of the movie *Apocalypse Now* ten years later, the main soundtrack was Vietnam-era helicopters bringing the acts and supplies to the festival, now that (unknown to us) the Thruway was jammed shut. That stage became our magnetic north and as I stared and stared gradually I realized that no one was going to collect my ticket.

Finally the most godlike stentorian voice I ever heard, which would usually be the determinedly mellow Chip Monck, boomed across the field announcing Richard Havens. Havens came on in what looked like a long robe, whipcrack-strumming his guitar and roaring out one of his anthems, and it was on.

Friday night was basically folk and acoustic night. It also featured the festival's steadiest guest performer: rain. Some may remember the beautiful shot from the film of Joan Baez playing while rain fell into spotlit puddles behind her. It was like that the whole late afternoon and night right into the early morning hours.

Having brought my old poncho, I spent Friday night cocooned in it watching the performers. Ravi Shankar had commented that he was sick of the "go man go" attitude toward his sitar, but he wanted people's ears opened, so there he was reprising his set of ragas from the film *Monterey Pop* bathed in silver light refracted through the raindrops on my eyes.[4] Tim Hardin did some great folk picking in the rain. When a surprise guest was announced, many of us stood up and cheered, anticipating Dylan, who was always rumored to be showing up; instead Melanie was announced and we shrank back into our ponchos with groans. Not Ms. Safka's fault. She gave a radiant performance, and was so inspired by lit matches held up by her fans she wrote her biggest hit

"Lay Down Candles (In The Rain)." Everyone there was a bit prone to exaggeration.

Arlo Guthrie poked the show to life with his good-natured wisecracking, irresistible performance look (long black hair, mischievous eyes) and a true spine to his music inherited from his father. It was he who told us that the New York State Thruway was closed. "Lotta freaks." Afterwards Joan Baez, glowing in a turquoise dress, brought the show to a close in appropriately reverential folk fashion, with intimate storytelling from American and her own history, including tales of her draft-resisting husband in prison, as she led a small folk-rock band before performing a hair-raising a cappella "Swing Low Sweet Chariot" that, like so many of the performances to come, would pick up high voltage emotional fulsomeness from the unprecedented crowd.

As I wrote in my high school article, "we were The Crowd … the pleasures of just existing in the midst of that experience … manifested itself in seismic cheers at every announcement… everyone purring with kindness… thrilling kinship." It's hard to describe how exhilarating that feeling was, except to say that on Friday night the biggest moment wasn't from any of the performers but when the announcer boomed out that though the promoters would lose their money, we were now at the world's largest free concert. We had just seen the first night go until about four in the morning despite a steady rain, and could easily figure out the rest of the weekend would be wall-to-wall music, all for free. The whole darkened field roared. I took my three tickets and tore them up and threw them into the air, along with hundreds of people. It was like a horde of gnats in the glow of the stage lights. Those little souvenirs would later be worth a lot more than eighteen bucks, but given how waterlogged my jeans would become, I doubt they would have survived anyway.

And so with a warning—"there's a hell of a lot of us, so if we're gonna make it, you better remember the guy next to you is your brother"—we knew the performance schedule was off, normal time frames and expectations were off, the rules were off. We were castaways on a counterculture island on the trip of our lives. The night closed with Chip Monck soothing the crowd to find a place to sleep and to say goodnight to the person next to you—my oldest buddy, as it turned out. I looked out at the bowl-shaped pasture filled with the dim masses of strangers and felt I was in one of the friendliest, safest, most familial spaces I'd ever been in.

The only problem was it was about three hours before dawn and with the rain never stopping there wasn't much sleep to be had. I listened to be what had to be the quietest sheltering-in-place of three hundred thousand people ever, occasionally shouts or guitar strums like crickets echoing across the fields, until finally under a cold and dimly lightening sky I unwrapped myself from my poncho feeling as stiff as I ever had up to that point, and once again greeted that amazing crowd. Food was shared, including hot cereal cooked over Sterno cans. The sun gradually came out as the hours drowsed on, and there was, as I vaguely remember, a yoga and a meditation session, and I grabbed a little sleep between sunlit warmup acts like an eerie madrigalesque set by the Incredible String Band and a spaced-out but nonetheless very moving performance by John Sebastian. Country Joe McDonald woke us all up with his spirited strumming of his anti-Vietnam "Fixin' to Die Rag" and the famous F-I-S-H cheer changed into a 300,000-voice roar of "What's that spell? FUCK!" Getting tired again, I wondered if I should sleep through Santana, whom I'd seen twice as a warmup band at the Fillmore East.

No way. Bill Graham, impresario of the Fillmore East, had insisted on having Santana on the bill at Woodstock, figuring they were about to break out, and they did so in spectacular fashion, bringing the crowd to their feet with conga-and-percussion-driven Afro-Cuban jamming.

From that point on, the Saturday lineup soared off into, for this audience member, the greatest show ever. It was the last blast of the San Francisco/New York "Summer of Love," dominated by mid-to-late '60s West Coast jam and psychedelic bands with that kind of luminous and anarchic spirit, except for new bands like Creedence Clearwater Revival, Sly and the Family Stone, and Santana, all of whom had been warmup acts at the Fillmore, and who would point the way to more disciplined and hit-single-driven performances while maintaining that same incandescence.

Canned Heat played the sunset with a gutbucket raw blues sound that very few white bands would ever duplicate. Mountain was like an optical illusion in orange light with then three-hundred-pound Leslie West in white buckskin on lead guitar, or perhaps I saw them slightly tilted because a motherly blonde woman was cradling my head in her lap and stroking my hair. Creedence in blue and forest green lighting was tight and crisp and intense, and driven by an absolutely hotwired John Fogerty, who barked commands at the sound crew, and led a great set with passion and old-school professionalism.

This was my first time seeing the Grateful Dead, and as with the first time I saw Led Zeppelin, I didn't get them back then. I was watching through the rainbow-colored lighting on the stage, the glow of what now seemed to be huge Christmas lights dangling from the towers, and the mist of yet another rainstorm, trying to figure out what was going on, though I was certainly responding to beautiful keyboard music and Garcia's lyrical filigrees of guitar. I remember only a combination of barely disciplined performing and the band's desire to flee the crackling equipment, and then suddenly they were gone. As is shown on the extra CD of performances in *Woodstock Director's Cut: Forty Years On*, The Dead actually succeeded with one of their freest jams. First they had to induce a totally tripped-out fan to leave the stage. "Pigpen" Ron McKernan finally got to start singing "Turn On Your Love Light," after which Garcia started soloing with the two drummers, and Bob Weir joined Pigpen for soul-blues choruses that built and built and built. Finally the jam ended as (literally, on film) one of the drummers, Mickey Hart, seemed to disappear in a puff of smoke, but had actually fled the stage when part of the equipment exploded. Garcia later said he had felt the presence of invisible time-travelers from the future, which no doubt fueled the trippy exuberance of their set.

While all this was going on a mini-town was being built. There were concessions and Port-O-Sans, which I once visited, but after a very bad burger and worse bathroom experience, I somehow found my way back to my seat and never left it again. Hugh Romney, a.k.a. Wavy Gravy, announced free kitchens at his one-hundred-member Hog Farm tent and services for people on bum acid trips, whom he called "hobo voyagers." The Hog Farm had its own way of treating them, not knocking them out with Thorazine, preferring to let the bum trippers work through and finish the trip with whatever lessons it had for them, after which they'd talk down the next bum tripper—or occasionally cradle the heads of hallucinating strangers in their arms.

And at one point came a Woodstock PSA, a warning that "the brown acid ... is not specifically too good,"[5] whereupon someone else grabbed the mike and said no, it was just fine (a kind of Woodstock example of what was then in media called the Fairness Doctrine).

Janis Joplin, as shown in eerily beautiful flash fade-ins-and-outs in the *Woodstock Director's Cut*, gave a sorrowful performance of "Work Me, Lord," and hers was one of the most emotional performances, from that number to the joy of her dancing before her horn line on "Can't Turn You Loose." Sly and the Family Stone then not only stole the show but the later movie and the whole collective memory of the event. Fronting a a racially integrated and choreographed line of guitars, drums, and horns, Sly, in what can only be called an early rap (as in speech fully synched to the beat) asked us to sing along while also shouting out anti-authoritarianism symbolized by the peace sign. He danced with the crowd as spotlights swept out into the night, raising his arms and buckskin sleeves (as slow-motion in the movie revealed) like white flames, and everyone went "Higher" as they could.

The Who somehow followed that by giving a full performance of *Tommy* that had us all standing up and lighting matches and, despite the wee hours of the morning exhaustion, never sitting down as they brought in the sunrise. The smartest and most literate band in rock pulled off the most physically dazzling of all the gigs, with Daltrey in full young buck microphone-tossing mode; Townsend at his leaping, windmilling the guitar, mod clockwork-orange-y best; and Keith Moon showing why Elvin Jones, in a blind test administered by *Life* Magazine, had once called him one hell of a drummer. Townsend apparently hated Woodstock at the time; whatever the reason, he got to work the anger off when Abbie Hoffman jumped up and interrupted their set and shouted (in ironical agreement with Townsend) "I think this is all a crock of shit while John Sinclair rots in prison." Townsend jabbed him with his guitar and he fell off the stage. Years later, at a Woodstock reunion show, he would apologize for that and play a touching tribute to Abbie; as for the rest of us at that moment, while we were bewildered at what had happened, we were just thrilled with the fantastic set.

The Airplane closed it out in the light of day, Grace Slick in a vestal white dress singing "We must begin here and now, a new continent of earth and fire..." A terrific set that ended for me when Jack Casady went into a bass solo I'd heard about ten times by then. I collapsed to the ground, and awoke to a happy freak offering me raisins.

One of the dreariest aspects of aging is all the what-might-have-been bullshit. By that morning, two of the girls in my group were freaking out from bad drugs, the rest us sixteen-to-eighteen-year-olds, myself the only one not taking drugs, were muddy and exhausted, and we decided to leave, although we felt horrible about it all the way back home, and never did New York City look drearier than after two days in the mud. I've since watched every tape I could (on You Tube and elsewhere) and listened to many recordings of that Sunday show I missed. Given the violence of that thunderstorm that hit after Joe Cocker's set, we probably would've fled anyway; by the time Hendrix closed the show there were about 30,000 out of 400,000 people left, a sodden mess of tents and ponchos stretching out behind them. And besides I'd seen or would see all of Sunday's performers.

But if, as in the movie *What Dreams May Come*, there's a heaven where wishes across time and space are granted, I'll ask for Day Three at Woodstock, with better foul-weather gear.

If Saturday saluted for the most part the *Monterey Pop*/Summer of Love bands of the '60s, Sunday, except for the Berkeley-based Country Joe and the Fish, signaled the approach of the '70s with, among other acts, Joe Cocker's gospel-tinged rock; Crosby, Stills, Nash, and Young, heralding the wave of upcoming "supergroups" with members of the Byrds, Hollies, and Buffalo Springfield merging into acoustic and electric country rock; and Jimi Hendrix summing up where African American electric music had been and where it was going.

Cocker and his Grease Band proclaimed themselves with a fiery set that nonetheless failed to deter a virtual monsoon, as anyone who saw the movie experienced vicariously. Amazingly the crew kept the set and the electronics intact during the deluge, after which Country Joe and the Fish gave a fast-paced thoroughly professional show, setting the tone for the rest of the festival. It was as if chaos had already spoken and been respectfully acknowledged, and the bands and the roadies and the engineers could now concentrate on the music.

Both Led Zeppelin and the Jeff Beck Group had been invited but didn't show up, so big time Brit blues-rock was solely represented by Ten Years After and lead guitarist Alvin Lee. I'd seen them blow away the crowd second on the bill at the Fillmore, and they did the same at Woodstock with Lee's masterfully developed and flying-fingered "Going Home," one of the best sequences in the later movie—perhaps because it was easier to pull off bravura editing to a song with huge dynamic contrasts and a steady rockabilly beat.

The Band performed a warm and beautifully orchestrated set, an amalgam of rock and bluegrass and folk music steeped in an older America, and were welcomed with great affection by the crowd (however much they screamed for Dylan), since, after all, they were probably the only part of actual Woodstock at the festival. The chart-topping and chart-driven Blood, Sweat and Tears struggled with the difficulty of performing a highly rehearsed set at whatever time after midnight it was, but David Clayton-Thomas did an excellent heartfelt job of blue-eyed-soul singing on "I Love You (More Than You'll Ever Know)." Johnny Winter, whom I'd been amazed by at the Fillmore, a long-haired albino dressed in black under violet light, played some of his hardest and best delta-blues-rooted guitar. Crosby, Stills, Nash and Young, premiering what would become their standard three-hour part-acoustic, part-electric set, were, as has been well-documented, the highlight of the evening, and surrendered full-blast to the emotions of that night on their "Long Time Gone."

But still to come after sunrise were The Paul Butterfield Blues Band with Butterfield in fine voice and some topnotch horns. The mock doo-wop early-rock-and-roll band Sha-Na-Na, as hysterically showcased on the *Woodstock Forty Years On* extra disc, performed "Teen Angel" before a crowd that at first watched with stoned worn-out bewilderment, then laughed and cheered; on the sidelines with a beatifically smiling clearly-digging-it expression was Jimi Hendrix.

Hendrix and his "Star-Spangled Banner", with its barrage of melody and sound and genuine emotional (and even patriotic) fervor, rightly became the symbol of the festival and it still brings me what Hawaiians call "chicken skin" when I watch or hear it. But what's often forgotten is not just the earlier part of the set, which he and drummer Mitch Mitchell lashed together out of what was a brand new band, but the sequence after the national anthem. Hendrix segues to "Purple Haze," then a whole series of composed-on-the-spot pieces including a roaring high-speed Malaguena-esque guitar solo and a beautiful ballad-like stretch to bid the crowd farewell. That's when you realize that, tragically, this was rock's John Coltrane in full-flight improvisation in one of his last great shows.

The Movie

Fortunately, we do have a hell of a memory of all that on film.

While we in the crowd were absorbed in the peak of outdoor music festivals, around us was transpiring the peak of on-the-fly rockumentary filmmaking. Shot with 1963 Éclair cameras, much of *Woodstock The Movie* was hand-held with a wide-angle lens (very difficult if you've ever tried it), helped by ingenious adaptations like the building of a lip on the stage the filmmakers could rest the Éclairs on. While all of the tumultuous and chaotic music and action was taking place, the film magazines had to be switched out and rethreaded in changing bags where you couldn't see your hands. The filmmakers would've had to do that frequently—plus, as director Michael Waldleigh has stated, because of the volume of the bands you couldn't hear when the film ran out and you'd just have to guess, which, as a former film school student, gives me shudders just thinking about it.

These were only a few of the difficulties Waldleigh and his crew had to combat while making a documentary that somehow replicated the time-warping fullness of this 24/7 three-day celebration. They did it in part by using B roll (cutaways from the main action) more imaginatively over double and triple split screens and at a greater length than any documentary before, not to comment on the action, but actually create filmic space and time. For instance, the repetitions of the crowd on split-screens coming in to the festival, the repeated processions of every kind of visitor (too bad night photography could only catch oncoming headlights and not the scene on the roofs of the cars, but then again portable lights would've definitely changed the vibe), all to the tune of "Wooden Ships."

Somehow the filmmakers scrambled and adapted to a giant community as it grew around them, and even covered the previous community that welcomed the almost half million newcomers. The film gives plenty of time to show the calm good sense of the townspeople (while also giving voice to angry ones), and the industriousness of the festival staff setting up campgrounds, facilities, the fence—and then getting overwhelmed but somehow dealing with it.

There were glimpses of new sexual mores on the outskirts of the show (the skinny-dipping at the lake), and trying out modes of communal living. A rhythm was set up between a variety of interviews on one screen panel—as when a young couple very thoughtfully commented on the generation gap vis-à-vis religion and politics—and people walking around and interacting in any number of ways on other panels, which gave the audience the feeling of what it was like to be sitting in that field between the acts. Other interviewees narrated the help of the US Army and doctors treating people for free, resulting in successful births and only two deaths. Above all there was the bravura filmmaking of the rainstorm sequence and the festivalgoers sliding through mud and partying in adversity.

All of this flows with a slow, immersive momentum between music sets that are thematically rather than chronologically organized: Arlo Guthrie's "Coming Into Los Angeles" becomes the soundtrack to a montage of dope-smoking. John Sebastian's "Younger Generation" segues into a sequence on children at the festival that should come with a three-hanky warning for childless adults.

The almost four-hour *Woodstock: Director's Cut* features additional sequences of Janis Joplin and Jimi Hendrix, who died within two months of each other in 1970, the year of the original release of the film. The music, with its overtones of both tragedy and joy, is of course the main event of the movie (though when I think of moments like one wide-angle moving follow shot that tracked a huge log being brought to the stage, or a beautiful silhouette of man dancing while "Going Up Country" plays on the soundtrack, the music sets didn't necessarily provide the most adventurous cinematography). The filming was done under extraordinary pressure, as was the music itself, which was also performed in the midst of drug use that could not be timed according to a constantly mutating schedule, along with all sorts of equipment problems. But the singing is fueled by unabashed ecstasy, and moments like the tracking of Hendrix's huge hands, racing up and down the guitar fretboard, and his rapt expression as he performs the "Star-Spangled Banner"; or Roger Daltrey and his microphone tosses with Pete Townsend leaping behind him; or Sly Stone prancing across the stage are unforgettable.

The true triumph of *Woodstock The Movie*, both the musical sequences and the slower documentary coverage of the festival's unfolding, was in the editing room. The principal editor was Thelma Schoonmaker, and her assistant (and assistant director) was Martin Scorsese. They would later flip that relationship around to some success, of course, and its fascinating to see how the editing techniques that would make Scorsese films such riveting cinematic experiences were first tried out on *Woodstock*.

The quiet nature of Joan Baez's set provided a perfect introduction to the two-and-three-screen motif that would be a landmark feature of the film. As Baez performed in a pool of rainswept light on the right of the screen, the left was in darkness until her profile was gracefully faded in.

The film had been shot in 16mm, but was blown up to 70mm so the three-screen process could be used. At a time when such optical effects were all engineered and printed laboriously step by step in film labs, with generations of layered effects sent back and forth from lab to editing and mixing rooms, frames were optically placed side by side in the widescreen format, while the 70mm gauge also allowed for manipulation of numerous audio tracks. In essence the Schoomaker-Scorsese team mastered a whole new way of combining editing and the optical (picture and sound) technology of the time, on full display in the Who set, where during the songs the three screens show different views of the band at different speeds, with interspersed slow-motion sequences and freeze-frames, and then the famous left-right-center mirroring technique that would occasionally flash into superimpositions. It perfectly depicted the way the band could shift on a dime from stillness to rock fury, and it anticipated the later slow-motion and freeze-frame editing that was such a vital part of *Raging Bull* and *Goodfellas*.

The last sequence of the film is a masterpiece. After Hendrix goes into the zone at the end of his set—he eerily has look on his face like he's in some sort of waking dream as he pulls off his guitar sheets of sound—his slower ballad music is juxtaposed against a deserted Woodstock, becoming a soundtrack to an exhausted wasteland, the garbage cleaned up by a few hundred diehards, the sprig of a plant rising above the debris. In his *Directors' Cut* Waldleigh extends that melancholic sequence, including the Felliniesque image of a girl with a color wheel umbrella walking alone through the festival's remains, and that was originally how he wanted to end the movie. Warner Brothers felt it was too depressing, while Waldleigh fought for his elegiac tone. In the studio release Waldleigh's sequence was abbreviated, but a balance is struck in the Directors' Cut: the wasteland sequence is the length Waldleigh wanted, but the movie still ends with an aerial pan over the giant crowd screaming for more. For once, a compromise between director and studio that's perfect.

The Holding On

Okay, great show, great movie. But isn't the canonization of three days listening to music in the mud the greatest example of baby boomer self-absorption and total believing of the hype? Trying once again to find Xanadu and get carried away? A forty-eighth anniversary of completely vanished youth? The absurdity of that aspect of it was captured in a hysterically funny Pepsi commercial several years back, which satirized a Woodstock reunion filled with middle-aged people in a muddy field with all their middle-aged sags and drags and proclivities, fortunately sparing us the satire of what the Port-O-San lines would've been like. The latest actual attempt to recapture the magic of '60s music and its greatest surviving performers at a festival, Desert Trip, was a thoroughly professional version of Coachella that you had to be pretty wealthy to attend.

And so hold on to what exactly?

One can go back to the immediate reactions to the festival for some answers as to what we all hold on to. *Life* Magazine, after covering Woodstock as a kind of victory snatched from the jaws of disaster, later realized that its joy and musical cornucopia required a rare special issue, which is replicated in the *Forty Years On* boxed set. That issue was a celebration of the bands, the "make love not war" spirit, the esprit de corps and "fast but orderly" exit. *Life* called Woodstock "a total experience, a phenomenon, a happening."[6] There was one cautionary article about the numbing effects of "rock-dope as a religion" from a writer who stayed until the end of the festival, and it's true that many festivalgoers drugged themselves out to near-stupors and, by the last act, some erratic behavior. But sheer burnout happened in those three days with or without drugs, and it was accepted as part of the experience. Joe Cocker knew how to take that in stride with his onstage greeting of "Good afternoon ... yeah, I know all about that."[7]

How special was that experience? One festival organizer, John Roberts, said "I don't think I lived before this weekend." Janis Joplin mused that "there's lots and lots and lots of us, more than anybody ever thought before. We used to think of ourselves as little clumps and weirdos." Jack Casady observed "You saw musicians getting soaked in the rain. The egos all melted away."[8]

Woodstock The Movie was released in March of 1970. Waiting on the line to get in was reminiscent of moments of the festival itself. The first run of the movie was one of those rare film releases that didn't need a wave of publicity to become an event, and included the placement of speakers in theaters that was one of the first attempts at a "surroundsound" system and that somehow captured the effect of that speaker voice booming across the fields. I've seen it at least three more times in theaters over the years, and it provokes reactions like no other movie. Audiences live differently within the running time. I've seen long bull sessions after one college screening, couples take off their clothes, people sit in the aisles and indulge however they wished.

The film virtually saved Warner Brothers, which was in the midst of a string of flops, and as can be seen on interviews in the *Forty Years On* boxed set, the experience was transforming for the filmmakers. Martin Scorsese, though not going into details, said that being with that music "fixed him … it was extraordinarily cathartic."[9] It certainly pointed him in the direction of becoming the greatest documentarian of the rock music of the era. Producer Dale Bell talks about it being "symbolism … being infused with the spirit."[10]

Perhaps Woodstock's main spirit-symbol was the whole concept of love and basic decent American unity and music being opposed to hatred and war. You can see it not just in those segments of the movie that focus on the "grooviness" of the true believers, their smoking dope and foreplay by the lake, but sequences where the town's chief of police proclaims the kids good citizens, where interviewees bring out that if it weren't for the Army and their choppers Woodstock would never have happened. Even the Port-O-San cleaner gets an (oddly subtitled) sequence—we don't know why until he reveals he has one son in Vietnam, one at the festival. Above all, the festival's organizers always told the concertgoers that the crowd's welfare was their main concern, and that keyed the event in the most affirmative possible way. "Make love, not war" truly got an airing, in life and on film.

That vibe took a pretty big hit in the winter of 1969, in an event that also underscored just how scary the crowd situation at Woodstock might have become. By the time the movie *Woodstock* was released, everyone knew what had happened at Altamont, which would later be showcased to the world in the Maysles Brothers documentary *Gimme Shelter*.

The film horrifically and indelibly recorded Altamont's anti-Woodstock, the nastiest musical event ever, in a way that suggested the counterculture itself was a drugged-out, empty, dying fraud. Altamont had been the perfect example of why the original Woodstock would remain unrecapturable. Sure it was free concert with a sensational lineup including Santana, The Flying Burrito Brothers, Crosby, Stills, Nash & Young, and Jefferson Airplane, with the Rolling Stones as headliners. But Altamont replaced three days of live and let live and of being together with a standard one-day show. It replaced hundreds of acres of beautiful green farmland with a packed desert speedway. The Stones image and charisma was the type that roused and cranked up rather than sweetened a crowd. And the Stones' management hedged its bets on love and peace by hiring the Hell's Angels as security and paying them with unlimited beer, figuring they'd get with the vibe. The result was a concert constantly interrupted by crowd agitation, fights that climaxed with an assault on the Airplane's Marty Balin, and the murder of a young black man by the Hell's Angels right at the front of the stage.

Altamont would forever become the shadow of Woodstock in '60s popular culture. But fortunately the example of Woodstock rose above that, the good trip beating the bad one.

Woodstock rescued the whole concept of the rock festival from any fear or opprobrium, leading to not only the whole forty-year-plus chain of large-scale shows that lives on in events such as Coachella and Desert Trip, but all the great fundraising concerts like Concert for Bangladesh, Farm Aid, Live Aid, and Live 8. And when you include the fact that Woodstock consolidated the listening audience for the mass success of AOR (Album-Oriented Rock)—forget abstract values, it's literally incalculable all the material good, in terms of money being applied in beneficial ways, Woodstock made possible through the '70s, '80s, and beyond.

But what about the Woodstock spirit and where did it go and where do we go with it? Or as a character put it in Pete Townsend's darkest concept album, 1993's *Psychoderelict*, "Whatever happened to all that lovely hippie shit?"[11]

Think about that brilliant touch by Roger Daltrey and Pete Townsend in the song "My Generation": the "g-g-g" stammer suggesting a childish speech freeze-up from too much pent-up thought, too much to say with the singer not quite having the strength and the smarts yet to fully say it. Didn't that freeze-up, sadly, by the '80s, become a total loss of '60s language of ideals and change and a complete freeze-out? Hasn't the end result of it all as of November 9, 2016 been what Radiohead sang in "Planet Telex," that everything is broken? Or even—given the apparent abandonment of the great dream of Presidents from John F. Kennedy to Ronald Reagan of controlling and abolishing nuclear weapons—what back in the '60s folk singer Barry McGuire called the "Eve of Destruction"?

Neither Woodstock nor its aftermath would have that much of a direct or practical impact on the lifestyle or political arena of its world. This was not a space, physical or psychological, in which any civil rights demonstration would be held, any resister would burn his draft card or her bra, any great work of fiction would be created, or any principles of the coming computer revolution would be organized, although Steve Jobs and Steve Wozniak, who would later put on a series of "Us" rock festivals in Los Angeles, could easily have been in that crowd. But it is where a lot of the music-and-pleasure-loving energy and righteous belief that would leaven such great tasks and tough decisions was gathered and generated. This was not a peace-and-love-and-dissent army ready to suffer and go to prison like in Czechoslovakia, but it was unity based on that kind of thinking and feeling that would have gainful effects far into the future. And when we forgot in the '80s that "if we're all gonna make it ... the guy next to you is your brother," the loss would be profound and lasting as well.

"We thought we could change the world" is a plaintive and tiresome baby boomer refrain. If you're a baby boomer, you were watching the previous generation try and change the world. Most veterans of the Woodstock stage are now in their mid-to-late seventies, which means by definition they weren't baby boomers. The cultural and political movements of the '60s were nurtured by the World War II and Korean War generations from the ashes of a cataclysm. Those men and women were, to use a recent phrase, the real change-makers.

Baby boomers were the inheritors. We did later change the world in the form of the digital revolution, and in ways initially informed by the '60s values of Jobs and Wozniak. So did the Internet, until it devalued creative endeavor and free sharing of information; as Camus might have put it, the digital mogul rebels became revolutionaries and imposed their own systems of "free"-marketing and control. That was the final stage of how the baby boom generation, having prepared for a changed world in a liberating way, then flipped over to its opposite. From peace and love to sex, drugs, and rock-and-roll to money, money, and money. From power to the people to corporate power. The boomers have, for the most part, endangered their inheritance in ways we're just beginning to contemplate. This is something we have to live with, along with the consequences for the planet.

But don't blame Woodstock, or even include Woodstock. Because for every, to quote Zappa, "phony hippie" from a "psychedelic dungeon," there were genuine artists, back-to-nature environmentalists, and activists starting lifelong missions that were sparked by Woodstock and what it represented (It would've been great to have had Zappa and the Mothers at Woodstock, not to mention the Doors, but they might not have exactly fit the room).

What ultimate good was all that ... entertainment? The very word "entertain" means hold between, however and with whatever you choose to do that, and in that sense, it's about education and almost always about love—which, as the angriest but also smartest Beatle told us, is all you need. And we desperately need that loving entertainment because, as we've just learned, there's another kind of entertainment, and it's all we fear.

Woodstock was a demonstration space for Eastern and Native American religious borrowings; the chords with which Joni Mitchell would swathe her own version of her "Woodstock" song reflect the native American/First Nations Canada influence. The festival showcased ways of living lightly on the earth: the geodesic domes scattered among the tent cities, the cooperative Hog Farm-related food services that sprang up. And then there were the values espoused by the musicians—antiwar as exemplified by Joan Baez and Country Joe McDonald; anti-religious hucksterism and groupthink, as exemplified by the Who's performance of *Tommy*; interracial peace, as exemplified by Sly and the Family Stone; and building a counterculture with its own vision of America, as sung by bands like Jefferson Airplane and Crosby, Stills, Nash, and Young, and as embodied by Jimi Hendrix playing "The Star Spangled Banner." With the schedule falling apart, with the bands one after another performing in a concert that blurred all day-night boundaries, with various teachers and speakers filling the breaks, it all amounted to a non-stop instilling of those values into an incredibly receptive audience. A protected space and time for those values to be absorbed in a life-changing way. A space of free play on every level.

In short Woodstock would become a feeling, a totem, something to be cherished in memory and drawn on for inspiration as an example of agape, brotherly love toward creative redemptive good. Sure it was on one level a kind of benign orderly camp counseling while people waited to see bands, but still ... accidents can happen ... and suddenly that alchemized into an Aquarian counterculture convention to balance that violent Chicago one. A confronting of a society that was already getting programmed by mass media and advertising (long before "fake news" and data mining) with sheer unmediated humanity in a space where, as promoter Michael Lang stated, "you can't buy this ... the turnabout is to realize what's really important, to live together and be happy."[12]

But not just quiescent happiness: freedom. The freedom of music. The freedom of make love not war, for, as our current culture forgets in its relishing of the all-conquering action hero who can in a fantasy world do whatever (s)he wants, nothing, as Stanley Kubrick's films dramatize, is more mechanical and enslaving than the actual war machine. And that dedication to love will help us in the future when we may have to comfort and protect distraught young women, fellow Muslim citizens, and imperiled Latinos without the right "papers."

And how different from core American values, or as Jefferson would say, principles as opposed to style, was Woodstock? Perhaps one reason we celebrate the original Woodstock Festival is: what could be more quintessentially American? Life, liberty and the pursuit of happiness—all on display. Freedom of expression? Couldn't beat Woodstock for that. Also present was everything that would addle and curdle Woodstock Nation's American dream: the too-much-ain't-enough, the excess of artificial energy, the hippie capitalism. But that weekend rain and music managed to wash all that away, leaving only the music and the massively peaceful and cooperative environment and its visitors who left the land the way they found it.

ALL AFTER

Once upon a time, in an America far far away, a generation was told it was wonderful and that all its problems could be solved at their parents' knees or in the halls of government and science. Television showed harmony nested in cozy suburban dens. Science (as showcased in Life *Magazine, especially in the International Geophysical Year) seemed to have answers for everything, and outer space was the backdrop for a triumphal march to the moon.*

But in winter 2017, this is the episode where Wally and The Beaver head for the family den for help to find the door locked and a note from June and Ward that reads "Mom and Dad are on a long vacation. Good luck with this one, boys, you're on your own." This is the week where the sheriff's not in town. The astronaut's not on the launch pad. The *Ed Sullivan Show* is off due to a blackout and the comedy and music albums sit beside a dead stereo. Batman isn't answering Commissioner Gordon, and the Joker is laughing.

For as perhaps its last politically significant act, our g-g-g-goddam generation has elected a president (yes, it was mainly "older voters," and that's not the boomers' ninety-year-old or dead parents anymore) who manifests the side of the baby boomers utterly self-seeking, self-absorbed, self-satisfying, and irresponsible via sex and stocks and tech and gun collections and Porsches and "he who dies with the most toys wins" and in its long decline (and how often was *The Apprentice* referred to this way?) "guilty pleasures." The story that began with the Age of Aquarius may now end, after the hype of the Me Decade and I Want My MTV and the Digital Revolution, with the Age of Trump.

We're on a runaway train. Pre-Inauguration, we heard "Now boarding, Runaway Train on Track 2017" and with faith in our institutions we peacefully transitioned to our seats on the runaway train. We'd last seen the conductor of the train at an impromptu press conference with Don King by his side dressed in what looked like a costume dredged up from a dumpster, laughing and flag-waving and seemingly under the influence (of patriotism). So we're hoping against hope some of the billionaire train crew care about the passengers and have some savvy about how to implement that. We're hoping there's an "In case of emergency, break glass" that works. Or at the very least we're hoping for a heroic first responder effort so when the train crashes it's not a mass casualty incident but a disaster that most people recover from.

But it's not all the boomers' fault. The country from Generation X to Z has developed a Stockholm syndrome with regard to the superrich and ultra-brutal, real or imagined. A Christmas Fiat commercial featured a Trumpian rich executive Santa Claus flanked by two gorgeous elf babes coming in to buy a Fiat and referring to his sleigh as his "trade-in." We've come to that. In the words of William Blake from his *Visions of the Daughters of Albion*, which betray the sexual biases of his eighteenth century but are still trenchant and powerful, "Their daughters worship terrors and obey the violent." Much has been said about the Left neglecting the concerns of the working and middle-class as a contributing factor to Trump's election and this book has concurred. But Trump's crazily impulsive and violence-evoking campaign statements were on display for months and young and old voted for that. What were they expecting, that they'd be the captives who'd get more time out of "Room"? No one's getting out of "Room" for at least four years.

It's frightening that in the same week we lost the great American astronaut, politician, and hero John Glenn, one of the icons of the '60s, we received word that the Russians, our geopolitical foes then and now, exerted a powerful, maybe even decisive influence on our election, and elements of our own government intervened to stop us from receiving a timely warning about that interference. But it's encouraging that in this same year Bob Dylan has received the Nobel Prize. For looking back at the '60s, we will now need the spirit of both John Glenn and Bob Dylan. JFK and Muhammad Ali. Alexander Hamilton and Martin Luther King. And, in the strangest of all possible historical conjunctions, the old peace and civil rights movements *and* the military. For just as the Army helped at Woodstock with those choppers we may need their support again, for relief from disasters environmental or manmade or both. And they'll need the spirit of those great '60s movements to keep this a country that will not send them to needless wars of choice and will, above all, be worth their sacrifices.

Time to face the defeated facts.

Time to turn off the devices and social media that own you as much as you own them and start talking to each other.

Time for the return of the repressed.

Above all, time to maintain hope. Because as the existentialist philosopher Gabriel Marcel stated, when you abandon hope, you've made yourself God—and from boomers to millennials our population has been narcissistic enough.

Something started on Day One after the election. Spontaneous demonstrations. People showing how heartsick they are on television, something that was common in the '60s but hasn't been seen much except in certain key events (Bush-Gore, Hurricane Katrina) since then. Speeches rallying the public to resist.

Meanwhile Trump's Inauguration and his remarks before the CIA memorial wall horrified us, then galvanized us. The extraordinary Women's March and successive marches against the Muslim-ban-by-another-name have become the drumbeat of modern political life.

The antibodies of democracy are getting to work. People of different views and abilities reaching out to each other rhizomatically. Decentralized experimentation. Cities, towns as "laboratories of democracy," not just states. Day by day and local. An interchange of ideas and resources financial and otherwise. And being patient. As Springsteen sang at what was supposed to be a Hillary Clinton victory rally, it's "gonna be a long walk home."[13]

The '60s circumstances that triggered a public wave of transparently loving, honest, nonadversarial, sharing and caring behavior will probably never come back. But that doesn't mean that, through smaller and more close-knit organizations and gatherings, and through more underground art, music, literary, and political communications and celebrations, there can't be a sustaining undercurrent. That doesn't mean the values and techniques and feeling of the '60s can't be rediscovered and fostered in different ways. And those of us who have had that experience and have children can teach their children well, especially over the next four years.

At that point a balance may start to be restored. Not transformation of the whole country, but a countervailing reemphasis on, yes, love, peace, and freedom. In the '60s and early '70s those who took the counterculture or even aspects of it to mind and heart never became the motor of American life—just part of the steering and the brakes. In the words of Camus, they remained in permanent rebellion without choosing revolution. Whether their instrument became a guitar or a paintbrush or a pen, an operating room or a court room, they accepted a life of tension and limits, less money and painful compromise, but also creativity and nonconformity and public service and peace.

Let's briefly imagine if the '60s had never happened. No antiwar movement. No civil rights movement. Especially important in a time of planetary climate cancer, no ecology movement. No Stonewall. No initial feminist rebellion, which would ultimately prepare women not only for gaining control of their own bodies but filling the need to join the workforce alongside men. No computer chieftains being influenced in ways that they've credited as helping them help usher in the greatest revolution in information and communication since the Gutenberg printing press. We owe all this to the rebels, the reformers, the nonviolently fighting enlightened.

The '60s may have landed badly, but pilots have a saying: "any landing you can walk away from." Remember that that flight was truly about integrity vs. the big lie, human rights vs. racism, sanctity of the earth vs. destruction of nature for cash, love and peace vs. hatred and war. Learn and fly on.

Woodstock played its part, and its memory, especially through that great film, will as well. For when the tease of pop was distilled and highly concentrated into this Aquarian Exposition of the counterculture, it could and did energize a different approach to life, which is at least a beginning and potentially a great end. It was finally as much an Eastern festival as a Western one. It wasn't that dissimilar to one of those Hindu festivals in India that, as many cultural anthropologists have stated, foster a kind of sacred distorted time. One such Indian festival, Kumbh Mela at Prayag, has been called an "ephemeral mega city" that creates a sustainable environment working with the forces of nature. Within that city class distinctions are destroyed, new behaviors and celebrations are allowed, new forces come into play, and contact with the divine seems to occur.

To see what hundreds of thousands of happy people looked like on a rainy morning and a sunny afternoon, dancing to Santana, holding up matches in the sunrise to greet The Who and the "morning maniac music" of the Airplane, doing basic yoga together, creating a giant event together, and then to carry back home, as my friends and I did, souvenirs of the weekend, both physical (in my case, an old sweater) and spiritual we'd never throw away—that's as close to sacred time as I ever got. As a high-schooler, I wrote, "It changed me, and I hope it's the first breath of change." That hope, not hype, based on our generation's one good short-lived Xanadu remains. It's still breathing. For the old and the young.

Three days in the mud. Nothing but fun and music. But Woodstock was also a vision incarnate. Like all visions it was out of the blue, elemental yet utterly fragile, but for myself I hope it lasts long enough to be one of the last visions I remember.

You had to be there.

POSTSCRIPT

"Won't you try
With love before we're gone
Won't you try
Won't you try. . ."

Won't You Try/Saturday Afternoon,
— **Jefferson Airplane**

Grace Slick, Marty Balin, Jorma Kaukonen,
Jack Casady, Spencer Dryden (1938–2005)
and Paul Kantner (1941–2016)

FIFTY YEARS AGO TODAY

NOTES

Some Life *Magazine articles do not have credited authors, and some page numbers have crumbled away with the passage of time. I have done my best to locate all such information.*

Introduction: We Wanted the World

The Doors. "Five to One." Words and Music by the Doors. From *Waiting for the Sun*. CD. [1968] 1982. Elektra EKS 74024.

Bob Dylan. "The Times They Are A Changin'." Bob Dylan. From the album of the same name. Vinyl. 1964. Columbia Records CL2105.

1. The Doors. "When The Music's Over." Words and Music by the Doors. From *Strange Days*. Vinyl. 1967. Elektra 9 74014-2.
2. Quoted in A.O. Scott, "In Love with Pop, Uneasy with the World," New York Times, Sept. 30, 2007, http://www.nytimes.com/2007/09/30/arts/music/30scot.html, accessed November 30, 2016.
3. Paul Kantner and Jefferson Starship. "Hijack." Paul Kantner, Grace Slick, Marty Balin, and Gary Blackman. From *Blows Against the Empire*. Vinyl. 1970. RCA Victor LSP-4448.
4. Bob Dylan. "It's All Right Ma, (I'm Only Bleeding)." From *Bringing It All Back Home*. Vinyl. 1965. Columbia Records CS 9128.
5. Buffalo Springfield, "For What It's Worth." Stephen Stills. From *Retrospective: The Best of Buffalo Springfield*. Vinyl. 1969. Atco SD33-283.

THE MUSIC

Quoted in Charles R. Cross, *Backstreets: Springsteen, the Man and His Music* (New York: Harmony, 1989), p. 81.

Why the Music Isn't Over
Originally posted on **March 30, 2015**

1. The Beatles. "Your Mother Should Know." Lennon-McCartney. From *Magical Mystery Tour.* Vinyl. 1967. Capitol Records 4CL-2835
2. Jon Pareles. "Jon Renbourn, Eclectic Guitarist Who Founded the Pentangle, Dies at 70," *New York Times*, March 27, 2015, http://www.nytimes.com/2015/03/29/arts/music/john-renbourn-eclectic-guitarist-who-founded-the-pentangle-dies-at-70.html?_r=0, accessed November 30, 2016.

Sweet and Dirty Water
Originally Posted on **July 15, 2015**

1. Fred Powledge, "Wicked Go The Doors," *Life* Magazine. April 12, 1968, p. 89.
2. The Doors. "The Crystal Ship." Words and Music by the Doors. From *The Doors*. Vinyl. 1967. Elektra EKS-74007.
3. The Mothers of Invention. "Trouble Comin' Every Day." Frank Zappa. From *Freak Out!* Vinyl. 1966. Verve Records V6-5005-2, V6/5005-2.

Dylan, Cash, and the New Nashville Skyline
Originally posted on **June 14, 2015**

1. Notes from the CMA Gene Autry exhibit.
2. Quoted in Anthony DeCurtis, Matt Diehl, Austin Scaggs and David Wild, "Remembering Johnny," *Rolling Stone*, Issue 933, Oct. 16, 2003, www.rollingstone.com/music/news/remembering-johnny-20031016, accessed November 30, 2016
3. Notes from "Dylan, Cash, and the Nashville Cats" exhibit.
4. Ibid. See also *Dylan, Cash and the Nashville Cats: A New Music City* published by the Country Music Association, Nashville, 2015, or the CD collection of the same name.

When Britain Rocked the Waves

1. Hugh Fielder, "Ten Years After—Reeling In The Years," *Classic Rock Magazine*, August 2003.
2. The Beatles. "Rock 'n' Roll Music." Chuck Berry. From *Rock 'N' Roll Music*. Vinyl. [1965] 1976. Parlophone UK PCSP 719, 0C 180 0.

Farewell Starman
Originally posted on **January 11, 2016**

1. David Bowie. "I'd Rather Be High." David Bowie. From *The Next Day*. CD. 2013. ISO Records 88765 46186 2.
2. David Bowie. "Life On Mars." David Bowie. From *Hunky Dory*. Vinyl. 1971. RCA Victor P8S-1850.
3. Bowie. "Ashes to Ashes." David Bowie. From *Scary Monsters*. Vinyl. 1980. RCA AQS1-3647.
4. Bowie. "All the Madmen." David Bowie. From *The Man Who Sold the World*. Vinyl. 1970. Mercury MC8 61325.
5. Bowie. "Modern Love." David Bowie. From *Let's Dance*. Vinyl. 1983. EMI America – SO-17093.
6. Bowie. "Heroes." David Bowie. From *Heroes*. Vinyl. 1977. RCA AFL1-2522.

7. Bowie. "I'll Take You There." David Bowie. From *The Next Day*. CD. 2013. ISO Records 88765 46186 2.
8. Bowie. "I'd Rather Be High." Ibid.

Farewell Starship, and Hail *Blackstar*
Originally posted on **February 12, 2016**

1. Quoted in William Grimes, "Paul Kantner, a Founder of Jefferson Airplane, Dies at 74," *New York Times*, January 28, 2016, http://www.nytimes.com/2016/01/29/arts/music/paul-kantner-of-jefferson-airplane-dies-at-74.html?_r=0.
2. Gavin Allen. "Paul Kantner Talks Woodstock, Jefferson Starships, and Smashed Cars," *Wales Online*, 28 March 2013, www.walesonline.co.uk/lifestyle/showbiz/paul-kantner-talks-woodstock-jefferson-2070790.
3. As quoted in Ronald Wright, *A Short History of Progress* (New York: Carroll and Graft, 2004).
4. Bob Dylan. "Not Dark Yet." Bob Dylan. From *Time Out of Mind*. CD. 1997. Columbia. CK 68556.
5. David Bowie. "Blackstar." David Bowie. From *Blackstar*. CD. 2016. ISO Records, Columbia, Sony Music 88875173862.
6. Bowie. "Lazarus." Ibid.
7. Bowie. "Sue." Ibid.
8. Bowie. "Dollar Days." Ibid.
9. Bowie. "I Can't Give Everything Away." Ibid.

Love and Mercy and California Nightmares
Originally posted on **July 4, 2015**

1. *Love and Mercy*. Directed by Bill Pohlad. Roadside Attractions. DVD. New York: Lionsgate Films, 2015.
2. Quoted in Jules Siegel, "Goodbye Surfing, Hello God: Brian Wilson's Tortured Effort to Finish 'Smile,'" *Rolling Stone*, November 3, 2011.
3. Neil Young. "This Old Guitar." Neil Young. From *Prairie Wind*. CD. 2005. Reprise Records. CDW 49395-2.

Music Hyphenation and the Changing of the Bards

1. Phil Ochs. "Here's to the State of Mississippi." Phil Ochs. From *I Ain't Marching Anymore*. Vinyl. 1965. Elektra EKL-287.
2. "The Angry Young Folk Singer," *Life* Magazine, April 10, 1964, 109–114.
3. Bob Dylan. "Like A Rolling Stone." From *Bob Dylan Live: 1966: The Bootleg Series, Vol. 4*. CD. Columbia. COL 491485 2.

4. Frank Zappa, "The Oracle Has It All Psyched Out," The New Rock, *Life Magazine*, June 28, 1968, pp. 82–86, 88, 91, www.afka.net/Articles/1968-06_Life.htm, accessed December 15, 2016.
5. Bob Dylan. "Roll On John." Bob Dylan. From *Tempest*. CD. 2012. Columbia 88725457602.
6. Bob Marley and The Wailers. "Trenchtown Rock." Bob Marley. From *Bob Marley and the Wailers Live!* Vinyl. 1975. Island Records ILPS 9376.

Get Off Our Great Lawn
Originally posted on **September 29, 2014**

1. See "Woodstock and All After," this volume.
2. Global Citizen, https://www.globalcitizen.org/en/. See also https://www.globalcitizen.org/en/content/jeffrey-sachs-talks-music-and-activism/

On Hearing Jimi Hendrix in a Cologne Commercial
Originally posted on **March 19, 2015**

1. *Bleu De Chanel: The Film*. February 25, 2015. https://www.youtube.com/watch?v=A8FvBrIKfDY.
2. *Bleu De Chanel The Interview*. February 5, 2015. https://www.youtube.com/watch?v=0adDm9-g-Oc.
3. Jimi Hendrix Experience. "If 6 Was 9." Jimi Hendrix. From *Axis: Bold As Love*. Vinyl. 1967. Reprise Records R 6281.
4. Jimi Hendrix Experience. "All Along the Watchtower." Bob Dylan. From *Electric Ladyland*. Vinyl 2LP. 1968. Reprise Records 2rS 6307.
5. Radiohead. "Anyone Can Play Guitar." Radiohead. From *Pablo Honey*. CD. 1992. Capitol Records C4 81409.
6. Jimi Hendrix, "Watchtower," ibid.

The Velvet Motherland and the City of Dreams

1. See "Expo '67: Movies that Blitz the Mind," *Life* Magazine 63(2), July 4, 1967. The National Film Board of Canada has long been famous for experimental works by, for example, filmmaker Norman McLaren ("Pas de Deux").
2. Young, Peter, "Czechoslovakia: Death of the Bright Young Freedom," *Life* Magazine, August 30, 1968, pp. 13–26.
3. Frank Zappa and the Mothers of Invention. "Who Needs the Peace Corps" and "Mom and Dad." Frank Zappa. From *We're Only In It for the Money*. Vinyl. 1968. Verve Records V6 5045X.
4. Frank Zappa quoted in David Walley, *No Commercial Potential: The Saga of Frank Zappa* (Boston: DaCapo, 1996).

5. Frank Zappa and the Mothers of Invention. "Plastic People" and "Brown Shoes Don't Make It." Frank Zappa. From *Absolutely Free*. Vinyl. 1967 Verve Records. V V6-5013X.
6. The Velvet Underground. "Venus in Furs" and "Heroin." Lou Reed. From *The Velvet Underground and Nico*. Vinyl. 1966 Verve Records V6 5008.
7. Quoted in Tom Stoppard, "Introduction," in *Rock 'n' Roll*, by Tom Stoppard. (New York: Grove/Atlantic, 2006.) Kindle edition, Loc. 157.
8. Tom Stoppard, Ibid., Loc. 132.
9. Tom Stoppard, Ibid., Loc 198.
10. Ziggy Marley and the Melody Makers. "When the Lights Gone Out." Ziggy Marley. From *One Bright Day*. CD. Virgin Records 7 91256-2.
11. Radiohead. "Lucky." Radiohead. From *OK Computer*. CD. Capitol Records CDP 7243 8 55229 2 5.
12. Tom Stoppard, *Rock 'n' Roll*, Loc. 1819.
13. Václav Havel, "The Politics of Hope," in *Disturbing The Peace* by Václav Havel (New York: Knopf, 1990), p. 181.

It Was Fifty Years Ago Today

1. The Beatles. "Help!" Lennon-McCartney. Vinyl. 1965. Parlophone PMC 1255.
2. "Paul McCartney on *Pet Sounds*," commentary. The Beach Boys. *Pet Sounds* (40th Anniversary Edition). Brian Wilson. CD. 2006. Capitol Records 0946 3 69940 2 4.
3. The Beatles. "She Said She Said" and "Tomorrow Never Knows." Lennon-McCartney. From *Revolver*. Vinyl. 1966. Parlophone. PMC 7009.
4. Paul McCartney, "Commentary to *Pet Sounds*."
5. Quoted in Peter Blake, "Commentary," p.4. The Beatles. *Sgt. Pepper's Lonely Hearts Club Band*. CD. 1987 [1967] Capitol/EMI Records CDP7-46442 2.
6. Thomas Thompson, "The New Far-Out Beatles," *Life* Magazine, Feb. 28, 1967, p. 105.
7. All songs whose lyrics are quoted are from *Sgt. Pepper's Lonely Hearts Club Band* unless otherwise stated.

THE MEDIA

The Ultimate '60s Filmmaker
Originally posted on **August 8, 2014**

1. Quoted in Loudon Wainwright, "The Strange Case of *Strangelove*," *Life* Magazine, March 13, 1964.
2. For Michael Herr's excellent and truly in-depth appreciations of Kubrick as an artist and a man, see the August 1999 VANITY FAIR article, http://www.vanityfair.com/hollywood/classic/features/kubrick-199908, and the April 2000 VANITY FAIR article, available at http://mentalfoto.tripod.com/herr/herr.html.

3. Shannon Vallor, *Technology and the Virtues* (Oxford: Oxford University Press, 2016).
4. From a discussion by Malcolm McDowell at a Museum of Modern Art screening of *A Clockwork Orange*.
5. One can play an enjoyable symmetry mirror game with Kubrick's body of work, starting with, in the center, *Clockwork Orange/Barry Lyndon* (rake survives/rake destroyed); and going on to *2001/The Shining* (monolith evolution/hotel ghosts devolution); *Strangelove/Full Metal Jacket* (protagonist can't stop the world's destruction/protagonist ends the deadly threat and survives); and *Lolita/Eyes Wide Shut* (deadly sexual jealousy/fruitful sexual reconciliation). It gets even weirder when you realize, had Kubrick lived longer to finish other planned projects, it might have gone on to *Spartacus/Napoleon* (slave revolt leader/arch-conqueror) and *Paths of Glory/The Aryan Papers* (victims of World War I destroyed/victim of the Holocaust survives).

Bonnie and Clyde: From Theme to Meme
Originally posted on **October 17, 2014**

1. *Bonnie and Clyde.* Directed by Arthur Penn. 1967. Tatria-Hiller Productions. Burbank, CA: Warner Bros./Seven Arts. DVD. Warner Home Video. 1986.
2. *They Live By Night.* Directed by Nicholas Ray. 1949. Los Angeles, CA: RKO Radio Pictures. DVD. Warner Home Video. 2007.
3. *Thieves Like Us.* Directed by Robert Altman. 1974. George Litto Productions. Los Angeles, CA: United Artists. DVD. Kino Lorber. 2014.
4. *Badlands.* Directed by Terrence Malick. 1973. Pressman-Williams. Burbank, CA: Warner Bros. DVD. The Criterion Collection. 2013.
5. *The Sugarland Express.* Directed by Steven Spielberg. 1974. Zanuck/Brown. Universal, CA: Universal Pictures. DVD. MCA/Universal Home Video. 1992.
6. *Beyoncé and Jay Z On the Run.* Directed by Jonas Åkerlund. An HBO Concert Event. 2014. Black Dog Films. New York: HBO Films.

Lawrence of Arabia to W of Iraq

1. *Lawrence of Arabia.* Directed by Sir David Lean. 1962. Horizon Pictures. Los Angeles, CA: Columbia Pictures. DVD. Sony Pictures Home Entertainment. 2008.

Gumping on the '60s
Originally posted on **August 28, 2014**

1. *Forrest Gump.* Directed by Robert Zemeckis. 1994. Steve Tisch/Windy Finerman. Hollywood, CA: Paramount Pictures. DVD. Paramount Home Entertainment. 2009.

2. *Who Framed Roger Rabbit?* Directed by Robert Zemeckis. 1988. Amblin Entertainment. Universal City, CA: Touchstone Pictures. DVD. Touchstone Home Entertainment. 2013.
3. *The Curious Case of Benjamin Button.* Directed by David Fincher. 2008. The Kennedy/Marshall Company. Hollywood, CA: Paramount Pictures (with Warner Bros.). DVD. Paramount Home Entertainment. 2009.

War Is Hell Yeah
Originally posted on **November 4, 2014**

1. *Fury.* Directed by David Ayer. 2014. QED International. Los Angeles, CA: Columbia Pictures. DVD. Sony Pictures Home Entertainment. 2015.

Tomorrowland: Beauty and the BS
Originally posted on **June 2, 2015**

1. *Tomorrowland.* Directed by Brad Bird. 2015. A113. Buena Vista, CA: Walt Disney Studios. DVD. Walt Disney Studios Home Entertainment. 2015.

Our Fair Lady
Originally posted on **July 31, 2015**

1. *My Fair Lady.* Directed by George Cukor. 1964. Burbank, CA: Warner Bros. DVD. Warner Home Video. 2014.
2. *My Fair Lady*, n.a., Warner Bros. promotional program, 1965, p. 5.

Selma and the '60s
Originally posted on **January 3, 2015**

1. *Selma.* Directed by Ava DuVernay. 2015. Harpo Films. Los Angeles, CA: Paramount Pictures. DVD. Paramount Home Entertainment. 2015.
2. The Who. "Won't Get Fooled Again." Pete Townsend. From *Who's Next.* Vinyl. 1971. Decca Records. 6-9182.

Selma and the Dramatization of History
Originally posted on **January 11, 2015**

1. John Lennon. "Gimme Some Truth." John Lennon. From *Imagine.* Vinyl. 1971. Apple Records. PAS 1004.

2. *Zero Dark Thirty*. Directed by Kathryn Bigelow. 2012. Annapurna Pictures. Los Angeles, CA: Columbia Pictures. DVD. Sony Pictures Home Entertainment. 2013.
3. Jeff Bailey. "The '*Selma* Controversy' Isn't About History; It's About Oscars." *Flavorwire*. http://flavorwire.com/496620/the-selma-controversy-isnt-about-history-its-about-oscars.
4. Todd Aaron Jenson. "A Friend's Goodbye." *Writers Guild of America West*. January 9, 2015. www.wga.org/writers-room/features-columns/the-craft/2015/american-sniper-jason-hall.
5. Not that James Comey has anywhere near the psychological problems of J. Edgar Hoover, but it's too bad President Obama didn't apply that leash lesson to his relationship with his FBI director.

The '60s and the Films of 2014
Originally posted on **January 28, 2015**

Loved It Madly, But Not the History
Originally posted (as "Mad Props to *Mad Men*") on **May 19, 2015**

1. Marshall McLuhan, *Understanding Media: The Extensions of Man*, New American Library (New York: McGraw Hill/Signet, 1964), p. 201.
2. Ibid., p. 202.
3. Tim Molloy, "Matthew Weiner to Stephen Colbert: Boomers Have a 'Child's View' of the '60s." Video. University of North Carolina School of The Arts, *The Wrap*, May 21, 2014, www.thewrap.com/matthew-weiner-tells-stephen-colbert-boomers-have-a-childs-view-of-the-60s-video/.

The N-Word and Other Shocks to The System.

1. Philip Roth on *Philip Roth Unmasked*, American Masters, Thirteen, WNET, PBS. Air date: 3/19/2013.
2. James Baldwin on *Pioneers of Thirteen*, WNET, PBS. Air date: 9/10/2016.
3. "Lenny Bruce on the Steve Allen Show April 5, 1959." Historic Films Stock Footage Archive. YouTube. Published Nov. 2, 2016. https://www.youtube.com/watch?v=G3QgxmiBfNY.
4. "Sex in the Lively Arts: How Far is Far Enough?" Various authors, *Life* Magazine, April 14, 1969, 21–23.
5. Nora Sayre, *Sixties Going On Seventies* (New York: Arbor House, 1973).
6. The Godfathers. "If I Only Had Time." Coyne/Coyne/Dollimore/Gibson/Mazur. From *Birth, School, Work, Death*. CD. 1988. Epic BFE-40946
7. Max Metzger, "Old Hollywood Elite Were the Last To Use LSD for Therapy," *Vice*, Oct. 20, 2014, http://www.vice.com/en_us/article/cary-grant-lsd-old-hollywood-289. LSD's bizarre and sometimes horrific early years in both the

cultural and military establishments (the inhumane and unethical MKULTRA psychwar program experiments) are chronicled in the book *Acid Dreams* (see References). LSD use, however mystical it became, was in some ways an outgrowth of the '60s overall scientific outlook coupled with faith in and heavy reliance on pharmaceuticals—from valium to psilocybin—by both hippies and suits. Acid trips were at one point described, only half-mocking the slogan of the mighty DuPont corporation, as "better living through chemistry."
8. *Dionysus in 69*. Richard Schechner, director. The Performance Group, producer; a film by Brian De Palma, Robert Fiore, and Bruce Rubin. Hemispheric Institute Digital Video Library. http://hidvl.nyu.edu/video/000031372_enhanced.html.
9. Living Theater. Quoted from flyer of The Living Theater, 1969, *Paradise Now*, Presented by the Open Theater and produced by the Radical Theater Repertory at Hunter College Assembly Hall.

Marshall McLuhan: Medium of the Media
Originally posted on **April 25, 2015**

1. Marshall McLuhan, *Understanding Media: The Extensions of Man*, New American Library (New York: McGraw Hill/Signet, 1964), p. 24.
2. Ibid, p. 20.
3. Marshall McLuhan. "Living in an Acoustic World," University of South Florida 1970, Public Lecture, p. 3., http://www.marshallmcluhanspeaks.com/media/mcluhan_pdf_6_JUkCEo0.pdf.
4. See Jac Holzman, President of Elektra Records, quoted in Fred Powledge, "Wicked Go The Doors," *Life* Magazine, p. 89. "They're creating, essentially, scenarios and you supply the pictures in your mind; they supply the mood and the words."
5. McLuhan, *Understanding Media*, p. 187.
6. Attributed to Andrew Lewis of MetaFilter, August 26, 2002.
7. McLuhan, *Understanding Media*, p. 311.
8. Ibid., p. 23.
9. Ibid., p. 19.
10. Ibid., p. 57.
11. Ibid, p. 310.
12. Ibid., p. 267.
13. Comparisons between Donald Trump and Adolf Hitler have become excessive. But McLuhanist linking of political success to mastery of new media "oppressing" old media yields one fruitful analogy: Hitler's mastery of the new media of its time, radio, and Donald Trump's mastery of Twitter. And with all the condemnation of Trump's use of Twitter, there hasn't been enough McLuhanist focus on the power of Twitter itself. Hopefully more focus on the medium rather than the message (Trump's insomniac vitriol) will lead to, for example, more education about the power and the drawbacks of this new medium, not to mention constant doublechecking and critiquing of Twitter's corporate moguls' adoption of an "anything goes" attitude toward their platform's increasingly antisocial content.

Finally, President Trump seems more aware of Twitter's impact as media than many pundits and scholars: he disinvited Twitter from his tech summit reportedly because of their refusal to allow him to sponsor and use a "crooked Hillary" emoji he knew would've planted itself in his followers' brains. But this at least opens up an intriguing possibility: Twitter, having already been blackballed by Trump, may, when faced with the possibility of massive lawsuits if Trump continues to tweet-target individuals for possible cyber- and dangerous "in real life"-reprisals, consider restricting the President's use of the medium he rode to the White House.

14. McLuhan, *Understanding Media*, 73. Giving more torque to this dystopic insight is McLuhan's description of the possible effect of a global information system on human temperament: "As we submit our humanity to information systems, technology requires utter human docility and quiescence of meditation such as befits an organism that now wears its brain outside its skull and its nerves outside its hide." (Ibid., p.54).
15. A few months after I wrote this, a branch of the government tried to do just this with a graphically gruesome video "Welcome to ISIS-Land ... Think hard/turn away." It was of course ultimately withdrawn by worried, culturally sensitive elements of the government in favor of ... pleas and lectures.
16. McLuhan, *Understanding Media*, p. 267, McLuhan could also have been speaking directly about Trump's use of Twitter here.
17. Ibid., p. 75, see also p. 311, and Marshall McLuhan, "Classrooms Without Walls," in *Explorations in Communication*, edited by Edmund Carpenter and Marshall McLuhan (Boston: Beacon, 1960).
18. W. Terrence Gordon, July 2002, www.marshallmcluhan.com/biography/, accessed 4/25/15. See also W. Terrence Gordon, *Marshall McLuhan: Escape into Understanding* (New York: Basic Books, 1997).
19. Marshall McLuhan. 1974. "Living at the Speed of Light," in *Understanding Me: Lectures and Interviews* (Cambridge, MA: The MIT Press, 2005), p. 230.

THE ISSUES

Frank Zappa and the Mothers of Invention, "Trouble Comin' Every Day." From *Freak Out!* Vinyl. 1966. Verve Records V6-5005-2.

JFK: 1963, 1991, and the Twenty-First Century

1. Richard Hofstadter, "The Paranoid Style in American Politics," *Harper's*, November 1964, http://harpers.org/archive/1964/11/the-paranoid-style-in-american-politics/.
2. "The Warren Report: How The Commission Pieced Together the Evidence," Various authors, *Life* Magazine, Oct. 2, 1964.
3. "Warren Report," *Life*, Gerald R. Ford, p. 42.
4. Ibid., p. 50.
5. Ibid., "A Matter of Reasonable Doubt," n.a. and Governor John Connally, pp. 37–49, 49.

6. *JFK: The Director's Cut.* Directed by Oliver Stone. 1991. Ixtlan Productions. Los Angeles, CA: Warner Bros. DVD. Warner's Home Video. 2001.
7. Commentary to *JFK: The Director's Cut.*
8. Ibid.
9. *JFK.*

Ferguson Won, Occupy Nothing
Originally posted on **September 10, 2014**

1. Ann Heppermann and Kara Oehler, "This Weekend in 1968: The Legacy of Resurrection City," Weekend America, *American Public Media*, May 10, 2008, weekendamerica.publicradio.org/display/web/2008/05/08/1968_resurrection/.
2. Phillip Agnew, "Activist for a New Generation," *Democracy Now!* Aug. 19, 2014, www.democracynow.org/2014/8/19/activist_for_a_new_generation_ferguson.
3. To be fair, the subsequent remarkably impressive Bernie Sanders campaign for president did owe some of its success to the nucleus of resistance built by the Occupy movement.
4. Interview with Antonio French. CNN Transcript *Anderson Cooper 360 Degrees.* August 25, 2014. transcripts.cnn.com/TRANSCRIPTS/1408/25/acd.02.html.
5. Since the writing of this article, a Justice Department investigation has revealed that Ferguson police, through ticket quotas and fines aimed primarily at African Americans, were working together to conduct in effect a shakedown operation on that community.

The New York PBA: Bringing Back the Ghetto
Originally posted on **December 23, 2014**

1. Robbins, Christopher. "'Blood on Many Hands': Police Unions Blame DeBlasio for Death of Two Cops." *The Gothamist*, Dec. 21 2014, gothamist.com/2014/12/21/cops_shot_nyc_nypd.php#photo-1.
2. Commissioner Bratton did in fact did step down on Sept. 16, 2016.

99 Homes and America Ain't One
Originally posted on **October 6, 2015**

1. *99 Homes.* Directed by Rahmin Bahrani. 2015. Hyde Park Entertainment. Los Angeles, CA: Broad Green Pictures. DVD. 2015.
2. Sam Roberts, "The Port Huron Statement at 50," *New York Times*, March 4, 2012, p. 5.

Black Mass for Citizens
Originally posted on **September 21, 2015**

1. *Black Mass*. Directed by Scott Cooper. 2015. Cross Creek Pictures. Burbank, CA: Warner Bros. DVD. Warner Home Video. 2016.
2. M.A. Farber, "The Con Man," *The New York Times Magazine,* June 21, 1987.
3. Ward Churchill and Jim Vander Wall, *The COINTELPRO Papers: Documents from the FBI's Secret Wars Against Dissent in the United States* (Brooklyn, NY: South End Press, 2001).
4. "COINTELPRO: Who Were the Targets?" In *Takin' It To The Streets.* Edited by Alexander Bloom and Wini Breines, 2nd ed. (Oxford: Oxford University Press, 2003), p. 319.
5. For further information on the "Citizens Committee" burglary, see Mark Mazzetti, "Burglars Who Took On F.B.I. Abandon Shadows," *New York Times,* January 7, 2014, www.nytimes.com/2014/01/07/us/burglars-who-took-on-fbi-abandon-shadows.html.
6. All letters alluded to which originated as confidential FBI communications, as well as quotes derived from the letters, are in photocopy form on the website www.freedomarchives.org/Documents/Finder/Black%20Liberation%20Disk/Black%20Power!/SugahData/Government/COINTELPRO.S.pdf

Fury Road Lingo and American Ecospeak
Originally posted on **August 12, 2015**

1. *Mad Max: Fury Road.* Directed by George Miller. Burbank, CA: Warner Bros. DVD. Warner Home Video. 2015.
2. Rachel Carson, *Silent Spring* (Boston: Houghton Mifflin, 1962).
3. George Orwell, *Animal Farm* (New York: Harcourt, Brace, and World, 1954).
4. George Orwell, *1984* (New York: Harcourt, Brace, and World, 1949).
5. "Politics and the English Language," NPR Ombudsman, www.npr.org/blogs/ombudsman/Politics_and_the_English_Language-1.pdf.
6. www.politifact.com/florida/statements/2015/jun/08/rick-scott/rick-scott-says-we-have-record-funding-environment/.
7. Familyfarmdefenders.org, http://www.corp-research.org/cargill.
8. http://www.deepwaterhorizoneconomicsettlement.com/docs/Promotional%20Fund_Final%20Recommendations_Media%20List.pdf.

Punch the Hippie, Kill the Planet

1. Annabel Leventon. "Easy to be Hard." Galt MacDermot, James Rado, Gerome Ragni. From *Hair: Original Cast Recording of London Production.* Vinyl. 1968. ATCO Records SD 7002.

2. *Rickover: The Birth of Nuclear Power.* Directed by Michael Pack. Washington, DC: Manifold Productions. Air date: December 9, 2014. PBS Video. The USS *Thresher* did sink in 1963, and the USS *Scorpion* in 1968, the first during deep diving tests, the second at sea, but no nuclear material was released.
3. Mark Lynas, "How I Got Converted to G.M.O. Food," *NY Times*, Sunday Review: Opinion, April 24, 2015. http://www.nytimes.com/2015/04/25/opinion/sunday/how-i-got-converted-to-gmo-food.html.

Helluva Good Country Once

1. *Easy Rider.* Directed by Dennis Hopper. 1969. Raybert Productions. Los Angeles, CA: Columbia Pictures. DVD. 1999.
2. James Brown. "The Payback." John Starks. From the album of the same name. Vinyl. 1973. Polydor PD2-3007.
3. Jimi Hendrix. "If 6 Was 9." Jimi Hendrix. From *Axis: Bold As Love*. Vinyl. 1968. Reprise, SKAO 91441.

Peace Then

1. R.E.M. "Losing My Religion." R.E.M. From *Out of Time*. CD. 1991. Warner Bros. Records 1-26496, 9 26496-1
2. John T. Elson, "Is God Dead?" *Time Magazine*, April 8, 1966. Bob Dylan's reply quoted in Seth Rogovoy, *Bob Dylan: Prophet, Mystic, Poet* (New York: Simon and Schuster, 2009), p. 226.
3. Peter Manseau. *One Nation, Under Gods* (New York: Little, Brown, and Company, 2015).
4. Leo Tolstoy. *The Kingdom of God Is Within You* (New York: Scribners, 1989 [1929]).
5. "Doubling the Draft: When They Tag You 1A," *Life* Magazine, 122–129.
6. Edward K. Kaplan, "Heschel and the Vietnam War," *Tikkun* 22(4):14–68. See also *National Humanities Center. The 20th Century. Religion in Post-World War II America*. Joanne Beckman Duke University ©National Humanities Center Links to online resources, http://nationalhumanitiescenter.org/tserve/twenty/tkeyinfo/trelww2.htm.
7. Daniel Lewis, "Daniel J. Berrigan, Defiant Priest Who Preached Pacifism, Dies at 94," *New York Times*, Obituaries, May 1, 2016, A1, p. 21.
8. Various authors. "The Day of Dissent," *Life* Magazine, Oct. 24, 1969, p. 33.
9. *Nixon.* Directed by Oliver Stone. Buena Vista Pictures. 1996. DVD. Walt Disney Home Entertainment. 2008.

Hiroshima
Originally posted on **May 27, 2016**

1. *Hiroshima Mon Amour*. Directed by Alain Resnais. Argos Films. 1959. DVD. The Criterion Collection. 2015.
2. John Hersey. *Hiroshima* (New York: Knopf, 1946). To read John Hersey's magazine-length-account of Hiroshima (Aug. 31, 1946) online: www.newyorker.com/magazine/1946/08/31/hiroshima, accessed January 3, 2017.
3. To watch President Obama's speech at Hiroshima (from PBS NewsHour May 27, 2016): www.youtube.com/watch?v=NDYiEHPfXRo, accessed January 3, 2017.

Sticking to Our Guns

1. District of Columbia v. Heller, 554 U.S. 570 (2008).
2. Truman Capote, *In Cold Blood* (New York: Random House, 1966).
3. "The Run on Guns: A Lethal National Problem," *Life* Magazine, August 27, 1965, 59–65.
4. Ibid., p. 60.
5. Joseph McBride, *Searching for John Ford: A Life* (New York: St. Martin's, 2003), p. 560.

Generation Gapped

1. Vaughan, Roger, "The Gulf Between Parents and Children," *Life* Magazine. 104A–114.
2. Ibid., 104B.
3. Ibid., 114.
4. Ibid., 108.
5. *The Invisible War*. Directed by Kirby Dick. 2012. Rise Films and ITVS. New York: Cindedigm. DVD. New Video.
6. Don DeLillo. *White Noise* (New York: Viking, 1985).
7. For a powerful and courageous personal account of that experience in Horace Mann, read Stephen Fife's *The 13th Boy* (Seattle: Cune Press, 2015).
8. Nigel Planer and Terence Blacker. *Neil's Book of the Dead* (New York: Viking, 1984.)
9. Joel Stein Millennials: The Me Me Me Generation, *Time Magazine*, May 20, 2013, http://time.com/247/millennials-the-me-me-me-generation/, accessed January 2, 2017.
10. Annika Hammerschlag, "Work-Study, Manhattan Style: Thousands of NY Students Turn to Sex Work to Make Ends Meet " *Village Voice*, May 17, 2016, www.villagevoice.com/news/work-study-manhattan-style-thousands-of-ny-students-turn-to-sex-work-to-make-ends-meet-8626389, accessed January 2, 2017, and Nancy Jo Sales, "Daddies, 'Dates,' and the Girlfriend Experience: Welcome to the New Prostitution Economy," *Vanity Fair*, July 7, 2016, www.vanityfair.com/style/2016/07/welcome-to-the-new-prostitution-economy.

11. Alex Gray, "The Troubling Charts That Show Young People Losing Faith In Democracy," World Economic Forum, www.weforum.org/agenda/2016/12/charts-that-show-young-people-losing-faith-in-democracy, Dec. 1, 2016, accessed January 2, 2017, and Amanda Taub, "How Stable Are Democracies? 'Warning Signs Are Flashing Red'," The New York Times, November 29, 2016, www.nytimes.com/2016/11/29/world/americas/western-liberal-democracy.html?_r=1, accessed January 2, 2017.
12. Jason Fagone, "The Serial Swatter," NY Times Magazine, November 24, 2015, www.nytimes.com/2015/11/29/magazine/the-serial-swatter.html, accessed January 2, 2017.

When Students Struck and Won

1. Columbia timeline. Columbia University 1968, Frank da Cruz, Columbia University Academic Information System, fdc@columbia.edu, April 1998, updated August 24, 2004
2. Quoted in Mark Alden Branch, Yale Alumni Magazine, July/Aug. 2016, from Doug Rae and Paul Bass, Murder in the Model City (New York: Basic Books), p. 41.
3. Quoted in Kathryn Day Lassila. "Race, Speech, and Values: What Really Happened At Yale," Yale Alumni Magazine. January/February 2016, p. 41.
4. Quoted in Nick Chiles and Lily Engbith, "Of Color, At Yale," Yale Alumni Magazine, January/February 2016, p. 48.
5. Quoted in Kathryn Day Lassila. "Race, Speech, and Values: What Really Happened At Yale," Yale Alumni Magazine. January/February 2016, p. 47.
6. Quoted in Mark Alden Branch, "Christakis Steps Down from Silliman," Yale Alumni Magazine. July/Aug. 2016, p. 18.
7. Lassila, Yale Alumni Magazine, p. 47. See the "Future Plans" segment.
8. Ibid., Yale Alumni Magazine, p. 45.
9. Richard Pérez-Peña, Mitch Smith And Stephanie Saul, "University of Chicago Strikes Back Against Campus Political Correctness," New York Times, August 26, 2016, www.nytimes.com/2016/08/27/us/university-of-chicago-strikes-back-against-campus-political-correctness.html?_r=1
10. Ibid.
11. Arthur Unger, "Danny Kaye Talks About His Role in the Complex Drama Skokie." Christian Science Monitor. November 13, 1981.
12. Carl Reiner and Mel Brooks. 2000 Years With. Vinyl. 1960. Capitol Records W 1529.
13. Natasha Singer. "On Campus, It's One Big Commercial," New York Times, September 10, 2011, www.nytimes.com/2011/09/11/business/at-colleges-the-marketers-are-everywhere.html.
14. Alexis Hauk. "Salaries of Public-University Presidents Rocket Despite Spiraling Student Debt," Time Magazine, May 19, 2014, http://time.com/104243/salaries-of-public-university-presidents-rocket-despite-spiraling-student-debt/.
15. Fredrik DeBoer, "Why We Should Fear University Inc.", New York Times, Education Issue, Sept. 9, 2015 p. 65, 66, 68.

16. See Marshall McLuhan, "Classrooms Without Walls," in *Explorations in Communication*, edited by Edmund Carpenter and Marshall McLuhan (Boston: Beacon, 1960).

When Teachers Struck and Won—and Lost.

1. Nora Sayre, "New York for Natives: The States of My City," in *Sixties Going on Seventies*, by Nora Sayre, p. 215 (New York: Arbor House, 1973).
2. Ibid., p. 216
3. Ibid.
4. Charles Isaacs, *Inside Ocean-Hill Brownsville: A Teacher's Education* (New York: SUNY Press, 2014).
5. Richard D. Kahlenberg. "Rebuilding: Recruiting the Paraprofessionals, Launching the 'Where We Stand' Column, and Seeking Teacher Unity (1969–1972)." In *Tough Liberal: Albert Shanker and the Battles Over Schools, Unions, Race, and Democracy* (Columbia University Press, 2007), 125-144.
6. Richard D. Kahlenberg and Halley Potter, "The Original Charter School Vision," *New York Times*, Aug. 30, 2014. https://www.nytimes.com/2014/08/31/opinion/sunday/albert-shanker-the-original-charter-school-visionary.html.

Tom Hayden and American Freedom
Originally posted on **October 25, 2015**

1. Václav Havel, *Disturbing the Peace* (New York: Knopf, 1990), p. 167.
2. From "The New Jerusalem" by William Blake.
3. Sam Roberts, "The Port Huron Statement at 50," *New York Times*, March 4, 2012, p. 5.
4. Tom Hayden, "Letter to the New Left," quoted in *Takin' It to the Streets: A Sixties Reader*, edited by Alexander Bloom and Wini Breines (Oxford: Oxford University Press), p. 60.
5. Hayden, "The Politics of the Movement," ibid., pp. 73–77
6. Tom Hayden speaking on Columbia Campus. Also see "Columbia Timeline," cited in this volume, "When Students Struck and Won," note 1.
7. Hayden, "Create Two, Three, Many Columbias," *Streets*, p. 334.
8. "Tasks for Radicals: Revive Our Tradition"—Tom Hayden Speaking at the 2013 DSA National Convention, posted 2/26/2014, http://www.dsausa.org/tasks_for_radicals.
9. Tom Hayden. "Commemorating the American War in Vietnam." *The Peace and Justice Resource Center*. April 30, 2013,
10. Tom Hayden. "Who Will Tell the Story of the Peace Movement?" *The Nation*, April 30, 2015, https://www.thenation.com/article/who-will-tell-story-peace-movement/.
11. Hayden, "The Politics of The Movement," in *Takin' It To The Streets*, p. 77.

THE COUNTERCULTURE: BACK-AND-FORWARD

Albert Camus, *The Plague*, Translated by Stuart Gilbert (New York: Vintage International, 1975), p. 253.
Monty Python's Flying Circus, "The Spanish Inquisition," uploaded on YouTube by jumperbean2 on November 17, 2007, https://www.youtube.com/watch?v=T ym0MObFpTI&index=6&list=RD7WJXHY2OXGE, accessed January 4, 2017.

Bad Xanadus
Originally posted on **March 9, 2015**

1. Donald Fagen. "I.G.Y." From *The Nightfly*. CD. 1982. Warner Bros. Records 9 23696-1, 1-23696.
2. Donald Fagen, *Eminent Hipsters* (New York: Penguin Books, 2014), p. 34.
3. Wlliam Greider, *The Secrets of the Temple* (New York: Simon and Schuster, 1987).
4. Weseltier, Leon. "Among The Disrupted." www.nytimes.com/2015/01/18/books/review/among-the-disrupted.html, accessed 3/7/15. *New York Times* Sunday Book Review, Jan 7, 2015.
5. See Andrew Lewis on MetaFilter, http://www.metafilter.com/user/15556, although the quote has also been attributed to Richard Serra and others.

Moon Age Daydreams and TV Reality
Originally posted on **April 12, 2015**

1. Tom Wolfe, *The Right Stuff* (New York: Farrar, Strauss and Giroux, 1979).
2. *Medium Cool*. Directed by Haskell Wexler. 1969. H & J Films. Hollywood, CA: Paramount Pictures. DVD. The Criterion Collection. 2013.

The Left Is Senator Goldwater Now.

1. Thomas Thompson, "An Interview with Jean-Jacques Servan Schreiber," *Life* Magazine, 26–29.
2. Philip K. Howard, *The Death of Common Sense* (New York: Random House, 1994).
3. Peter Georgescu, "Capitalists, Arise: We Need to Deal With Income Inequality," Sunday Review, *New York Times*, August 7, 2015, www.nytimes.com/2015/08/09/opinion/sunday/capitalists-arise-we-need-to-deal-with-income-inequality.html, accessed January 3, 2017.
4. Thomas Paine, *Agrarian Justice* (New York: Simon and Schuster, 2013).
5. It needs to be considered that, especially if we lose net neutrality, the Internet and in particular Facebook might be subject to or go along with authoritarian top-down suppression as in other international regimes. That will make Twitter all the

more important. It will also make it necessary, especially given how unhackable and un-data-mine-able older media are, to rediscover printers and copying machines. The term for underground unpublished hard copy manuscripts in the '60s-era Soviet empire was *samizdats*. So, with a nod to David Byrne and Talking Heads, much future written dissent may be *samizdat* ever was.

Woodstock and All After

1. Bing Crosby, Crosby Classics Vol. 2, Columbia, MM 62 1933
2. Sly and the Family Stone. "Stand!" Sylvester Stone. From the album of the same name. Vinyl. 1969. Epic BN26456.
3. *Woodstock: The Director's Cut*. Directed by Michael Waldleigh. 1970. Waldleigh-Maurice. Burbank, CA: Warner Bros. Warner Home Video. 2010. Part of "40th Anniversary Ultimate Collectors Edition Boxed Set."
4. Borgzamer, John. "Close Up: Ravi Shankar: His Sitar Sound Rocks the U.S." *Life* Magazine. 1967, p. 40.
5. *Woodstock: The Director's Cut*, and personal recollection.
6. "Woodstock," *Life* Magazine special issue, 40th Anniversary Special Edition Reprint, 1969, included in 40th Anniversary Directors' Cut boxed set.
7. "Untold Stories" extra disc in boxed set.
8. Ibid.
9. Ibid.
10. Ibid.
11. Pete Townsend. *Psychoderelict*. Pete Townsend. CD. 1993. Atlantic 7 82494-2.
12. "Untold Stories" disc.
13. Bruce Springsteen. "Long Walk Home." Bruce Springsteen. From *Magic*. CD. 2007. Columbia 88697 17060 2, CD, 2007.

REFERENCES / FOR FURTHER READING

Consider this a purely introductory list; there are many hundreds of books on the subject of the ideas and events of the '60s, their origins, and their impacts on contemporary American culture, politics, and history.

Bentley, Eric. *Bernard Shaw.* New York: New Directions, 1947.

Bloom, Alexander, and Wini Breines, eds. *Takin' It To The Streets.* 2nd ed. Oxford: Oxford University Press, 2003.

Branch, Taylor. *Parting of The Waters: America in the King Years, 1954–1963.* New York: Simon and Schuster, 1988.

Branch, Taylor. *Pillar of Fire: America in the King Years, 1963–1965.* New York: Simon and Schuster, 1998.

Branch, Taylor. *At Canaan's Edge: America in the King Years, 1965–1968.* New York: Simon and Schuster, 2006.

Camus, Albert. *The Plague.* Translated by Stuart Gilbert. New York: Vintage International, 1975.

Camus, Albert. *The Rebel.* Translated by Anthony Bower. New York: Vintage International, 1984.

Cannato, Vincent. *The Ungovernable City: John Lindsay and His Struggle To Save New York.* New York: Basic Books, 2001.

Capote, Truman. *In Cold Blood.* New York: Random House, 1966.

Caro, Robert. *The Passage of Power.* New York: Knopf, 2012.

Carson, Rachel. *Silent Spring.* Boston: Houghton Mifflin, 1962.

Churchill, Ward, and Jim Vander Wall. *The COINTELPRO Papers: Documents from the FBI's Secret Wars Against Dissent in the United States.* Brooklyn, New York: South End Press, 2001.

Collins, Ronald K. L., and David M. Skover. *The Trials of Lenny Bruce: The Fall and Rise of an American Icon.* Naperville, IL: Sourcebooks MediaFusion 2002.

Cross, Charles R. *Backstreets: Springsteen, the Man and His Music.* New York: Harmony, 1989.

Cross, Charles. *Roomful of Mirrors: A Biography of Jimi Hendrix*. New York: Hyperion, 2005.

DeLillo, Don. *White Noise*. New York: Viking, 1985.

Deponte, Paige, and Mark Berry. *Gaia II: Song of the Vanishing Tribe*. Maui, HI: Global Art in Action, 2002.

Didion, Joan. *The White Album*. New York: Simon and Schuster, 1979.

Doctorow, E.L. *Book of Daniel*. New York: Random House, 1971.

Duras, Marguerite. *Hiroshima Mon Amour*. Screenplay Marguerite Duras, Director Alain Resnais. New York: Grove, 1961.

Dylan, Bob. *Chronicles*. New York: Simon and Schuster, 2004–.

Fagen, Donald. *Eminent Hipsters*. New York: Penguin Books, 2014.

Garbus, Martin. *Ready for the Defense*. New York: Farrar, Strauss, and Giroux, 1971.

Ginsberg, Allan. *Howl and Other Poems*. San Francisco: City Lights Books, 1997.

Gitlin, Todd. *The Sixties: Years of Hope, Days of Rage*. New York: Bantam, 1987.

Gordon, W. Terrence. *Marshall McLuhan: Escape into Understanding*. New York: Basic Books, 1997.

Gottehrer, Barry. *The Mayor's Man*. New York: Doubleday, 1975.

Greider, William. *The Secrets of the Temple*. New York: Simon and Schuster, 1987.

Havel, Václav. *Disturbing the Peace*. New York: Knopf, 1990.

Hersey, John. *Hiroshima*. New York: Knopf, 1946.

Hopkins, Jerry, and Daniel Sugerman. *No One Here Gets Out Alive: The Biography of Jim Morrison*. New York: Warner Books, 2006 [1980].

Howard, Phillip K. *The Death of Common Sense*. New York: Random House, 1994.

Isaacs, Charles. *Inside Ocean-Hill Brownsville: A Teacher's Education*. New York: SUNY Press, 2014.

Kahlenberg, Richard D. *Tough Liberal: Albert Shanker and the Battles Over Schools, Unions, Race, and Democracy.* New York: Columbia University Press, 2007.

Lane, Mark. *Rush to Judgment.* New York: Dell, 1975.

Lawrence, T.E. *Seven Pillars of Wisdom.* Garden City, NY: Doubleday, 1935.

Lee, Martin A., and Barry Shlain. *Acid Dreams.* New York: Grove Weidenfeld, 1992.

Lerner, Alan Jay. *My Fair Lady.* Adapted from *Pygmalion* by Bernard Shaw. New York: Signet, 1956.

Loewen, James. *Lies My Teacher Told Me.* New York: Simon and Schuster, 1995.

Mailer, Norman. *Miami and the Siege of Chicago.* New York: Signet/New American Library, 1968.

Mailer, Norman. *Armies of the Night: History as a Novel, the Novel as History.* New York: Signet/New American Library, 1968.

Mailer, Norman. *Of A Fire on the Moon.* Boston: Little Brown, 1970.

Manseau, Peter. *One Nation, Under Gods.* New York: Little, Brown, and Company, 2015.

Marcus, Greil. *The Old Weird America.* New York: Picador, 2011.

Martin, George, and William Pearson. *With A Little Help From My Friends: The Making of Sgt. Pepper.* New York: Little, Brown, and Co., 1995.

McBride, Joseph. *Searching for John Ford: A Life.* New York: St. Martin's, 2003.

McGinniss, Joe. *The Selling of the President 1968.* New York: Trident, 1969.

McLuhan, Marshall, *Explorations in Communication.* Edited by Edmund Carpenter and Marshall McLuhan. Boston: Beacon, 1960.

McLuhan, Marshall. *Understanding Media: The Extensions of Man,* New American Library. New York: McGraw Hill/Signet, 1964.

McLuhan, Marshall. *Understanding Me: Lectures and Interviews.* Cambridge, MA: The MIT Press, 2005.

O'Brien, Tim. *The Things They Carried.* New York: Broadway, 1998.

Orwell, George. *1984.* New York: Harcourt, Brace, and World, 1949.

Orwell, George. *Animal Farm*. New York: Harcourt, Brace, and World, 1954.

Orwell, George. "Politics and the English Language," *NPR Ombudsman*, http://www.npr.org/blogs/ombudsman/Politics_and_the_English_Language-1.pdf.

Paine, Thomas. *Agrarian Justice*. New York: Simon and Schuster, 2013.

Rae, Doug, and Paul Bass. *Murder in the Model City*. New York: Basic Books, 2006.

Rimbaud, Arthur. *Collected Poems*. Translated by Martin Sorrell. New York: Oxford University Press, 2001.

Roth, Phillip. *Portnoy's Complaint*. New York: Random House, 1969.

Sarris, Andrew. *Interviews with Film Directors*. New York: Avon, 1967.

Sayre, Nora. *Sixties Going On Seventies*. New York: Arbor House, 1973.

Sheehan, Neil, Hedrick Smith, et al. *The Pentagon Papers: The Secret History of the Vietnam War*. As published by *The New York Times*. New York: Bantam, 1971.

Slick, Grace, and Andrea Cagan. *Somebody To Love?* New York: Warner Books, 1998.

Stein, Michael Eric. *Cats' Eyes*. New York: CreateSpace/Streetlight Books, 2014.

Stoppard, Tom. *Rock 'n' Roll*. New York: Grove/Atlantic, 2006.

Takiff, Michael. *Brave Men, Gentle Heroes: American Fathers and Sons in World War II and Vietnam*. New York: Morrow, 2003.

Tolstoy, Leo. *The Kingdom of God Is Within You*. New York: Scribners, 1989 [1929].

Vallor, Shannon. *Technology and the Virtues*. Oxford: Oxford University Press, 2016.

Walker, Alexander. *Stanley Kubrick Directs*. A Visual Analysis. New York: Harcourt, Brace, Jovanovich. 1971.

Walker, Daniel, and the National Commission on the Causes and Prevention of Violence. *Rights in Conflict: The Violent Confrontation of Demonstrators and Police in the Parks and Streets of Chicago during the Week of the Democratic National Convention of 1968*. New York: Bantam, 1968.

Walley, David. *No Commercial Potential: The Saga of Frank Zappa*. Boston: DaCapo, 1996.

Warren Commission. *The Warren Commission Report on the Assassination of John F. Kennedy: A Concise Compendium*. With an Introduction by Robert Donovan. New York: Popular Library Edition, 1964.

White, Theodore. *Making of The President 1960*. New York: Atheneum, 1961.

Wolfe, Tom. *Radical Chic and Mau-Mauing the Flak Catchers*. New York: Farrar, Strauss, and Giroux, 1970.

Wolfe, Tom. *The Right Stuff*. New York: Farrar, Strauss and Giroux, 1979.

Wolfe, Tom. *The Electric Kool-Aid Acid Test*. New York: Bantam, 1999 [1968].

Wright, Ronald. *A Short History of Progress*. New York: Carroll and Graft, 2004.

Zappa, Frank, with Peter Occhiogrosso. *The Real Frank Zappa Book*. New York: Poseidon Press, 1989.

FIFTY YEARS AGO TODAY